First World War
and Army of Occupation
War Diary
France, Belgium and Germany

16 DIVISION
Headquarters, Branches and Services
Commander Royal Engineers
18 December 1915 - 25 June 1919

WO95/1961/1

The Naval & Military Press Ltd
www.nmarchive.com
Published in association with The National Archives

Published by

The Naval & Military Press Ltd

Unit 10 Ridgewood Industrial Park,

Uckfield, East Sussex,

TN22 5QE England

Tel: +44 (0) 1825 749494

www.naval-military-press.com

www.nmarchive.com

This diary has been reprinted in facsimile from the original. Any imperfections are inevitably reproduced and the quality may fall short of modern type and cartographic standards.

© Crown Copyright
Images reproduced by permission of The National Archives, London, England, 2015.

Contents

Document type	Place/Title	Date From	Date To
Heading	WO95/1916. 16 Division Headquarters Branches & Services Dec 1915-Jun 1919 Commander Royal Engineers		
Heading	16th Division C.R.E. Dec 1915-Jun 1919		
War Diary	Blackdown	18/12/1915	18/12/1915
War Diary	Farnborough	18/12/1915	18/12/1915
War Diary	Southampton	18/12/1915	18/12/1915
War Diary	Le. Havre	19/12/1915	20/12/1915
War Diary	Fouquereuil	20/12/1915	20/12/1915
War Diary	Drouvin	21/12/1915	31/12/1915
War Diary	Drouvin Bomy	01/01/1916	07/01/1916
War Diary	Amettes	08/01/1916	10/01/1916
Heading	C.R.E. 16th Div. Vol I & II Dec 18-31st Jan 16		
War Diary	Amettes	11/01/1916	31/01/1916
Heading	C.R.E. 16th Div Vol 3		
War Diary	Amettes	01/02/1916	26/02/1916
War Diary	Busnes	27/02/1916	29/02/1916
Heading	CRE 16 Div Vol 4		
War Diary	Busnes	01/03/1916	08/03/1916
War Diary	Lillers	09/03/1916	29/03/1916
War Diary	Noeux-Les Mines	30/03/1916	30/06/1916
Miscellaneous	Report on Consolidation of new Harrison's and Hart's Craters.	29/06/1916	29/06/1916
Map	Hart's Crater.		
Heading	War Diary Headquarters 16th Divl. Engineers 1st. July to 31st. July 1916. Volume No. 8 16 Infy CRE 16 Div Vol 8		
Map	Harrison's Crater.		
War Diary	Noeux Les Mines	01/07/1916	31/07/1916
Heading	War Diary. 16th Div. Engineers H.Q. Month Of August, 1916. Volume 9		
War Diary	Noeux-Les-Mines	01/08/1916	25/08/1916
War Diary	Raimbert	26/08/1916	28/08/1916
War Diary	In Train	29/08/1916	29/08/1916
War Diary	Corbie	30/08/1916	30/08/1916
War Diary	Forked Tree	31/08/1916	01/09/1916
Operation(al) Order(s)	16th Divisional Engineers. Operation Order No. 1.	23/08/1916	23/08/1916
Miscellaneous	March Table to accompany 16th D.E. O.O. No. 1.	23/08/1916	23/08/1916
Operation(al) Order(s)	16th Divisional Engineers. Operation Order No. 2.	24/08/1916	24/08/1916
Miscellaneous	March Table to accompany 16th Div. Engineers O.O. No. 2.	24/08/1916	24/08/1916
Heading	War Diary 16th Div. Engineers Head Quarters For Month Of September, 1916. Volume 10		
War Diary	Forked Tree	01/09/1916	04/09/1916
War Diary	Mindenpost	05/09/1916	09/09/1916
War Diary	Citadel	10/09/1916	10/09/1916
War Diary	Corbie	11/09/1916	17/09/1916
War Diary	Hallancourt	18/09/1916	20/09/1916
War Diary	Westoutre	21/09/1916	30/09/1916

Heading	War Diary Month Of October, 1916. Volume 11 16th Div. Engineers Headquarters Vol 11		
War Diary	Westoutre	01/10/1916	31/10/1916
Heading	War Diary. For Month Of November, 1916. Volume 12 Headquarters 16th Div Engineers		
War Diary	Westoutre	01/11/1916	30/11/1916
Heading	War Diary For Month Of December, 1916. Volume 13 Headquarters 16th Div Engineers		
War Diary	Westoutre	01/12/1916	31/12/1916
Heading	War Diary for month of January, 1917. Volume 14 Hd Qrs. 16th Div. Engineers		
War Diary	Westoutre	01/01/1917	31/01/1917
Heading	War Diary. For Month Of February, 1917. Volume 15 Unit:- H.Q. 16th Div. Engineers.		
War Diary	Westoutre	01/02/1917	28/02/1917
Heading	War Diary For Month Of March, 1917. Volume 16 Unit:- Headquarters 16th Div. Engineers		
War Diary	Westoutre	01/03/1917	30/03/1917
War Diary	Canada Corner (M.17.c.5.4) (Sheet 28. S.W.)	31/03/1917	31/03/1917
Heading	War Diary For Month Of April, 1917. Volume 17 Unit:- H.Q. 16th Div Engineers		
War Diary	Canada Corner (M.17.C.5.4) Sheet 28 S.W	01/04/1917	30/04/1917
Heading	War Diary. Volume:- 18 For Month Of May, 1917. Unit:- Headquarters 16th Div Engineers		
War Diary	Canada Corner	01/05/1917	31/05/1917
Operation(al) Order(s)	C.R.E'S Order No. 101. App 1	15/05/1917	15/05/1917
Operation(al) Order(s)	C.R.E'S Order No. 102.	16/05/1917	16/05/1917
Operation(al) Order(s)	C.R.E'S Order No. 103.	27/05/1917	27/05/1917
Operation(al) Order(s)	C.R.E'S Order No. 104.	31/05/1917	31/05/1917
Miscellaneous	Instructions For The Offensive Issued By C.R.E., 16th Division. App 2		
Miscellaneous		29/05/1917	29/05/1917
Operation(al) Order(s)	16th Divisional Engineers Operation Order No. 27. App 3	08/05/1917	08/05/1917
Operation(al) Order(s)	16th Divisional Engineers Operation Order No. 28. App 4	10/05/1917	10/05/1917
Miscellaneous	Schedule Showing Change Over Of Work On 12-5-17.	12/05/1917	12/05/1917
Operation(al) Order(s)	16th Divisional Engineers Operation Order No. 29. App 5	22/05/1917	22/05/1917
Heading	War Diary. For Month Of June, 1917. Volume 19 Unit:- Headquarters 16th Div Engineers		
War Diary	Scherpenberg	01/06/1917	11/06/1917
War Diary	Canada Corner	11/06/1917	18/06/1917
War Diary	Merris	19/06/1917	20/06/1917
War Diary	Godwaesvelde	20/06/1917	20/06/1917
War Diary	Poperinghe (Sh. 27.) L.11.d.	21/06/1917	30/06/1917
Operation(al) Order(s)	C.R.E's Order No. 104.	31/05/1917	31/05/1917
Miscellaneous	C.R.E'S Instructions For The Offensive. Addenda No. 1.	04/06/1917	04/06/1917
Miscellaneous	Provisional Instructions for Advance to Oosttaverne Line issued by C.R.E. 16th Division.	04/06/1917	04/06/1917
Miscellaneous	C.R.E'S Instructions For The Offensive. Addenda No. 2.	05/06/1917	05/06/1917
Miscellaneous	C.R.E's. Instructions For The Offensive. Addenda No. 4.	06/06/1917	06/06/1917

Miscellaneous	Provisional Instructions for Advance to Oosttaverne Line issued by C.R.E. 16th Division.	04/06/1917	04/06/1917
Operation(al) Order(s)	C.R.E's Order No. 105.	05/06/1917	05/06/1917
Operation(al) Order(s)	C.R.E's Order No. 106.	06/06/1917	06/06/1917
Operation(al) Order(s)	C.R.E's Order No. 107.	06/06/1917	06/06/1917
Miscellaneous	16th Division R.E. Narrative of Events.	07/06/1917	07/06/1917
Operation(al) Order(s)	16th Divisional Engineers Operation Order No. 30.	12/06/1917	12/06/1917
Operation(al) Order(s)	16th Divisional Engineers Operation Order No. 31.	17/06/1917	17/06/1917
Miscellaneous	Table To Accompany 16th Divisional Engineers O.O. No. 31.		
Miscellaneous	Distribution		
Operation(al) Order(s)	16th Divisional Engineers Operation No. 32.	17/06/1917	17/06/1917
Operation(al) Order(s)	16th Divisional Engineers Operation Order No. 33.	20/06/1917	20/06/1917
Miscellaneous	Table To Accompany 16th Div. Engineers O.O. No. 33.	20/06/1917	20/06/1917
Miscellaneous	Distribution.		
Heading	War Diary. For Month Of July, 1917. Volume 20 Unit:- H.Q. 16th Div Engineers		
War Diary	Poperinghe (Sht. 27.) L.11.d.	01/07/1917	31/07/1917
Operation(al) Order(s)	C.R.E's Order 'Y' 1.	04/07/1917	04/07/1917
Miscellaneous	Chief Engineer, XIX Corps.	09/07/1917	09/07/1917
Miscellaneous	C.R.E'S Instructions For The Offensive. No. 1 General Plan And Preliminary Dispositions.	25/07/1917	25/07/1917
Miscellaneous	C.R.E'S Instructions For The Offensive No. 2. March Discipline.	26/07/1917	26/07/1917
Miscellaneous	C.R.E's Instructions For The Offensive No. 3.	28/07/1917	28/07/1917
Operation(al) Order(s)	C.R.E's Order 'Y' 1.	04/07/1917	04/07/1917
Operation(al) Order(s)	Operation Order By C.R.E. 16th Division. No. 'Y' 2.	29/07/1917	29/07/1917
Miscellaneous	C.R.E's Instructions For The Offensive. No. 4. Reconnaissance For Enemy Mines And Dugouts.	31/07/1917	31/07/1917
Heading	War Diary. For Month Of August, 1917. Volume 21 Unit Headquarters 16th Div Engineers		
War Diary	Poperinghe (Sht 27) L.11.d.6.8.	01/08/1917	03/08/1917
War Diary	Brandhoek H.7.C.8.6 (Sheet 28)	04/08/1917	15/08/1917
War Diary	Brandhoek H.7.C.8.6.	16/08/1917	18/08/1917
War Diary	Watou Sh 27. K.4.6.	19/08/1917	26/08/1917
War Diary	Moyenneville (57C) A.3.d.0.0.	27/08/1917	31/08/1917
Miscellaneous	O.C. 155th Field Coy. R.E. O.C. 157th Field Coy. R.E. Appendix. 1	01/08/1917	01/08/1917
Miscellaneous	Headquarters, 16th Division "G". Appendix 2.	01/08/1917	01/08/1917
Miscellaneous	Engineer Report. 15th Division Front.	01/08/1917	01/08/1917
Operation(al) Order(s)	16th Divisional Engineers Operation Order No. 35. Appendix 3	03/08/1917	03/08/1917
Miscellaneous	Table To Accompany 16th Div. Engrs. O.O. No. 35.		
Miscellaneous	Addendum to 16th Divisional Engineers Operation Order No. 35 Appendix 3	03/08/1917	03/08/1917
Miscellaneous	Headquarters, 16th Division 'G'. Appendix 4	03/08/1917	03/08/1917
Miscellaneous	C.R.E's Report. 3rd August, 1917	03/08/1917	03/08/1917
Miscellaneous	H.Q.R.E. 16th Division Scheme for Work in the Line. Appendix 5	05/08/1917	05/08/1917
Miscellaneous	Amendment to Scheme for Work in the Line. Appendix 6	06/08/1917	06/08/1917
Miscellaneous	C.R.E's Instructions For The Offensive No. 5. Appendix 7	13/08/1917	13/08/1917
Operation(al) Order(s)	Operation Order No. Y.4. by C.R.E. 16th Division. Appendix 8	14/08/1917	14/08/1917

Operation(al) Order(s)	Operation Order No. 'Y' 5. by C.R.E. 16th Division. Appendix 9	14/08/1917	14/08/1917
Miscellaneous	Move Table to accompany C.R.E's O.O. No. 'Y' 5.	14/08/1917	14/08/1917
Miscellaneous	16th Division. Report on R.E. Operations. 15th/16th August. Appendix 10	20/08/1917	20/08/1917
Diagram etc	16 Div. R.E. Situation At Zero 16-8-17		
Operation(al) Order(s)	16th Divisional Engineers Operation Order No. 36. Appendix 11	24/08/1917	24/08/1917
Miscellaneous	Table to accompany 16th Div. Engrs. O.O. No. 36.	24/08/1917	24/08/1917
Heading	War Diary. For Month Of September, 1917. Volume 22 Unit:- H.Q. 16th Div. Engineers.		
War Diary	Moyenneville	01/09/1917	17/09/1917
War Diary	Behagnies.	18/09/1917	30/09/1917
Miscellaneous	155th Field Company, R.E. Technical assistance for 16th Div. Artillery. Appendix (1)	01/09/1917	01/09/1917
Miscellaneous	16th Division. Scheme for R.E. and Pioneer Work. Appendix (2)	02/09/1917	02/09/1917
Diagram etc	Drawing To accompany C.R.E. No 3334/12.		
Heading	War Diary For Month Of October, 1917. Unit H.Q. 16th Div Engineers Volume Number 23		
War Diary	Behagnies.	01/10/1917	31/10/1917
Heading	War Diary For Month Of November, 1917. Volume 24 Unit:- H.Q. 16th Div Engineers.		
War Diary	Behagnies.	01/11/1917	30/11/1917
Map	C.R.E. F.C. 2/6		
Miscellaneous	Scheme Of Work (R.E. and Pioneers) after capture of Tunnel Trench and Tunnel Support. Appendix 1.	05/11/1917	05/11/1917
Miscellaneous	Amendment To F.C. 2 of 5th Nov. 1917.	06/11/1917	06/11/1917
Operation(al) Order(s)	C.R.E's Operation Order No. F. C. 7. Appendix 2.	17/11/1917	17/11/1917
Miscellaneous	O.C. 155th Field Company, R.E. C.R.E'S Instructions as to action in the Event of an Enemy Withdrawal. No. 3. Appendix. 3.	01/11/1917	01/11/1917
Miscellaneous	C.R.E's Instructions as to Action in the event of an Enemy Withdrawal. No. 4.	15/11/1917	15/11/1917
Miscellaneous	Third Army No. G.13/7		
Miscellaneous	C.R.E's Instructions as to Action in the event of an Enemy Withdrawal. No. 5	18/11/1917	18/11/1917
Miscellaneous	Consolidation Of Tunnel Trench And Tunnel Support. Synopsis of proposed Work. Appendix 4	25/11/1917	25/11/1917
Heading	War Diary For Month Of December, 1917. Volume 25. Unit: Headquarters 16th Div. Engineers.		
War Diary	Behagnies.	01/12/1917	02/12/1917
War Diary	Behagnies Ytres	03/12/1917	03/12/1917
War Diary	Ytres	04/12/1917	04/12/1917
War Diary	Ytres & Peronne	05/12/1917	06/12/1917
War Diary	Villers Faucon	07/12/1917	31/12/1917
Operation(al) Order(s)	C.R.E'S Order No. 40.	23/12/1917	23/12/1917
Operation(al) Order(s)	C.R.E'S Order No. 40/1.	26/12/1917	26/12/1917
Operation(al) Order(s)	C.R.E's Order No. 41.	27/12/1917	27/12/1917
Heading	War Diary, For Month Of January, 1918. Volume 26 Unit:- H.Q. 16th Div. Engineers.		
War Diary	Villers Faucon	01/01/1918	21/01/1918
War Diary	Tincourt J.17.b.	22/01/1918	31/01/1918
Heading	War Diary. For Month Of February, 1918. Volume 27. Unit:- H.Q. 16th Div Engineers		
War Diary	Tincourt J.17.b.9.6.	01/02/1918	28/02/1918

Type	Description	Date 1	Date 2
Operation(al) Order(s)	C.R.E'S Order No. 45.	01/02/1918	01/02/1918
Operation(al) Order(s)	C.R.E'S Instructions No. 46.	10/02/1918	10/02/1918
Operation(al) Order(s)	C.R.E'S Order No. 47.	11/02/1918	11/02/1918
Operation(al) Order(s)	C.R.E'S Order No. 48. Warning Order.	24/02/1918	24/02/1918
Operation(al) Order(s)	C.R.E's Order No. 49.	26/02/1918	26/02/1918
Operation(al) Order(s)	C.R.E'S Order No. 50.	27/02/1918	27/02/1918
Operation(al) Order(s)	C.R.E's Order No. 51.A.	28/02/1918	28/02/1918
Operation(al) Order(s)	C.R.E'S Order No. 52.	28/02/1918	28/02/1918
Heading	16th Divisional Engineers C.R.E. 16th Division March 1918		
War Diary	Tincourt J.17.b.9.6	01/03/1918	22/03/1918
War Diary	Doingt I.36a. & Advanced at Tincourt J.17.b.9.6	22/03/1918	22/03/1918
War Diary	Doingt I 36 a	22/03/1918	23/03/1918
War Diary	Biaches H.30d.2.7	23/03/1918	23/03/1918
War Diary	Herbecourt H.25.d.	23/03/1918	23/03/1918
War Diary	Cappy E.24.C.	24/03/1918	24/03/1918
War Diary	Morlancourt K.8.6.7.3.	24/03/1918	25/03/1918
War Diary	Morlancourt	25/03/1918	25/03/1918
War Diary	Lamotte en Santerre P.36.a.	25/03/1918	26/03/1918
War Diary	Hamel P.10.C.	26/03/1918	27/03/1918
War Diary	Fouilloy O.10.a	28/03/1918	28/03/1918
War Diary	Bois De Vaire P.14d	28/03/1918	28/03/1918
War Diary	P.20.a.2.8	28/03/1918	28/03/1918
War Diary	Fouilloy. O.10.a.	28/03/1918	30/03/1918
War Diary	Fouilloy	30/03/1918	31/03/1918
Operation(al) Order(s)	C.R.E's Operation Order No. 56. Appendix. 1.	21/03/1918	21/03/1918
Operation(al) Order(s)	C.R.E's Operation Order No. 57. Appendix. 2.	21/03/1918	21/03/1918
Miscellaneous	O.C. 156th Field Company, R.E. Appendix 3.	21/03/1918	21/03/1918
Operation(al) Order(s)	C.R.E.s Order No. 60. Appendix 4	25/03/1918	25/03/1918
Heading	M.G. Taylor P With the Royal Engineers Of The Irish Division 21st March 1918 4th April by C.R.E.		
Miscellaneous	Foreword.		
Miscellaneous	Appendix. Special Order Of The Day By General Sir H. de la P. Gough, K.C.B., K.C.V.O., Commanding Fifth Army.	26/03/1918	26/03/1918
Miscellaneous	16th (Irish) Division Line Of Retreat. 21st-27th March 1918	21/03/1918	21/03/1918
Miscellaneous	Central Registry. Subject, And Office Of Origin.		
Miscellaneous	D.E.S.	09/11/1918	09/11/1918
Miscellaneous	Brigadier General P. Leveson-Gower. C.M.G., D.S.O. Commanding 49th Inf. Brigade.	29/08/1918	29/08/1918
Miscellaneous	Major-General Sir. C.P.A. Hull. K.C.B. G.O.C. 16th (Irish) Division.	02/09/1918	02/09/1918
Miscellaneous	Foreword.		
Miscellaneous	Appendix. Special Order Of The Day By General Sir H. de la P. Gough, K.C.B., K.C.V.O., Commanding Fifth Army.	26/03/1918	26/03/1918
Miscellaneous	Brigadier-General P. Leveson-Gower, C.M.G., D.S.O. Commanding 49th. Infantry Brigade.	01/09/1918	01/09/1918
Miscellaneous	16th (Irish) Division Line Of Retreat.	21/03/1918	21/03/1918
Heading	HQ RE 16 D Vol 29 April 1918		
War Diary	Fouilloy	01/04/1918	03/04/1918
War Diary	Saleux.	03/04/1918	04/04/1918
War Diary	Cerisy	05/04/1918	09/04/1918
War Diary	Gamaches	10/04/1918	10/04/1918
War Diary	Fauquembergues	11/04/1918	15/04/1918

Type	Description	Start	End
War Diary	Aire	15/04/1918	26/04/1918
War Diary	H.28.C.7.7	27/04/1918	29/04/1918
War Diary	Aire	29/04/1918	30/04/1918
Operation(al) Order(s)	C.R.E's Order No. 61. Appendix No. 1	08/04/1918	08/04/1918
Operation(al) Order(s)	C.R.E's Order No. 62. Appendix No. 2	13/04/1918	13/04/1918
Operation(al) Order(s)	C.R.E.s Order No. 62/1 Appendix No. 3.	14/04/1918	14/04/1918
Map	France		
Miscellaneous	Appendix No 4 W.D. April 1918 H.Q.R.E.		
Miscellaneous	C.R.E's Instructions For Work On Reserve Lines. No. 1. Appendix No. 5.	15/04/1918	15/04/1918
Miscellaneous	C.R.E's Instructions For Work On Reserve Lines. No. 2. Appendix No. 6.	16/04/1918	16/04/1918
Miscellaneous	C.R.E's Instructions For Work On Reserve Lines. No. 3. Appendix No. 7.	16/04/1918	16/04/1918
Miscellaneous	C.R.E's Instructions For Work On Reserve Lines. No. 4. Appendix No. 8	16/04/1918	16/04/1918
Miscellaneous	C.R.E's Instructions For Work On Reserve Lines. No. 5. Appendix No. 9	18/04/1918	18/04/1918
Miscellaneous	C.R.E's Instructions For Work On Reserve Lines. No. 6. Appendix No. 10	19/04/1918	19/04/1918
Miscellaneous	C.R.E's Instructions For Work On Reserve Lines. No. 7. Readjustment Of Labour. Appendix. No. 11	23/04/1918	23/04/1918
Miscellaneous	C.R.E's Instructions For Work On Reserve Lines. No. 8. Appendix No. 12		
Miscellaneous	C.R.E's Instructions For Work On Reserve Lines. No. 9 Appendix No. 13	24/04/1918	24/04/1918
Miscellaneous	C.R.E's Instructions For Work On Defence Lines. No. 10. Appendix No. 14.	25/04/1918	25/04/1918
Miscellaneous	C.R.E's Instructions For Work On Reserve Lines. No. 11. Appendix No. 15	28/04/1918	28/04/1918
Miscellaneous	C.R.E's Instructions For Work On Reserve Lines. No. 12. Appendix No. 16	29/04/1918	29/04/1918
Miscellaneous	C.R.E's Instructions For Work On Reserve Lines. No. 13. Appendix No. 17	29/04/1918	29/04/1918
Miscellaneous	C.R.E's Instructions For Work On Reserve Lines. No. 14. Appendix No. 18	30/04/1918	30/04/1918
War Diary	Aire Sheet 36A H.28.c.7.8.	01/05/1918	14/05/1918
War Diary	Aire.	15/05/1918	17/05/1918
War Diary	Samer	17/05/1918	31/05/1918
Miscellaneous	C.R.E's Instructions For Work On Reserve Lines. No. 15. Appendix No. 1	08/05/1918	08/05/1918
Miscellaneous	C.R.E's Instructions For Work On Reserve Lines. No. 16. Warning Order. Appendix No. 2	14/05/1918	14/05/1918
Miscellaneous	C.R.E's Instructions For Work On Reserve Lines. No. 17. Appendix No. 3.	14/05/1918	14/05/1918
Miscellaneous	C.R.E's. Instructions. A.3. Engineers Stores. Samer Area. Appendix No 4.		
Miscellaneous	C.R.E's Instructions No. A./4. Engineer Stores. Appendix No. 5	24/05/1918	24/05/1918
War Diary	Samer Rue de Breuil	01/06/1918	09/06/1918
War Diary	Samer	10/06/1918	30/06/1918
Operation(al) Order(s)	C.R.E's Order No.63. Appendix No. 1	07/06/1918	07/06/1918
War Diary	Samer	01/07/1918	31/07/1918
Operation(al) Order(s)	C.R.E's Order No. 66. Appendix No 1	17/07/1918	17/07/1918
Operation(al) Order(s)	C.R.E's Order No. 67. Appendix No. 1	17/07/1918	17/07/1918
Operation(al) Order(s)	C.R.E's Order No. 68. Appendix No 2	18/07/1918	18/07/1918

Operation(al) Order(s)	C.R.E's Order No. 69. Appendix No. 3.	24/07/1918	24/07/1918
Operation(al) Order(s)	C.R.E's Order No. 70. Appendix No 4	27/07/1918	27/07/1918
Operation(al) Order(s)	C.R.E's Order No. 72. Appendix No 5	29/07/1918	29/07/1918
Operation(al) Order(s)	C.R.E's Order No. 73. Appendix No 6	30/07/1918	30/07/1918
War Diary	Samer	01/08/1918	19/08/1918
War Diary	Anvin	20/08/1918	22/08/1918
War Diary	Ruitz	23/08/1918	31/08/1918
Operation(al) Order(s)	C.R.E's Order No. 74. Appendix No 1	01/08/1918	01/08/1918
Operation(al) Order(s)	C.R.E's Order No. 75. Appendix No 2	12/08/1918	12/08/1918
Operation(al) Order(s)	C.R.E's Order No. 76. Appendix No 3.	16/08/1918	16/08/1918
Operation(al) Order(s)	C.R.E's Order No.77. Appendix No 4.	17/08/1918	17/08/1918
Miscellaneous	Table 'A' (Moves by bus and lorry) to accompany C.R.E's Order No.77.		
Miscellaneous	Table B (Transport).		
Operation(al) Order(s)	C.R.E's Order No. 78. Appendix No 5	27/08/1918	27/08/1918
Operation(al) Order(s)	C.R.E's Order No. 79. Appendix No 6	28/08/1918	28/08/1918
War Diary	Ruitz	01/09/1918	23/09/1918
War Diary	Drouvin	24/09/1918	30/09/1918
Miscellaneous	Preliminary Instructions As To Action In The Event Of An Enemy Retirement. Appendix No 1	01/09/1918	01/09/1918
Operation(al) Order(s)	C.R.E's Order No. 80. Appendix No 2	02/09/1918	02/09/1918
Operation(al) Order(s)	C.R.E's Order No. 81. Appendix No. 3	06/09/1918	06/09/1918
Operation(al) Order(s)	C.R.E's Order No. 82. Appendix No. 4	07/09/1918	07/09/1918
Operation(al) Order(s)	C.R.E's Order No. 83. Appendix No. 5	15/09/1918	15/09/1918
Operation(al) Order(s)	C.R.E's Order No. 85. Appendix No 6	21/09/1918	21/09/1918
Operation(al) Order(s)	C.R.E's. Order No. 88. Appendix No 7	21/09/1918	21/09/1918
War Diary	Drouvin	01/10/1918	05/10/1918
War Diary	Sailly Labourse	06/10/1918	16/10/1918
War Diary	Billy Berclau	17/10/1918	18/10/1918
War Diary	Phalempin	19/10/1918	20/10/1918
War Diary	Templeuve	21/10/1918	31/10/1918
Operation(al) Order(s)	C.R.E's Order No. 87. Appendix No 1	05/10/1918	05/10/1918
Operation(al) Order(s)	C.R.E's Order No. 88. Appendix 2	14/10/1918	14/10/1918
Operation(al) Order(s)	C.R.E's Order No. 89. Appendix 3	15/10/1918	15/10/1918
Operation(al) Order(s)	C.R.E's Order No.90. Appendix 4	25/10/1918	25/10/1918
Operation(al) Order(s)	C.R.E's Order No. 91. Appendix 5	31/10/1918	31/10/1918
War Diary	Templeuve	01/11/1918	08/11/1918
War Diary	Florent	09/11/1918	16/11/1918
War Diary	Attiches.	17/11/1918	30/11/1918
Operation(al) Order(s)	C.R.E's Order No. 92. Appendix No. 1	03/11/1918	03/11/1918
Miscellaneous	Reference C.R.E's Instructions No. 4 App. No 2	06/11/1918	06/11/1918
Miscellaneous	C.R.E's Instructions No. 4. Appendix 2.	06/11/1918	06/11/1918
Operation(al) Order(s)	C.R.E's Order No. 93. Appendix No. 3.	26/11/1918	26/11/1918
War Diary	Attiches	01/12/1918	31/12/1918
Heading	War Diary Of The 16th Divisional Engineers. from January 1st to January 31st. 1919 Vol 38		
War Diary	Attiches.	01/01/1919	31/01/1919
Heading	War Diary of The 16th Divisional Engineers. From February 1st. 1919 to February 28th 1919 Vol 39		
War Diary	Attiches	01/02/1919	28/02/1919
Miscellaneous	D.A.G. 3rd Echelon.	03/04/1919	03/04/1919
Heading	War Diary H.Q. 16th Divisional Engineers. 1st to 31st March 1919 Vol 40		
War Diary	Attiches	01/03/1919	31/03/1919
Operation(al) Order(s)	C.R.E's Order No. 94 Appendix 1	28/03/1919	28/03/1919

Heading	War Diary. H.Q. 16th Divisional Engineers. April 1919. Vol 41		
War Diary	Attiches.	01/04/1919	01/04/1919
War Diary	Avelin.	02/04/1919	30/04/1919
Heading	War Diary. H.Q.R.E. 16th Division May 1919. Vol 42		
War Diary	Avelin	01/05/1919	31/05/1919
Heading	War Diary. H.Q.R.E. 16th Division June 1919. Final Sheets Vol 43		
War Diary	Avelin	01/06/1919	25/06/1919

WO 95/1916.

16 Division
Headquarters Branches
& Services

Dec 1915 - Jun 1919.

COMMANDER ROYAL
ENGINEERS

16TH DIVISION

C. R. E.

DEC 1915 - JUN 1919.

Army Form C. 2118.

WAR DIARY
or
INTELLIGENCE SUMMARY.
(Erase heading not required.)

Head Quarters
19th Div'l Engineers

Instructions regarding War Diaries and Intelligence Summaries are contained in F. S. Regs., Part II. and the Staff Manual respectively. Title pages will be prepared in manuscript.

Place	Date	Hour	Summary of Events and Information	Remarks and references to Appendices
	1915 Dec		(Dec 15 – Jan 16)	
BLACKDOWN	Dec 18th	1.10pm	Leave BLACKDOWN and march via FRITH HILL & S.W. of FARNBOROUGH on way to join Bedford Rupert Jones	
FARNBOROUGH	18th	4.10pm	Entrain for SOUTHAMPTON with Div'l Head Qtrs	
SOUTHAMPTON	18th	5.30pm	Arrive SOUTHAMPTON	
SOUTHAMPTON	18th	8 pm	Leave SOUTHAMPTON on H.M.S. MAIDAN with Div'l H.Q. Staff etc.	
LE HAVRE	19th	4.30am	Arrive at LE HAVRE and waited for tide to proceed up Pier	
"	19th	9 am	Commenced to disembark, and then marched to Dock Rest Camp	
"	19th	11 pm	March to Point 4 and commenced to entrain with H.Q. & Div'l Sig Coy	
"	20th	3.20am	Left LE HAVRE for ST OMER	
FOUQUEREUIL	20th	11.55pm	Detrain and proceed to billet at DROUVIN arrived at billets 6.10am on 21.12.15	
DROUVIN	21st		Rest	
"	22nd		C.E. 4th Corps calls for Recon to take over & Corps gd at MINX etc & Rutment at NOEUX LES MINES, and to assume S.C. Rutments at MAZINGARBE and Reserve vice SAILLY LA BOURSE	
"	23rd		Convoy with R.W. MINX for stores for huts at DROUVIN. Sam 15/th to MAZINGARBE and 155 Coy at PHILOSOPHE. Gd at 200* away from their billets & has been heavily shelled in the morning	
"	24th		Entrain to lay trench at BETHUNE but cab told on-fated as wa. See 11th HANTS about entry R.E. at NOEUX LES MINES and furthers or copier. Issued at NOEUX LES MINES, for O.E. 11th HANTS	

Army Form C. 2118.

Head Quarters
S/16 Divisional Engineers 2.

WAR DIARY
or
INTELLIGENCE SUMMARY.
(Erase heading not required.)

Instructions regarding War Diaries and Intelligence Summaries are contained in F. S. Regs., Part II. and the Staff Manual respectively. Title pages will be prepared in manuscript.

Place	Date	Hour	Summary of Events and Information	Remarks and references to Appendices
DROUVIN	25 Dec	—	Go to Div. Engr. Hts NOEUX LES MINES and look at Coys at BETHUNE and find men outside for billets	
"	26th		Visit 155 Coy at PHILOSOPHE and 157 at MAZINGARBE	
"	27 Dec		Go to Foss 6 and see work of different parties, billeting carried by 2 Coys 11th Hants and 1/2 Coy 156 3d Coy	
"	28 Dec		Visit Cat at NUEUX and see work started.	
"	29 Dec		Start w/ part of 3000 Brans at LA BUSSIERE from Army Corps	
"	30 "		In Car arrivals stay near DROUVIN	
"	31st		Pack up and arrange for move. 2 Sects 157 Coy quen MAZINGARBE for AMETTES on their	
"	1 Jan		way to BOMY	

Army Form C. 2118.

Head Quarters
16th Divisional Engineers

WAR DIARY
or
INTELLIGENCE SUMMARY.
(Erase heading not required.)

Instructions regarding War Diaries and Intelligence Summaries are contained in F. S. Regs., Part II. and the Staff Manual respectively. Title pages will be prepared in manuscript.

Place	Date	Hour	Summary of Events and Information	Remarks and references to Appendices
DROUVIN	1st Jan	9.am	Leave DROUVIN for BOMY, 2 Sects 157 Coy arrive GREUPPE	
BOMY	1st Jan	12.40am	arrive BOMY and arrange billets and CRES yard	
"	2 Jan		Sale Vauxhall car to look for baggage wagon and trace it to Aire	
"	3 Jan		Visit LILLERS and start stores for new yard. Also arrange for general supplies of material	
"	4th Jan		Recommend huts at BEAUMETZ. 155 Coy attached to 2nd division Canadian 156 & 1/2 157 attached 47th Divn 2 Sects 157 Coy 9th SENUS	
"	5 Jan		Visit H.2. 48th brigade and find out requirements for mine Pits	
"	6 Jan		Knowegate HOINENGHEM on divn H.2. last find to hoplon	
"	7 Jan		Change to billets for H.2. RE and 2 sects 157 Ju. G. Ile at AMETTES. Also arrange for workshop and store yard	
AMETTES	8 Jan		Arrive AMETTES, CRE arrange for target firing at MINX, also sees 6th Coy and 11th Hants	
"	"		156 Coy taken over work from 11th Hants for construction/Puits at VIEUX LES MINES	
"	"		H.d.2 & two 1 & 2 Sects 157 Coy report to work under 1st Divn	
"	9th Jan		See. 41 & 48th Brigades about targets, baths, etc.; arrange for material for hut	
"	"		R.E Park LILLERS and OC 73 3rd Coy LILLERS	
"	10th		Go to 4 RE Park LILLERS, also arrange to g' huts at MAZINGHEM and by tents etc at AIRE	

Ore. 16th Div:
Vols I & II

Dec 15-31st
Jan '16

Army Form C. 2118.

Head Quarters
16th Divisional Engineers

WAR DIARY
or
INTELLIGENCE SUMMARY.
(Erase heading not required.)

Instructions regarding War Diaries and Intelligence Summaries are contained in F. S. Regs., Part II. and the Staff Manual respectively. Title pages will be prepared in manuscript.

Place	Date	Hour	Summary of Events and Information	Remarks and references to Appendices
AMETTES	11th Jan		Arrange for lunch at St HILAIRE, also make purchases at AIRE and BETHUNE, also see 156, 157 and 155 Coys at their respective billets, also arrange for showers baths at MINX.	
"	12.1.16		Buy steel, iron timber etc at AIRE and LILLERS	
"	13.1.16		See LILLERS, BETHUNE, MINX and DROUVIN purchasing material	
"	14.1.16		See AIRE and LILLERS for more material etc.	
"	15.1.16		Arrange to get stop for weeks and run standing from AUCHEL	
"	16.1.15		Following letter received from Adjt 2 – C.R.E., please convey to Colr BREMNER and all Officers and men of the 155th FIELD COY. R.E. who were engaged on this work my appreciation of their efforts and my thanks for having saved this horse for the Division. Sd W.B. HICKIE MAJ-GEN 14th Jan 1916. Letter from C.R.E. 1st Divisional to Adjt 2nd Divisional Divn – "The 155th FIELD COY R.E. of yours was lucky on Thursday even am very fortunate. From the 2nd December 1915 under the 1st Jan 1916 the Coy was shelled in Laures which were much shewn to the fire and would have were all against its luck so setted down really and P.T.O.	

T2134. Wt. W708-776. 500000. 4/15. Sir J. C. & S.

Army Form C. 2118.

WAR DIARY
or
INTELLIGENCE SUMMARY.
(Erase heading not required.)

Head Quarters
10th Divisional Engineers

Place	Date	Hour	Summary of Events and Information	Remarks and references to Appendices
AMETTES	17.1.16		Returned very crowded. The Sections were employed in our front line and in carrying bombs at the mine craters. They came under a lot of fire and being quite new to the work were only have been most useful. but they stuck to their work well and gave a very favorable impression of the men and of their Officers. The Sections were also employed on the reconnaissance of Left Flow Enemy Line and were settling down well to their work of forming and handling large parties of Infantry labouring to difficult situations. Sd. S.D.A. CROOKSHANK, Lt. Col. R.E. 23.1.16	
"	18.1.16		Away for 2 Rd. at AUCHEL.	
"	19.1.16		Buy timber at AUCHEL also arrange for sand at ST HILAIRE and ROMBLEY. Go A.H.2. : BETHUNE & MINX, hay for Bde. at BEAUMETZ.	
"	20.1.16		Went to NOEUX LES MINES. PHILOSOPHE & MASINGARBE	
"	21.1.16		Buy turf, wood, and tube w. Adjt at ST HILAIRE. go to AIRE in afternoon.	
"	22.1.16		Arrange for baths for 1 Brigade at AMETTES and also for disinfection of cloths at doctors village near LIERES	

Army Form C. 2118.

WAR DIARY
or
INTELLIGENCE SUMMARY.
(Erase heading not required.)

Head Quarters 16th Divisional Engineers

Instructions regarding War Diaries and Intelligence Summaries are contained in F. S. Regs., Part II. and the Staff Manual respectively. Title pages will be prepared in manuscript.

Place	Date	Hour	Summary of Events and Information	Remarks and references to Appendices
AMETTES	23.1.16		Arrange for horse shelters for Divl. AMN. Column and go to 16th Divl. Bomb School. Recon. information. Lieut GEORGE CARLYLE wounded in chest when in billets 157th Coy.	
"	24.1.16		Capt. ASSHER suffering from shell shock	"
"	25.1.16		C.R.E. visited 155 Coy at PHILOSOPHE and 157 Coy at MAZINGARBE.	
"	26.1.16		Go to LILLERS and AIRE for materials & tools	
"	27.1.16		Get moved from LILLERS.	
"	28.1.16		Decide to arrange for Brigade Umbrella. Go AIRE in afternoon	
"	29.1.16		Go to selecting point to see about shelters and platform. Go hayfork and saw in Rotary range in afternoon	
"	30.1.16		iiLT FRANCIS JAMES COLLEY & ii LT HAROLD MARSTON SIMMS joined for duties with 157 Fd Coy R.E.	
"	31.1.16			

T2134. Wt. W708—776. 500000. 4/15. Sir J. C. & S.

CRC 16ᵃ Die Vol 3

Army Form C. 2118.

WAR DIARY
or
INTELLIGENCE SUMMARY.
(Erase heading not required.)

Headquarters,
16th Divisional Engineers

Instructions regarding War Diaries and Intelligence Summaries are contained in F. S. Regs., Part II. and the Staff Manual respectively. Title pages will be prepared in manuscript.

Place	Date	Hour	Summary of Events and Information	Remarks and references to Appendices
AMETTES	1.2.16		Visit 155, 156 & 157 Fd Coys RE and tell 2 new officers to join 157 Fd Coy at MAZINGARBE	
"	2.2.16		Go AIRE and LILLERS for work	
"	3.2.16		Divisions is going to be attached to 1st Corps shortly. Go AIRE LILLERS and 47th Bdy HQ	
"	4.2.16		C.E. 1st Corps sees C.R.E at AMETTES	
"	5.2.16		Visit C.R.E. 12th Div at BUSNES	
"	6.2.16		C.R.E brings Capt MACGEORGE forward to be O i/c MAZINGARBE	
"	7.2.16		Go to AIRE for guns etc	
"	8.2.16		C.R.E to PHILOSOPHE and visits 2nd Line trenches with Capt BREMNER	
"	9.2.16		See C.R.E. 12th Div in front of NIEPPE. Suffolks 1st Corps in evening to MAZINGARBE	
"	10.2.16		To AIRE and LILLERS for stores	
"	11.2.16		To BETHUNE. 155 Fd Coy PHILOSOPHE to HOUCHIN	
"	12.2.16		155 Fd Coy RE HOUCHIN to NEDON	
"	13.2.16		155 Fd Coy RE NEDON to MONT CORNET & RANNEVILLE	
"	14.2.16		157 Fd Coy R.E MAZINGARBE to AMETTE	
"	15.2.16		156 " " NEUX LES MINES to GUHEM	
"	16.2.16		CRE sees 156 Field Coy	

WAR DIARY or INTELLIGENCE SUMMARY

Army Form C. 2118.

Headquarters, 16th Divisional Engineers.

Place	Date	Hour	Summary of Events and Information	Remarks and references to Appendices
AMETTES	17.2.16		G.O.C. visits 155th Coy R.E. and was very pleased with turnout	
"	18.2.16		" 156 "	
"	19.2.16		" 157 "	
"	20.2.16		Meeting at Div. H.Q. as to state Brigade Work etc.	
"	21.2.16		Go route to NIEPPE and BETHUNE	
"	22.2.16		See 155 Coy. at RANNEVILLE. Heavy fall of snow.	
"	23.2.16		Go to see about watering arrangements of new DIVL ARTILLERY. Hard frost and snow	
"	24.2.16		Hard frost and snow continues	
"	25.2.16		"	
"	26.2.16		Arrange Billets for 157 F'd Coy at and for H.Q. R.E. at BUSNES	
BUSNES	27.2.16		Move to BUSNES. 156 3rd Coy to LA MIQUELLERIE	
"	28.2.16		156 move to BEUVRY	
"	29.2.16		157 3rd Coy move to LA MIQUELLERIE. 155 F'd Coy to BOUREC	

JMS

CRE
16 DW
Vol 4

Instructions regarding War Diaries and Intelligence Summaries are contained in F. S. Regs., Part II. and the Staff Manual respectively. Title pages will be prepared in manuscript.

WAR DIARY
or
INTELLIGENCE SUMMARY.
(Erase heading not required.)

Headquarters, 16th Divisional
Engineers

C. 2118.

Place	Date	Hour	Summary of Events and Information	Remarks and references to Appendices
BUSNES	1.3.16		Company pushing forwards at ISBERGUES	
	2.3.16		Hostile aeroplanes over LILLERS 10 am	
	3.3.16		156 Field Coy from BEUVRY to FOSSE du BRAQUEMONT to 1st DIV	
	4.3.16		157 field Coy attd to 12TH DIV	
	5.3.16		157 field Coy to ANNEQUIN	
	"		156 field Coy to LES BREBIS	
	6.3.16		Divn ordered to new area	
	7.3.16		Snow in morning about 1½" thaws during day	
	8.3.16		3" Snow in morning 155 field Coy move to Du REVEILLON	
	9.3.16		Arrive LILLERS fm BUSNES Lt F J COLLEY 157 Coy wounded	
LILLERS	10.3.16		Lt R. on work fm 138 Army troops Coy	
	11.3.16		Lt C. on stone fm LILLERS yard.	
	12.3.16		do do go to 157 Coy at ANNEQUIN	
	13.3.16		Arrange to various works in the area	
	14.3.16		See C.R.E. 12TH Div	
	15.3.16		156 Fd Coy fm LES BREBIS to LAPUGNOY	

Headquarters, 16th Divisional Engineers.   Army Form C. 2118.

WAR DIARY
or
INTELLIGENCE SUMMARY
(Erase heading not required.)

Place	Date	Hour	Summary of Events and Information	Remarks and references to Appendices
LILLERS	16.3.16		Arrange for Reorg. of the plate glass at ST OMER. 157 Fd Coy to CAUCHY A LA TOUR.	
	17.3.16		See C.R.E. 15th Div re Canadian ovens	
	18.3.16		C.R.E. walks over Village lines	
	19.3.16		Following letter received from O.C. 156 Coy R.E.: At BULLY GRENAY at about 9.30 a.m. stand-to fire. The enemy opened a heavy 5.9" shell fire on the village, when the vehicles of this Company were parked. One shell exploded under one tool cart damaging the cart, killing one L.Cpl. and wounding the guns-cart thrown about. Cpl. BAILEY, N.C.O. i/c Guard over vehicles, with his guard, but not the Cpl. and horses, removed the overturns remaining from being fired. Having had the road left of the vehicles & the shell road continued detonation. 6 S/n OGDEN, seeing that shells were bursting near the vehicles, immediately collected a party from billets, proceeded to the mine and removed the remaining vehicles (tool carts and limbered wagons) from damage and also (removing the explosives from being set off and damaging) the mine buildings. This was done under shell fire - one shell landed within a	

WAR DIARY
or
INTELLIGENCE SUMMARY
(Erase heading not required.)

Headquarters, 16th Divisional Engineers. Army Form C. 2118.

Place	Date	Hour	Summary of Events and Information	Remarks and references to Appendices
LILLERS		19.3.16	couple of yards from the hole, just luckily it was a blind shell. The N.C.O's and men who carried out this plucky and praiseworthy action were:— 107476. C.S.M. OGDEN. W. 53947. SERGT. CARTER. E. 97817. 2/CPL. UTTLEY. F. 97654. SAPR. BARROW. T. 97645. SAPR. CUNNINGHAM. J. 101325. SAPR. FIELD. J. 97914. SAPR. HARRIS. T. 97929. SAPR. MARSTON. G. 108477. SAPR. SCOTT. W. 94803. SAPR. STONE. C. 97913. SAPR. BURTON. W. 69961. SAPR. DENMAN. H. 69811. SAPR. MORGAN. W. GUARD:— 97842. CPL. BAILEY. N. 98322. SAPR. GEAR. N. 101540. SAPR. HUNT. J. 98260. SAPR. CASTLE. W.	as R. of W. MARSDEN, Lieut. R.E. O.C. 156th Field Coy R.E.
		17.3.16	Reply:- O.C. 156 Field Coy R.E. The W.R.E. notes with very great satisfaction the gallant conduct of 107476. C.S.M. OGDEN. W. 53947. SERGT. CARTER. E. 97817. 2/CPL. UTTLEY. F. 97842. CPL. BAILEY. W. Their names have been noted in this office.	Col. L. E. Baker Collyer R.E. Asst. 16th Divl. Engrs.
		19.3.16		

Headquarters, 16th Divisional Engineers. Army Form C. 2118.

WAR DIARY
or
INTELLIGENCE SUMMARY
(Erase heading not required.)

Instructions regarding War Diaries and Intelligence Summaries are contained in F. S. Regs, Part II. and the Staff Manual respectively. Title pages will be prepared in manuscript.

Place	Date	Hour	Summary of Events and Information	Remarks and references to Appendices
LILLERS	19.3.16		C.R.E. to NOEUX LES MINES to take over from C.R.E. 13th DIV	
	20.3.16		C.R.E. at NOEUX LES MINES.	
	21.3.16		C.R.E. returns LILLERS	
	22.3.16		C.R.E. sees Village Line with C.E.	
	23.3.16		1 Section 155 Fd Coy and 156 Fd Coy to PHILOSOPHE to take over Machine gun emplacements	
	24.3.16		Capt BREMNER to MAZINGARBE, Capt HUNT to PHILOSOPHE to take over Divisional Dump	
	24.3.16		Capt MARSDEN to PHILOSOPHE 3" of Snow during the Night	
	25.3.16		155 Fd Coy less 1 section to MAZINGARBE	
	26.3.16		156 " " " to PHILOSOPHE	
	27.3.16		157 Field Coy to PHILOSOPHE	
	28.3.16		The following letter received from the O.C. 156th Fd R.E.:-	

No. 59402. Serg.t T. NORMANTON. N. No. 97432 Sapr. C.E.;-
No. 2nd RE 6 NOEUX LES MINES. Hd 2nd RE 6 NOEUX LES MINES.
Sapr. THOMAS L.

About 1.0 a.m. on the 27.3.16, during the repair and consolidation of trenches damaged by the explosion of a mine at H.13.5, the above N.C.O and men worked with great energy under machine gun

WAR DIARY
or
INTELLIGENCE SUMMARY.

Headquarters, 16th Divisional Engineers. Army Form C. 2118.

Place	Date	Hour	Summary of Events and Information	Remarks and references to Appendices
			and rifle grenade fire, and received three men of the 9. R.M.F. who were burned and wounded. Artificial respiration was successfully applied in one case, & all three were carried up, all admitted to a place of safety. I saw in this party during the above mentioned (sd) R.W. Morgan Capt RE O.C. 156th Fd Co RE	
	29/7	Reply.	O.C. 156th Fd Co RE The C.R.E. is very gratified with the fine work done by No 59402 Sergt Normanton W. No 97432 Sapr Clenley W. No 98257 Sapr Thomas L. and has had their names noted in this office. (sd) L.E. Bear Capt RE Adjutant 16. Div. Eng.	

WAR DIARY or INTELLIGENCE SUMMARY

**Headquarters, 16th Divisional Army Form C. 2118.
Engineers.**

Place	Date	Hour	Summary of Events and Information	Remarks and references to Appendices
	3/3/16		The following letter received from the O.C. 157th Field Coy R.E.— "I wish to report on gallantry displayed by No 3 Section, 157th Field Coy R.E. while attached to the 12th Division.— On night of 14/15th March 1916, Nos. 2 and 3 Sections under Lieut. Greenlow & Lieut Sirapo respectively were ordered to assist in consolidation of No 3 Crater. No 3 Section were in the act of trenching along the top with ties to No. 3 Crater followed by No. 2 Section. The head of the party was about 10 yards from the entrance to the Crater. At this moment, two Rifle Grenades or small Trench Mortar Bombs (probably the latter from the dangerous) fell among the Infantry Garrison who were lining the two lips of the Crater. Of the Garrison (12 strong) 5 were killed and 6 wounded. Their Stretcher Bearers were instructed the killed & wounded	

Headquarters, 16th Divisional Engineers.

Army Form C. 2118.

WAR DIARY
or
~~INTELLIGENCE SUMMARY~~
(Erase heading not required.)

Place	Date	Hour	Summary of Events and Information	Remarks and references to Appendices
			Capot. Rae of N°3 Section unnecessarily dashed into the Crater followed by Lieut. Simms & Sergt. Stubbs. On inquiry what had happened, and my sent to Lieut. Greenhead who withdrew No Section and sent N°3 so as to allow wounded to be carried into the Fap. I went to see the Infantry that N°3 Crater was without a Garrison.	
			Meanwhile Rme men of N°3 Section went into the Crater to assist with the wounded. Despite the fact that small French Parties (or say the Grenadiers) were taking Clinjon & around the Crater had been sentenced at the end, this report rested first-aid to the wounded & carried them out of the Crater. They handed one over to the Infantry Stretcher Bearers & carried the remaining five to the nearest Dressing Station which was over la mile away.	

T2134. Wt. W708—776. 500000. 4/15. Sir J. C. & S.

WAR DIARY

Headquarters, 16th Divisional Engineers.

Army Form C. 2118.

Instructions regarding War Diaries and Intelligence Summaries are contained in F. S. Regs., Part II. and the Staff Manual respectively. Title pages will be prepared in manuscript.

Place	Date	Hour	Summary of Events and Information	Remarks and references to Appendices
			in B. to Alley. One of the Infantry was too badly wounded to render any first-aid to & he died before he reached the Dressing station. (half his chest was blown away) Ten field dressings were used in the crater on the Infantry Sergeant. Specially good work was done by :— 2nd Lieut. H.M. Sims R.E. No. 40474 Sergt. Hobbs N.L. No. 97088. Pionr. Joe J.N. (enre promoted for the job) No. 113780. Sapr. Miller A. No. 58226. Sapr. Jones E.E. The following also gave valuable assistance in look= =ing after work on the Crater, in rendering the wounded from the Crater & in carrying wounded to the dressing station. No. 53613. L. Cpl. Reeves J. No. 95932. Sapr. Underwood N. No. 45772. Sapr. Davis G. No. 103560. Sapr. Thomas F. (sd.) K.J. Neo Geo. Lyt. Cor. 26.3.16 OC. 154th Field Coy. RE	

WAR DIARY
or
INTELLIGENCE SUMMARY.

(Erase heading not required.)

Army Form C. 2118.

Headquarters, 16th Divisional Engineers.

Instructions regarding War Diaries and Intelligence Summaries are contained in F. S. Regs., Part II. and the Staff Manual respectively. Title pages will be prepared in manuscript.

Place	Date	Hour	Summary of Events and Information	Remarks and references to Appendices
NOEUX LES MINES	30TH		C.R.E. goes over Village line with C.E.	
	31st		C.R.E. to 155 and 156 Field Coys to arrange about new trench work tR. R.R.	

....
Captain, R.E.
Adjutant R.E. 16th Division

Army Form C. 2118.

WAR DIARY
or
INTELLIGENCE SUMMARY.
(Erase heading not required.)

Headquarters,
16th, Divisional Engineers.

Instructions regarding War Diaries and Intelligence Summaries are contained in F.S. Regs., Part II. and the Staff Manual respectively. Title pages will be prepared in manuscript.

Place	Date	Hour	Summary of Events and Information	Remarks and references to Appendices
NOEUX LES MINES	April 1		Staff Divisional Cinema	
"	2		C.R.E. to transfer with 157 Fd Cy C.O to decide on two new approaches to Village line	
"	3		C.R.E. to transfer with G.S.O.1	
"	4		C.R.E. goes with G.O.C. 16th divn and C of S Commander to see the front line trenches, at a meeting in the evening it is decided that some counter measures must be taken against the Boches mining efforts on our front.	
"	5		S.O.C. Conference at MAZINGARBE CHATEAU	
"	6		It absolute necessity for a Divisional Unit. As more and more efforts on trench guns arise at all events for the the Stationary siege warfare. It is quite essential of a section of R.E with an officer should be attached to A.2 R.E and included in the establishment.	
"	7th		New trench W of CHALK PIT WOOD COMMENCED	
"	8th		Instructions for listening galleries sent out	
"	9th		The following received from the O.C. 156 Field Coy R.E:- "I have men self extremely forwarded for your information. These men did extremely"	

Army Form C. 2118.

Headquarters,
16th, Divisional Engineers.

WAR DIARY
or
INTELLIGENCE SUMMARY.
(Erase heading not required.)

Place	Date	Hour	Summary of Events and Information	Remarks and references to Appendices

available work in war time and keeping grip at work.

8 April 1916.   L. E. M. Evans Captain
                                 O.C. 156 Div Co R.E.

O.C. 156 Fld Coy R.E.

I beg to report that yesterday morning the
to Company was digging out a working party on the front
No 10,852 Sapr GEDDES. P No 101,409 Sapr HEYMAN A N° 9317
Sapr YENDLE T. On the 3rd April 1916 the men of Fly dug
out by digging out a Trench which was blown
after the existence of a mine believed to be a mine
men killed at once. The Cuirassiers which were doing
were sent in dug and his close to the immediately
reported of once, but be to the enemy and blown
Lieut [?] not [?] spanner. But the rifle grenades and his
killed and were working and dug the Sers GEDDES and his
men for the say in which they carried out this work.

Army Form C. 2118.

WAR DIARY
or
INTELLIGENCE SUMMARY.
(Erase heading not required.)

Headquarters,
16th, Divisional Engineers.

Instructions regarding War Diaries and Intelligence Summaries are contained in F. S. Regs., Part II. and the Staff Manual respectively. Title pages will be prepared in manuscript.

Place	Date	Hour	Summary of Events and Information	Remarks and references to Appendices
	April			
	10th		regretty as was planned & owing to incurring list their services to flood in neighborhood of evacuation (Sapr. PICKLES. G. 10830 & Sapr. NEWMAN.A. 14404 these former volunteered to go to site but it was decided [illegible] not required.) [illegible] R. E. 16 [illegible]	
NOEUX LES MINES				
"	11th		Bury angle new and T new at AIRE for frames for overhead cover near listening galleries when construction in Ft fort Ont.	
"	12		C.R.E sees 253 Tunnelling Coy re new listening galleries. Listening galleries commenced.	
	13th		FOSSE 3 Store shelled with 8" 10000 sand bags set on fire	
	14th		C.R.E to Village Line and junction of new line with Indian SECTOR	
	15th		NOEUX LES MINES shelled in the evening	
	16th		FOSSE 3 again shelled in the evening	
	17th		11th Hants Queens dig MEATH Trench and deepen RAILWAY ALLEY	
	18th		widen RAILWAY ALLEY	

Army Form C. 2118.

WAR DIARY
or
INTELLIGENCE SUMMARY

(Erase heading not required.)

Instructions regarding War Diaries and Intelligence Summaries are contained in F.S. Regs., Part II. and the Staff Manual respectively. Title pages will be prepared in manuscript.

Place	Date	Hour	Summary of Events and Information	Remarks and references to Appendices
NOEUX LES MINES	19		Supn CHALK PIT ALLEY (11th HANTS)	
"	20		Made R.E. Site Plan Scheme for Entering Galleries	
"	21		Gone with rain. C.R.E. to Village Line with G.O.C.	
"	22		Gone with rain	
"	23		A fine day. BRAQUEMONT SHELLED slightly	
"	24		CAPT BREMNER to NOEUX & at C.R.E. during C.R.E's Recce.	
"	25		Meeting at MAZINGARBE CHATEAU	
"	26th		C.R.E. gone on Recce.	
"	27th		Gas alarm at 5.30 am. tear shells fell in NOEUX LES MINES at 6.30 am. Dense cloud / smoke and gas from 7 to 7.30 am so thick that the sun could scarcely be seen through it, all enemy ejected from CHALK PIT WOOD by 11.30 am	
"	28th		Day quite except for gas alarm at 8 pm	
"	29		Gas alarm at 4.15 am but gas did not reach NOEUX LES MINES	
"	30		Day passed quietly	

Headquarters,
16th, Divisional Engineers.

H.M. Bertin
Captain R.E.
for C.R.E. 16th, Division.

Army Form C. 2118.

WAR DIARY
or
INTELLIGENCE SUMMARY.
(Erase heading not required.)

Headquarters,
16th Divisional Engineers.

Instructions regarding War Diaries and Intelligence Summaries are contained in F. S. Regs., Part II. and the Staff Manual respectively. Title pages will be prepared in manuscript.

Place	Date	Hour	Summary of Events and Information	Remarks and references to Appendices
NOEUX LES MINES	1.5.16		Quiet day, first Coy in HULLUCH SECTION relieved by Hants Pioneers	
	2.5.16		Arrange scheme for men showers baths at MAZINGARBE	
	3.5.16		Lecture on gas by first army expert	
	4.5.16		Weather very wet. Quiet day	
	5.5.16		C.R.E. arranges work for attached Pioneer Battalions and Field Coys	
	6.5.16		C.R.E. shows O.C. 12th Div Pioneers over work	
	7.5.16		C.R.E. returns from leave	
	8.5.16		1st Shower Bath now in use hourly completed	
	9.5.16		Normal day – Capt Beckm R.E. goes on leave	
	10.5.16		Normal day	
	11.5.16		Artillery barrage at PHILOSOPHE	
	12.5.16		Normal day	
	13.5.16		"	
	14.5.16		"	
	15.5.16		"	
	16.5.16		"	

J.W. Beckm
Captn
Adjt 16th Div Engineers

Vol. 11

WAR DIARY
or
INTELLIGENCE SUMMARY.

Headquarters,
16th Divisional Engineers Army Form C. 2118.

(Erase heading not required.)

Place	Date	Hour	Summary of Events and Information	Remarks and references to Appendices
NOEUX LES MINES	17.5.16		Normal Day	
	18.5.16		" "	
	19.5.16		" "	
	20.5.16		" "	
	21.5.16		Normal day except for slight shelling of NOEUX les MINES. — Capt Baker returns	
	22.5.16		Normal day — heavy enemy aerial work to epitaphs by Lt Hickey	
	23.5.16		Normal Day	
	24.5.16		C.R.E to see LOOS	
	25.5.16		Noeux shelled at about 4 pm	
	26.5.16		Normal	
	27.5.16		Working parties called up on account of possible attack	
	28.5.16		Working parties all to be in billets by daylight on account of possible attack	
	29.5.16		Same as 28.5.16	
	30.5.16		" "	
	31.5.16		" "	

Army Form C. 2118.

Vol 7

WAR DIARY
or
INTELLIGENCE SUMMARY.
(Erase heading not required.)

Headquarters,
16th Divisional Engineers.

Instructions regarding War Diaries and Intelligence Summaries are contained in F. S. Regs., Part II. and the Staff Manual respectively. Title pages will be prepared in manuscript.

Place	Date	Hour	Summary of Events and Information	Remarks and references to Appendices
NOEUX LES MINES	1.6.16		2 Companies of Suffolk Regt. 12th Division attached for work	
	2.6.16		2 More Companies of Suffolk Regt. 12th Div. attached for work	
	3.6.16		Normal	
	4.6.16		Normal	
	5.6.16		C.R.E. goes on billeting Rec.	
	6.6.16		5 Battalion Regiment relieve Suffolk regiment at 12 noon for work under C.R.E.	
	7.6.16		Normal	
	8.6.16		2 Sections 157 Coy to the LOOS ABATTOIR & MAZINGARBE areas drilled small sheds	
	9.6.16		229th Field Coy attached for work.	
	10.6.16		C.R.E. to LOOS	
	11.6.16		One Coy 7th Yorks Regiment Juniors attached C.R.E. for work	
	12.6.16		Normal	
	13.6.16		C.R.E. to Northern Sub Redoubt 5th Hallants & 11th Middlesex attached 12th Div.	
	14.6.16		2 Coys 12th Yorks Regiment arrive for work under C.R.E	
	15.6.16		640 Loaves for LOOS WAKERI dumped in the avenues	
	16.6.16		80 loaves completed 83 Sub trenches	

Army Form C. 2118.

WAR DIARY
or
INTELLIGENCE SUMMARY.
(Erase heading not required.)

Headquarters,
16th Divisional Engineers.

Instructions regarding War Diaries and Intelligence Summaries are contained in F. S. Regs., Part II. and the Staff Manual respectively. Title pages will be prepared in manuscript.

Place	Date	Hour	Summary of Events and Information	Remarks and references to Appendices
NOEUX LES MINES	17.6.16		600 Special Issues sent to trenches also 40 waggons 300 to LOOS 300 to POSEN Street	
	18.6.16		252 and 223 have placed in position in Southern and Northern Sectors respectively	
	19.6.16		a practically impossible task almost carried out in filling the above locations	
			Major A.H.2. called within the hundred difficulties & work in the trenches and guns seem to hopefully organise and make revisions and were satisfactory work called to date	
	20.6.16		Vn and Vn M.G. emplacements in Village Line adjusted	
	21.6.16		Find Hpets Bomb dugout ruined the shelters in the Village Line sent to the T.R.h. into shelters	
	22.6.16		Intd. over Village Line with R.E.	
	23.6.16		Inwood	
	24.6.16		Inwood	
	25.6.16		The wells down in front of Village Line	
	26.6.16		Lt. JENNINGS and Lt. O'SULLIVAN 155 Field Coy Consolidate HARTS and HARRISBURG Saler ander any fire, fire during raids.	
	27.6.16		Crater Consolidation started on account of bombardment	

WAR DIARY
~~INTELLIGENCE SUMMARY~~

Headquarters,
16th Divisional Engineers

Army Form C. 2118.

Place	Date	Hour	Summary of Events and Information	Remarks and references to Appendices
NOEUX LES MINES	28.6.16		Crater Consolidation Carried on	
	29.6.16		C.R.E. on village. Rain not to previous O.P.s to view HARTS and HARRISON'S CRATERS	
	30.6.16			

Meiklejohn
Capt. R.E.
Adj. 16th Divl. Engineers

SECRET

ROYAL ENGINEERS
No. 566
18TH DIVISION

Report on Consolidation of new HARRISON'S and
HART'S Craters.
----

(1) HARRISON's CRATER.

The party under Lieutenant R.B. JENNINGS, R.E. consisted of 25 R.E., 2nd Lieutenant DARCY and 52 6th Connaught Rangers.

The party followed the raiding parties out to front line wire.

Lieutenant JENNINGS went up the crater, selected position for bombing post and left 1 N.C.O. and 6 Sappers to get on with the work. He then returned to 2nd Lieut DARCY who was getting the diggers out and together they lined them on a trench to connect bombing post with existing front line trench.

He then shewed 2nd Lieut. DARCY where the wire should go, and went off to get the party with the wooden shelter frames. He could only find one Sapper whom he told to look for the others and bring them up to the front.

He then returned to the crater, and adjusted the position of the wire which had been got out. The wooden frames not arriving and knowing that it was all important that the work on bombing post and shelter should not be delayed Lieut. JENNINGS got together a party to get any available timber from the old front line.

When the shelter was half completed the frames arrived and some were fitted in the shelter.

The wire was by this time finished and the party was put on to clear out the front line and old sap.

By 2.0am. the fire was getting hot and several men were hit in the open whilst carrying material up to the shelter.

Soon after this the shelter was finished so the men were cleared off the top and work concentrated on the communication trench and post. At 2.30.am. the shelter and post were finished and the trench dug to a depth of 3'6" and work ceased.

I consider that Lieutenant R.B. Jennings conduct on this occasion deserves recognition. His intrepidity, coolness and foresight under a very hot fire contributed largely to the success of the work. There were 5 casualties among the R.E. of this party.

He was most ably assisted by 2nd Lieutenant DARCY of the 6th Connaught Rangers who was always in the right spot at the right time and was of the greatest help in keeping his men going and getting them on their work.

Lieut Jennings also reports that every man of the 6th Connaughts in his party worked splendidly.

He also specially mentions Sapper WILD his orderly as being absolutely invaluable in finding material, guiding men to it, and getting them off to the bombers post at a time when every minute was of value.

(2) HART'S CRATER.

This party under Lieutenant J.O'SULLIVAN, R.E. consisted of 15 R.E. and 50 Infantry under 2nd Lieutenant BLAKE O'SULLIVAN.

They were ordered to advance in rear of raiding party No. 6, on getting on to the front line 1 N.C.O. and 4 Sappers, specially detailed, were to advance with the R.E. Officer in charge to make a bombing post to command the new crater, the Officer in charge Infantry party was to accompany this party so as to get to know the ground, the remainder of the party were to remain in the front line and await orders.

After party No. 6 had been ordered to advance, Lieut. J. O'SULLIVAN proceeded with his special party to reconnoitre for a suitable bombing post, but could not discover any new crater, and thought the new mine must have more or less coincided with the old one. While on this reconnaissance, word was brought to him that his party had been given orders to go back. He then sent 2nd Lieut. BLAKE O'SULLIVAN with his own orderly to collect any of the party he could discover, after a considerable time some of the party were collected and the following work done to works which had been damaged by the explosion:-

Two old Saps A to B and F to J cleared and deepened.
Two Covered Shelters D and G repaired.
Snipers Post at H repaired.
A new Bombers Post made at C.

At 2.50 am. just when it was getting light, Lieut. J.O'SULLIVAN discovered the mound J to the left of the old crater and from what he could see in the bad light it did not appear to be a large one. With the help of some men 2nd Lieut. BLAKE O'SULLIVAN collected, a Snipers Post at I was put up so as to cover the ground between our lines and this mound.

The party was withdrawn at 3.20 am. after having reported to the O.C. Left Party, Captain PHILLIPS.

Lieut. J.O'SULLIVAN draws attention to the excellent work done by 2nd Lieut. BLAKE O'SULLIVAN, 6th Connaught Rangers in his initiative in collecting and getting men on their work and who by his coolness and disregard of danger gave great confidence to his men and got the best out of them.

The whole work was carried out under a very heavy fire of all sorts.

I also consider that Lieutenant J.O'SULLIVAN, R.E. deserves great credit for his initiative and arrangements when he found his working party had gone wrong and the crater was not where it was expected, the whole of these arrangements having to be made under a heavy fire.

29th June 1916.

Lieut-Colonel, R.E.
C.R.E. 16th Division.

W A R   D I A R Y

Headquarters
16th Divl. Engineers

1st. July to 31st. July 1916.

VOLUME No. 8

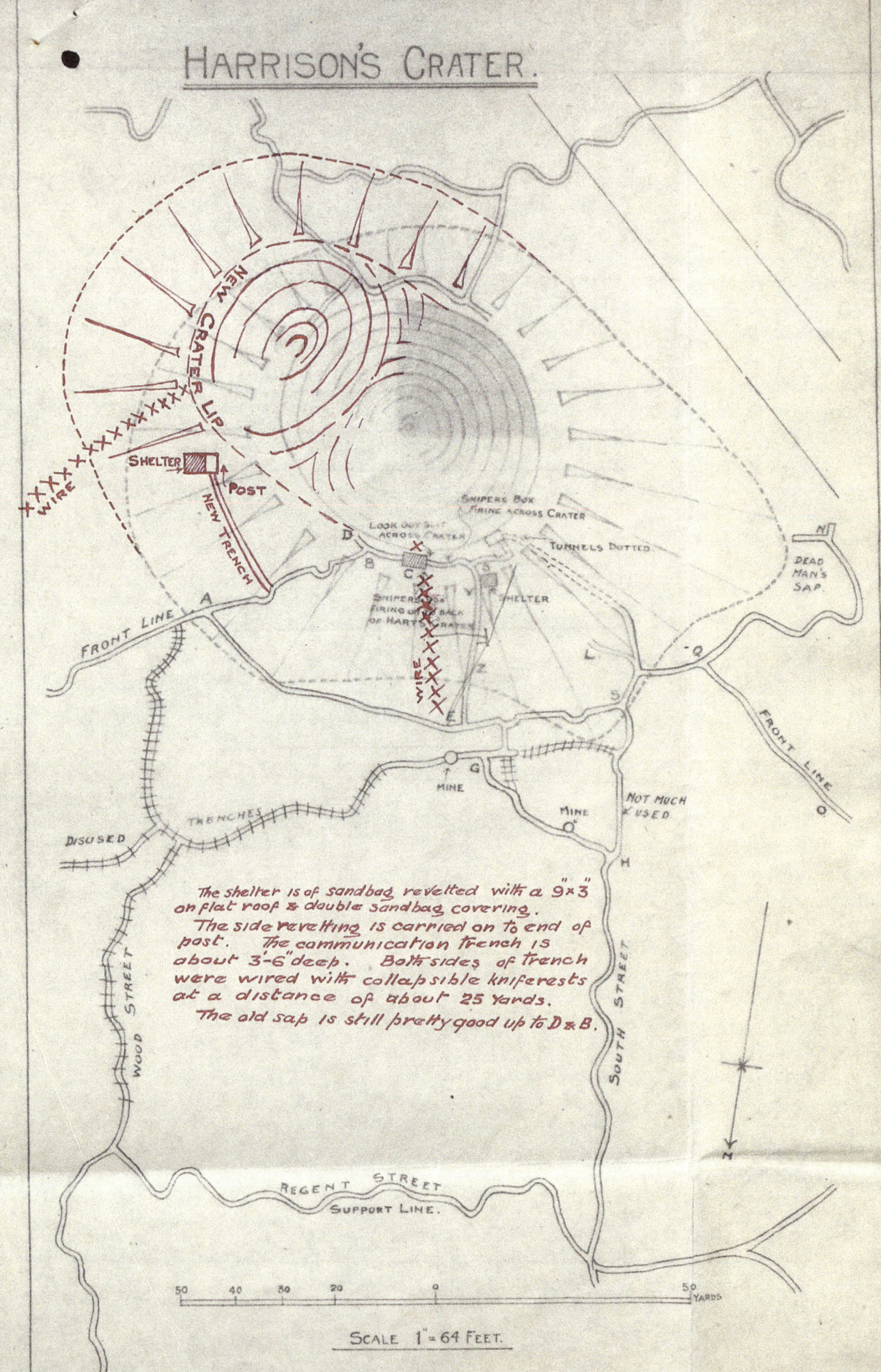

WAR DIARY
or
INTELLIGENCE SUMMARY.

(Erase heading not required.)

Headquarters 16th Division Artillery. From 1st to 31st July 1916.

Instructions regarding War Diaries and Intelligence Summaries are contained in F. S. Regs., Part II. and the Staff Manual respectively. Title pages will be prepared in manuscript.

Place	Date	Hour	Summary of Events and Information	Remarks and references to Appendices
NOEUX LES MINES	1.7.16		Normal	
"	2.7.16		" Mazingarbe shelled	
"	3.7.16		MAZINGARBE little shelled.	
	4.7.16		Normal	
	5.7.16		M.O. talk from Bosw and Lucl. Cellular	
	6.7.16		Normal	
	7.7.16		Normal	
	9.7.16		2 Sections 155th Bty to LOOS Blur, Arrival taken over Command Western Sector	
	10.7.16			
	11.7.16		Normal. C.R.E. Reports Lamberts shell etc	
	12.7.16		Hon Countin RE Field Coy in 2 Corps Division for 8th Divn arrives	
	13.7.16		Lieutenant Light Hants / Division orders pack to 3rd Divn	
	14.7.16		Normal	
	15.7.16		Lt Hughes & Lt Hagarty 155 Field Coy Evacuated hospital Enteric	
	16.7.16		Normal	
	17.7.16		Normal.	

WAR DIARY
INTELLIGENCE SUMMARY

Headquarters 16th Divisional Engineers.

Army Form C. 2118.

(Erase heading not required.)

Place	Date	Hour	Summary of Events and Information	Remarks and references to Appendices
	18.7.16		Normal	
	19.7.16		Normal. Lt MAC HAFFIE R.E. arrives for 155/Fd Coy	
	20.7.16		Normal.	
	21.7.16		Move of a Brigade front to the North	
	22.7.16		2 Sections 156 Field Coy from LOOS to PHILOSOPHE	
	23.7.16		C.R.E. Egerton our relieve part of 47 Div	
	24.7.16		drew 1500 ﾖ from A.E. 1st Corps.	
	25.7.16		None	
	26.7.16		None — Colonel LE BECHER R.E. assumed duties of O.C. 1 Army Workshops BETHUNE— ment (with Captain) R.E. STRADLING R.E. assumed duties Ad. P.E.	
	27.7.16		None	
	28.7.16		"	
	29.7.16		"	
	30.7.16		"	
	31.7.16		D.H.Q. conference	

B.B.Keatley Capt RE
Adj / 16 Div Engrs

WAR DIARY.

16th Div. Engineers A.A.

MONTH OF AUGUST, 1916.

VOLUME :- 9

Army Form C. 2118.

WAR DIARY Headquarters, 16th Divisional Engineers.

INTELLIGENCE SUMMARY.

(Erase heading not required.)

Instructions regarding War Diaries and Intelligence Summaries are contained in F.S. Regs., Part II. and the Staff Manual respectively. Title pages will be prepared in manuscript.

Place	Date	Hour	Summary of Events and Information	Remarks and references to Appendices
NOEUX-LES-MINES	1/8/16		Normal day	
"	2/8/16		"	
"	3/8/16		"	
"	4/8/16		"	
"	5/8/16		"	
"	6/8/16		"	
"	7/8/16		"	
"	8/8/16		"	
"	9/8/16		"	
"	10/8/16		Change of Divisional front - New front HULLUCH ROAD to LOOS SECTOR	
"	11/8/16		Normal day	
"	12/8/16		"	
"	13/8/16		"	
"	14/8/16		"	LW.
"	15/8/16		"	LW.
"	16/8/16		"	LW

Army Form C. 2118.

WAR DIARY Headquarters, 16th Divisional Engineers.
~~INTELLIGENCE SUMMARY.~~
(Erase heading not required.)

Instructions regarding War Diaries and Intelligence Summaries are contained in F. S. Regs., Part II. and the Staff Manual respectively. Title pages will be prepared in manuscript.

Place	Date	Hour	Summary of Events and Information	Remarks and references to Appendices
NOEUX-LES-MINES	17/8/16		None	
,,	18/8/16		,,	
,,	19/8/16		,,	
,,	20/8/16		,,	
,,	21/8/16		,,	
,,	22/8/16		,,	
,,	23/8/16		Orders received re move of Field Coys. Field Coys cleared work.	
,,	24/8/16		157th Coy left for VERQUIN, 156 FdCoy to RUITZ, 157 FdCoy to RUITZ. Received orders re further move of Field Coys.	
,,	25/8/16		Handed over to CRE 40", CRE 8" and CE (per OC 31st A.T.Coy) Drew 1000hs. 7d Coy to prelim – 155 – Caundy à la Tour, 156 – HURIONVILLE, 157 – MARLES LES MINES	
RAIMBERT	26/8/16		H.Q. R.E. moved to RAIMBERT	
,,	27/8/16		Rest & liesh	
,,	28/8/16		,, ,,	
In train	29/8/16		Entrained at FOUGUEREIL ~~FONQUERO~~ for LONGUEAU	
CORBIE	30/8/16		Handed from LONGUEAU to CORBIE arrived 12 midday. 7d Coys 155 CORBIE, 156 DAOURS 157 SERLEY LE SEC.	
FORKED TREE	31/8/16		Moved from CORBIE (10AM) to FORKED TREE. 7/Coys. 155 – ~~HAPPY VALLEY~~ SANDPIT 156 – CITADEL, 157 – HAPPY VALLEY.	

T2131. Wt. W708–776. 500000. 4/15. Sir J. C. & S.

Army Form C. 2118.

WAR DIARY Headquarters,
or
INTELLIGENCE SUMMARY. 16th Divisional Engineers.
(Erase heading not required.)

Place	Date	Hour	Summary of Events and Information	Remarks and references to Appendices
FORUED IEES	1-9-16		Appended hereto — Covering herewith — Reserved reports & war of Infantry Brigades for Sep 1916	
			Appendice "A" 16th Divisional Engineers O.O. No. 1 dated 28.8.16	
			" "B" " " " " O.O. No 2 " 26.8.16	

R.O.Stamer(?)
Capt & Adjt 16th Divl Engrs.

"A"

S E C R E T.

Copy No. 6

16th Divisional Engineers.
Operation Order No.1.

23rd August 1916.

1 MARCH ORDER.

Field Companies will move away from their present Billets to-morrow 24th August, 1916, as per attached March Table.

2. ADVANCE PARTIES.

1 Officer and 4 Other Ranks per Company.
Interpreters will be arranged to meet the parties.

3. REPORTS.

Reports will be made on arrival at destination to:-

1. Divisional Headquarters.
2. Headquarters, Divisional Engineers.

4. RATIONS. - Will be obtained at usual supply dump unless otherwise instructed.

R.E. Stradley Captain R.E.
Adjutant 16th Divisional Engineers.

Copy No:-

1. Retained.
2. 155th Field Company, R.E.
3. 156th Field Company, R.E.
4. 157th Field Company, R.E.
5. H.Q. 16th Division (for information).
6.
7.

Copy No. 6

March Table to accompany 16th D.E. O.O. No.1. dated 23/8/16.

Unit.	Date.	Time.	Route.	Destination.	Remarks.
155th Field Coy. Advance Party. Transport (less Bridging wagons). Dismounted.	24/8/16.	7.0.am. 10.45.am. 11.0.am.	} MAZINGARBE - NOEUX. }	VERQUIN.	Transport moves at 50 yards interval E. of NOEUX. Dismounted by Sections at 200 yards interval E. of NOEUX.
156th Field Coy. Advance Party. Transport (less Bridging wagons) Dismounted.	24/8/16.	7.0.am 10.15.am. 10.30.am.	} MAZINGARBE - NOEUX. }	RUITZ.	TRANSPORT. All bridging wagons and as much transport as possible will reach NOEUX to-night (23/8/16) during hours of darkness.
157th Field Coy. Advance Party. Transport (Less Bridging wagons). Dismounted.	24/8/16.	7.0.am. 9.45.am. 10.0.am.	} MAZINGARBE - NOEUX. }	RUITZ.	ALL Companies to be clear of NOEUX by 12.30. p.m. 24th August 1916. NB Transport at Khevul na pt Sains on 24/8/16

B'

Copy No. 6

16th Divisional Engineers.

Operation Order No. 2.

24th August 1916.

1. The 155th, 156th, and 157th Field Companies, R.E. will move as per attached March Table on 25th August 1916.

2. BILLETING PARTIES. Arranged by O.C. Field Companies. Interpreters will be arranged by C.R.E.

3. Reports on arrival in new area to :-

    1. Headquarters, 16th Division.

    2. Headquarters, 16th Divisional Engineers.

4. RATIONS. Any change in Ration Dumps will be notified.

Issued at 4.20 p.m.

Captain R.E.
Adjutant 16th Div. Engineers

Copy No.
1. retained.
2. 155th Field Company, R.E.
3. 156th Field Company, R.E.
4. 157th Field Company, R.E.
5. Headquarters, 16th Division (for information.

March Table to accompany 18th Div.Engineers O.O. No.2. dated 24/6/16.

Unit.	ROUTE.	DESTINATION.	Remarks.
155th Fld.Coy.	Road Junction J.17.b. and Railway Crossing J.4.c.	ONJON - A - LA - TOUR.	To follow 156th Company and to be clear of road junction J.17.b. by 8.30. a.m. Come under orders of C.O.R. 48th Inf. Bde. on arrival.
156th Fld.Coy.	Road Junction J.17.b. Railway crossing J.4.c.	HURIONVILLE.	To follow 157th Company and to be clear of road junction J.17.b. by 8.20. a.m. Come under orders of C.O.C. 47th Inf. Bde on arrival.
157th Fld.Coy.	Road Junction J.17.b. via Railway crossing J.4.c.	MARLES - LES - MINES.	To follow 7th LEINSTER REGIMENT and to be clear of road junction J.17.b. by 8.10. am. Come under orders of C.O.C. 49th Inf. Bde. on arrival.

WAR DIARY

16th Div. Engineers Head Quarters

FOR MONTH OF SEPTEMBER, 1916.

VOLUME 10

WAR DIARY
or
INTELLIGENCE SUMMARY
(Erase heading not required.)

Army Form C. 2118.

Alfred Russell
1/6 Lieutenant Engineers

Place	Date	Hour	Summary of Events and Information	Remarks and references to Appendices
FORKED TREE 1-0-C			Occupied Since - hand entrenchments - received orders re road bays, camps for 66. XIII	
"	2-9-16		adj with AMIENS to purchase of green canvas (fray sheet)	
"	3-9-16		Movement of 48th Aug 1st Brigade (and attached Fd Coys) - 1ST Fd Cy to BILLON FARM (F.29.L). 157 to CITADEL (F.21.d.&b). (47th Brigade relief 48th Northumberland.)	
"	4-9-16		Orders received re taking over of portion of line from 20th Div.	
MINDEN POST 5-9-16			H.Q. moved from FORKED TREE to MINDEN POST. C.R.E.15.16th arrived MINDEN POST 9. A.M. took over fm C.R.E. 20th Div. 1ST Fd Cy worked under 48th Inf Brigade, 156 in reserve, 157 under 49th Inf Brigade. on night 5th/6th Lieut MORRES R.E. - killed. 156 Fd Cy relieved 1ST Fd Cy R.E.	
"	6-9-16		156 - CRATERS, 157 - BRIQUETERIE, [156 &157 under Bicourcy]	
"	7-9-16		Orders received for the three Fd Cys to proceed to GUILLEMONT as garrison. COMMANDANT - GUILLEMONT - Oc. 11th Hows.(P). Transport ordered to park near MINDEN POST. under Lieut HUGHES	
"	8-9-16		Orders received fw attach to GINCHY. 157 Fd coy proceeded	

Head Quarters
16 Divisional Engineers

Army Form C. 2118.

WAR DIARY
or
INTELLIGENCE SUMMARY.
(Erase heading not required.)

Instructions regarding War Diaries and Intelligence Summaries are contained in F. S. Regs., Part II. and the Staff Manual respectively. Title pages will be prepared in manuscript.

Place	Date	Hour	Summary of Events and Information	Remarks and references to Appendices
MINDEN POST	8.9.16		Reconnoitred. Orders received to relieve 47th Div. by Guards Div. Preliminary arrangements to C.R.E. GUARDS	
	9.9.16		Orders received to relieve 16th Div by Guards Div. Preliminary arrangements to C.R.E. Guards. 3rd Cys ordered to withdraw from line on night 9/10 Sept & concentrate at MINDEN POST. 16th Division attacked GINCHY & obtained objective. Good work of 157 ½ Coy in consolidation of left flank.	
CITADEL	10.9.16		Passed over work to C.R.E. GUARDS. Moved back to CITADEL WEST — FIELD COYS to HAPPY VALLEY.	
CORBIE	11.9.16		Moved to CORBIE. 155 – CORBIE, 156 – VAUX-SUR-SOMME, 157 – SAILLY LE SEC. Refitting billets.	
"	12.9.16			
"	13.9.16			
"	14.9.16			
"	15.9.16		Capt MacGeorge (155th) admitted hospital — (Port Thee Fleet)	
"	16.9.16			
"	17.9.16		Orders received to HALLENCOURT — Transport started to-night at LACHAUSSEE.	
HALLENCOURT	18.9.16		Move by motorlins to HALLENCOURT. — 155 + 156 under orders of 47th Bdg + 157 under 49 ½	

Major Powers
16 Divisional Engineers

WAR DIARY
or
INTELLIGENCE SUMMARY.
(Erase heading not required.)

Army Form C. 2118.

Place	Date	Hour	Summary of Events and Information	Remarks and references to Appendices
HALLAYCOURT	19.9.16		Rest. Weeks	
"	20.9.16		CRE & Interpr. went on by car to WESTOUTRE to take over from 4 Can. Div.	
WESTOUTRE	21.9.16		Adjutant + remainder of H.Q. R.E. travelled by train to WESTOUTRE.	
"	22.9.16		CRE & adj. went round work. Cellar at BERVIE FARM have 155+157 + 12" Can. Fd. Cy	
"	23.9.16		Worken hutty schemes. 155 + 157 with new work " in line	
"	24.9.16		Hutting work — Coys work under Bergeheren — CRE. hutty etc	
"	25.9.16		ditto	
"	27.9.16		"	
"	28.9.16		"	
"	29.9.16		"	
"	30.9.16		"	

R.Studdy Capt RE
Adj. 16 Div Engs.

WAR DIARY

MONTH OF OCTOBER, 1916.

VOLUME 11

16th Div. Engineers HeadQuarters

Army Form C. 2118.

WAR DIARY
or
INTELLIGENCE SUMMARY.
(Erase heading not required.)

Headquarters,
18th Divisional Engineers.

Instructions regarding War Diaries and Intelligence Summaries are contained in F. S. Regs., Part II. and the Staff Manual respectively. Title pages will be prepared in manuscript.

Place	Date	Hour	Summary of Events and Information	Remarks and references to Appendices
WESTOUTRE	1/9/16		R.E. work – 2 Coys – line. 1 in reserve.	
"	2/10/16		R.E. work – 3 Coys – line (1 with each Bde) 2 Pioneer Coys on "Stokes bomb" – 2 in Reserve work (hutting)	
"	3/10/16		ditto	
"	4/10/16		ditto	
"	5/10/16		ditto	
"	6/10/16		ditto. Lt. Col. BUTTERWORTH R.E. arrived & took over duties of CRE.	
"	7/10/16		ditto. 2nd Lt. Palmer buried new work 15 N.C.O. hutment	
"	8/10/16		ditto	
"	9/10/16		O.O. No 8 (N. Div. Engrs) ditto	
"	10/10/16		O.O. No 9 (18. Div. Engrs) move ordering change of R.E. work organisation	
"	11/10/16		1 Section R.E. from each F. Coy. placed in DIZON Camp and used for work in hutting in their Brigade area. 1 Coy of Hants Pioneers divided between the 3 Brigade areas for hutting. 3 Coy Pioneers in line work – 2 Strong point – 1 Communication Trench	
	12.10.16		normal day	
	13.10.16		"	
	14.10.16		"	

Army Form C. 2118.

WAR DIARY
or
INTELLIGENCE SUMMARY.
(Erase heading not required.)

Headquarters, 16th Divisional Engineers.

Place	Date	Hour	Summary of Events and Information	Remarks and references to Appendices
WESTOUTRE	15.10.16		Normal day	
"	16.10.16		"	
"	17.10.16		"	
"	18.10.16		"	
"	19.10.16		"	
"	20.10.16		"	
"	21.10.16		Orders issued re relief of Sappers in trenches	
"	22.10.16		Normal day	
"	23.10.16		69 & 171 Coys in trenches relieved	
"	24.10.16		Normal day	
"	25.10.16		"	
"	26.10.16		"	
"	27.10.16		"	
"	28.10.16		"	
"	29.10.16		"	
"	30.10.16		"	

Army Form C. 2118.

WAR DIARY
or
INTELLIGENCE SUMMARY.

Headquarters, 16th Divisional Engineers.

(Erase heading not required.)

Instructions regarding War Diaries and Intelligence Summaries are contained in F. S. Regs., Part II. and the Staff Manual respectively. Title pages will be prepared in manuscript.

Place	Date	Hour	Summary of Events and Information	Remarks and references to Appendices
WESTOUTRE	31.10.15		Experiments on trench cutting with H.E. — NORMAL DAY	

R.J. Shuels?
Capsel
A.D.16 Div Engr.

WAR DIARY.

FOR

MONTH OF NOVEMBER, 1916.

VOLUME 12.

Headquarters 16th Div Engineers

Army Form C. 2118.

WAR DIARY
or
INTELLIGENCE SUMMARY.
(Erase heading not required.)

Headquarters, 16th Divisional Engineers.

Instructions regarding War Diaries and Intelligence Summaries are contained in F. S. Regs., Part II. and the Staff Manual respectively. Title pages will be prepared in manuscript.

Place	Date	Hour	Summary of Events and Information	Remarks and references to Appendices
WESTOUTRE	1.11.16		Handing over 1st 2nd Lt Cr. B. Breen R.E. by Adjutant (Greene) NORMAL DAY	
	2.11.16		C.P.R.E.STACKPOLE (Adjutant) proceeded on leave. Duties of Adjutant taken on by Lt BOLTON. — CRE visits Sir, Park R.E.	
			— NORMAL DAY. —	
	3.11.16		NORMAL DAY	
	4.11.16		NORMAL DAY	
	5.11.16		NORMAL DAY	
	6.11.16		155 & 157 Fd. Coy. Hutting section changed (G.O. No 11) NORMAL DAY	
	7.11.16		NORMAL DAY New Hutting section blank work	
	8.11.16		156th Coy. Hutting section changed (O.O. No 11) NORMAL DAY	
	9.11.16		NORMAL DAY	
	10.11.16		NORMAL DAY	
	11.11.16		NORMAL DAY	
	12.11.16		NORMAL DAY. — Experiments by 157th Coy. to test new Stokes Gun Platform 2nd Army attended and trial considered very satisfactory.	
	13.11.16		Adjutant returned from leave took out duties from Lt Bolton — Normal day	
	14.11.16		Normal day.	

T2134. Wt. W708-776. 500000. 4/15. Sir J. C. & S.

Army Form C. 2118.

WAR DIARY
or
INTELLIGENCE SUMMARY.
(Erase heading not required.)

Headquarters, 16th Divisional Engineers.

Instructions regarding War Diaries and Intelligence Summaries are contained in F.S. Regs., Part II. and the Staff Manual respectively. Title pages will be prepared in manuscript.

Place	Date	Hour	Summary of Events and Information	Remarks and references to Appendices
WESTOUTRE	15.11.16		Lt Col BUTTERWORTH goes on leave W/ENGLAND — CAPTAIN R.W. MARSDEN took over duties of CRE	
	16.11.16		NORMAL DAY	
	17.11.16		" "	
	18.11.16		" "	
	19.11.16		Relief of 2nd Section by 4th Section (157 F.C.) NORMAL DAY	
	20.11.16		NORMAL DAY	
	21.11.16		" " (Lt Boetta went on leave to Channel Islands)	
	22.11.16		" "	
	23.11.16		" "	
	24.11.16		" "	
	25.11.16		Lt Col Butterworth returned from leave NORMAL DAY	
	26.11.16		Capt. Marsden rejoined his company (156) NORMAL DAY	
	27.11.16		NORMAL DAY	
	28.11.16		" "	
	29.11.16		" "	
	30.11.16		" "	

WAR DIARY FOR MONTH OF DECEMBER, 1915.

VOLUME B

Headquarters 16th Div Engineers

Army Form C. 2118.

WAR DIARY
or
INTELLIGENCE SUMMARY.
(Erase heading not required.)

Headquarters,

16th Divisional Engineers.

Instructions regarding War Diaries and Intelligence Summaries are contained in F. S. Regs., Part II. and the Staff Manual respectively. Title pages will be prepared in manuscript.

Place	Date	Hour	Summary of Events and Information	Remarks and references to Appendices
WESTOUTRE	1/12/16		NORMAL DAY — orders received re change in divisional front — BOCHE NEW BATHS finished &	
	2/12/16		handed over to A.D.M.S.	
	3/12/16		NORMAL DAY	
	4/12/16		" "	
	5/12/16		2 Sections 158 Fd Coy R.E. moved to BUS FARM (SPANBROEK SECTION) — NORMAL DAY	
	6/12/16		HQ. 151 Fd Coy R.E. moved to LUEGAN CAMP — NORMAL DAY	
	7/12/16		NORMAL DAY	
	8/12/16		" "	
	9/12/16		" "	
	10/12/16		CRE spent whole day in line observing work.	
	11/12/16		" "	
	12/12/16		" "	
	13/12/16		" "	
	14/12/16		" "	
	15/12/16		" "	
	16/12/16		" "	

WAR DIARY
or
INTELLIGENCE SUMMARY.
(Erase heading not required.)

Army Form C. 2118.

Headquarters, 16th Divisional Engineers.

Instructions regarding War Diaries and Intelligence Summaries are contained in F. S. Regs., Part II. and the Staff Manual respectively. Title pages will be prepared in manuscript.

Place	Date	Hour	Summary of Events and Information	Remarks and references to Appendices
WESTOUTRE	17/12/16		NORMAL DAY	
"	18/12/16		"	
"	19/12/16		"	
"	20/12/16		"	
"	21/12/16		"	
"	22/12/16		Paid for horse at Kemmel.	
"	23/12/16		"	
"	24/12/16		"	
"	25/12/16		"	
"	26/12/16		"	
"	27/12/16		Orders issued for change of hasty return	
"	28/12/16		"	
"	29/12/16		Hutt. orders changed	
"	30/12/16		"	
"	31/12/16		"	

WAR DIARY for month of JANUARY, 1917.

VOLUME 14

Hd. Qrs. 16th Div. Engineers

Army Form C. 2118.

WAR DIARY
or
INTELLIGENCE SUMMARY.
(Erase heading not required.)

ROYAL ENGINEERS,
H.Q.
16TH DIVISION.

Instructions regarding War Diaries and Intelligence Summaries are contained in F.S. Regs., Part II. and the Staff Manual respectively. Title pages will be prepared in manuscript.

Place	Date	Hour	Summary of Events and Information	Remarks and references to Appendices
WESTOUTRE	1/1/17		Normal Day —	
"	2/1/17		" " — Inspected fresh Huts in divisional area	
"	3/1/17		" " — Major R.W.M. MARSDEN R.E. notified as which shelter R.E. Sterlite Between Huts for receiving military Cross —	
	4/1/17		Normal day —	
			OC. 155 Tu Coy RE (Maj. Reynolds) left for leave. Officer Comdr. 157 TU CO HOT	
			2nd Lieut Johnstone RE joined 155 Tu Coy RE	
	5/1/17		Normal day	
	6/1/17		" "	
	7/1/17		" "	
	8/1/17		" "	
	9/1/17		Capt R.P. PAKENHAM–WALSH R.E. joined as OC. 155 172 Coy RE	
	10/1/17		Normal day	
	11/1/17		" "	
	12/1/17		" " — Normal day —	
	13/1/17		" "	

Army Form C. 2118.

ROYAL ENGINEERS,
H.Q.
18TH DIVISION.

WAR DIARY
or
INTELLIGENCE SUMMARY.
(Erase heading not required.)

Instructions regarding War Diaries and Intelligence Summaries are contained in F. S. Regs., Part II. and the Staff Manual respectively. Title pages will be prepared in manuscript.

Place	Date	Hour	Summary of Events and Information	Remarks and references to Appendices
WESTOUTRE	14.1.17		Normal day — Capt. E.K. GREENHOW RE. joined 157 Fd Coy RE. on 2ⁿᵈ in command	
	15.1.17		2ⁿᵈ Lieut F.O.D. BURKE-GAFFNEY RE joined 157 Fd Coy RE	
	16.1.17		Normal day — visit of ARMY COMMANDER to area.	
	17.1.17		Normal day	
	17.1.17		" " — 2ⁿᵈ Lieut T.B. FRANK RE (from ETC NEWARK) attached 1/7/8 Fd Coy for instruction	
	18.1.17		" "	
	19.1.17		" "	
	19.1.17		" "	
	20.1.17		" "	
	21.1.17		" " — Presentation of 2nd Cav/M Parchment Certificate by C.R.E. to R.E.	
	22.1.17		Normal Day	
	23.1.17		" "	
	24.1.17		" "	
	25.1.17		" "	
	26.1.17		" "	
	27.1.17		" "	

Army Form C. 2118.

WAR DIARY
or
INTELLIGENCE SUMMARY.
(Erase heading not required.)

Instructions regarding War Diaries and Intelligence Summaries are contained in F. S. Regs., Part II. and the Staff Manual respectively. Title pages will be prepared in manuscript.

ROYAL ENGINEERS.
H.Q.,
16TH DIVISION.

Place	Date	Hour	Summary of Events and Information	Remarks and references to Appendices
WESTOUTRE	28-1-17		Normal Day —	
	29-1-17		" " — Chacing organisation of Run. Front — 2 Engineers in Line — in pleure of 3 Inspectors — 155 Fd Coy in left sector — 157 " 157 Field Coys in Right sector.	
	30-1-17		Normal Day —	
	31-1-17		" "	

R.C. Stendali
Captain
A.D. 16 Division

W A R   D I A R Y.

FOR   MONTH   OF   FEBRUARY,   1917.

VOLUME 15

UNIT:- H.Q. 16th Div. Engineers.

Vol 15

Army Form C. 2118.

WAR DIARY
or
INTELLIGENCE SUMMARY.
(Erase heading not required.)

Headquarters,
16th Divisional Engineers.

Instructions regarding War Diaries and Intelligence Summaries are contained in F. S. Regs., Part II. and the Staff Manual respectively. Title pages will be prepared in manuscript.

Place	Date	Hour	Summary of Events and Information	Remarks and references to Appendices
WESTOUTRE	1.2.17		Normal Day	
	2.2.17		"	
	3.2.17		" — Received orders re transfer of 2nd Lieut NOLMAN (157 T.Coy) to 196 L.D. Coy and transfer of 2nd Lieut LEACH (196 L.D. Coy) to 155 T. Coy R.E.	
	4.2.17		Normal Day	
	5.2.17		"	
	6.2.17		"	
	7.2.17		"	
	8.2.17		"	
	9.2.17		"	
	10.2.17		" — Capt Carlyle (155 T.Coy) starts to take over duties of Adjt. R.E.	
	11.2.17		} NORMAL	
	12.2.17			
	13.2.17			
	14.2.17			
	15.2.17			

Army Form C. 2118.

WAR DIARY
or
INTELLIGENCE SUMMARY.
(Erase heading not required.)

Headquarters,
16th Divisional Engineers.

Instructions regarding War Diaries and Intelligence Summaries are contained in F. S. Regs., Part II. and the Staff Manual respectively. Title pages will be prepared in manuscript.

Place	Date	Hour	Summary of Events and Information	Remarks and references to Appendices
WESTOUTRE	16.2.17		⎫	
	17.2.17		⎬ NORMAL.	
	18.2.17		⎬	
	19.2.17		⎬	
	20.2.17		⎬	
	21.2.17		⎬	
	22.2.17		⎬	
	23.2.17		⎭	
	24.2.17		Capt R.E. STRADLING R.E. returned from leave & took on duties of Adjutant.	
	25.2.17		Capt G. CARLYLE rejoined his company (156th Fld Coy) - Relief of huts positions	
	26.2.17		NORMAL DAY.	
	27.2.17		Advance visited BERGUES [?] steam patrol - NORMAL DAY.	
	28.2.17		NORMAL DAY.	

R.E. Stradling
Capt.
CRE 16 Div.

WAR DIARY
FOR MONTH OF MARCH, 1917.

VOLUME 16

UNIT:- Headquarters 16th Div. Engineers

Vol 16

Army Form C. 2118.

WAR DIARY
or
INTELLIGENCE SUMMARY.
(Erase heading not required.)

Head Quarters
1st Div Engrs

Place	Date	Hour	Summary of Events and Information	Remarks and references to Appendices
WESTOUTRE	1/3/17		NORMAL DAY	
"	2/3/17			
	3/3/17			
	4/3/17		156th + 155th Fd Coys Hutts sections relieved	
	5/3/17			
	6/3/17		156 section returned LURGAN CAMP	
	7/3/17			
	8/3/17			
	9/3/17			
	10/3/17		Orders received (16 Div. O.O. N°80) reference relief of SPANBROEK section by 36th Div.	
	11/3/17		157 Fd Coy returned relieved of charge of	
	12/3/17		Operation order N°19 (16 Div Engrs) issued re relief of 157 Fd Coy mining sections in G.H.Q. mines by 36 Division — continued mining on G.H.Q. mines	
	13/3/17		158 Fd Coy relieved by 36 Division — continued mining on G.H.Q. mines	
	14/3/17		Continued mining on G.H.Q. mines	
	15/3/17		" " " " " — normal day	
	16/3/17		Continued work on M.G. dugouts HT.H.Q. Huts — 16 D. Ecc O.O. N°20 issued	

Army Form C. 2118.

WAR DIARY
or
INTELLIGENCE SUMMARY.
(Erase heading not required.)

Instructions regarding War Diaries and Intelligence Summaries are contained in F. S. Regs., Part II. and the Staff Manual respectively. Title pages will be prepared in manuscript.

Place	Date	Hour	Summary of Events and Information	Remarks and references to Appendices
WESTOUTRE	16/3/17		CRE & order McGowan to work parties — Received A.O. 2 & O.O. 83.	
	17.3.17		Normal Day — NEW ENCAMPMENT near CROIX du POPERINGHE Contract workers cutting, Rads VIERSTRAAT SWITCH — artly new encampment chapel — recital wind gear started — 156 Fd Coy ordered to move from LURGAN CAMP to BALDOYLE. — Normal day —	
	18.3.17		O.O. 84 received — Normal day	
	19.3.17		156 Fd Coy arrive BALDOYLE CAMP. — Normal day	
	20.3.17		O.O. 87 received (Bombs between 16"×6" Dis) wheeled to Camp. — Normal Day	
	21.3.17		O.O. 21 (16th Dio Engr) sent to Camp — to move of 156 Fd Coy to FLETRE — Normal Day	
	22.3.17		O.O. 88 received and orders = 156 Fd Coy moves to FLETRE. — Normal day — 82 Fd Coy RE CofR 16 pers in BIEBUYCK ALL SECTOR.	
	23.3.17		Two altered at 11 pm (Relieve 12 mash/lt) — Normal day	
	24.3.17		Normal day —	
	25.3.17		O.O. 89 received & A.O. No.3 received — Normal day. — Major MARSDEN arrived	
	26.3.17		O.O. 90 received Note: was elected — going ABQ Bullerworth DSO RE western lines	
	27.3.17		O.O. 91 received — Normal day — O.O. 29.10 received — powers — O.O. (19 Div Engr) No 30 received	

Army Form C. 2118.

WAR DIARY
or
INTELLIGENCE SUMMARY.
(Erase heading not required.)

Instructions regarding War Diaries and Intelligence Summaries are contained in F. S. Regs., Part II. and the Staff Manual respectively. Title pages will be prepared in manuscript.

Place	Date	Hour	Summary of Events and Information	Remarks and references to Appendices
WESTOUTRE.	28/3/17		Normal Day —	
"	29/3/17		Normal Day —	
"	30/3/17		O.O. H'Qrs R.A.M.C. received :- 156 Fd Coy R.E. relieved 155 Fd Coy R.E. in line — 156 Fd Coy in billets Reg Fearns — 155 Fd Coy R.E. FLÊTRE AREA — Normal day —	
CANADA-CORNER (M.17.c.5.4) (Not 28 Sw)	31/3/17		CO.'s Notice moved from Westoutre to WESTOUTRE to CANADACORNER (M.17.c.5.4) (Sheet 28 Sw) — Bns. HQ moved to LOCRE. — 156 Fd Coy + 157 Fd Coy present over horse standing to 19" Div — Tactical horse standing in LOCRE — Normal day.	
"				

R.E. Shurely
CPRE
A57. 16 Division

31/3/17

WAR DIARY FOR MONTH OF APRIL, 1917.

VOLUME:- 14

UNIT:- H.Q. 16th Div Engineers

Army Form C. 2118.

WAR DIARY
or
INTELLIGENCE SUMMARY.
(Erase heading not required.)

Instructions regarding War Diaries and Intelligence Summaries are contained in F. S. Regs., Part II. and the Staff Manual respectively. Title pages will be prepared in manuscript.

Place	Date	Hour	Summary of Events and Information	Remarks and references to Appendices
CANADA CORNER (M17.c.S.4) Sheet 28SW	1.4.17		Normal day —	
	2.4.17		Normal day —	
	3.4.17		Normal day —	
	4.4.17		" "	
	5.4.17		" "	
	6.4.17		" "	
	7.4.17		" "	
	8.4.17		" "	
	9.4.17		" "	
	10.4.17		" "	
	11.4.17		Lieut. Col. Butterworth D.S.O.,R.E. returned from leave — Normal day	
	12.4.17		" " resumed duties of C.R.E. — Normal day	
	13.4.17		Major Munden R.E. rejoined his company — Normal day	
	14.4.17		Normal day	
	15.4.17		Normal day — McDo. Engr. O.O. no 25 issued re relief of ½ Co. C.R.	

1

WAR DIARY
or
INTELLIGENCE SUMMARY.
(Erase heading not required.)

Army Form C. 2118.

Instructions regarding War Diaries and Intelligence Summaries are contained in F. S. Regs., Part II. and the Staff Manual respectively. Title pages will be prepared in manuscript.

Place	Date	Hour	Summary of Events and Information	Remarks and references to Appendices
CANAL ON LOENSE	16.4.17			
M17c 5.4 (Sheet 28 Sw)	17.4.17		⎱ Normal routine work – ⎰	
	18.4.17			
	19.4.17			
	20.4.17			
	21.4.17			
	22.4.17			
	23.4.17			
	24.4.17			
	25.4.17			
	26.4.17			
	27.4.17			
	28.4.17			
	29.4.17		16th Div Engr O.O. No 26 issued re taking over PILCKEM sector – 155 Fd Coy to take work in new sector – 156 Fd Coy over PILCKEM sector 157 Fd Coy to take charge VIERSTRAAT sector.	
	30.4.17		Sorting over arrangements made –	R.Stracey Smyth Lt Col RE

WAR DIARY:
-----------oOo-----------

VOLUME:- 18

FOR MONTH OF MAY, 1917.

UNIT:- Headquarters 16th Div Engineers

Army Form C. 2118.

WAR DIARY
or
INTELLIGENCE SUMMARY.
(Erase heading not required.)

Instructions regarding War Diaries and Intelligence Summaries are contained in F.S. Regs, Part II. and the Staff Manual respectively. Title pages will be prepared in manuscript.

Place	Date	Hour	Summary of Events and Information	Remarks and references to Appendices
CANADA CORNER	1.5.17		Divisional R.E. took over work & watermill etc. detailed for work store. — 1st Fd Coy + 1 Coy Pioneers — DAIPENDAL SECTOR. — 155 Fd Coy (156) + 2 sections (157) together with 3 Coy Pioneers — work in VLIETSTRAAT SECTOR. Normal Day —	
	2.5.17		" "	
	3.5.17		" "	
	4.5.17		" "	
	5.5.17		Night 5/6" about 8pm enemy opened fire on R.E. FARM & forward R.E. dump & Pt fire to workshops & farm — Continued intermittent shelling of this & other roads & track areas — 1 Officer + 2 O.R. casualties. Fd Coy ordered to withdraw to BRADOYLE & DEZON — O/C (Lt Colonel BUTTERWORTH DSO, R.E.) approved his action whilst superintending to put out fire —	
	6.5.17		O/C not able to leave his room — 2 sections 156 & elk R.E. Farm — such areas shelled during night 6/7 " 15 helbits in cellars	
	7.5.17		Normal Day —	

Army Form C. 2118.

WAR DIARY
or
INTELLIGENCE SUMMARY.
(Erase heading not required.)

Instructions regarding War Diaries and Intelligence Summaries are contained in F.S. Regs., Part II. and the Staff Manual respectively. Title pages will be prepared in manuscript.

Place	Date	Hour	Summary of Events and Information	Remarks and references to Appendices
CANADA CORNER	8.5.17		Orders received re relief of 16th Div by 19th Div in DIEPENVAL SECTOR — G.O. No 27 (16 Div. Engs.) issued — showing distribution of Fd Coys.	Annexe 3
	9.5.17		Relief started	
	10.5.17		Op. Ord. No 28 (16 Div S. Engs) issued showing rearrangements of reliefs and work —	Annexe 4
	11.5.17		Fd Coys. moved over reliefs as per O.O. No 28 — Normal day	
	12.5.17			
	13.5.17		Normal — work on M.O. details pushed forward.	
	14.5.17		CRE's order No 101 issued — see appendix (1)	
	15.5.17		CRE's order No 102 issued see appendix (1)	
	16.5.17			
	17.5.17			
	18.5.17		horse working by night & by Instructions for RE cars (or Fd Coys forward dumps)	
	19.5.17		etc.	
	20.5.17		Relief forward dumps & pushing the general preparation — normal	
	21.5.17			

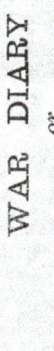

T2134. Wt. W708—776. 500000. 4/15. Sir J. C. & S.

WAR DIARY or INTELLIGENCE SUMMARY.

Army Form C. 2118.

(Erase heading not required.)

Place	Date	Hour	Summary of Events and Information	Remarks and references to Appendices
CANADA	22.5.17		Divisional Order No. 29 issued	Appendix 5
CORNER	23.5.17		General preparations pushed forward — normal day —	
	24.5.17			
	25.5.17			
	26.5.17			
	27.5.17		C.R.E's order No. 105 issued see appendix (1). — normal day — night 27/28 — raid by 47th Bde accompanied by 16 Saplers — Trench + emplacements found so levelled about by previous shell fire that no way inside R.E. work was done — About 30 prisoners taken — normal work	Appendix 01
	28.5.17			
	29.5.17		CRE's INSTRUCTIONS FOR OFFENSIVE issued as appendix (2) Normal work for Offensive	Appendix (2)
	30.5.17		D.H.Q. 447th R.E. moved to SCHEPPEN BERG.	
	1.5.17		CRE's ORDER No. 104 issued as appendix (0)	Appendix (0)

R.B. Greenslyer

SECRET.

APP 1

C. R. E'S ORDER No. 101.

15th May, 1917.

R.E. DUMPS.

1. The filling of Dumps will now commence in accordance with the attached list.

2. The position of the Dumps is as follows:-

MAIN R.E. DUMP.	CANADA CORNER.
RESERVE R.E. DUMP.	R.E. FARM.
INTERMEDIATE DUMP.	RIGHT BRIGADE.
	ROSSIGNOL. N.22.a.5.8.
	LEFT BRIGADE.
	SANDBAG VILLA. N.16.d.5.8.
ADVANCED DUMP.	RIGHT BRIGADE.
	ALBERTA. N.25.d.2.6.
	TIT ROAD. N.23.b.7.4.
	LEFT BRIGADE.
	FOSSE. N.17.d.2.4.
	TURNERSTOWN. N 17.d.5.7.

3. Care is to be taken to make the dumps as inconspicuous as possible, by making use of any natural cover, spreading the stores, and using camouflage. Each dump is to be enclosed by a wire fence, and a notice board erected.

4. All tools are to be kept in one place, and rough boxes, or compartments, provided for the small tools such as pliers, saws, etc.

5. A R.E. Storeman will be put in charge of each dump as soon as it is filled, with one (or two) attached Infantry as assistants.

He will not issue any operation stores until ordered by his Field Company Commander.

Later it will be his duty to keep a check on stores issued, and inform his Field Company Commander of his daily requirements to keep the dump up to its authorised complement.

6. Field Company Commanders will forward a statement with their Weekly Progress Report showing the stores actually dumped.

Sd. R.F.A. BUTTERWORTH, Lt.Col.R.E.

C. R. E. 16th Division.

SECRET.

C. R. E'S ORDER No. 102.

16th May, 1917.

FORWARD ROADS FOR R.F.A.

O.C. 156th Field Company, R E. will carry out the construction of the bridges shewn on attached Blue Print - 11 bridges in all.

The following instructions are to be carefully followed:-

(1) Bridges to take a load of 1½ tons on a pair of wheels.

(2) 6'6" head-room above trenches, except disused trenches.

(3) Approaches to be ramped, and rammed or packed solid.

(4) All work to be disguised, and all woodwork painted, including floor. Posts and Rails green.

    Floor. Brown or green, according to site.

    Across water. Band of light blue on floor corresponding with water underneath, remainder brown or green.

The work is urgent, as the routes will be used in a few day's time.

                        Sd. R.E. STRADLING, Capt.R.E.
                              for Lt.Colonel, R.E.

C. R. E. 16th Division.

C. R. E'S ORDER No. 103.

27th May, 1917.

PACK TRANSPORT.

A pack Section consisting of 20 animals with leaders will be formed and trained by each Field Company.

2. 16 packs per Unit will be supplied by D.A.D.O.S. 16th Division, the remaining 4 being on present establishment.

3. A good N.C.O. will be placed in charge of the pack Section, which will be organised into 4 Sub-Sections, each of which can work independently with one of the Field Company Sections if required.

4. Packs will be adapted for carrying wire, pickets, picks and shovels, or sandbags.

Sd. R.F.A. BUTTERWORTH, Lt.Col.R.E

C. R. E. 16th Division.

SECRET.
==========

C. R. E'S ORDER No. 104.

31st May, 1917.

The programme of work of preparation now being complete O.Cs. 156th and 157th Field Companies, R.E. will withdraw their Sappers from the line, leaving behind one Section with an Officer to carry out ordinary trench maintenance, and to assist Brigadiers 47th and 49th Brigades in any special work of preparation, which they may require.

This order will become operative after work to-morrow.

O.C's Field Coys. will visit Brigadiers daily to keep in touch with the situation in their respective Brigade areas.

The maintenance of the main communication trenches from YORK ROAD to CHINEZE WALL LINE is being carried out by O.C. 11th Hants (P).

Sd. R.E. STRADLING, Captain, R.E.
for C. R. E. 16th Division.

APP 2
War Diary

SECRET. 3324/72. Copy No. 10

INSTRUCTIONS FOR THE OFFENSIVE ISSUED BY

C. R. E., 16th DIVISION.

(1)   The Military Situation and intention of the Divisional Commander.

(2)   Employment of the R.E. and 11th Hants Pioneers in accordance with (1).

(3)   Control of and responsibility for work.

(4)   Liaison and Reports.

(5)   Distribution and location of Field Companies and 11th Hants (Pioneers).

(6)   System of Dumps, issue of Stores, responsibility for refilling during operations.

(7)   Field Company Transport.

(8)   Roads and Tramways.

(9)   Maps.

(10)   Caution.

(1).

(1).

    (a)   The enemy is to be attacked by IX Corps on a front extending from the WULVERGHEM - WYTSCHAETE ROAD to the DIEPENDAAL BEEK.

    (b)   Corps Order of Battle:-

Right.	36th Division.
Centre.	16th Division.
Left.	19th Division.
In Reserve.	11th Division.

    (c)   The boundaries of the 16th Division and objectives are shown on Map G/16/1, a copy of which is issued herewith.

    The following will be the time of arrival on, and departure from the various coloured lines:-

RED LINE.	Zero plus. (0.35 (1.05
BLUE LINE.	Zero plus. (1.40 (3.40
GREEN LINE.	Zero plus. (4.10 (4.20
BLACK LINE.	Zero plus. (4.40

    (d)   The assault will take place on Zero (Z) Day.

    The five proceeding days will be referred to as U, V, W, X, Y days.

    Days before U DAY.   Z Minus 6 etc.

    Three days after Z DAY.   A, B, C, days.

    Days after C DAY   Z plus 4 etc.

    (e)   16th Division Order of Battle:-

    Right Attack.   47th Inf. Bde.
    156th Field Coy.R.E.
    'C' Coy. 11th Hants (P).

    Left Attack.   49th Inf. Bde.
    157th Field Coy.R.E.
    'D' Coy. 11th Hants (P).

    Divisional Reserve.
    48th Inf. Bde.
    155th Field Coy.R.E.
    11th Hants (less 2 Coys).

    The dividing line between the two attacking Brigades is shown on Map G/16/1.

    Each Brigade will attack with two Battalions in front line and one in reserve, the fourth providing mopping up and carrying parties, and Garrisons for Strong Points.

/(f)

(2).

(f) Divisional Battle Headquarters.   SCHERPENBERG.

   2nd Echelon.   LOCRE.

   Brigade, Artillery Group and Battalion Battle Headquarters are shewn on Trench Map C.R.E. 169.

(g) Lines of Assembly.

   (1) CHINEZE WALL LINE.   (Flanks to Attacking Brigades, Centre to Reserve Brigade)

   (2) PARK LINE.

   (3) FRONT LINE.   (excluding N.18.1., N.24.10., N.24.9).

   (4) Additional for Left Brigade.
       WREN TRENCH between trench junction BIRR TRENCH and CROWBAR.

(h) Communications.

   Main.   Right Attack.   VIA GELLIA and Overland Route (C) (OUT).

                           ROSSIGNOL and Overland Route (D) (IN).

           Left Attack.   THE FOSSE and Overland Route (E) (OUT).

                           WATLING STREET and Overland Route (F) (IN).

   Subsidiary.

           Right Attack.   LEEMING LANE, BROADWAY, OAK TRENCH, PARK LANE, PARK STREET, ASH LANE, FIR LANE.

           Left Attack.   BIRR TRENCH, CROWBAR, MAYO STREET, CHOW STREET, USNACH STREET, CLARE STREET, TARA STREET.

(j) Action of Artillery.

   The systematic destruction of the enemy defence system is now being carried out, and will culminate in an intense bombardment prior to the assault.
   Barrages will then be created by ordnance of all calibre to synchronize with the timed advances of the attacking brigades on the coloured lines.

(k) Special barrages of machine guns, Trench Mortars and Special R.E. projectiles will also be employed.

/2.

2. Employment of the R.E. and 11th Hants (Pioneers).

(a) The programme of work of preparation for which detailed instructions have been issued will be completed by night 31st May/1st June, and all will be in readiness for occupation and use by troops on 1st June.

(b) Following on the assault the following work will be required of the technical troops.

Right Brigade Sector.

(1) Maintenance of VIA GELLIA and ROSSIGNOL TRENCHES, OAK TRENCH - ASH LANE from YORK ROAD to the front line.

(2) Junction of ASH LANE with NANCY STREET - NANCY DRIVE, and clearing of the latter towards the HOSPICE. Erection of notice boards at trench junctions in German line.

(3) Extension of Overland Route D to ROUND POND with necessary bridges, so as to be available for advance of guns at earliest possible moment.

(4) Junction of VIA GELLIA with NAP DRIVE, and clearing towards WYTSCHAETE as for (2).

(5) Extension of Overland Route C to PECKHAM - WYTSCHAETE ROAD N.24.d.3.4. as for (3).

(6) Construction of Strong Points at:-

    (i) N.24.d.58.70. NAP POST.
   (ii) O.19.c.25.85. WOOD POST.
  (iii) O.19.b.20.10. CHURCH POST.

(7) Searching for and opening up water supplies in WYTSCHAETE Village:-

On road N. of Church, at O.19.b.20.35 and BRASSERIE O.19.d.52.92.

(8) Refilling Advanced Dumps 1 and 2 from Intermediate Dump No.1.

(9) Forming advanced dump near ROUND POND O.19.a.48.15.

Responsibility for the above:-

156th Field Coy.R.E.

6 (i), subsequently 6 (ii), (iii), 7, 8, 9.

Hants Pioneers.

1, 2, 3, subsequently 4, 5.

Left Brigade Sector.

(1) Maintenance of FOSSE, and WATLING STREET - MAYO STREET.

/(2).

(4).

- (2) Junction of BIRR TRENCH with NAME DRIVE, and clearing latter towards SOUTHERN BRICKSTACK. Erection of notice boards at trench junctions.

- (3) Extension of Overland Route E to BLACK COT for early advance of guns.

- (4) Junction of MAYO STREET with NAIL DRIVE, and clearing latter towards SUNKEN ROAD.

- (5) Extension of Overland Route F to RED CHATEAU and NORTHERN BRICKSTACK.

- (6) Construction of Strong Points at:-

    - (i) O.13.c.15.90. RED POST.
    - (ii) O.13.c.40.25. BLACK POST.
    - (iii) O.19.b.30.80. OBVIOUS POST.

- (7) Searching for and opening up RED CHATEAU water supply N.18.b.80.28. and HOSPICE supply O.13.c.5.2.

- (8) Refilling Advanced Dumps Nos. 3 and 4 from Intermediate Dump No.2.

- (9) Forming an advanced dump near NORTHERN BRICKSTACK.

Responsibility for above.

157th Field Coy.R.E.

(6) (i) then 6 (ii), (iii), 7, 8, 9.

Hants Pioneers.

1, 2, 3, then 4 and 5.

- (10) Wiring of BLACK LINE. This will be carried out by 48th Inf.Bde. with such R.E. assistance as may be required by the Brigadier.

- (11) Repair of Dug-outs for Command Headquarters.

Responsibility for above.

155th Field Coy.R.E.

Work will be carried out progressively on the above lines subject to alterations necessitated by the tactical situation.

Carrying Parties.

O.C's Field Companies will arrange with Brigade Commanders of Sectors for necessary carrying parties in connection with portorage of stores from Advanced Dumps to sites for Strong Points, and for refilling Advanced Dumps and forward new Dumps.

3. Control and Responsibility for Work.

All technical personnel acting under the orders of the C.R.E. will be carrying out definitely

allotted

allotted tasks, as directed by the Divisional Commander after consultation with Brigade Commanders.

No party therefore should be diverted from the work for which it has been sent without special reasons, and any such alterations will be at once reported to the C.R.E. by the unit concerned.

4. Liaison and Reports.

The O.C. Field Company will be attached to the Headquarters of the Brigade in whose Sector he is working.

He will arrange with the Brigadier for any carrying and working parties required, and receive his instructions as to when the R.E. and working parties can move forward to their tasks.

The O.C. Field Company will keep the C.R.E. informed of the sequence of events as affecting R.E. work, and send in a daily progress report of work done, state of dumps, and Engineer situation generally on the Brigade front.

In case of urgency the O.C. Field Coy. will pass on any orders received from the C.R.E. or Brigadier affecting their work to the Pioneer Company in the same Sector, though the normal procedure will be for orders to be sent to the O.C. 11th Hants by the C.R.E., and transmitted by him to the Companies concerned.

The O.C. 11th Hants will forward a daily progress report of the work of the Pioneers, and details of his requirements in stores.

5. The location of the R.E. (with attached Infantry) and Hants Pioneers on Z Day will be as follows:-

47th Brigade Front.

156th Field Coy. R.E.

Headquarters and three Sections.	R.E. FARM. G.H.Q. II. N.15.c.
1 Section (with 25 Infantry)	CHINEZE WALL.

Hants Pioneers.

'C' Company.

Headquarters and two Platoons.	G.H.Q. II N.15.a.
Two Platoons.	CHINEZE WALL.

49th Brigade Front.

157th Field Coy. R.E.

Headquarters and three Sections.	R.E. FARM and G.H.Q. II N.15.c.
1 Section (with 25 Infantry)	CHINEZE WALL.

Hants Pioneers.

'D' Company.

Headquarters and two Platoons.	G.H.Q. II N.15.a.
Two Platoons.	CHINEZE WALL.

In Reserve.

155th Field Coy. R.E.	CHATHAM CAMP.
Hants Pioneers (H.Q. and two Companies)	MOORE PARK CAMP.
R.E. Transport Line.	M.22.d.0.8.

6. **System of Dumps.**

    (a) Main R.E. Dump.   CANADA CORNER.
           Reserve R.E. Dump.   R.E. FARM.

           Intermediate Dump No.1. YORK ROAD. N.22.a.5.8.
                                     (ROSSIGNOL).

               do   do No.2. YORK ROAD. N.16.d.5.8.
                                     (SANDBAG VILLA).

           R.F.A. Dump.   YORK ROAD. N.16.d.05.40.
                                    (LAITERIE).

           Advanced Dump. No. 1.   ALBERTA. N.23.d.2.6.
              "   "   No.2.   TIT ROAD. N.23.b.7.4.
              "   "   No. 3. FOSSE.   N.17.d.2.4.
              "   "   No. 4. WATSONVILLE. N.17.d.5.7.

    (b) A list of stores stocked at each dump is issued herewith.
         A copy mounted on a board will be kept at each dump.

    (c) Advanced Dumps will be kept up to establishment by O.C⁸ Field Companies.
         The Main, Reserve and Intermediate Dumps will be filled under arrangements made by C.R.E. Normally a train will arrive nightly at 6.0. p.m. from ZEVECOTEN Corps Dump with stores for the Intermediate Dumps.

    (d) A R.E. Storeman will be put in charge of each Intermediate and Advanced Dump with an attached Infantryman as assistant. He will keep a check on all stores issued, and inform his Field Coy. Commander of his daily requirements to keep the dump up to complement. He will pack all stores in one-man loads.

         The R.F.A. will draw from their special dumps.

         The large German Dump at O.20.a.35.10 will be exploited for front line wiring and other work, and other enemy dumps as discovered made full use of to save transport.

7. **Transport.**

    (a) Tool Carts and Limbers will be taken forward by 156th and 157th Field Companies, and parked under cover at R.E. FARM.
         The remainder of the wagons, and all animals will be brigaded at the Transport Lines M.22.d.0.8., under the Command of a selected Officer R.E.

         Pontoons and Weldon Trestles will be dumped, and pontoon wagons fitted with a floor for carriage of stores.

    (b) Pack transport will be improvised by each Field Company as follows:-

            8 for coils of wire.
            4 for pickets.
            4 for odd tools.
       making a total of 20 pack animals per Company.

8. **Roads and Tramways.**

   The T.T.O. will arrange to patrol the Trench Tramway lines during the operations, and carry out necessary repairs; for this purpose spare track will be dumped at points on each line.

   The pushing forward of the ROSSIGNOL TRAM towards WYTSCHAETE and of V.C. Road to join SUICIDE ROAD near MAEDELSTEDE is being undertaken by the IX Corps.

9. The following Maps are issued herewith:-

   (1) Copy of Map G/16/1.
   (2) Trench Map C.R.E. 169.
   (3) 1/2,500 Survey of CHINEZE WALL. C.R.E. 186.
   (4) Routes. C.R.E. 187.

10. These Instructions and Maps are to be kept under lock and key, when not in use, and only such portions of the instructions will be communicated to Section Commanders, as may be necessary for the carrying out of their duties.
    Under no circumstances will these orders be taken East of VIERSTRAAT SWITCH, nor any marked Map of any sort.

29th May, 1917.

R.F.A. Butterworth
Lieut-Colonel, R.E.
C. R. E. 16th Division.

SECRET.　　　　　　　　　　　　　　　　　Copy No. 9

APP 3

16th DIVISIONAL ENGINEERS OPERATION ORDER NO. 27.

8th May, 1917.

1.　　　The 19th Division will relieve the 16th Division in the DIEPENDAAL SECTOR, relief commencing on 9th May, and command passing on night 9th/10th.
　　　81st and 82nd Field Companies, R.E. will take over the work in the line from 155th Field Company, R.E. on 10th inst.

2.　MOVES.　　The following will take place on the 9th May:-

155th Field Company, R.E.　　　Transport from BALDOYLE to LOCRE.

156th Field Company, R.E.　　　H.Q. and 2 Sections from DE. ZON CAMP to BALDOYLE CAMP.
　　　　　　　　　　　　　　　　2 Sections from DE ZON CAMP to R.E. FARM.

157th Field Company, R.E.　　　2 Sections from BALDOYLE CAMP to UPNOR CAMP.
　　　　　　　　　　　　　　　　Transport from LOCRE to UPNOR CAMP.

　　　All the above to be completed by 2.0. p.m. except 156th Fld. Coy. This Company to be clear of DE ZON CAMP by 10 a.m.
　　　The following will take place on the 11th instant:-

155th Field Company, R.E.　　　H.Q. and 2 Sections to M.23.b.8.8.
　　　　　　　　　　　　　　　　2 Sections to R.E. FARM.

156th Field Company, R.E.　　　H.Q. and 2 Sections to M.23.b.8.8.

TRANSFERS OF BILLETS:-

　　　O.C. 156th Field Company, R.E. will hand over DE ZON CAMP to O.C. 81st Field Company, R.E. on afternoonxxxx 9th inst. by 10 a.m.

　　　O.C. 155th Field Company, R.E. will hand over BALDOYLE and HALLEBAST CAMPS to O.C. 82nd Field Company, R.E. on morning of 11th inst.

WORK:-

　　VIERSTRAAT.　　Work will be carried on as usual.

　　DIEPENDAAL.　　O.C. 155th Field Company, R.E. will arrange to hand over all work and stores to O.C's 81st and 82nd Field Companies on 10th inst., withdrawing his parties on completion.

4.　NEW CAMP.　M.23.b.8.8.

　　　O.C's 155th and 156th Field Companies will start work to-morrow on preparation of the R.E. CAMP at M.23.b.8.8.

5.　LOCATION.　　On evening of 11th instant:-

　　155th Field Company, R.E.　　　H.QRS. and 2 Sections. M.23.b.8.8.
　　　　　　　　　　　　　　　　　2 Sections. R.E. FARM.
　　　　　　　　　　　　　　　　　Transport. LOCRE.

/156th

(5. contd).

    156th Field Company, R.E.   H.Q. and 2 Sections, M.23.b.8.8.
                                             2 Sections.   R.E. FARM.
                                             Transport.   LOCRE.

    157th Field Company, R.E.   UPNOR CAMP.

6.   Reports on completion of move to H.Q. R.E., CANADA CORNER.

7.   ACKNOWLEDGE.

                                                         R E Stradling
                                                                Captain, R.E.

                                      Adjutant 16th Divisional Engineers.

Copies to:-

    1. Retained.
    2. 155th Fld. Coy. R.E.
    3. 156th Field Coy. R.E.
    4. 157th Field Coy. R.E.
    5. 'G' 16th Div.
    6. 'Q' 16th Div.
    7. C.R.E. 19th Div.
    8. 16th Div. Sigs.
    9. War Diary.)
  10.   "   "   )

SECRET. App 4   Copy No. 14

16th DIVISIONAL ENGINEERS OPERATION ORDER No. 28.

10th May, 1917.

1. Consequent upon return of 155th Field Company, R.E. and 'C' Company, 11th Hants (P) from DIEPENDAAL SECTOR, the following readjustment of work in the line will take place from 12th instant.

    155th Field Coy. R.E.   H.Q. and 2 Sections WOULDHAM CAMP.

    For work in RIGHT SUB-SECTOR.   2 Sections.   R.E. FARM.

    156th Field Coy. R.E.   UPNOR CAMP.

    Training and administrative work under C.R.E.

    157th Field Coy. R.E.   H.Q. and 2 Sections WOULDHAM CAMP.

    2 Sections R.E. FARM.

    For work in LEFT SUB-SECTOR.

    Change over of work will be arranged between Field Company Commanders and will be in accordance with attached schedule.
    All moves to be completed by night 12th/13th May.

    ### 11th HANTS (P).

    'C' Company, 11th Hants will return to MOORE PARK CAMP and will be employed on Tramway extensions required to R.F.A. Ammunition supply.

2. 100 Infantry with complement of Officers and N.C.O's are being permanently attached to Field Companies for work and training.

    These will be billeted, rationed and administered by the Field Company concerned.
    These parties are being provided as follows:-

    155th Field Coy. R.E.   from 48th Inf. Bde.
    156th Field Coy. R.E.   from 47th Inf. Bde.
    157th Field Coy. R.E.   from 49th Inf. Bde.

    Field Company Commanders will arrange all details, as to taking over these parties, direct with Brigade Major of the Brigade concerned.

3. R.E. conference will be held this afternoon at 5.30 p.m. at MONT ROUGE. The following will attend:-

    Field Company Commanders.
    O.C. 11th Hants (P).

4. ACKNOWLEDGE.

Issued at 4.0. p.m.

R.E. Stradling
Captain, R.E.
Adjutant 16th Div. Engineers.

Distribution:-

1. Retained.
2. 155th Fld.Coy.R.E.
3. 156th Fld.Coy.R.E.
4. 157th Fld.Coy.R.E.
5. 11th Hants (P).
6. 'G' 16th Div.   )
7. 'Q' 16th Div.   )
8. 47th Inf.Bde.   )   For information.
9. 48th Inf.Bde.   )
10. 49th Inf.Bde.   )
11. A. D. M. S.   )
12. 16th Div.Sigs.   )
13. WAR DIARY.
14.   "   "

SCHEDULE SHOWING CHANGE OVER OF WORK ON 12-5-17.

Unit.	WORK.	Taken over by
156th Fld.Coy.	Reclamation of Front Line (L).	157th Fld.Coy.
"	Completing YUM YUM and SWATOW Trenches, and putting in small shelters.	"
"	Cutting and revetting USNACH Street.	"
"	Battalion H.Q. YUM YUM.	"
"	Company H.Q. SWATOW.	"
"	Work on M.T.M's. ( )	"
"	Work on H.T.M's. (V - VIII)	"
"	A. D. S. FOSSE.	"
"	Reclamation of Front Line (R)	155th Fld.Coy.
"	Completing PEKING including small shelters.	"
"	Company H.Q. S.P. 12.	"
"	Work on M.T.M's ( )	"
"	Work on H.T.M's (I - IV).	"
157th Fld.Coy.	VIERSTRAAT SWITCH. RIB and FOSSE. C.T's.	"
	2 Visual Signal Stations, FOSSE.	157th Fld.Coy.
	Signal Dug-out. SIEGE FARM.	"
	Signal Dug-out PALLAS FARM.	"
	Overland Routes. 1) 2)	"
	" " 3) 4)	155th Fld.Coy.
	A. D. S. Near PALLAS FARM.	156th Fld.Coy.
	Main Divisional Dump.	156th Fld.Coy.
	LOCRE LAUNDRY.	156th Fld.Coy.
	Work on Camps.	156th Fld.Coy.

NOTE:-   On the change over O.C's 155 and 157 Field Coys. will detail 1 Section each with an Officer for work on Gun Positions.

Copy No.

APP. 5

16th DIVISIONAL ENGINEERS OPERATION ORDER No.29.

22nd May, 1917.

1. 156th Field Company, R.E. will relieve 155th Field Company, R.E. in the Right Sub-Sector on 23rd/24th May, 1917.

2. All work in the line will be handed over by arrangements between the two Companies, the change-over to take place on the morning of 24th May.

3. O.C. 156th Field Coy. R.E. will retain the work on FOSSE DUG-OUTS, Signal Station, K.14 and Advanced Divisional Dump.

4. O.C. 155th Field Coy. R.E. will take over the administrative work from 156th Fld.Coy. as in para: 2.

5. 156th Field Coy.R.E. will move to CHATHAM CAMP, and 155th Field Coy.R.E. to UPNOR CAMP.
   Moves to be completed by 12 NOON on 24th May.

6. The Horse Lines now occupied by 155th and 157th Field Companies, R.E. will be vacated on 24th inst., and the following moves take place:-

    155th Field Coy.   to MONT ROUGE.

    156th Field Coy.)
    157th Field Coy.)   to M.22.c.6.3½.

    O.C's 155th and 157th Field Companies will have the horsestandings thoroughly cleaned and disinfected in accordance with 16th Div. No. Q/1173 forwarded under this Office No. 3324/53 dated 12th May,1917., so as to be fit for occupation by the troops, In each case an Officer will superintend the final clearing up.

7. No telephones will be removed by Field Companies, and a certificate will be obtained when handing over these instruments to an incoming Unit.

8. ACKNOWLEDGE.

Issued at 1.0 p.m.

R E Stradling
Captain, R.E.
Adjutant 16th Div.Engineers.

Distribution:-

1. Retained.
2. 155th Fld.Coy.R.E.
3. 156th Fld.Coy.R.E.
4. 157th Fld.Coy.R.E.
5. 16th Div. 'G'.   )
6. 16th Div. 'Q'   )
7. A.D.M.S.   )   For information.
8. A.D.V.S.   )
9. O.C. 11th Hants (P).)
10. 47th Inf. Bde.   )
11. 48th Inf. Bde.   )
12. 49th Inf. Bde.   )
13. 16th Div. Signals.   )
14.   (
15.   (War Diary.

WAR DIARY.

FOR MONTH OF JUNE, 1917.

VOLUME:- 19

UNIT:- Headquarters 16th Div Engineers

Army Form C. 2118.

WAR DIARY
or
INTELLIGENCE SUMMARY.
(Erase heading not required.)

Instructions regarding War Diaries and Intelligence Summaries are contained in F. S. Regs., Part II. and the Staff Manual respectively. Title pages will be prepared in manuscript.

Place	Date	Hour	Summary of Events and Information	Remarks and references to Appendices
SCHERPENBERG	1.6.17		7th Corps withdrawn from mud to line (ref Appendix 1) CRE's order No 104	
	2.6.17		Minor operations & filling of 2 advanced dumps (ARMSTP. ST. II ROAD) both hours were brought up by horses. Shell fire. These dumps were destroyed through T.M. ammunition being placed alongside	
	3.6.17		Refilling of 2 advanced dumps (ARMSTP cont'd) — following round 4 ces —	
	4.6.17		CRE Instructions for the offensive — ADDENDA No 1. (Appendix (1)) — Provisional Instructions for advance to OOSTTAVERNE LINE issued by CRE (Appendix (2))	Appendix (1) Appendix (2)
	5.6.17		Field Coys except 2section (1-156 & 1-157) in back billets — 2 forward sections employed on maintenance + CRE's order No 105 issued Appendix (3) — CRE's Instructions for offensive — (ADDENDA No 2) (Appendix No 1)	Appendix (3) Appendix (1)
	6.6.17		7th Corps C.O. 5.6.17 — Report on completion of small dumps on forward route at HARINGHEBEEK (marked "C"). — CRE's order No 106 issued Appendix (3) — CRE's Instructions for offensive ADDENDA No 4 issued — Appendix (1) CRE's order No 107 issued — Appendix (3) — 7th Corps move to battle positions during night 6/7th —	Appendix (3) Appendix (1) Appendix (3)

Army Form C. 2118.

WAR DIARY
or
INTELLIGENCE SUMMARY.
(Erase heading not required.)

Instructions regarding War Diaries and Intelligence Summaries are contained in F. S. Regs., Part II. and the Staff Manual respectively. Title pages will be prepared in manuscript.

ROYAL ENGINEERS 16th DIVISION

Place	Date	Hour	Summary of Events and Information	Remarks and references to Appendices
SOUERPENBERG	7/6/17		Messages received from Fd Coys. reports arrival at battle positions (157 reported 1.30AM) 156 & 155 reports received 2.12 AM.) — ZERO hour 3.10AM. —	
	8/6/17		for return of operation are attending (4) (CRE's report on operations) 156 157 FdCoys withdrew from work in line by 9AM on 9.6.17	
	9.6.17		155 Fd Coy withdrew at 7.30pm 9.6.17	
	10.6.17		Location of companies 155 Fd Coy HQ. – UPNOR CAMP – 156 & 157 Fd Coys HQ. – CHATHAM CAMP.	
	11.6.17		Lt.Col. Butterworth (CRE) went on leave – Major WM Marsden acting CRE – HQ R.E. moved to CANADA CORNER at 2.15pm –	
CANADA CORNER	12.6.17		HQ & O.O. No 30 issued —	
"	13.6.17		Fd Coys working under CRE under O.C. B"Coys on THE RIDGE DEFENCES	
	14.6.17			
	15.6.17			
	16.6.17			
	17.6.17		16" Div O.O. No 31 issued at 12.30 pm and cancelled at 11 pm orders received that Division will move to MERRIS area tomorrow	

Army Form C. 2118.

WAR DIARY
or
INTELLIGENCE SUMMARY.
(Erase heading not required.)

Instructions regarding War Diaries and Intelligence Summaries are contained in F. S. Regs., Part II. and the Staff Manual respectively. Title pages will be prepared in manuscript.

Place	Date	Hour	Summary of Events and Information	Remarks and references to Appendices
CANADA CORNER — MERRIS. —	18.6.17		1st Cup moved under Brigade orders to MERRIS AREA — CRE's Office to MERRIS	
	19.6.17		orders received that 16th Div. is to be transferred from 2nd Army to 5th ARMY — 2d Cup & 11th Hants to attached for work to CE XIX Corps from 21st inst.	
MERRIS —	20.6.17		HQ R.E. move to GODAWAESVELDE — 2d Cup move under Brigade orders —	
GODAWAESVELDE			orders received that 1st Cup & 11th Hants (P) move under CRE's orders to XIX Corps area — 16 Div Eng. operation order No. 33 issued — (Appendix 4)	Appendix (4)
POPERINGHE	21.6.17		No R.E. & 2 2d Cup move to POPERINGHE area + 155th L.C. to ARNEKE —	
(P.27) L.11.d.			A.C.E. BUTTERWORTH returned from leave — Major Meredith rejoined his company —	
	22.6.17			
	23.6.17			
	24.6.17		work under CE XIX Corps	
	25.6.17			
	26.6.17			
	27.6.17			
	28.6.17			
	29.6.17			
	30.6.17			

SECRET.
===========

Copy No. 7.

C. R. E's Order No. 104.

31st May, 1917.

The programme of work of preparation now being complete O.C's 156th and 157th Field Companies, R.E. will withdraw their Sappers from the Line, leaving behind one Section with an Officer to carry out ordinary trench maintenance, and to assist Brigadiers 47th and 49th Brigades in any special work of preparation, which they may require.

This order will become operative after work to-morrow.

O.C's Field Coys. will visit Brigadiers daily to keep in touch with the situation in their respective Brigade areas.

The maintenance of the main Communication Trenches from YORK ROAD to CHINEZE WALL LINE is being carried out by O.C. 11th Hants (P).

Sd. R.E. STRADLING, Captain, R.E.
for C. R. E. 16th Division.

SECRET.   3524/34.   Copy No. 6

C.R.E'S INSTRUCTIONS FOR THE OFFENSIVE.
ADDENDA No. 1.

1. **DUMPS.**

The sites of all dumps and establishment of stores are shewn in C.R.E's Instructions for the Offensive.

Advanced Dumps will supply the needs of the troops for consolidation during the advance, and for the special R.E. work on Supporting Points, etc.

Pack Mules should be loaded at the Intermediate Dumps.

Advanced Dumps are allotted for R.E. work on Z Day as follows:-

ALBERTA.	156th Field Company, R.E.
TIT ROAD.) POSSE.)	158th Field Company, R.E., to include stores for wiring BLACK LINE.
WATLING ST.	167th Field Company, R.E.

Each Company will arrange for refilling of these dumps during the night following Z Day, or sooner if practicable.

Instructions regarding formation of Dumps in the German lines will be issued later.

2. **COMMUNICATIONS.**

1. The O.C. 11th Hants has arranged a complete system of communications, telephone, visual and runners.

A copy of his instructions is attached for information.

The Field Companies will make use of this system as much as possible, to save sending special runners back from the Companies.

2. Three Cyclists from each Company will be attached to H.Q.R.E. for use in emergency, reporting on the night Y/Z.

R J Butterworth

4th June, 1917.

Lieut-Colonel, R.E.
C. R. E. 18th Division.

S E C R E T.   Copy.No.
=========

[Stamp: ROYAL ENGINEERS No. 3324/25 16TH DIVISION]

Provisional Instructions for Advance to
OOSTTAVERNE LINE issued by C. R. E. 16th Division.
==

1. The 33rd Infantry Brigade and 68th Field Company, R.E. are attached to the 16th Division for this further advance.

2. The BLACK LINE should be completely in our hands by Zero plus 5 hours.

   The consolidation of this line will be carried out by the 47th and 49th Brigades assisted by wiring parties from the 48th Brigade.

3. At Zero plus 5 hours and 30 minutes the 48th Brigade will push forward strong patrols which will establish themselves in the MAUVE LINE.

4. In the event of considerable success the 33rd Inf. Bde. will carry out a further advance to capture and consolidate the OOSTTAVERNE LINE between O.28.b.7.1 and O.16.c.4.2.

5. The MAUVE LINE and OOSTTAVERNE LINE will be consolidated and prepared to resist counter-attacks.

   155th FIELD COMPANY, R.E.

6. The 155th Field Company, R.E. will assist the 48th Brigade in the work of consolidation of the MAUVE LINE, and will conform to the forward movements of this Brigade.

   This Company will also furnish R.E. supervision for the wiring of the BLACK LINE in accordance with para: 2.

   The move to the Preliminary Assembly Position, and Advanced Assembly Position will be carried out without further orders in accordance with programme.

   The subsequent forward moves, will be in accordance with the tactical situation, and when ordered by the Brigadier.

    (1) Preliminary Assembly Position. G.H.Q. II. N.15.c.

    (2) Advanced Assembly Position. (H.Q. and 2 Sections. MACAW.
                                         (2 Sections SHANTUNG.

    (3) Rendezvous for Working Sections. BLACK COT - HOSPICE.

    (4) Objective. LEG COPSE - TORREKEN FARM.

   The move to (1) will take place on Y/Z night.

   The move from (1) to (2) on Z Day as soon as the Brigade moves out of the CHINEZE WALL LINE.

/Work

(2).

WORK:— Construction of Supporting Points as follows:—

      (1) FARM POST.   0.20.d.3.4.

      (2) LEG POST SOUTH.   0.20.b.80.15.

      (3) LEG POST NORTH.   0.20.b.6.6.

Two selected by the Brigadier to be made first.

68th FIELD COMPANY, R.E.

(7)   The 68th Field Company, R.E. will assist the 33rd Brigade in the work of consolidation of the OOSTTAVERNE LINE, and conform to the movements of the Brigade as follows:—

    (1) Preliminary Assembly Position. G.H.Q. LINE.

    (2) Advanced Assembly Position.   VIERSTRAAT SWITCH.

    (3) Rendezvous of Working Sections. (a) OOSTTAVERNE WOOD.
                                                  (b) TORREKEN FARM.

    (4) Objective. OOSTTAVERNE - MATHIEU FARM LINE.

The move to (1) will take place under Brigade arrangements on Y/Z Night. From (1) to (2) as soon as the Brigade moves forward from G.H.Q. LINE.

The moves from (2) to (3) will be decided by Field Company Commander after consultation with Brigadier, from (3) to (4) when the Section Commander is satisfied that the OOSTTAVERNE LINE is held, and work possible on Supporting Points detailed.

WORK:— Construction of Supporting Points as follows:—

    (1) POACHER'S POST.   0.28.a.15.85.

    (2) FORESTERS POST.   0.21.d.5.5.

    (3) PEEL POST.   0.21.b.9.9.

WORKING PARTIES:—

A Platoon will be handed over to each Section R.E. at the Preliminary Assembly Position as follows:—

    (1) From 6th LINCOLNS to assist in work on POACHER'S POST.

    (2) From 9th SHERWOOD FORESTERS to assist on FORESTERS POST.

    (3) From 6th BORDERERS to assist on PEEL POST.

8. TOOLS AND STORES:—

All parties will carry up the necessary tools including a proportion of picks, shovels, wire-cutters and hedging gloves.

Pack Mules should be got forward as soon as feasible from the Intermediate Dumps with wiring material etc.

/It

(3).

It is probable however that the preliminary work will be done with stores available on the site.

German Dumps exist at

    O.20.a.3.1.   )
    TORREKEN FARM.) 155th Field Company, R.E.

    O.15.c.1.4.   )
    O.16.c.6.1.   ) 68th Field Company, R.E.

Further there is a lot of erected wire which may be improved to form obstacles or taken up for re-erection elsewhere.

9. RECONNAISSANCE.

No party should be sent forward until the exact site has been reconnoitred. The work should then be traced out by a small advance party, and the remainder brought up by guides.

R.H. Butterworth

4th June, 1917.

                                                  Lieut-Colonel, R.E.

                               C. R. E. 16th Division.

SECRET. 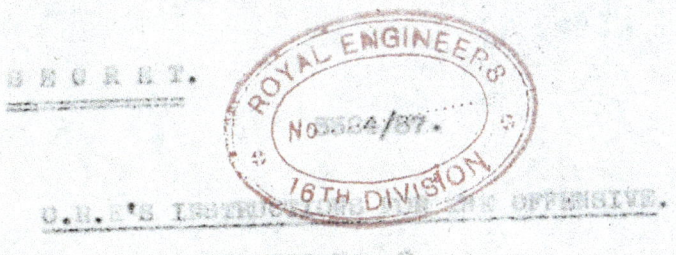 Copy No. 11

C.R.E.'S INSTRUCTIONS FOR THE OFFENSIVE.
ADDENDA No. 2.

1. **EMPLOYMENT OF TUNNELLING COMPANIES.**

Reference General Staff Instructions para: 61 the three Officers and 30 Sappers detailed to reconnoitre captured dug-outs will be accommodated at S.P.13 under arrangements made by O.C. 250th Tunnelling Company, R.E.

2. They will proceed to S.P. 13 on Y/Z Night, taking two day's rations with them.

3.
(a) The Officer in charge of the party will detail his Officers and men for the search of defined areas in the captured trenches, and will carry out repairs to suitable dug-outs.

(b) He will have boards fixed in the dug-outs showing accommodation.

(c) He will forward a report each evening to O.C. 250th Tunnelling Company, R.E. giving location of habitable dug-outs.

(d) He will communicate direct with C.R.E. 16th Division in case of urgency, through Signals S.P.13.

4. The time for the party to go forward on Z Day will be synchroneous with advance of 49th Brigade, but O.C. Tunnelling Party will use his discretion as to the possibility of being able to go forward and do useful work.

He will subsequently work independently at such time as the situation admits, reporting progress to O.C. 250th Tunnelling Coy. as in para: 3 (c).

5th June, 1917.

Lieut-Colonel, R.E.
C. R. E. 16th Division.

S E C R E T.  Copy No. 12

C.R.E.'S INSTRUCTIONS FOR THE OFFENSIVE.

ADDENDA No. 2.

1. EMPLOYMENT OF TUNNELLING COMPANIES.

Reference General Staff Instructions para: 61 the three Officers and 30 Sappers detailed to reconnoitre captured dug-outs will be accommodated at S.P.13 under arrangements made by O.C. 250th Tunnelling Company, R.E.

2. They will proceed to S.P. 13 on Y/Z Night, taking two day's rations with them.

3.
  (a) The Officer in charge of the party will detail his Officers and men for the search of defined areas in the captured trenches, and will carry out repairs to suitable dug-outs.

  (b) He will have boards fixed in the dug-outs showing accommodation.

  (c) He will forward a report each evening to O.C. 250th Tunnelling Company, R.E. giving location of habitable dug-outs.

  (d) He will communicate direct with C.R.E. 16th Division in case of urgency, through Signals S.P.13.

4. The time for the party to go forward on Z Day will be synchroneous with advance of 48th Brigade, but O.C. Tunnelling Party will use his discretion as to the possibility of being able to go forward and do useful work.

He will subsequently work independently at such time as the situation admits, reporting progress to O.C. 250th Tunnelling Coy. as in para: 3 (c).

5th June, 1917.   Lieut-Colonel, R.E.
                                              C. R. E. 16th Division.

SECRET.   Copy No. 4

G.S.G.S. INSTRUCTIONS FOR THE OFFENSIVE.

ADDENDA No. 4.

1. DESTRUCTION OF ENEMY GUNS.

O.C's 69th and 158th Field Companies, R.E. will send forward a supply of guncotton, detonators, and fuses, with their working sections for the destruction of guns.

2. In the event of a battery being taken, two sappers will be detached to prepare each gun for demolition, and they will remain with the battery until recalled, or until the battery is taken over by the Artillery.

   No gun will however be destroyed, unless it is in imminent danger of being recaptured.

3. An effective method of destruction is to open the breech, and tie a slab against the hinge. For a heavy gun or howitzer two slabs should be used.

4. Each working Section will take 12 slabs of guncotton ready primed, with means of ignition (detonators, fuse, patent lighters) carried separately.

   A small reserve of explosives will be stored at the Company Advanced Headquarters.

                                    R M Butterworth
                                    Lieut-Colonel, R.E.
6th June, 1917.
                                    C. R. E. 19th Division.

S E C R E T.      Copy.No. 20

Provisional Instructions for Advance to
OOSTTAVERNE LINE issued by C. R. E. 16th Division.
==

1. The 33rd Infantry Brigade and 69th Field Company, R.E. are attached to the 16th Division for this further advance.

2. The BLACK LINE should be completely in our hands by Zero plus 5 hours.

   The consolidation of this line will be carried out by the 47th and 49th Brigades assisted by wiring parties from the 48th Brigade.

3. At Zero plus 5 hours and 30 minutes the 48th Brigade will push forward strong patrols which will establish themselves in the MAUVE LINE.

4. In the event of considerable success the 33rd Inf. Bde. will carry out a further advance to capture and consolidate the OOSTTAVERNE LINE between O.29.b.7.1 and O.16.c.4.2.

5. The MAUVE LINE and OOSTTAVERNE LINE will be consolidated and prepared to resist counter-attacks.

155th FIELD COMPANY, R.E.

6. The 155th Field Company, R.E. will assist the 48th Brigade in the work of consolidation of the MAUVE LINE, and will conform to the forward movements of this Brigade.

   This Company will also furnish R.E. supervision for the wiring of the BLACK LINE in accordance with para: 2.

   The move to the Preliminary Assembly Position, and Advanced Assembly Position will be carried out without further orders in accordance with programme.

   The subsequent forward moves, will be in accordance with the tactical situation, and when ordered by the Brigadier.

   (1) Preliminary Assembly Position.   S.H.Q. II.
                                         H.18.c.

   (2) Advanced Assembly Position.   (H.4. and 2
                                        (Sections. MACAW.
                                        (
                                        (2 Sections
                                        (SHANTUNG.

   (3) Rendezvous for Working Sections. BLACK COT -
                                         HOSPICE.

   (4) Objective.   LIM COPSE -
                                         TORREKEN FARM.

   The move to (1) will take place on Y/Z night.

   The move from (1) to (2) on Z Day as soon as the Brigade moves out of the CHINESE WALL LINE.

                                                    /More

(2).

WORK:- Construction of Supporting Points as follows:-

    (1) FARM POST.   O.20.d.3.4.

    (2) LMG POST SOUTH.   O.20.b.80.15.

    (3) LMG POST NORTH.   O.20.b.6.6.

Two selected by the Brigadier to be made first.

88th FIELD COMPANY, R.E.

(7) The 88th Field Company, R.E. will assist the 33rd Brigade in the work of consolidation of the OOSTTAVERNE LINE, and conform to the movements of the Brigade as follows:-

    (1) Preliminary Assembly Position.   S.H.Q. LINE.

    (2) Advanced Assembly Position.   VIERSTRAAT SWITCH.

    (3) Rendezvous of Working Sections.   (a) OOSTTAVERNE WOOD.
                                    (b) TORREKEN FARM.

    (4) Objective.   OOSTTAVERNE - MATHIEU FARM LINE.

The move to (1) will take place under Brigade arrangements on Y/Z Night. From (1) to (2) as soon as the Brigade moves forward from S.H.Q. LINE.

The moves from (2) to (3) will be decided by Field Company Commander after consultation with Brigadier, from (3) to (4) when the Section Commander is satisfied that the OOSTTAVERNE LINE is held, and work possible on Supporting Points detailed.

WORK:- Construction of Supporting Points as follows:-

    (1) POACHER'S POST.   O.28.d.15.85.

    (2) FORESTERS POST.   O.21.d.5.5.

    (3) PEEL POST.   O.21.b.9.9.

WORKING PARTIES:-

A Platoon will be handed over to each Section R.E. at the Preliminary Assembly Position as follows:-

    (1) From 6th LINCOLNS to assist in work on POACHER'S POST.

    (2) From 9th SHERWOOD FORESTERS to assist on FORESTERS POST.

    (3) From 8th BOMBARDERS to assist on PEEL POST.

8. TOOLS AND STORES:-

All parties will carry up the necessary tools including a proportion of picks, shovels, wire-cutters and hedging gloves.

Pack Mules should be got forward as soon as feasible from the Intermediate Dumps with wiring material etc.

/It

(3).

It is probable however that the preliminary work will be done with stores available on the site.

German Dumps exist at

    O.20.a.3.1.   )
    TORREKEN FARM.) 155th Field Company, R.E.

    O.15.c.1.6.   )
    O.15.c.8.1.   ) 68th Field Company, R.E.

Further there is a lot of erected wire which may be improved to form obstacles or taken up for re-erection elsewhere.

3. RECONNAISSANCE.

No party should be sent forward until the exact site has been reconnoitred. The work should then be traced out by a small advance party, and the remainder brought up by guides.

R J Butterworth

4th June, 1917.

Lieut-Colonel, R.E.

C. R. E. 16th Division.

SECRET.   Copy No. 12.
===========

C. R. E's ORDER No. 105.
================================ ==============

5th June, 1917.

Reference 1/10,000 Map.

1. 155th, 156th and 157th Field Companies, R.E. and 'C' and 'D' Companies, 11th Hants (Pioneers) will move into Assembly Positions on the night Y/Z under cover of darkness.

2. 1 Section from each of 156th and 157th Field Companies and 2 Platoons from each of 'C? and 'D' Companies, 11th Hants (Pioneers) that are to occupy positions of assembly in the 47th and 49th Inf.Bdes. assembly areas will move to their assembly positions with the Brigade to which they are attached under the orders of the Brigadiers concerned.

3. 155th Field Company, 156th Field Company, (less 1 Section) 157th Field Company (less 1 Section), will move under the arrangements of the O.C. Companies to R.E. FARM and G.H.Q. II

        Route -   BRULOOZE - NUT ROAD - POMPIER ESTAMINET.

4. All Units to pass BRULOOZE CROSS ROADS 12 midnight (Y/Z) and to be in position by 2.0 .a.m Z Day.

5. O.C. 11th Hants will arrange for O.C. 'C' and 'D' Companies, to proceed as detailed in 3 and 4.

6. On East of LOCRE - LA CLYTTE ROAD all movement is to be by sections or platoons.

7. Completion of assembly is to be reported to H.Q.R.E. by the use of the Code Word

                  FIXT.

8. The 68th Field Company, R.E. will assemble under orders of the Brigadier 33rd Brigade.

9. The brigading of transport, 155th, 156th and 157th Field Companies, R.E. will take place under the direction of Captain E K. GREENHOW, R.E. in horse lines at M.22.d.0.8. To be completed by 7.pm. on Y Day.

10. Tool-carts and Pack Mules will be taken forward to place of assembly.
    Tool-cart teams will be sent back to the horse lines and the pack mules picketed in as covered position as possible near place of assembly.

11. In addition to Iron Ration the Ration for Z Day will be taken forward.
    Subsequent arrangmenets will be made by Units concerned.

                          R.E. STRADLING, Captain, R.E.
                            for C. R. E. 16th Division

C. R. E's ORDER No. 106.

6th June, 1917.

(1)　The following move to VIERSTRAAT SWITCH of Company H.Qrs. will take place consequent on the advance of working parties on Z Day.:-

    155th Field Coy.　　to MACAW TRENCH.
    156th Field Coy.　　to STORK TRENCH.
    157th Field Coy.　　to PARRET TRENCH.

On arrival O.C. Field Companies will report to their respective Brigades and C.R.E. giving exact location.

(2)　Captain BOYD, R.A.M.C. will proceed with Field Companies to R.E. FARM (in accordance with C.R.E's Order No 105) and form an A.D.S. Post there on Y/Z Night.

When Headquarters of Companies move forward to VIERSTRAAT SWITCH he will proceed to LAITERIE A.D.S. where he will report for general duties to the Senior Officer in Charge.

(3)　FORWARD DUMPS.

Reference forecast of work already issued.
The following forward dumps will be formed as soon as possible under arrangements by Os.C. 156th and 157th Field Company's.

    No. 1　ROUND POND. M 0.19.a.4.1.

    2. Near BLACK POST.　O.13.c.4.3.

The chain of dumps will then be;-

LEFT.	RIGHT.
No. 2 Intermediate.	No. 1 Intermediate.
WATSONVILLE (WATLING ST.)	TOT ROAD (Now PUNCH BOWL)
BLACK POST.	ROUND POND.

C. R. E. will make arrangements for filling PUNCH BOWL and WATSONVILLE DUMPS thence Field Coys. will carry by pack mule to new advanced dumps near ROUND POND and BLACK POST.

ALBERTA and FOSSE advanced dumps will cease to exist as such on formation of the two dumps in German lines. These latter will be marked by conspicuous notice boards lettered "D"　These have already been sent to R.E. FARM.

Sd. R.E. STRADLING, Captain, R.E.

for C. R. E. 16th Division.

C. R. E's ORDER No. 107.

6th June, 1917.

Reference 1/10,000 Map.

1. Reference para: 5 C.R.E's Order No. 105.
   O.C. 11th Hants will arrange for 1 Platoon from each of 'A' and 'B' companies to accompany 'C' and 'D' Companies to their position of assembly on Y/Z Night.

2. These two Platoons will work on 'C' and 'F' Overland Routes taking the time to start from the Brigadiers concerned under the same arrangements as 'C' and 'D' companies.

3. Some ladders are required by the R.F.A. to connect up the OUT and IN Routes behind their gun position.
   The site of the batteries is shewn on attached map.

   O.C. 11th Hants will arrange this work in accordance with progress of work on the routes concerned.

Sd.R.F.A. BUTTERWORTH, Lieut-Col.R.E.

C. R. E. 16th Division.

3324/103.

16th DIVISION R.E.

Narrative of Events.   7th of June, 1917.

1. Preliminary Dispositions.

(a) Personnel.

Unit.	Location.	Remarks.
155th Field Company, R.E. and attached Infantry.	G.H.Q. II and R.E. FARM.	Reserve Company.
156th Field Company, R.E. and attached Infantry.	G.H.Q. II and R.E. FARM.	1 Section & 25 Infantry CHINEZE WALL
157th Field Company, R.E. and attached Infantry.	G.H.Q. II and R.E. FARM.	1 Section & 25 Infantry SHANTUNG.
Section, 250th Tunnelling Company, R.E.	S.P.13.	
68th Field Company, R.E.	G.H.Q. III	Attached to 33rd Brigade.
11th Hants Pioneers. H.Q., 'A' and 'B' Coys.	MOORE PARK CAMP.	* 4 platoons in CHINEZE WALL LINE.
'C' and 'D' Companies (less 4 platoons)*	G. H. Q. II.	
Special Wiring Party.	FOSSE TRENCH.	1 R.E. Officer 128 Infantry.

NOTE:- Tool Carts and 20 Pack Mules were taken forward to G.H.Q. Line. Remaining transport brigaded under C.R.E. at MONT ROUGE.

(b) Dumps.

Main Reserve Dump.	R.E. FARM.	
Intermediate Dumps.	No.1 ROSSIGNOL.) No.2 PARRET FARM.)	In YORK ROAD.
Advanced Dumps.	No.1 ALBERTA.) No.2 PUNCHBOWL.) No.3 FOSSE.) No.4 WATSONVILLE.)	In CHINEZE WALL LINE.

2. Sequence of Events.

3.10 a.m.   Attack launched on enemy front line.

5.0 a.m.   BLUE LINE taken.

155th, 156 (H.Q. and 3 Sections), 157 (H.Q. and 3 Sections) to VIERSTRAAT SWITCH.

2.

6.50 a.m.		Advance on BLACK LINE.

2 Sections 155 Company to S.P.13.

2 Companies 11th (Hants Pioneers) to CHINEZE WALL LINE.

8.0 a.m. BLACK LINE taken.

8.15 a.m. Advanced Sections 156 and 157 Coys. with attached Infantry move forward to construct S.P's NAP POST and RED POST. Advanced Platoons 11th Hants move up to start work on Overland Routes D and E, and extension of Communication Trenches (ASH and BIRR) across NO MAN'S LAND.

8.45 a.m. Parties move forward to work as follows:-

156th Company, R.E. 2 Sections with attached Infantry to construct S.P's WOOD POST and CHURCH POST. ½ Section to search for an open up Wells in WYTSCHAETE Village.
½ Sections with pack mules to form forward dump near ROUND POND.

157th Company, R.E. 1 Section with attached Infantry to construct S.P. BLACK POST.
½ Section with pack mules to form dump at BLACK COT.
1 Section to construct heavy bridge for 6" Howitzers, across VIERSTRAAT SWITCH.

11th Hants (Pioneers).

'C' Company.	(Half Company.	Overland Route D.
	(Half Company.	Extension of ASH Lane C.T.
'D' Company.	(Half Company.	Overland Route E.
	(Half Company.	Extension of BIRR C.T.
1 Platoon 'A' Company.		Overland Route F.
1 Platoon 'B' Company.		Overland Route C.

10.0 a.m. MAUVE LINE held by patrols.

Special Wiring Party ordered to go forward, and wire BLACK LINE.

Pioneers taken off Communication Trenches, and concentrated on the Overland Routes.

10.15 a.m. Section 250th Tunnelling Company, R.E. proceeds to locate and clear dug-outs in WYTSCHAETE WOOD and Village.

10.35 a.m. Two Pontoon Wagons sent up to carry wire from R.E. FARM to PUNCHBOWL Dump, for forward dump ROUND POND.

1.0 p.m. Artillery unable to get forward on D Route. Two Platoons Pioneers sent forward from MOORE PARK CAMP by motor lorry to hasten work.

1.30 p.m. Two Sections 155 Field Company with attached Infantry move forward to construct S.P's near LEG COPSE.

2.0 p.m.   68th Field Coy. R.E. move up to CHINEZE HILL, and S.P. 13.

3.0 p.m.   3 Sections 68th Field Coy.R.E. go up to construct S.P's FORESTER'S POST and POACHER'S POST.

3. Short Narrative.

156th Field Company, R.E.

Within an hour of the capture of the BLACK LINE three Sections were on their way, to construct Supporting Points NAP POST, WOOD POST and CHURCH POST.

Each Section was accompanied by 25 attached Infantry, and the garrison of the Post (20 Infantry). Stores were taken forward from PUNCHBOWL and ALBERTA Dumps, by Pack Mule, and the Infantry parties.

The Section Officer went ahead in each case to reconnoitre the site, and lay out the work. The O.C. sent for his Pontoon Wagons, and refilled PUNCHBOWL Dump during the afternoon.

The 4th Section formed a forward dump by pack mules near the ROUND POND on the rear slope of WYTSCHAETE RIDGE, and sent small parties to locate and open up water supplies in the Village.

Work on WOOD POST and CHURCH POST was delayed at times by shrapnel fire, and the Section on NAP POST being finished their work at 5.0 p.m, went up to help them.

WOOD POST and CHURCH POST were completed by 7. p.m.

157th Field Company, R.E.

Three Sections went forward at the same time as 156th Field Coy. to construct Supporting Points RED POST, BLACK POST and OBVIOUS POST.

One Section remained in Reserve, and was called upon later to rebuild a bridge for the forward move of 60-pdr. guns.

Stores

4.

Stores were taken up by pack mule, and a forward dump formed near BLACK POST.

Small parties searched known sites for wells at RED CHATEAU, BLACK COT, and HOSPICE. A good well was found near WYTSCHAETE Church. This was opened up, and a sample sent back for test. Subsequently a pump was carried up, and installed.

The party working on BLACK POST suffered some casualties, and were slightly disorganised. However a fresh start was made, and the work got through. The progress of a Tank through this post, also delayed work somewhat.

RED POST was completed by 5.0 p.m., and the party went up to help the other Posts. BLACK POST and OBVIOUS POST were completely dug and wired by 7.30 p.m.

The casualties of this Section were 2 Sappers wounded, 1 Infantry Officer wounded, and 2 O.R. killed, 2 O.R. Missing.

155th Field Company, R.E.

This Company was working with the 48th Brigade, whose task was to capture and consolidate the MAUVE LINE.

The O.C. took forward 2 Sections at 1.30 p.m. to NORTH HOUSE, then went up with the Section Officers to reconnoitre sites for Supporting Points, LEG COPSE, NORTH and SOUTH.

Meanwhile the Sections were caught in a barrage, and suffered some casualties. The Infantry parties were rather shaken, and O.C. decided to send them back.

He sent for fresh parties, and got them on to the work by 6 p.m. The two points were laid out, and completed wired by 9.15 p.m.

Stores

5.

Stores were taken forward by pack mule, and a forward dump formed near BLACK COT.

Casualties.

    R.E.   2 Officers wounded.
                   1 Sergt. and 4 O.R. killed.

    Infantry.   10 O.R. wounded.

68th Field Company, R.E.

This Company was working with the 33rd Brigade, whose task was the capture and consolidation of the GREEN (OOSTTAVERNE) LINE.

Two Sections went forward from S.P.13 at 3. p.m. to construct Supporting Points FORESTER'S POST and POACHER'S POST. A third Section went forward to construct PEEL POST, but was diverted, and instructed to assist at the other Posts.

The change of programme in the further advance upset the arrangements for working parties, the Battalions detailed to supply them having been ordered to make the attacked, instead of remaining in support. It was also responsible for the abandonment of work on PEEL POST, as this Point became outside the 33rd Brigade area of operations.

However the two points were laid out and work started, a small Infantry party being obtained for each from the Battalion in the front line. Both posts were sufficiently well dug to be able to be manned, and some wire was erected. This wire had to be taken from German entanglements, as the carry up was found to be impracticable from the CHINEZE WALL advanced dumps.

The parties were interfered with by shell fire, and work had to be stopped on occasions during bombardments.

The Officer and men stuck to their work well under trying circumstances.

The casualties were not heavy, except for the sad mischance of Lieut. GILLOTT being killed by a shell

from

from one of our batteries.

Section 250th Tunnelling Company, R.E.

The O.C. organised his Section into three parties, and gave each an area for search. They went forward at 10.0 a.m., and found some dug-outs in WYTSCHAETE WOOD, and others in the Village. Clearing and repairs were put in hand. A location report was furnished the same evening.

Special Wiring Party.

This party consisted of 4 squads each of 32 Infantry, under the command of Lieut. DIXON, R.E.

Their task was to wire the BLACK LINE.

They were sent up under orders from the Division at 10.a.m., arriving on the task at 1. p.m.

The party carried up sufficient wire and pickets for the whole task.

Work had to be done during lulls of enemy fire, and so the progress of work was slow.

However by 5 p.m. a 30 yards width of strong wire had been erected along the whole front. There were practically no casualties.

11th Hants (Pioneers).

Shortly after taking the BLACK LINE work was started by the forward platoons on 2 trenches across NO MAN'S LAND and 2 Overland Routes (D and E). The remainder of the parties followed, and work was started by a platoon each on C and F Routes.

The Divisional Commander decided to stop work on the trenches, and to concentrate on the Overland Routes. An order to this effect was sent out, and the necessary alterations made, the parties on C and F Routes being augmented by 1 platoon each.

Thus there were a Company (less a platoon) on each of D and E Routes, and ½ Company on each of C and F.

D

D Route was a slow job, as the enemy had done much damage from the CHINEZE WALL to our front line. The R.F.A. wired that they were waiting to get their guns up. Two more platoons were despatched by motor lorry from MOORE PARK CAMP, and the track was made practicable by 3. p.m.

By the end of the day all routes were through into NO MAN'S LAND, and the two Northern ones as far as the old German line.

The Pioneers had the following casualties, but their work was practically uninterrupted:-

    3 O.R. wounded.
    4 O.R. wounded at duty.

4. Summary of Work done.

1. Supporting Points.

Six Strong Points, Cruciform pattern, to take a garrison of 25 men with 2 machine guns, were completely dug and wired.

Two Strong Points, Cruciform pattern, were traced and completely wired.

Two Strong Points of irregular shape were partly dug and wired in rear of the most forward line.

2. Wiring.

The Divisional Front (BLACK LINE) was strongly wired by a special party soon after capture.

3. Routes.

    (1) 4 Overland Routes were carried forward from the line of the CHINEZE WALL into NO MAN'S LAND.

    (11) A heavy bridge was erected for passage of heavy artillery over VIERSTRAAT Trench.

4. Communication Trenches.

The 4 Main Communication Trenches were kept clear by special parties of Pioneers during the first stage of the battle.

5. Water.

Many wells located and examined. Samples of water sent back for test.

6. Dumps, etc.

Two German dumps were located and made use of.

Two forward dumps were formed on the rear slope of WYTSCHAETE Village.

A supply of wire and pickets was organised for the use of the Infantry.

7. Dug-outs.

A start was made on clearing and repairing German dug-outs. Sufficient accommodation was made ready by nightfall for Battalion Command Headquarters.

5. Remarks.

(1) All work was carried out on prearranged lines under the orders of the C.R.E., who kept in close touch with the Field Company Commanders.

(2) The sites for the Strong Points worked out well on the ground. The relief model at LA CLYTTE was of great assistance in siting these.

(3) Pack mules were invaluable for taking forward material. The work could not have been done without them. YUKON Packs were also very useful.

(4) The permanently attached Infantry parties proved of great value, and no application was made to Brigadiers for working parties, except by 68th Field Company, R.E.

(5) The Garrisons of the Strong Points went up with the R.E. Party, and helped in carrying up and construction.

(6) 68th Field Coy. R.E. were handicapped in their work by not having permanent Infantry parties.

Four platoons were earmarked for work under them, but these were absorbed into the fight, on the change of the afternoon plan of attack.

(7) A Horrocks Set was available at one of the advanced Company H.Q. for testing water for poison. This saved a lot of time. It is considered that Companies should have four sets, one for each Section on establishment.

(8) Care should be taken when working on captured dug-outs that the men are not under observation, or an important command post may be subsequently shelled.

(9) German Dumps.

Arrangements should be made for the earliest possible reconnaissance of enemy dumps, as the labour in taking up stores across the shattered trench area is a very serious matter.

(10) Material.

The system of dumps worked well, but there was not enough wire in the advanced dumps. The transport of the long screw pickets was a difficulty, much lighter pickets are required.

(11) General.

Thanks to the splendid system of artillery barrage, the Infantry went forward steadily and punctually to their objectives. Thus it was possible to get the R.E. forward to do useful work earlier than is usual. Further the conformation of the ground gave the parties working on the reverse slope of WYTSCHAETE RIDGE the benefit of dead ground.

10th June, 1917.
Sd. R.F.A. BUTTERWORTH,
Lieut-Col.R.E.
C. R. E. 16th Division.

S E C R E T.   Copy No. _____
==========

16th DIVISIONAL ENGINEERS OPERATION ORDER No.30.

12th June, 1917.

1. The Field Companies and attached Infantry are to be employed, under the C.R.E., and under orders to be issued by Chief Engineer, IX Corps, on the construction of the Defences of the WYTSCHAETE RIDGE, which will be known as " THE RIDGE DEFENCES ".

2. (a) Consequent upon this the following moves will take place to-morrow. The Field Companies and attached Infantry will move to Camp on VIERSTRAAT RIDGE, approximate location being:-

   155th Field Company, R.E.   N.17.a.2.0.

   156th Field Company, R.E.   N.17.a.2.4.

   157th Field Company, R.E.   N.17.a.2.5.

   (b) The Field Companies will move complete except pontoon equipment, which may be left for the present at CANADA CORNER.

   (c) The tents and bivouacs at CHATHAM and UPNOR CAMPS will be taken forward by the Companies, but 2 caretakers left in each Camp in charge of the remaining huts.

   (d) A motor lorry will be at (1) UPNOR CAMP (for 155th Field Coy), (2) at CHATHAM CAMP (for 156th and 157th Field Companies) at 10 a.m. to-morrow. These may be employed until move is complete.

   These lorries must be instructed to report at CANADA CORNER before rejoining their Park.

   (e) Telephone instruments will be carried with the Field Companies, who will be responsible for same until further orders.

3. C.R.E's Office will remain at CANADA CORNER for the time being.

4. Completion of move to be reported by wire to this Office.

5. ACKNOWLEDGE.

Issued at 10. p.m.

R E Studdring

Captain, R.E.

for C. R. E. 16th Division.

Copies to:-
1 Retained.
2. 155th Field Coy. R.E.
3. 156th Field Coy. R.E.
4. 157th Field Coy. R.E.
5. 16th Div. 'G'.   ) for
6. 16th Div 'Q'.   ) information.
7. 16th Div. Train.   )
8. A.D.M.S.   )
9. A.D.V.S.   ) for
10. 11th Hants (P)   ) informa-
11. C.E. IX Corps.   ) tion.
12. 16th Div. Sigs   )
13. War Diary.
14. "   "

SECRET.   Copy No. 1

16th DIVISIONAL ENGINEERS OPERATION ORDER No.31.

                                              17th June, 1917.

1.   The 16th Division is to relieve the 19th Division in the LEFT SECTOR of the line held by the IX Corps.

2.   (a) On 18th June and night 18th/19th June. The 47th Inf. Bde. will relieve 58th Inf. Bde. in the LEFT SECTION of the line.

        (b) On 19th June and night 19th/20th June. The 49th Inf. Bde. will relieve the 57th Inf. Bde. in the RIGHT SECTION of the line.

        (c) Both these reliefs will be carried out under orders of G.O.C. 19th Division.

        (d) On 20th June.

            (i) 16th Divisional Headquarters will be established on the SCHERPENBERG.

            (ii) Command of the LEFT SECTOR of the line will pass from G.O.C. 19th Division to G.O.C. 16th Division at 9 a.m. on June, 20th.

3.   Consequent on above, the reliefs of technical personnel will take place as shewn on attached table.

4. BILLETS.

        156th and 157th Field Companies, R.E. will remain in their present Camps.

        155th Field Company, R.E. will withdraw to R.E. FARM on 18th June, 1917, taking over from O.C. 94th Field Company, R.E., who will take over the present 155th Field Coy. Camp.

5.   C. R. E's Office remains at CANADA CORNER.

6. DUMPS.

        R.E. FARM DUMP becomes main divisional store and VIERSTRAAT DUMP (N.18.a.7.8.) an Advanced R.E. Store.

7.   ACKNOWLEDGE.

Issued at 12.30 p.m.

                                         R.E. Stradling
                                         Captain, R.E.
                                      for C. R. E. 16th Division.

TABLE TO ACCOMPANY 16th DIVISIONAL ENGINEERS O.O. No.31.

Date of taking or handing over 1917	UNIT Handing Over.	UNIT Taking Over	Date Unit taking over starts new work. 1917	WORK.	REMARKS.
18th June.	C.R.E. 16th	C.R.E. 19th	19th June.	The RIDGE DEFENCES.	
18th June.	O.C. 82nd Fld. Coy.	O.C. 156th Fld. Coy.	19th June.	In LEFT SECTION.	
18th June.	O.C. 81st Fld. Coy.	O.C. 157th Fld. Coy.	19th June.	In RIGHT SECTION.	
18th June.	O i/c R.E. FARM DUMP.	Lt. O'SULLIVAN 155th Fld.Coy	18th June.	O i/c R.E. FARM DUMP.	
18th June.	N.C.O. i/c VIERSTRAAT DUMP.	N.C.O. 155th Fld. Coy.	18th June.	N.C.O. i/c VIERSTRAAT DUMP.	
18th June.	—	O.C.155th Fld. Coy.	19th June.	Formation of Divisional R.E. Dump at R.E. Farm and VIERSTRAAT DUMP (N.18.a.7.8.)	Details of VIERSTRAAT ROAD DUMP (N.18.a.7.8) will be issued later.
18th June.	11th Hants (P)	S.W.B. (P)	19th June.	Work on tramways, roads, etc.	
18th June.	S.W.B. (P).	11th Hants (P)	19th June.	Work on tramways, roads, etc.	

Distribution:-

Copy No.
1. Retained.
2. 155th Fld. Coy.
3. 156th Fld. Coy.
4. 157th Fld. Coy.
5. 11th Hants (P).
6. 16th Div. 'G'.   )
7. 16th Div. 'Q'.   )
8. A. D. M. S.   )
9. A. D. V. S.   ) For
10. 47th Bde.   ) information.
11. 48th Bde.   )
12. 49th Bde.   )
13. C.R.E. 19th Div.   )
14. War Diary.
15.   "   "

S E C R E T. Copy No. 1

16th DIVISIONAL ENGINEERS OPERATION No. 32.

17th June, 1917.

1. 16th Div. Engineers O.O. No.31 is cancelled.

2. 16th Division (less Divisional Artillery) will proceed to MERRIS AREA on 18th June, 1917.

3. Field Companies will proceed from present billet by cross-country track to CANADA CORNER in order;- 500 yards interval between Companies.
   155th Field Company.
   156th Field Company.
   157th Field Company.

   The head of 155th Field Company, R.E. to be at CANADA CORNER at 10am.

4. One motor lorry per Company will report at CANADA CORNER during the morning. One guide per Company will take lorry to Company Camp to pick up surplus stores.

5. C.R.E. will warn caretakers at CHATHAM and UPNOR CAMPS to pick up Field Companies at CANADA CORNER.

6. O.C. Field Company or representative will report at C.R.E's Office at 9.30 a.m. to-morrow to receive instructions as to billeting areas.

7. ACKNOWLEDGE.

Issued at 11.30 p.m.

R E Shoeling
Captain, R.E.
for C. R. E. 16th Division.

Copies to:-
1. Retained.
2. 155th Fld. Coy.
3. 156th Fld. Coy.
4. 157th Fld. Coy.
5. 16th Div. 'G'.
6. 16th Div. 'Q'.
7. War Diary.
8. " "

S E C R E T.
==========

Copy No. 18

16th DIVISIONAL ENGINEERS OPERATION ORDER NO.33.

Reference. Sheets 27 and 28. 1/40,000.

20th June, 1917.

1.   The three Field Companies, R.E. and 11th Hants (P) will march to XIX Corps Area to-morrow, 21st inst. for work under CHIEF ENGINEER.

2.   Starting Point.
        156th Field Coy.)
        157th Field Coy.) K.35.d.5.5. at 7 a.m.
        11th Hants (P)   )

   155th Field Coy. to be Clear of STEENVORDE by 7. a.m.

   For further details see attached table.

3.   Distances of 500 yards will be kept between Units.

4.   O.C. 157th Field Company will detail one mounted Officer to precede column and warn Traffic Control Posts of its approach. This Officer to be at K.35.d.5.5. at 6.50 a.m.

5.   Tents will be drawn from O.O. XIX Corps Troops, 26 PLACE BERTHEN, POPERINGHE, at the scale of 1 tent per 2 Officers or 14 men and will be camouflaged before being put up. Material for same will be issued with tents.
   1 Motor lorry will report at 5.30 a.m. at each of 156th and 157th Field Coys. to pick up advance party under an Officer to draw tents and obtain guides from Town Major, POPERINGHE.

6.   RATIONS.
   156th and 157th Field Companies will be attached to XIX Corps Troops Supply Column for rations.
   155th Field Company. Lorry will report at Town Major's Office ARNEKE (Sheet 27, H.24.) on 22nd inst. about noon with rations for 22nd. Company Supply Wagons will wait for lorry.
   Night of 22nd. Refilling will take place at WATTEN (Sheet 27.A.L .14) and thence daily. R.S.O. WATTEN will give information as to refilling.
   11th Hants will be attached to 55 Div. for rations.

7.   BILLETS.

   155th Field Company will report to Town Major, ARNEKE for billets for night 21st/22nd and to Commandant XIX Corps School MERCKEGHEM on night 22nd/23rd and following days.

8.   WORK.
   O.C 155th Field Coy. will be employed on construction of School at MERCKEGHEM, details of which will be issued later.

9.   H.Q.R.E. will close at GODEWAERSVELDE at 9.0 a.m. and reopen at L.12.c.2.6. (Sheet 27) on arrival.

10.   ACKNOWLEDGE.

R E Strackling

Captain, R.E.
for C. R. E. 16th Division.

TABLE TO ACCOMPANY 16th DIV. ENGINEERS O.O. No.33. dated 20th June, 1917.

DATE. 1917	UNIT.	STARTING POINT.	TIME.	DESTINATION	REMARKS.
21st June.	11th Hants (P)	K.35.d.5.5.	7 a.m.	H.Q. and 2 Coys Camp (Sh.28) G.8.c.9.1. 2 Coys. Camp (Sh.28) H.7.c.6.3.	
21st June.	156th Fld.Co.R.E.	K.35.d.5.5.	7.20 am.	Camp (Sh.27) L.11.d.8.4.	
21st June.	157th Fld.Co.R.E.	K.35.d.5.5.	7.40 am.	Camp.(Sh.27) L.12.c.2.6.	
21st June.	155th Fld.Co.R.E.	To be clear of STEENVOORDE	7. am.	ARNEKE (Sh.27) H.24.	Apply to Town Major for billets for night 21/22
22nd June.	155th Fld.Co.R.E.	To be clear of ARNEKE	9. a.m.	MERCKEGHEM (Sh.27) A.27.	Apply to Commandant, XIX Corps School for billets for 22/23 onwards.

Distribution.

1. Retained.
2. 155th Fld. Coy.
3. 156th Fld. Coy.
4. 157th Fld. Coy.
5. 11th Hants (P).
6. 16th Div.'G'   )
7. 16th Div.Sigs.   )
8. 16th Div.'Q'   )   For information.
9. C.E. XIX Corps.   )
10. A.D.M.S.   )
11. A.D.V.S.   )
12. War Diary.
13.   "   "

WAR DIARY.

FOR MONTH OF JULY, 1917.

VOLUME :- 20

UNIT :- H.Q. 16th Divl Engineers

Army Form C. 2118.

ROYAL ENGINEERS,
H.Q.
16TH DIVISION.
No.............
Date............

WAR DIARY
or
INTELLIGENCE SUMMARY.
(Erase heading not required.)

Instructions regarding War Diaries and Intelligence Summaries are contained in F. S. Regs., Part II. and the Staff Manual respectively. Title pages will be prepared in manuscript.

Place	Date	Hour	Summary of Events and Information	Remarks and references to Appendices
POPERINGHE (Sh 27) L.11.d.	1.7.17		Work under C.E. XIXth Corps on Wells, Magine dugouts, Battery positions	
	2.7.17			Appendix 1.
	3.7.17		ditto — CRE's order No. Y.1. issued (see appendix (1))	
	4.7.17			
	5.7.17			
	6.7.17		work under C.E. as above	
	7.7.17			
	8.7.17			
	9.7.17		Work under C.E. — hutments re hory of Tilleys. (3331/8) (see appendix 2)	Appendix 2.
	10.7.17		"	
	11.7.17		"	
	12.7.17		"	
	13.7.17		"	
	14.7.17		"	
	15.7.17		157 Fd Coy RE. to WINNEZEELE area for training	

Army Form C. 2118.

WAR DIARY
or
INTELLIGENCE SUMMARY.
(Erase heading not required.)

Instructions regarding War Diaries and Intelligence Summaries are contained in F.S. Regs., Part II. and the Staff Manual respectively. Title pages will be prepared in manuscript.

ROYAL ENGINEERS.
H.Q.
16TH DIVISION.
No............
Date...........

Place	Date	Hour	Summary of Events and Information	Remarks and references to Appendices
POPERINGHE	16.7.17		Work under CE XIX Corps as above Capt R.E STRADLING R.E to leave	
ELVERDINGHE	17.7.17		" " " " " "	
	18/7/17		" " " " " " Capt J.C. BOYD R.A.M.C & leave.	
	19/7/17		Work as above.	
	20/7/17		157 Fld Coy (less 1 section) to WINNE ZEELE area for training	
	21/7/17		C.R.E. ETAPLES. Major R.W. MARSDEN 157 Fld Coy acting CRE	
	22/7/17		833 A/T moved to Calais, 157 Fld Coy 574 Inf. Bde. Group.	
	23/7/17		CRE from ETAPLES	
	25/7/17		CRE's Instruction for Offensive No 1 issued.	Appendix 3
	26/7/17		CRE's Instruction for Offensive No 2 issued.	Appendix 4
	27/7/17		Capt R.E STRADLING R.E from leave. 155 Fld Coy RE to WATOU G.15.c.9.1.	
	28/7/17		CRE's Instruction for Offensive No 3 issued	Appendix 5
	30/7/17		155 Fld Coy 155 Fld Coy 157 Fld Coy to BRANDHOEK area this evening. Capt J.C. BOYD R.A.M.C. from leave	Appendix 6
	29/7/17		CRE's Order No Y.2. issued	
	31/7/17 9.20am		155 Fld Coy RE to VLAMERTINGHE. H.16.a.7.9. 155 Fld Coy RE to BRANDHOEK. 28.Q.11.c.7.5. 7pm	
	1/8/17		CRE's Order Y.3 issued	Appendix 7

1/8/17
R.W. Marsden Major
Lieut.-Col. R.E.
C.R.E. 16th Division.

SECRET.   Copy No 4

C. R. E's ORDER 'Y' 1.

4th July, 1917.

The Field Companies will reorganise their Pack Sections of 20 on the same lines as those for last offensive.

A special Mounted N.C.O. is to be told off to take charge directly under Captain of Company.

Pack Saddles (16) will be issued by Division and these are to be equipped to carry wire, screw pickets, and tools.

Officers Commanding Field Companies will submit design of box or other form of carrier by 15th July, in order that pattern may be selected and adopted for Field Companies.

Practices of Pack Sections will be carried out at least once per week, either by drawing rations or some other practical way.

R P Stradling
Captain
for
Lieut-Colonel, R.E
C. R. E. 16th Division.

Copies:-
1. C.R.E.
2. 155th Fld. Coy.
3. 156th Fld. Coy.
4. 157th Fld. Coy.
5. 16th Div 'G'
6. 16th Div 'Q'
7. File.
8. War Diary.

SECRET.   3331/8.

Chief Engineer,
    XIX Corps.

        In view of the forthcoming offensive, in
which I understand the 16th Division is to take part,
it is of urgent necessity that the Field Companies, R.E.
shall have an opportunity to refit and train.

        Prior to the battle of MESSINES the Field
Companies each had a fortnight in which to carry out
training with their attached Infantry, and to organise
and work Pack Sections, etc.   As a result satisfactory
work was done in the way of consolidation, provision of
dug-outs, water supply and opening up of communications,
immediately following on the capture of the Ridge.

        Since the battle, the R.E. have been working
continuously, firstly on the captured MESSINES position,
and since 21st June in the XIX Corps (and VIII Corps)
Areas, and their attached Infantry (100 per Field
Company) have been sent back to their Battalions. Unless
an opportunity is afforded for each Company to again
work and train with its attached Infantry prior to
operations, the great advantage to the R.E. Field
Company Commander of having Infantry Officers and men,
whom he knows and has trained, will be lost.

        I commanded a Field Company last Summer in
the SOMME offensive, which was in and out of the battle
for a month, and I know the great difficulty in
collecting a working party during operations, and of
organising work, and of the small results achieved.

                                                    I

I request therefore, that, having due regard
to the importance of this matter from the point of
view of the Division, and without unduly interferring
with the work of preparation on the Corps front,
it may be arranged for the Field Companies to be
handed over for training with their attached
Infantry for a period of at least 14 days prior to
their being required for active operations.

    The same argument applies to the 11th
Hants (Pioneers), and I strongly urge that this
Unit also be released for refit and training, if
the best results are to be expected later on.

9th July, 1917.   Lieut-Colonel, R.E.

                                              C. R. E. 16th Division.

Copies to:-

    H.Q. 16th Div.
    11th Hants (P).
    War Diary.
    Office File.

SECRET.   Copy No. 5

C. R. E's INSTRUCTIONS FOR THE OFFENSIVE. No.1

GENERAL PLAN AND PRELIMINARY DISPOSITIONS.

1. Offensive operations on a large scale, in which the XIXth Corps is to take part, will shortly commence.

2. GENERAL PLAN OF ATTACK.

   (a) The attack will take place on "Z" day; the exact time and date will be notified later. It will be preceded by an artillery bombardment of some/day's duration.

   (b) The attack will be carried out in three stages as under:-

   1st Objective.

   To capture and consolidate the enemy's front system of trenches up to, and including, the BLUE LINE.

   2nd Objective.

   To capture and consolidate the enemy's 2nd line system of trenches (STUTZPUNKT LINE) up to, and including, the BLACK LINE.

   3rd (Final) Objective.

   To capture and consolidate the enemy's 3rd line system (GHELUVELT - LANGEMARCK LINE) up to, and including, the GREEN LINE.

   The various objectives, and the times of leaving them, are shown on the attached Map "A".

3. DISPOSITIONS FOR THE ATTACK.

   (a) The XIXth Corps is to attack on a front of about 2,800 yards, with the 15th Division on the right, the 55th Division on the left and the 16th and 36th Divisions in Corps Reserve.

   The frontages and objectives of the two attacking divisions are shown on Map "A". Each of these divisions will deliver the first assault with two brigades in the front line and one brigade in reserve.

   (b) The IInd Corps will be attacking on the right of the XIXth Corps. Its left attack will be delivered by the 8th Division supported by the 25th Division.

   (c) The XVIIIth Corps will be attacking on the left of the XIXth Corps. Its right attack will be delivered by the 39th Division, the 11th and 48th Divisions being in reserve.

4. SITUATION OF DIVISION AT ZERO.

   (a) On Y/Z night the 16th Division (less Divisional Artillery and certain other units) will be disposed as follows in the BRANDHOEK Area:-

                                                        Div H.Q.

Div. H.Q.	POPERINGHE (G.1.d.5.1).
48th Inf. Bde.	"B" Bde. (or Southern) Area.
Bde. H.Q. at BRANDHOEK (H.7.a.2.1).	
49th Inf. Bde.	"A" Bde. (or Northern) Area.
Bde. H.Q. at "A" Camp (H.2.c.2.7).	
47th Inf. Bde.	"C" Bde. (or Western) Area.
Bde H.Q.	POPERINGHE (G.2.c.2.2.)

The boundaries and accommodation of the above areas are given in 16th Div. Administrative Instruction No.4.

(b) The 16th Divisional Artillery will be in action under the orders of C.R.A. 15th Division.

(c) The 47th Machine Gun Coy. will be under the orders of the Corps Machine Gun Officer to assist in the machine gun barrages until the GREEN LINE is taken. At Zero plus 8 hours 20 minutes, when the protective barrage is lifted off the front of the GREEN LINE, the 47th Machine Gun Coy. will revert to the 16th Division.

(d) The 11th Hants (Pioneers) have been placed at the disposal of the Chief Engineer XIXth Corps for work.

5. ACTION AT ZERO.

At Zero the 48th Inf. Bde. and 155th Field Coy. R.E., will move forward from the BRANDHOEK Area to an assembly area in H.10 and H.16 where they will be in Corps Reserve and ready to move at one hour's notice.

The remainder of the 16th Division in the BRANDHOEK Area will be held in readiness to move at two hour's notice.

6. PROBABLE ROLE OF DIVISION.

As far as possible, the 16th Division will be used to support the 15th Division and the 36th Division to support the 55th Division.

It is not however the intention of the Corps Commander to use his Reserve Divisions before the capture of the GREEN LINE if he can avoid doing so, and when the 16th Division finally relieves the 15th Division it is hoped that it will be the prelude to a further advance. Should the battle proceed on the above lines it is the intention of the Divisional Commander that the 48th and 49th Inf. Bdes. with their affiliated R.E. Companies should relieve the Right and Left Brigades respectively of the 15th Division, and that the 47th Inf. Bde. and 156th Field Coy. R.E. should be in reserve.

In arranging all preliminary reconnaissance and dispositions these intentions as to the probable role of the division should be borne in mind.

7. TRAFFIC ARRANGEMENTS IN THE FORWARD AREA.

The attached Map G/16/X of the XIXth Corps Forward Area shows:-

A.

(3).

      A.   The communication trenches now in use.

      B.   The various tracks that have been prepared.

      C.   The roads and traffic circuits that will eventually come into use.

8.   A. <u>COMMUNICATION TRENCHES.</u>

There are four main communication trenches in the 15th Division Sector.

EAST and WEST LANES.	OUT.
PICCADILLY.	IN.
HAYMARKET.	IN.
CURZON STREET.	OUT.

After Zero Hour PICCADILLY and HAYMARKET will if necessary be carried forward by the 15th Divisional Engineers so as to join up with ICE and IBERIA LANES in the present German lines.

9.   B. <u>TRACKS.</u>

Five tracks (Nos. 1 to 5), commencing in the neighbourhood of the MENIN and DIXMUDE GATES, have been carried forward as far as CAMBRIDGE TRENCH and OXFORD ROAD.

There are also two tracks ("C" and "F") which might be used as alternative routes to the GORDON'S TRACK road for bringing up Infantry should the latter road be subjected to heavy shelling. These two tracks are not passable by wheeled traffic and would be difficult, even for infantry, after heavy rain.

The above tracks are marked on the ground but should be reconnoitred before troops are taken along them. This is especially the case as regards "C" and "F" tracks.

After Zero hour the following tracks will be carried forward into the captured positions:-

(a) <u>By 15th Divisional Engineers.</u>

Two tracks wide enough for guns and horsed transport

  (i) From I.5.d.5.4. through BILL COTTAGE and D.2.a.7.4. to BOSTIN FARM.
      To be marked with white posts marked with one stroke.

  (ii) From I.5.b.1.4. through BAVARIA HOUSE to DELVA FARM.
      To be marked with white posts with two strokes.

(b) <u>By 55th Divisional Engineers.</u>

  (i) No. 5 track (for Pack Transport) to be carried forward from OXFORD ROAD to the BLUE, and subsequently the BLACK LINE.

  (ii) Two other forward tracks will also be marked out.

(4).

10. At 5 p.m. on "Z" + 1 day further instructions as to Traffic Circuits will come into force. A map showing these further Circuits will be issued later to all concerned.

11. ENGINEER WORK AND CONSOLIDATION.

The following arrangements for Engineer work and Consolidation have been made by the two attacking Divisions.

15th DIVISION.

(a) Infantry Brigades are responsible for the consolidation of objectives gained.

(b) One Section R.E. will be attached to each of the two attacking Infantry Brigades.

(c) The remainder of the Engineers (and attached Infantry) will be employed under the C.R.E.

(d) The Officers Commanding Field Coys. working in each Infantry Brigade area will be present at Brigade Headquarters and will keep the C.R.E. in touch with technical requirements.

(e) The C.R.E. will make a very early reconnaissance of the captured area and will report on roads, streams, tramways and water supply. Captured Engineer material is to be utilized in the consolidation of the position and information where it is to be found is to be given to battalions by R.E. personnel carrying out the reconnaissance.

(f) After the capture of the GREEN LINE an R.E. Stores Dump will be established as far forward as possible. When the position of this Dump has been decided, the C.R.E. will inform Infantry Brigades.

(g) The following work will be carried out under C.R.E's orders:-

(i) Open up the POTIJZE - FREZENBERG road, making it fit for artillery and limbered wagons.

(ii) Open up the two forward tracks mentioned in ~~15th Div. G.S. Instruction No.2.~~ Para 9.(ii)

(iii) If required to do so, prolong PICCADDILLY and HAYMARKET TRENCHES to join up with ICE and IBERIA LANES.

(iv) Construct Strong Points at the following places:-

        D.26.a.7.2.
        D.20.c.7.2.
        D.20.a.5.9.

12. 55th DIVISION.

(h) Infantry Brigades are responsible for the construction of any Strong Points located in or in advance of captured objectives.

(j)

(5).

(j) One Section R.E. will be attached to each of the two attacking Infantry Brigades. One Company of Pioneers will work under the Orders of C.E. XIXth Corps.

(k) The following work will be carried out by the remainder of the 55th Divisional Engineers and Pioneers.

   (i) Open up the SAINT JEAN - GRAVENSTAFEL road.

   (ii) Carry forward No. 5 Track from OXFORD ROAD to the BLACK LINE.

   (iii) Mark out two other forward tracks.

   (iv) Construct Supporting Points (as distinguished from Strong Points made by the Infantry) at about the following places:-

      C.18.c.50.85.
      C.24.a.90.60.
      D.19.c.05.60.
      D.7.d.05.50.
      D.7.d.60.20.
      D.13.b.75.00.
      D.14.c.55.20.

The garrison of each of these Supporting Points will be 1 Machine Gun, 1 Lewis Gun and ½ platoon of infantry.

13. The 11th Hants (Pioneers) will be employed as follows after Zero Hour under the orders of the C.E. XIXth Corps:-

Headquarters.   H.7.c.5.3.

Three Coys.   (Re-construction of POTIJZE-
                       (FREZENBERG road beyond German
                       (Front line.

One Coy.   Light railway construction.

14. With reference to the above work on roads, the allocation of responsibility for repairs to roads between Corps and Divisions is as follows:-

(a) At the present time the Corps undertakes no work on roads in the forward area, but at Zero plus 4 hours it will take over the responsibility up to the road junction 200 yards East of BAVARIA HOUSE on the POTIJZE road, and up to BOSSAERT FARM on the ST. JEAN road.

(b) This arrangement leaves it to the Divisions to maintain and open up the roads East of YPRES up to Zero plus 4 hours. They will confine themselves to the two main forward roads and to making the crossing of our own trenches and the German first line system practicable for Divisional Artillery.

(c) The Corps will improve and strengthen those forward roads so as to make them fit for the passage of heavy guns and lorries. They will also open up the HELLFIRE - POTIJZE - ST. JEAN road and the CAMBRIDGE and OXFORD roads.

(d)

(6).

(d)   The lines defining the responsibilities of Transportation, Corps and Divisions will be moved forward during operations as opportunity occurs. Local conditions alone cannot decide on whether Transportation can take over any particular roads or sections of roads. It is on these conditions that the advancing of the lines will depend.

(e)   Divisions will throughout be responsible for making the roads assigned to them practicable for Field Artillery. The Corps for their temporary improvement so that heavy artillery and lorries can use them. Transportation for further improvement of a more permanent nature.

25th July, 1917.

R.H.Butterworth
Lieut-Colonel, R.E.
C. R. E. 16th Division.

Copy. No:-

1. C. R. E.
2. 155th Fld. Coy.
3. 156th Fld. Coy.
4. 157th Fld. Coy.
5. War Diary.

SECRET.   Copy No. 5

C.R.E's INSTRUCTIONS FOR THE OFFENSIVE No.2.

MARCH DISCIPLINE.

1. The normal hourly halts are to be observed throughout a march unless orders are given to the contrary.

2. Horsed vehicles of all kinds must keep to the right side of the road.
   Riding horses will, during halts, be drawn up on the right side of the road facing inwards.

3. Whenever columns of troops or vehicles halt, cross roads and road junctions must be left clear. Whenever possible, heads of columns should be halted at least 50 yards short of cross roads and road junctions.

4. All ranks, whether mounted or dismounted, must march in the column, and not abreast of it.

5. All details marching with transport will carry their arms and equipment and will march under proper Command.
   The one man per vehicle told off to attend to the brakes will march fully equipped immediately in rear of his vehicle.
   Cooks may be allowed to put their packs on the cooks wagon, but will otherwise march fully equipped.

6. No man, except the driver, will ride on any vehicle unless in possession of a written permit signed by an Officer.

7. The current days forage may be carried on vehicles, with the exception that nothing beyond the authorised loads is to be carried.
   Whenever a road is not broad enough for three lines of traffic vehicles of all kinds, whether halted or on the move, must leave gaps between each group of 6 vehicles to act as "refuges" for single vehicles, and so enable meeting traffic to pass.

TRAFFIC CONTROL.

1. Up to Z day the system of Traffic Control laid down in Provisional Traffic Orders, dated 19th July, 1917, remains in force. From W/X night to 5 p.m. on Z plus 1 day traffic is restricted as laid down in movement table issued with XIX Corps Order No. 73, and any subsequent G orders which may be issued.

2. On Z day all traffic East of VLAMERTINGHE except Ammunition Wagons, Ammunition lorries, Road Material Wagons, Road Material Lorries, R.E. Stores, Water Supply Vehicles, Ambulances and Buses for Wounded will be by Pack Animals, which must be kept off the traffic routes.

3. At 5 p.m. on Z plus 1 day the traffic circuits shown on the Fifth Army Forward Traffic Circuit Map will be brought into Force. This map will be issued to all concerned.

   The IInd Corps have the right to use XIX Corps Roads from SHRAPNEL CORNER through LILLE GATE to MENIN GATE from Z - 6 hours onwards for movement of Heavy Artillery of XIX Corps. Horse-Drawn Artillery will have precedence of Tractor drawn.

Water

(2).

WATER SUPPLY EAST OF POPERINGHE.

1. The initial water points in the forward Area for the supply of drinking water are located as follows (Sheet 28), water bottles, water carts and water tank lorries will be able to refil at these points:-

   Tank No. 4 at G.7.d.9.5. yielding daily 7,400 Gallons.
   "   5 at G.3.c.7.2.   - do -   25,250 "
   "   6 at G.15.b.2.6.   - do -   11,700 "
   "   9 at H.14.a.9.6.   - do -   7,000 "
   "   11 at G.10.c.4.9.   - do -   15,500 "
   "   14 at H.8.b.9.9.   - do -   5,000 "
   "   14a at H.2.d.8.3.   - do -   3,200 "
   "   14b at H.3.c.2.5.   - do -   3,200 "
   "   32 at G.12.c.5.1.   - do -   4,000 "
   "   43 at G.12.a.9.9.   - do -   5,000 "

2. The First Forward Water Point will be established for operations just off the road, west of existing pumping house near the Swimming Bath in the North East corner of YPRES.

3. It is hoped to establish the Second Forward Water Point on the SAINT-JEAN - WIELTJE road, West of WIELTJE.

4. A Section of the No.2 Water Column has been allotted to the Corps and is located at L.17.b.4.3. (Sheet 27). It consists of 16 150 gallon tanks and 2 500 gallon tanks. An additional 4 600 gallon tank lorries from 64th Aux. Petrol Co. are joining later. Any formation requiring water to be delivered to their location will forward an application to O i/c Det. Water Column, c/o S.M.T.O. giving the following particulars:-

   (a) Unit.
   (b) Location (with map reference)
   (c) Quantity required (in gallons) daily.
   (d) Time required.
   (e) For what purpose.

   All applications must be rendered by 6 p.m. the day previous to requirements.

5. As soon as tanks are established at the Second Forward Point the Tank Lorries will fill at the Initial Water Points and fill the tanks at the Second Forward Water Point. As soon as this has been done, water carts and water bottles can be filled from the Second Forward Water Point. Until then, water carts will fill at Initial Water Points or First Forward Water Point.

6. A 4" pipe line will be run forward from the First to the Second Forward Water Points concurrently with the supply of the latter from the former by tank lorry.

7. As soon as the pipe line is completed, the tank lorries will work from the Second to the Third Forward Water Points.

8. The Horse Water Supply is from existing streams and ponds, long shallow wells dug by the units themselves, from wells completed by R.E. and from tank supply.

   There are shallow wells at:-

BRANDHOEK

(2).

BRANDHOEK AREA No. 2 (Sheet 28).

G.10.d.1.2.   G.10.d.7.3.   G.10.b.10.3.
G.11d.6.1.   G.11.d.5.9.

9. WEST OF POPERINGHE.

No. 74 Water Point for water bottles, water carts and tank lorries is at L.11.a.6.8.

VETERINARY ARRANGEMENTS.

1. There will be a Veterinary aid post at H.11.b.9.9. (Sheet 28), to which units can take any animal for dressing, and where they can leave such animals as are unable to march to a Mobile Veterinary Section.

2. There will be a Mobile Veterinary Section at G.11.a.4.6. and one at G.14.b.5.4., and two others whose positions will be notified later.

LIGHT RAILWAYS.

1. The Light Railways used by the Corps are the Southern portion of the "B" System and the northern portion of the "D" System. Trains will be run over both these systems from WESTONHOEK (XCA) Railhead.

The location of the Corps Railhead Officer is now A.27.a.2.2. He has an Office at that location and also at WESTONHOEK and is on the telephone at both Offices.
Telephone Exchange S.X.

2. The following are the Refilling Points on, or to be put on, the System:-

   (a) Corps Reserves.
      ORILLIA H.1.b. and B.25.c.
      TAVISTOCK H.1.d.

   (b)   xxxxxxx

   (c) Right Division.
      VANCOUVER H.8.d.7.3.

   (d) Left Division.
      TORONTO. G.11.a.7.2.

TRAMWAYS.

1. No. 5 Army Tramway Co., has been allotted to the XIX Corps.

2. Its principle function is to lay tramways from the Light Railways to Battery Positions. When not required for this purpose it assists in the construction of Light Railways.

R.J. Butterworth
Lieut-Colonel, R.E.
C. R. E. 16th Division.

26th July, 1917.

Copy No. 1. C.R.E.   4. 157th Fld. Coy.
        2. 155th Fld. Coy.   5. War Diary.
        3. 156th Fld. Coy.

SECRET.
==========

Copy No. 6

C.R.E's INSTRUCTIONS FOR THE OFFENSIVE No. 3.

1. MAPS TO BE CARRIED BY EACH OFFICER.

    The following Maps will be carried by each Officer in the attack:-

    (a) 1/10,000 FREZENBERG (XIX Corps Front) Edition (2). (already issued).

    (b) Latest Edition of each of the following sheets of 1/10,000 Map.

    ST JULIEN.   )
    ZONNEBEKE.   ) already issued.
    ZILLEBEKE.   )

    WESTROOSEBEKE. To be issued.

    (c) Barrage maps of operation in which they are actually engaged. (Not issued to Divisions in Reserve).

    (d) Adequate number of Message Forms with Maps on the back. (To be issued).

2. S.O.S. SIGNALS.

    (a) The present S.O.S. Signal on the Fifth Army front is

        A succession of S.O.S. Rifle Rockets, each bursting into two RED and two GREEN lights simultaneously, until the artillery comply.

    (b) No alternative S.O.S. Signal to the above is to be used.

    (c) In the event of circumstances requiring a change of S.O.S. Signal, the new S.O.S. Signal will probably be made with coloured VERY Signal Cartridges.

3. TANKS.

    (a) ACTION.

        (i) Two Companies will be employed on each Divisional front against the BLACK LINE and two Companies against the GREEN LINE.

        (ii) In the event of the 15th Division advancing beyond the GREEN LINE with a view to consolidating a line EAST of it, No. 4 Section, No. 9 Coy., O. Battalion will co-operate and will remain with the Infantry until 4 a.m. on Z Plus 1 day as a support.

    (b) SIGNAL COMMUNICATION.

        (i) Infantry will signal to tanks in accordance with instructions contained in "TANK COLOURED DISC and LIGHT CODE" 2nd Edition.

        (ii) No other Signals will be used from TANKS to INFANTRY except the following which must be learnt by heart.

                                                        RED

RED and GREEN DISCS = "HAVE REACHED OBJECTIVE".
RED, RED and RED DISCS = "BROKEN DOWN".
RED, WHITE and WHITE DISCS = "NO ENEMY IN SIGHT".

(c) RALLYING FLAGS.

Tank Section Commanders will use Rallying Flags 2 feet square with the number of section on them. Colours as follows:-

       "C" Battalion.   GREEN.

       "F" Battalion.   RED and YELLOW.

R. Butterworth

28th July, 1917.
                  Lieut-Colonel, R.E.
                  C. R. E. 16th Division.

Copy No. 1.   C.R.E.
        2.   155th Fld. Coy.
        3.   156th Fld. Coy.
        4.   157th Fld. Coy.
        5.   Office.
        6.   War Diary.

SECRET.   Copy No ___

C. R. E's ORDER 'Y' 1.

4th July, 1917.

The Field Companies will reorganise their Pack Sections of 20 on the same lines as those for last offensive.

A special Mounted N.C.O. is to be told off to take charge directly under Captain of Company.

Pack Saddles (16) will be issued by Division and these are to be equipped to carry wire, screw pickets, and tools.

Officers Commanding Field Companies will submit design of box or other form of carrier by 15th July, in order that pattern may be selected and adopted for Field Companies.

Practices of Pack Sections will be carried out at least once per week, either by drawing rations or some other practical way.

R E Strudwick Captain
for Lieut-Colonel, R.E
C. R. E. 16th Division.

Copies:-
1. C.R.E.
2. 155th Fld. Coy.
3. 156th Fld. Coy.
4. 157th Fld. Coy.
5. 16th Div 'G'
6. 16th Div 'Q'
7. File.
8. War Diary.

SECRET.   Copy No. 6

OPERATION ORDER BY C.R.E. 16th DIVISION. No. 'Y' 2.

1. FORWARD MOVES.

   (a) 155th, 156th and 157th Field Companies, R.E. will move
       forward on Y/Z Night to Camp at G.11.d.1.5., under
       orders of 48th, 47th and 49th Brigades, respectively.

   (b) 155th Field Coy. R.E. will march under 48th Brigade
       orders on Z Day to H.16.

   (c) Subsequently Field Companies will conform to the
       movements of their Brigades unless otherwise ordered.

2. EMPLOYMENT OF R.E.

   (a) For the first stages of the battle Field Company
       Commanders will assist and advise their Brigadiers,
       and carry out any preliminary R.E. work that is
       possible. They should, however, keep C.R.E. fully
       informed of what is being done.

   (b) An early reconnaissance of main roads, tracks and
       railways is to be made and sent to C.R.E., also report
       on stores found locally, and probable immediate
       requirements.

   (c) Work under (a) will comprise:-

       (1) Preparation of forward tracks for Infantry
           and guns.

       (2) Construction of light bridges across streams, &c.

       (3) Provision of Brigade and Battalion H.Q.

       (4) Constructions of S.P's.

       (5) Collection of stores and formation of dumps.

       (6) Search for, and exploitation of Wells and
           Water supplies.

   (d) As soon as it is possible, a constructional scheme
       for work will be prepared, and carried out as a whole
       under the direction of the C.R.E.

3.   The following are proposed positions of Strong Points and
   Command Headquarters:-

   GREEN LINE.

   LEFT.   Brigade. H.Q.   C.30.d.35.75.

            Battalion H.Q. L.   DELVA FARM (dugouts)
            "   "   R.   COFFEE FARM.
            " Support.   L.   C.30.b.45.60.
                           R.   LOW FARM.

   RIGHT.   Brigade. H.Q.   VAMPIR FARM.

            Battalion H.Q. L.)   BREMEN
                           R.)   REDOUBT.
            " Support   D.26.b.2.5.

                                                Strong

(2).

    Strong Points:-

            Battery Post.   D.25.c.9.6.
            Square Post.   C.30.b.9.9.

RED LINE.

LEFT.   Brigade H.Q.   DELVA FARM
                                        (or COFFEE FARM D.20.c.15.15)

            Battalion H.Q. L.   OTTO FARM.
                          R.   DOCHY FARM
                                  (or BOURDEAUX)
             " Support. L.   DELVA FARM.
                      R.   COFFEE FARM.

    Strong Points:-   On reverse slope of ABRAHAM HEIGHTS.

            ABE POST.   D.15.b.3.7.
            HAM POST.   D.15.b.9.4.

RIGHT.   Brigade H.Q.   BOSTIN FARM.

            Battalion H.Q. Left.   SPRINGFIELD.
                        Right.   D.22.a.7.2.
                    Support.   ALMA.
                    Reserve.   WINDMILL. D.21.d.2.8.

    Strong Points:-   Approximate sites.

            PILL POST.   D.16.c.10.10.
            WOOD POST.   D.16.c.80.25.
            RAILWAY POST.   D.22.b.1.7.

4.   R.E. STORES.

      The 15th Div. Dump is at I.4.c.4.9.   This will eventually be taken over by 16th Div, but in the meantime stores will be issued on requisition of Field Company Commander, 16th Division.

5.   TRANSPORT.

      On moving forward from G.11.d.1.5. Field Companies will take their tool carts, limber wagons and water-carts.
      Other transport together with Mess, Office and Q.M.S. Store will remain at G.11.d.1.5.
      The Pontoon Wagons will be brigaded for transport of stores and material under Captain GREENHOW, R.E.

6.   COMMUNICATIONS.

      Each Company will detail 4 Cycle Orderlies to join at H.Q.R.E. on Z DAY.

7.   REPORTS.

      Reports to H.Q.R.E., L.11.d. central. (on SWITCH ROAD S.W. of POPERINGHE).

29th July, 1917.

                                                      Lieut-Colonel, R.E.
                                                      C. R. E. 16th Division.

Distribution:-

1. C. R. E.
2. 155th Fld. Coy.
3. 156th Fld. Coy.
4. 157th Fld. Coy.
5. Office.
6. War Diary.

SECRET.   Copy No. 6

C. R. E.'S   INSTRUCTIONS FOR THE OFFENSIVE.

No. 4.

RECONNAISSANCE FOR ENEMY MINES AND DUGOUTS.

1.   The Germans appear to be holding their front line (where occupied) by posts only, and we must consider the possibility of their making use of land mines.

2.   These mines are most likely to be found at the junction of firing lines and communication trenches. The duckboards in communication trenches should therefore be removed at intervals and the ground underneath searched for wires.
        The possibility of two complete sets of leads, one obvious and the other concealed, an example of which has already occurred, should not be overlooked.

3.   Detachments from Tunnelling Coys. have already been detailed by XIX Corps to reconnoitre for dugouts suitable for Brigade and Battalion Headquarters. These detachments will also investigate mining systems in view of the possibility of charged mines being left behind by the enemy. They will also be employed on searching for any land mines under roads or tracks, or in places in which men might collect.

                                            R. M. Butterworth

31st July, 1917.   Lieut-Colonel, R.E.
                                             C. R. E. 16th Division.

Copies:-
    1. C. R. E.
    2. 155th Fld. Coy.
    3. 156th Fld. Coy.
    4. 157th Fld. Coy.
    5. Office.
    6. War Diary.

WAR DIARY.

FOR MONTH OF AUGUST, 1917.

VOLUME 21

UNIT Headquarters 16th Div Engineers.

Vol 21

Army Form C. 2118.

ROYAL ENGINEERS,
H.Q.
16TH DIVISION.

WAR DIARY
or
INTELLIGENCE SUMMARY.
(Erase heading not required.)

Instructions regarding War Diaries and Intelligence Summaries are contained in F. S. Regs., Part II. and the Staff Manual respectively. Title pages will be prepared in manuscript.

Place	Date	Hour	Summary of Events and Information	Remarks and references to Appendices
PROVEN GHE (N27) L.11.d.6.8	1.8.17		CRE's order no. Y3. issued re. Reconnaissance of BLACK LINE (appendix 1)	Appendix 1.
	3.8.17		Report on 15th Divisional Front to date (appendix 2)	Appendix 2.
			16" Div R.E. Operation Order No. 35 issued and addendum (appendix 3) — M.O. 1/c R.E (Capt J.C. Boyd) attached to 113.F.A. for duty during offensive operations — CRE's report on Divisional Front issued (appendix 4)	Appendix 3. Appendix 4.
BRANDHOEK H.7.c.8.6 (Hut 26)	4.8.17		H.Q. R.E. move with DH.Q. to BRANDHOEK — Fd Corps as follows — 155 — H.7.a.3.9 — 156 H.7.b.2. 157 — G.12.b. — Work taken over from 15th Div. Engrs.	
	5.8.17		CRE's scheme of work (331/70) issued (appendix 5)	Appendix 5.
	6.8.17		Amendment to 6 (331/70) issued (appendix 6)	Appendix 6.
	7.8.17 to 12.8.17		Fd. Corps. employed on formation of forward Tracks and dumps — strengthening dugouts & posts	
	13.8.17		CRE's instruction for Offensive No.5 issued — then gives details of R.E. Arrangements (appendix 7)	Appendix 7.
	14.5.17		CRE's order Y4 (appendix 8) and Y5 (appendix 9) issued — re. relief of Fd Coys forward — detachments ad move to VLAMERTINGHE area	Appendix 8. Appendix 9.
	15.8.17		Field Companies and Pioneer Battalion move to assembly positions	

Army Form C. 2118.

ROYAL ENGINEERS.
H.Q.
16TH DIVISION.

WAR DIARY
or
INTELLIGENCE SUMMARY.
(Erase heading not required.)

Instructions regarding War Diaries and Intelligence Summaries are contained in F. S. Regs., Part II. and the Staff Manual respectively. Title pages will be prepared in manuscript.

Place	Date	Hour	Summary of Events and Information	Remarks and references to Appendices
BRANDHOEK I.7.c.8.6.	16.8.17	4.45 AM	Division attacks at 4.45 AM. — Fd Coys, many parties + 2 Coys. II Tanks on causeway position await orders — some forward — Situation obscure all day	
	17.8.17		— Fd Coy nil employed — Details of work etc given in Appendix 10. Fd Coys withdrew to Brandhoek camps.	
"	18.8.17		Hq R.E. move to WATOU (K.4.b.) — 155 Fd Coy to L.16.a.5.5. (Sh.27) Work handed over to C.R.E. 15" Div. — Fd Coys carry out attery dugouts for mines	
WATOU R27. K.4.b.	19.8.17		155 Fd Coy move to (Shy) L.7.a.9.6. — 157 Fd Coy. to (Sh.27) K.12. c.8.4. C.R.E. & refund in R.E. dugouts 15/16 moved (Appendix) 10	Appendix 10
	20.8.17			
	22.8.16		Hq R.E. move to 3rd Army area. — ACHIET LE - PETIT. 155 Fd Coy to COUCELLES LE COMTE. — 156 Fd Coy to GOMIE COURT. — 157 Fd Coy to ACHIET	
			LG - PETIT. with New Appendix Nos 36 issued Appendix re the Brigade groups 2nd DW R.E. — Hq R.E. to MOYENNEVILLE Took over workshops from	appendix 11.
MOYENNEVILLE [579] A.3.d.0.0	26.8.16 29.8.17		155 R.E.G — DOIRY DEZENGREMES — T.8.c.42. — 156 Fd Coy ST LEGER B.4.a 8.7	
	31.8.17		157 RECy — HAMBLINCOURT S.29.d.3.4.	R.O. Stanley Capt R.E. Adj. ReJohn for CRE

T2134. Wt. W708-776. 500000. 4/15. Sir J. C. & S.

Y.3 appendix

3331/57.

O.C. 155th Field Coy. R.E.
O.C. 157th Field Coy. R.E.

The General Staff ask for an Engineer Reconnaissance of the state of the Engineer work in connection with consolidation of the BLACK LINE i.e. Strong Points, wire, communications, also state of roads and tracks leading up.

Copy of Map 'A' forwarded to you, shows work projected by 15th Division.

The dividing lines between Brigades is approximately a line E. and W. through FREZENBERG, 49th Bde. N., 48th Bde. South of same.

Send an Officer to carry out reconnaissance in your Brigade Area.

The completed report and reconnaissance are required as early as possible, as the Division will in all probability take over to-night.

The Officers had better call ECOLE, collect information from the 15th Division Field Coys., and then visit forward as may be necessary. There will be no object in their going up into the front line in any case at present.

Sd. H.A.A. Butterworth.

1st August, 1917.

Lieut-Colonel, R.E.
C. R. E. 16th Division.

War Diary

SECRET.
==========

Headquarters,

    16th Division "G".

    Herewith Engineer Report on 16th Division Front on 1-8-17, as requested.

1st August, 1917.

                                                Lieut-Colonel, R.E.

                                      C. R. E. 16th Division.

Copies to:-

    C. R. E.
    155th Fld. Coy.
    156th Fld. Coy.
    157th Fld. Coy.
    — War Diary.

SECRET.

SECRET.   3331/62.

ENGINEER REPORT. 15th DIVISION FRONT.

FRONT LINE.

Line of outposts runs from about POTSDAM through VAMPIR, BORRY FARM in front of BECK HOUSE to D.19. Central.

BLACK LINE is being consolidated. This line has German wire in front of it, but is probably not continuous.

STRONG POINTS.

(1) I.6.b.95.50. Consists of 10 bays each 5 yards in length, excavated, but not wired. Wiring attempted this morning but impossible owing to M.G. fire.

(2) C.30.d.6.0. This point excavated but not wired. Wiring to-day prevented by M.G. fire.

(3) BATTERY POINT. D.25.c.9.6½. Situated in front line, excavated, but not yet wired.

(4) FREZENBERG REDOUBT. (German) In rear of BATTERY POINT. There are 7 dug-outs in this with 3 ft. Reinforced Concrete cover. Accommodation for 120 men (close).

(5) C.30.d.8.9. Excavated and wired all round.

(6) SQUARE S.P. C.30.b.9.9. (about). Excavated but not wired at present. SQUARE FARM has a Concrete Dug-out suitable for Battalion H.Q. This point commands ridge to East.

TRACKS.

No. 1 Track I.9.d.7.4. on MENIN ROAD to I.5.d.05.15. on CAMBRIDGE ROAD has been carried forward to approximately D.25.c.3.3. just South of FREZENBERG, 1st portion marked with White posts, 2nd with White posts and red rings on top. 10' 0" wide, passable for troops, in dry weather for light transport. Cut up by guns yesterday and impassable for transport to-day.

F and C Tracks good for Troops and Pack Transport, but not for vehicles owing to ramps near RAILWAY and LILLE ROAD. In good condition.

GORDON'S TRACK. Timbered road except for portions in I.14.d. Available for Horse Transport.

No. 3 Track carried forward and marked to BAVARIA to HOUSE C.30.c.65.35, ~~thence~~ along POTIZJE ROAD C.30.d.4.7. thence North to C.30.b.30.35., thence East by track to LOW FARM D.25.a.7.5. Available for Infantry but not for Transport during present weather.

TRENCHBOARD

(2).

TRENCHBOARD TRACKS.

Two Duckboard tracks are being made:-

(1) From about GULLY FARM to about I.6. central. thence through WILDE WOOD in direction of DOUGLAS VILLA. Very little progress at present.

(2) North Side of POTIZJE ROAD to be doubled later by track on South Side. Fair progress.

COMMUNICATION TRENCHES.

No Communication Trenches across NO MAN'S LAND. IBEX DRIVE (Old German) is wide and deep, and in fair condition.

BRIGADE HD. QRS.

44th INF. BDE. Deep dug-out at JAMES FARM I.4.d.6.2.

45th INF. BDE. Deep dug-outs at CAMBRIDGE TRENCH near HAYMARKET.

46th INF. BDE. Deep dug-out at MILL COTTS.

COMMAND DUG-OUTS.

The following Farms have good dug-out accommodation:-

SQUARE FARM. (Battalion H.Q. and Dressing Station.)

GREY RUIN, LOW FARM and FROST HOUSE.

STORES.

(1) POTIZJE. Chiefly screw pickets, wire, sandbags, tools ~~and some light bridges~~.

(2) MENIN ROAD I.9.d.1.6. (ECOLE) as above with Trenchboards. *and some light bridge*

No Forward Dumps have yet been formed.

No German dumps discovered. It is thought that some exist along the RAILWAY, but these are beyond our present forward line.

GENERAL REMARKS.

Ground is very sodden and heavy owing to recent rain, but it is not badly cut up past the forward German system of trenches and as soon as the weather improves it will be possible to make dry weather tracks following alongside and a short distance from Tracks 1 and 3.

1st August, 1917.

Lieut-Colonel, R.E.

C. R. E. 16th Division.

SECRET.   Copy No. 11

Appendix 3

16th DIVISIONAL ENGINEERS OPERATION ORDER No.35.

                                                 3rd August, 1917.
Reference Map. Sh. 28. 1/40,000.

1.   The 16th Division will take over the Right Sector of XIX Corps Front from 15th Division, command passing at 10 a.m. on 4th August, 1917.

2.   RELIEF OF 15th DIVISION FIELD COMPANIES.

        15th Division Field Companies will work on night 3rd/4th Aug.

        16th Division Field Companies will work on night 4th/5th Aug.

        O.C. 155th Field Coy. will arrange direct to take over work from O.C. 74th Field Coy. in Right Sub-Sector.

        O.C. 157th Field Coy. will arrange direct to take over work from O.C. 73rd Field Coy. in Left Sub-Sector.

3.   At present Field Companies are in Divisional Reserve and remain in their Camp at G.11.d.1.5.

        On receipt of further orders the moves shewn in attached table will be made.

4.   R.E. STORES.

        Divisional Dump and Workshops.   BRANDHOEK. H.7.a.3.9.
                                          (155th Fld. Co. billet)

        Advanced Dumps:-

            Left.   POTIJZE DUMP.   I.4.c.1.8.

            Right.   MENIN ROAD DUMP. I.9.d.0.5.

        O.C. 155th Field Coy. will take over MENIN ROAD Dump and arrange to relieve 15th Division Sapper in charge.

        O.C. 157th Field Coy. will take over POTIJZE DUMP and relieve 15th Division Sapper in charge.

        Daily reports will be forwarded to C.R.E's Office giving state of these dumps together with indents for any stores specially required.

5.   C.R.E's Office will be at H.7.c.8.6. from 10 a.m. 4th August, 1917.

7.   ACKNOWLEDGE.

                                        R E Stradling
                                        Capt RE
                                    for   Lieut-Colonel, R.E.
                                        C. R. E. 16th Division.

Distribution:-

1. C.R.E.
2. 155th Fld. Coy.
3. 156th Fld. Coy.
4. 157th Fld. Coy.
5. 16th Div. 'G'.   )
6. 16th Div. 'Q'   )
7. C.R.E. 15th Div.   ) For information
8. 16th Div. Sigs.   )
9. A.D.M.S.   )
10. D.A.D.V.S.   )
11. War Diary.
12.   "   "

TABLE TO ACCOMPANY 16th DIV. ENGRS. O.O. No.35.

Unit Relieving.	Unit to be relieved.		Remarks.
	Name.	Map Location	
155th Field Coy. R.E.	74th Fld. Coy.	H.7.a.3.9.	Location of Advanced Billets will be notified later.
H.Q. and 2 Sections.		H.7.b.5.2.	
Transport.			
2 Sections.		Advanced Billets.	
156th Field Coy. R.E.	91st Fld. Coy.	H.7.b.0.2.	
H.Q. and 2 Sections.		H.7.b.2.2.	
Transport.			
157th Field Coy. R.E.	73rd Fld. Coy.	G.12.b.5.6.	-- do --
H.Q. and 2 Sections.		G.12.b.5.6.	
Transport.			
2 Sections.		Advanced Billets.	

Appendix 3

Addendum to 16th Divisional Engineers Operation
Order No. 35.
==

Reference Para 3.

1. 2 Sections 155th Field Coy. R.E., and 2 Sections of 157th Field Company R.E., together with attached Infantry, will occupy advanced billets at the RAMPARTS YPRES about I.8.d.1.8.

2. Advance party will be sent forward early in the day to secure billets.

3. Sections and attached Infantry to leave camp at 3 p.m., and march via VLAMERTINGHE.

4. ACKNOWLEDGE.

3rd August 1917.

R.E. Stuckley
Captain R.E.

for C.R.E. 16th Division.

Addressed all recipients of
16th Div. Engineers O.O. No. 35.

Appendix 4

Headquarters,
    16th Division 'G'.

    Herewith ~~Copy No.1 of~~ C.R.E's Report
on Divisional Front, dated 3rd August, 1917.

3rd August, 1917.   R.E.Stradling
                                  for Lieut-Colonel, R.E.
                                  C. R. E. 16th Division.

Copies to:-
    C. R. E.
    155th Fld. Coy.
    156th Fld. Coy.
    157th Fld. Coy.
    War Diary.

SECRET.   3331/84.
==========

C. R. E's   REPORT.   3rd August, 1917.

(A) INFORMATION.

1. FRONT LINE.

   Approximately as shewn on attached Map.

   RIGHT.   held in small groups, partly in shelter trenches, partly in old German trenches.

   LEFT.   in the STUTZPUNKT Trench.

   Some attempt has been made to dig in, and improve existing trenches and cover, but the ground is now entirely waterlogged, and the trenches (except the quite shallow ones) fill with water and cave in.

2. SUPPORT LINE.

   RIGHT.   STUTZPUNKT Trench and FREZENBERG REDOUBT.

   LEFT.   Partly old German trenches, partly in shelter trenches.

3. LINE OF STRONG POINTS.

   5 have been constructed, the trenches are shallow, partly wired.

   A continuous line of wire has been commenced along the front of the S.P's, by the 15th Division Pioneers, they will work on this again to-night, and hope to complete an apron fence the whole length.

4. FREZENBERG REDOUBT.   A German system of trenches occupying a strong position on the forward slope of the FREZENBERG SPUR.

5. COMMUNICATIONS.

   POTIJZ -FREZENBERG ROAD is in good order, but under observation on a clear day, the portion about FREZENBERG is sniped by machine guns from the right.
   A trench-board track has been laid on the North of this road via RUPPRECHT FARM to GREY RUIN, which is reported to have reached.   It will be continued on to SQUARE FARM.

   A second trench-board track runs from GULLY FARM, and has reached I.6. Central. It is to be continued past the North of WILDE WOOD to DOUGLAS VILLA

6. COMMAND HEADQUARTERS.

    BRIGADE.   MILL COTT. Very good.

    BATTALION.   RUPPRECHT FARM. Concrete dug-out, very cramped and wet.

                    FREZENBERG. Good concrete dug-outs.

                    WILDE WOOD. Good concrete dug-out near old German Dump.

                    NORTH STN BUILDING. Good dug-out at about 100 yards N. of the building.

7. HANEBEEK. This stream was drain-framed by the Germans. It requires clearing to prevent valley being flooded.

B. PROPOSED WORK.

1. FRONT LINE.

It is considered that digging new trenches is out of the question for the time being, but the German STUTZPUNKT and other old trenches can be cleared and improved.

Some wire should be erected early in front of the line we hold.
Transport will be a difficulty, but a start might be made by putting up some 100 yard bands in the most vital places, e.g. in front of FREZENBERG REDOUBT.

2. SUPPORT LINE.

Improve old trenches as far as possible.

3. STRONG POINTS.

Complete strong points and strengthen wire, which is only a single fence at present.
                      apron

4. FREZENBERG REDOUBT.

Improve trenches, provide machine gun emplacements, wire front and flanks.

5. COMMUNICATIONS.

Continue work on trench board tracks to DOUGLAS VILLA and SQUARE FARM.

Double these tracks as soon as trenchboards are available, and construct a central track following line IBEX LANE and BILL COTTAGE to back of FREZENBERG.

6. HEADQUARTERS.

Improve RUPPRECHT FARM, and undertake construction of traverses at others to protect entrance from hostile fire.

7. Clear and revet HANEBEEK.

3.

C. **EMPLOYMENT OF R.E. and PIONEERS.**

R.E.   Two Sections 157th Field Coy. (with 50 attached Infantry) for Right Sector.
Two Sections 155th Field Coy. (with 50 attached Infantry) for Left Sector.

Assist Infantry to wire and improve trenches, front line and support. Complete Strong Points. Strengthen and improve Command Dug-outs.

PIONEERS.   Complete two trenchboard tracks. Double these, and construct a third.
Clear and revet HANEBEEK.

LOCATION OF R.E.

155th Fld. Coy.   H.Q. and 2 Sections. H.7.a.3.9.
                   2 Sections. RAMPARTS. - I.8.d.1.8.

156th Fld. Coy.   In reserve.   H.7.b.0.2.

157th Fld. Coy.   H.Q. and 2 Sections. G.12.b.5.6.
                   2 Sections. RAMPARTS. - I.8.d.1.8.

LOCATION OF PIONEERS.

H.Q. and 2 Coys.   H.7.c.7.2.
2 Coys. ECOLE.

3rd August, 1917.   Lieut-Colonel, R.E.

                                                     C. R. E. 16th Division.

SECRET.

Copy No. 12

Appendix 5

H.Q.R.E. 16th DIVISION

Scheme for Work in the Line.   5th August, 1917.

1. **FRONT AND SUPPORT LINE.**

    Wire is urgently required.
    A little has been put up by the 15th Division behind the line of Strong Points.

    Every effort will be made to arrange for transport of wire and pickets forward, for erection by Infantry assisted by R.E.

2. **STRONG POINTS.**

    The S.P's made by the 15th Division are practically non-existent.

    New S.P's on the BLUE LINE will be taken in hand, dug and wired.

    Machine gun emplacements will be required at various tactical points in the forward area. It is proposed to construct open emplacements, near existing concrete dug-outs in NORTH STN BUILDINGS, FREZENBERG REDOUBT, and also, if ~~possible~~ found suitable, in FROST HOUSE and LOW FARM.

3. **COMMUNICATIONS.**

    The only practicable routes at present are:-

    (1) The POTIJZE-FREZENBERG Road.

    (2) Trench-board Track "F" from CAMBRIDGE ROAD at about I.11.b.2.7. to IBEX RESERVE at about I.6.a.6.1.

    (3) Trench-board Track "G" from I.5.a.7.9. to about C.30.c.5.5.

    The mud tracks No. 1 and 3 made by the 15th Division have become impassable.

PROPOSALS.

(1) This road is being repaired and improved by the XIX Corps.

(2) "F" Track will be continued South of ~~GREY RUIN~~ to DOUGLAS VILLA ~~SQUARE FARM~~ .

(3) "G" Track will be continued to ~~DOUGLAS VILLA~~ South of GREY RUIN to SQUARE FARM.

(4) A lateral communication track will be laid from POTIJZE ROAD at about C.30.d.2.7. to junction with "G" Track at about 200 yards E. of DOUGLAS VILLA.

4

4. **TRENCH ROUTES.**

   (1) PICCADILLY TRENCH will be recovered from its junction with POTIJZE-HELL FIRE ROAD to Old British Front Line thence by trench-board track via OSKAR FARM to IBEX AVENUE.

   (2) Thence IBEX DRIVE will be recovered as far as FREZENBERG REDOUBT.

   (3) HAYMARKET will be recovered from its junction with POTIJZE ROAD up to old British Front Line, and thence by trench-board track to West end of "G" Track. (This will provide a switch way in case WHITE CHATEAU -MILL COTT end of POTIJZE ROAD is being shelled).

   (4) CAMEROON AVENUE - CAMEROON DRIVE will be recovered to provide a covered communication between RUPPRECHT FARM and SQUARE FARM.

5. **FORWARD DUMPS.**

   It is proposed to establish two forward dumps.

   These Dumps will contain wire, pickets and sandbags for use in Front and Strong Points lines.

   The exact location will be determined after a little more experience in the line.

   The Dump for the Left Brigade will probably be near SIX TREES at about C.30.d.3.6.

6. **DEEP DUG-OUTS.**

   1. All deep dug-outs in our old line are being systematically reconnoitred, and steps taken to provide or repair pumps.

   ST JAMES FARM and MILL COTT are both reasonably dry.

   2. German dug-outs are being reconnoitred and repaired, attached Map C.R.E. No. 220 shows the situation up to date.

   The FREZENBERG System will provide 2 good Advanced Brigade Headquarters.

7. **GENERAL.**

   (1) Screening of MENIN ROAD. A screen is required from ECOLE to HELL FIRE CORNER.

   (2) Additional accommodation at PRISON, YPRES, for the A.D.S. This will be provided by Steel Shelters, strengthened by concrete.

   (3) Maintenance of Bridges over YPRES Canal. There are 6 in all on West side of the town.

8. **RESPONSIBILITY FOR WORK.**

    1. Infantry Garrison assisted by R.E. (155th and 157th Coys).

    2. R.E. (155th and 157th) and attached Infantry, with any help obtainable from the Garrisons.

    3.   (2) 11th Hants (Pioneers).

        (3) 11th Hants (Pioneers).

        (4) 11th Hants (Pioneers).

    4.   (1) 155th Coy. R.E.

        (2) 11th Hants (Pioneers).

        (3) 157th Coy. R.E.

        (4) After completion of (2) by 11th Hants (P).

    5. Under organisation of R.E. (155 and 157). Carrying to be done by attached Infantry, special Infantry carrying parties, R.E. and Infantry Pack Mules.

    6.   (1) R.E. (155 and 157).

        (2) 171 Tunnelling Coy. R.E.

    7.   (1) 11th Hants (Pioneers).

        (2) 156th Coy. R.E.

        (3) 2, 2A, 3 by 155 Coy. R.E.   Remainder by 157th Coy. R.E.

5th August, 1917.

R.J. Butterworth
Lieut-Colonel, R.E.
C. R. E. 16th Division.

Distribution:-

1. G.O.C.
2. 16th Div. 'G'.
3. 47th Inf. Bde.
4. 48th Inf. Bde.
5. 49th Inf. Bde.
6. 155th Fld. Coy.
*7. 156th Fld. Coy.
8. 157th Fld. Coy.
*9. 11th Hants (P).
10. C.R.E.
*11. File.
*12. War Diary.

* C.R.E's Map No. 220 not attached.

SECRET. 3331/70/1.

Amendment to Scheme for Work in the Line.

Reference H.Q.R.E. 16th Division, Scheme for Work in the Line, dated 5th August, 1917.

3.   PROPOSALS:-

For
    (2) read. " "F" Track will be continued to DOUGLAS VILLA"

    (3) read " "G" Track will be continued South of GREY RUIN to SQUARE FARM.

6th August, 1917.
                                      Lieut-Colonel, R.E.
                                    C. R. E. 16th Division.

Addressed all recipients of 16th D.E. 3331/70.

SECRET.   3331/70/1.

Amendment to Scheme for Work in the Line.

Reference H.Q.R.E. 16th Division, Scheme for Work in the Line, dated 5th August, 1917.

3.   PROPOSALS:-

   For
    (2) read. " "F" Track will be continued to DOUGLAS VILLA"

    (3) read " "G" Track will be continued South of GREY RUIN to SQUARE FARM.

6th August, 1917.   Lieut-Colonel, R.E.

                                      C. R. E. 16th Division.

Addressed all recipients of 16th D.E. 3331/70.

SECRET.   Copy No. 18

appendix 7
appendix 7

C.R.E's INSTRUCTIONS FOR THE OFFENSIVE No.5.

1. (a) The Fifth Army is to continue the attack at an early date. The date ("Z" Day) and hour of attack (Zero Hour) will be notified later.

   (b) The XIXth Corps is attacking with the 16th Division on the right and the 36th Division on the left.

   (c) The 8th Division, IInd Corps, is attacking on the right of the 16th Division, its loft attack being carried out by the 23rd Infl. Bde.

   (d) The right attack of the 36th Division will be carried out by the 108th Inf. Bde. (H.Q. at WIELTJE).

2. (a) The German lines opposite the XIXth Corps front are held by two Regiments of the 3rd Reserve Infantry Division and one Regiment of the 221st Division. Each of the above divisions is holding the front line with one battalion, with two battalions in close support. The 3rd Reserve Division has one regiment in reserve; 221st Division has two regiments in reserve, both of which have been recently withdrawn from the line opposite the XIXth Corps front.

3. The 16th Division will attack and establish itself on the GHELUVELT - LANGEMARCK line, which was formerly known as the GREEN LINE. This line, which will henceforward be known as the DOTTED RED LINE, is shown in dotted red on the attached map B. The objectives of the neighbouring divisions, and the dividing lines between them and the 16th Division, are also shewn on Map B.

4. The attack will be carried out in two stages, as under:-

   (a) At Zero the Infantry will advance up to an intermediate line, where a pause of 20 minutes will take place. This intermediate line is shown in green on Map B. and will in future be referred to as the GREEN LINE.

   (b) After the pause of 20 minutes the Infantry will advance and capture the DOTTED RED LINE. The 36th Division is to establish a post at or near WURST FARM in order to have observation over the valley of the STROOMBEEK.

5. On reaching the DOTTED RED LINE the troops in possession of it will consolidate it and will push forward a line of posts in advance of it to the line of the Standing Barrage.

6.

6. The 16th Division will attack on a two brigade front; 48th Inf. Bde. (plus one battalion) on the right, 49th Inf. Bde. (plus one battalion) on the left.

The 47th Inf.Bde. will place one battalion at the disposal of each of the attacking brigades. One battalion will be employed on Special work under C.R.E.

47th Inf. Bde. (less 3 battalions and 47th M.G.Coy). will be in Divisional Reserve in VLAMERTINGHE No. 3 Area.

The final objective of the 48th Inf. Bde. will be the RED DOTTED LINE from Railway Crossing at D.26.b.90.40. (inclusive) to the ZONNEBEKE Stream (exclusive); that of the 49th Inf.Bde. will be the RED DOTTED LINE from the ZONNEBEKE Stream (inclusive) to point D.14.d.15.45.

The dividing line between the two attacking brigades which is shown in dotted brown on Map B, will run as follows:-

Point where RED DOTTED LINE crosses the ZONNEBEKE Stream -Building just S.E. of FROST HOUSE enclosure at D.25.a.75.05. (BREMEN REDOUBT to RIGHT Brigade) - I.5.Central.

7. (a) Each attacking Infantry Brigade will attack with two battalions in line, one in support and two in reserve.

(b) The support battalions will assist in mopping up and will garrison the following points with previously told off garrisons:-

48th Inf.Bde.

POTSDAM.
VAMPIR FARM.

49th Inf.Bde.

BORRY FARM.
DELVA FARM.
IBERIAN.

(c) The Reserve Battalions of each Brigade will take over the defences of the BLACK LINE and BLUE LINE in their Brigade Sectors.

(d) The Headquarters of these two Brigades will be as follows:-

48th Inf.Bde.   JAMES FARM.

49th Inf.Bde.   MILL COTTS.

8. ARTILLERY.

All Field Artillery allotted to the 16th Division will be under the command of C.R.A. 16th Division and will work under the orders of G.O.C. R.A. XIX Corps.

The

The Infantry advance will be preceded by a Creeping Barrage. This barrage will be put down 300 yards in advance of our front line at Zero. Enemy's position at BECK HOUSE will be specially treated. The first lift will take place at Zero plus 5 minutes, and the barrage will then move forward at the rate of 100 yards in 5 minutes, with a halt of 20 minutes in front of the GREEN LINE.

After the capture of the DOTTED RED LINE a standing barrage will be established 300 yards in front of it for a period of . one hour, after which the Field Artillery will be at the disposal of the Division.

Maps showing the above barrage will be issued later to all concerned.

9. TANKS.

One Section of Tanks from "C" Bn., Tanks Corps has been allotted to 16th Division.

These tanks will not be available unless the weather conditions improve. In any case they are only likely to arrive behind the Infantry in time to act as "Moppers Up" in cases where isolated positions continue to hold out.

10. SYNCHRONIZATION OF WATCHES.

Field Company Commanders will synchronize watches at nearest Bde. H.Q. daily.

11. Divisional Headquarters will be at H.7.d.0.4.

12. The following are the arrangements for employment of R.E., Pioneers and attached Infantry.

DETAIL OF WORK.   Map C.R.E. 224.

(1) Supporting Points (Machine Gun Fortins).

Right Brigade.

    (a) POTSDAM.   D.26.c.75.80.

    (b) VAMPIR.   D.26.a.05.50.
                               (or D.25.b.10.70).

Left Brigade.

    (c) IBERIAN FARM.   D.19.b.2.2.

    (d) DELVA FARM.   D.20.a.05.30.

Concrete dug-outs are known to exist in (a), (b) and (d). The exposed entrances will be traversed with sandbag wall and bursters, and the dug-out or group of dug-outs wired in.

Where no dug-outs exist the main building will be wired in, and protection added to the cellar, if such is found. Notches or embrasures for Lewis Machine Guns will be made /to dug-outs and cellars.

    adjacent

2. COMMUNICATIONS.

   (a) RIGHT BRIGADE.

   No. 2 Track will be carried forward to BOSTIN FARM.

   (b) LEFT BRIGADE.

   No. 3 Track will be carried forward to DELVA FARM.

   These tracks will be marked through to their destination with boards 6" square, with a red triangle and figure in black thus:-

   (c) Repairs will be carried out on the FREZENBERG - VAMPIR FARM ROAD.

3. BRIDGES.

   (I) Repairs to existing bridges or new bridges to take Pack Mules will be made at the following points:-

   (a) Over the STEENBEEK at D.26.a.7.3. and D.26.a.55.50.

   (b) Over the STEENBEEK at D.19.d.1.5., D.19.c.45.70. and D.19.c.40.80.

   (II) Infantry Bridges will be erected at the following points, approximately:-

   (a) STEENBEEK D.26.a.6.4. and D.26.a.7.3.

   (b) STEENBEEK D.19.d.75.20 (2).

   (c) The following existing foot-bridges will be repaired:-

   STEENBEEK D.19.d.35.45.
   ZONNEBEKE D.20.c.10.65.

   In the event of continuous fine weather the STEENBEEK will not present a serious obstacle, but the ZONNEBEKE is known to be 5' deep with marshy banks.

   There are many Willow trees along the banks of both rivers, so in the event of transport of light bridges not being feasible, a suitable tree will be felled here and there to form a bridge.

4. RECONNAISSANCE.

   (a) DUG-OUTS.

   The following localities will be examined for dug-outs and concrete M.G. Emplacements:-

   POTSDAM, VAMPIR, BECK HOUSE, IBERIAN FARM, DELVA FARM, BREMEN REDOUBT and German captured trenches (GHELUVELT - LANGEMARCK LINE).

(b) DUMPS.

The following German Dump will be reconnoitred, and early report sent back as to stores available.
D.25.d.6.2.

Other Dumps discovered will be reported on similarly.

(c) ROADS.

Reconnaissance of FREZENBERG-VAMPIR FARM road as far forward as possible, and Tracks Nos. 2 and 3.

5. WIRE.

Bays of wire entanglement will be put up as soon as possible after capture of DOTTED RED LINE. Approximately along the line of the GHELUVELT-LANGEMARCK Trench.

(1) D.26.b.4.3.
(2) D.26.b.2.6.
(3) D.20.d.05.00.
(4) D.20.c.95.45.
(5) D.20.a.80.00 (in Copse).
(6) D.20.a.75.80.

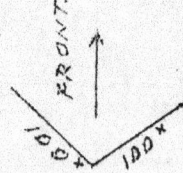

Each bay will consist of two arms 100 yards long. Arms being laid out in enfilade of machine guns at POTSDAM, VAMPIR, IBERIAN, DELVA.

Map reference refers to point of junction of the two arms.

The obstacle will consist of a single fence of long pickets 5 yards apart, with three strands of wire, later the fence will be strengthened by an apron.

6. RESPONSIBILITY FOR WORK.

155th Field Coy.R.E.   1. (a), (b). 3.(I) (a) and
(II) (a). 4 (b).

157th Field Company,   1. (c), (d). 3.(I) (b), (II) (b),
(c).   4 (b).

Detachment 171 Tunnelling Company,R.E.   4. (a).

11th Hants (Pioneers).   2. (a), (b), (c), and 4. (c).

Wiring party 7th Leinster Regt. 5. (1), (2) and (3).

Wiring party 6th Connaught Ran. 5. (4), (5) and (6).

7. STORES.

Advanced R.E. Dumps are being formed as follows:-

RIGHT BRIGADE.   C.30.d.7.1.

LEFT BRIGADE.   SIX TREES. C.30.d.5.7.

These

These contain wire, pickets (long and short), and sandbags, for work on Supporting Points, and SIX TREES Dump additional wire and pickets for special wiring.

There are also supplies of tools, Camouflage, notice boards and light bridges.

A list of stores available at each will be sent to all concerned, as soon as the Dumps are filled.

13. ASSEMBLY POSITION AND MOVES.

(1) 155th and 157th Field Companies, R.E. with attached Infantry, Pack Transport Sections, tool-carts and G.S. Wagons will assemble in H.18.a. on evening of Y/Z Night and there form bivouac.

They will move forward on Y/Z Night to selected positions in IBERIA RESERVE and IBEX RESERVE Trenches in old German Support Line. Mules and transport will be left in H.18.

Field Company Commanders will report at the Brigade Headquarters of their battle front, and get into touch with the situation before making plans to advance.

On the capture of the DOTTED RED LINE by XIXth and IInd Corps parties will be got forward as soon as possible. Parties should be halted on the reverse side of FREZENBERG SPUR, while the necessary reconnaissance of the job and locality is being made.

(2) 156th Field Company, R.E. will move forward on Z Day to H.18.a. and remain in Reserve at one hour's notice.

(3) O.C. 11th Hants (Pioneers) will detail two Companies for work on Tracks (2) and (3), moving to position of Assembly on Y/Z Night, as follows:-

4 Platoons HALF MOON TRENCH.

2 Companies (less 4 Platoons) in ECOLE.

H.Q. and 1 Company will remain in Reserve at H.16.d.5.9.

(4) WIRING PARTIES. 7th LEINSTERS and 6th CONNAUGHT RAN.

These will consist of 3 squads each of 1 Officer and 30 O.R. and 2 attached R.E. (156th Field Coy.).

They will move to position of Assembly near Field Coys. in H.18.a. on Y Day and then to IBEX SUPPORT TRENCH on Y/Z Night.

7th Leinster party will be in contact with 155th and 6 Con. Ran. with 157th Field Coy.R.E.
By this means the senior Officer of each party will keep in touch with progress of events. He will only send out his parties to wire in daylight, provided certain information is at hand that the IInd Corps as well as XIXth Corps have made good on the DOTTED RED LINE. Otherwise he will wait until dusk, and get his parties forward then.

14. **RATIONS.**

    Three day's rations will be taken forward to position of assembly, and two day's rations carried on each man on Z Day.

15. **DRESS FOR WORKING PARTIES.**

    Light Marching Order. Haversack to be worn in place of Pack, which will be left at H.18.a.

16. **REPORT CENTRES.**

H.Q.R.E.	H.7.d.0.4.
H.Q.R.E. Advanced Report Station.	RAMPARTS, I.8.d.1.8.
155th Field Coy.R.E.	MILL COTT.
157th Field Coy.R.E.	JAMES FARM.
156th Field Coy.R.E.	H.18.a.1.7.
11th Hants (Pioneers).	H.16.d.5.9.

13th August, 1917.

R J Butterworth
Lieut-Colonel, R.E.
C. R. E. 16th Division.

appendix 8

SECRET.   Copy No. 18

OPERATION ORDER No. Y.4. by C.R.E. 16th DIVISION.

                                            14th August, 1917.

1.   Reference C.R.E's Instructions for the Offensive
No.5 the following moves will take place:-

14th August.   Advanced Sections 155th and 157th Field
        Companies, R.E., and attached Infantry from RAMPARTS
        to Camp in BRANDHOEK.
            Os.C. will arrange times, and, if necessary,
        leave small detachments to complete any unfinished
        work.
            In any case Caretakers will be left in each
        billet to prevent the billets being taken over by
        other troops.

15th August.
        (1) 155th, 157th Field Companies, R.E. with attached
        Infantry, Pack Transport, Limber wagons and tool-
        carts will   move to position of Assembly in
        H.18.a., and there form bivouac.
            Move to be completed by 12 noon.
            H.Q. will be at H.18.a.1.1.

        (2) The Special Wiring Parties of 7th Leinsters
        and 6th Connaught Rangers will parade at 156th
        Field Company Camp at 9.0. a.m. (H.7.b.0.2).
            They will march to same position of Assembly
        in H.18.a. - route VLAMERTINGHE STN. - DEN GROENEN
        JAGER CABT - FARM H.17.c.9.4. - H.18.a.
            Lieut. CULVER, 156th Fld. Coy.R.E. will
        accompany the special wiring parties.

        (3) Advance parties of 155th and 157th Field Coys.
        will reconnoitre and allot bivouac areas to Field
        Coys. and Wiring Parties on their arrival.

2.   RATIONS.

        Three complete days rations will be taken forward
to Position of Assembly for every man and animal.

3.   WATER.

        Os.C. 155th and 157th Field Coys will arrange for
water for their attached Infantry.
        A special water-cart will be allotted to the
Wiring Parties, Leinsters and Connaught Rangers.

4.   COVER.

        Water-proof sheets and any available tarpaulins
and bivouacs will be taken forward, as there is no
shelter on the ground except that afforded by hedges.

                                                5.

5. PRECAUTIONS.

   All ranks must be kept close to the banks and hedges and not allowed to stray about, as it is essential that enemy aeroplanes should not notice movement in this area.

6. Orders will follow regarding forward move to old Gorman Support Trench.

Issued at 12.30 p.m.

R M Butterworth

Lieut-Colonel, R.E.

C. R. E. 16th Division.

Distribution:-

1. C.R.E.
2. 155th Fld. Coy.
3. 156th Fld. Coy.
4. 157th Fld. Coy.
5. 6th Con. Ran.
6. 7th Leinster Rgt.
7. 16th Div. 'G'.
8. 16th Div. 'Q'.
9. 47th Inf. Bde.
10. 48th Inf. Bde.
11. 49th Inf. Bde.
12. 11th Hants (P).
13. File.
14.
15.
16.   "
17.   "
18. War Diary.

SECRET.   Copy No. 12

OPERATION ORDER NO 'Y' 5. by C.R.E. 16th DIVISION.

                                          14th August, 1917.

1.   Moves of Units to assembly positions will be carried
out on Y day and Y/Z night in accordance with attached
move table. All moves to be completed by 2.30 a.m. on
Z day.

2.   The instructions contained in 16th Division No. E.S.
1276/22 (forwarded under this Office No. 3320/32 dated
26th June, 1917) will be strictly complied with.

3.   Approximate assembly areas are shown on the attached
Map. 225

4.   Completion of moves to be reported by wire by use of
the code word 'FIXT'.

5.   Acknowledge.

Issued at 6of p.m.

                                          Lieut-Colonel, R.E.

                                          C. R. E. 16th Division.

            Distribution:-

                1.   C.R.E.
                2.   155th Fld. Coy.
                3.   156th Fld. Coy.
                4.   157th Fld. Coy.
                5.   6th Con. Ran.
                6.   7th Leinsters.
                7.   16th Div. 'G'.
                8.   11th Hants (P).
                9.   File.
               10.   File.
               11.   File.
               12.   War Diary.

SECRET.

MOVE TABLE to accompany C.R.E's O.O. NO. 'Y' 5. dated 14th August, 1917.

Serial No.	Date.	Unit.	From	To	Move under orders of	Remarks.
1.	15th Aug.	155th Fld. Coy.) with 156th Fld. Coy.) attached Infantry. Wiring parties from 6th Connaught Rangers and 7th Leinsters.	BRANDHOEK No. 2 Area.	H.18.a.	Vide O.O. No. 'Y' 4 by C.R.E. 16th Div.	Moves to be completed by 12 noon. No restrictions as to route.
2.	15th Aug.	156th Fld. Coy. with attached Infantry.	BRANDHOEK No. 2 Area.	VLAMERTINGHE No. 3 Area. H.16.c.3.3.	O.C. 156th Fld. Coy. R.E.	Move to be completed by 12 noon. No restrictions as to route.
3.	Night Y/Z	155th Fld.Coy.) with 157th Fld.Coy.) attached Infantry and wiring parties.	H.18.a.	Area reserved for R.E. and Pioneers in IBEX and IBERIAN Reserve Trenches.	O.C. 155th Coy. and O.C. 157th Coy.	Not to reach MENIN GATE before 11.30 p.m. and to be in position by 2.30 a.m.
4.	Night Y/Z	2 Coys. 11th Hants.	H.16.d.6.8.	IBERIA and IBEX TRENCH -do- and SUPPORT new map 225	O.C. 11th Hants (P).	Not to reach MENIN GATE before 11.30 p.m. and to be in position by 2.30 a.m.

3331/105.

16th DIVISION.

Report on R.E. Operations.   15th/16th August.

1. SCHEME FOR R.E. WORK.

   This was based on the successful capture of the 16th Division objective (DOTTED RED LINE), and is described in detail in C.R.E's Instructions for the Offensive No.5 and Map 224, issued to all concerned on 13th August.

   It provided for:-

   (1) The wiring of the line of resistance along the German GHELUVELT - LANGEMARCK Trench.

   (2) The construction of Supporting Points (Machine Gun Fortins) at POTSDAM, VAMPIR, IBERIAN and DELVA FARMS.

   (3) The reconnaissance for and construction of two forward tracks in prolongation of Nos. 2 and 5 Tracks.

   (4) The bridging of the HANEBEEK and STEENBEEK.

   (5) The reconnaissance of captured German dug-outs.

2. PRELIMINARY DISPOSITIONS.

   (a) On Y Day (15th Aug) the Field Companies with attached Infantry, Pack Transport, Limber wagons and tool carts moved forward to Assembly Positions as follows:-

   155th Field Coy. R.E.   H.18.a.
   157th Field Coy. R.E.   H.18.a.
   156th Field Coy. R.E.   H.16.c.3.3.

   11th Hants (Pioneers) remained at H.16.d.5.9.

   Special Wiring Party - H.18.a.

   NOTE:- The special Wiring Parties consisted of 6 Squads, each 1 Officer and 30 O.R. trained to carry up and erect 200 yards single fence wire entanglement, 3 Squads were provided by the 7th Leinster Regt. and

3

3 Squads by the 6th Connaught Rangers.

Lieut. CULVER, 156th Field Coy.R.E. was in charge of the parties, and work.

(B) Simultaneous with above move C.R.E. established an Advanced Report Station in Advanced Divisional H.Q., RAMPARTS, YPRES.

3. On Y/Z Night the following moves took place:-

155th Field Coy.R.E.

    3 Sections   OLD GERMAN SUPPORT.
    1 Section   RAMPARTS.
    O.C. to 48th Bde. H.Q. JAMES FARM.

157th Field Coy.R.E.

    3 Sections   OLD GERMAN SUPPORT.
    1 Section   RAMPARTS.
    O.C. to 49th Bde. H.Q. MILL COTT.

2 Coys. 11th Hants (P).   OSKAR FARM.
        (Liaison Officer 49th Bde. H.Q.).

Wiring Party (6th Connaughts).   OLD GERMAN SUPPORT.
        (in liaison with 155th Coy).

Wiring Party (7th Leinsters)   OLD GERMAN SUPPORT.
        (in liaison with 157th Coy).

Attached diagram shows positions of all technical troops on Y Day and at Zero.

4. ACTION TAKEN.

The battle was of a see-saw nature, and on the withdrawal of the Left (49th) Brigade to their original line, it was evident that very little work on the prearranged plan would be possible.

Meanwhile the portion of the battle front between FREZENBERG RIDGE and the OLD BRITISH LINE was fairly quiet and the Pioneers were instructed to work forward on Tracks Nos. 2 and 3. They commenced work at Zero plus 4 (9. a.m) and worked through the day.

At about Zero plus 10 (3 p.m.) the Right (48th) Bde. were holding a line about D.26 (Central) - VAMPIR FARM - D.25.d.5.7. (exclusive of BORRY FARM which was still occupied by the enemy), to right of Left Brigade about LOW FARM.

The

The Divisional Commander instructed the C.R.E. to make plans to wire the line of the HANEBEEK, and to construct Supporting Points in rear of this line, thus forming a defensive line which was to include POTSDAM, VAMPIR and BORRY FARM. The work was contingent on the capture of BORRY FARM, orders for which were then being issued.

C.R.E. issued warning instructions to O.C. 155th Field Coy. and Wiring Parties 7th Leinsters.

At about 4.30 p.m. (Zero plus 12) the attack on BORRY FARM was postponed and reports came in from the Right (48th) Brigade that enemy machine guns were located near VAMPIR FARM, and THE BIT WORK.

At the same time the Left (49th) Bde. asked for reinforcements to hold his line in case of counter-attack. The Divisional Commander ordered C.R.E. to instruct the Special Wiring Parties to place themselves at the disposal of the G.O.C. 49th Bde. as reinforcements.

C.R.E. informed O.C. 155th Field Coy. that the scheme for wiring of the HANEBEEK, etc. was no longer possible, and instructed him to place himself at the disposal of G.O.C. 48th Bde. for any R.E. work that might be possible during the hours of darkness. This Company was not used, and was withdrawn next day to H.18.a.

The O.C. 157th Field Coy. R.E. was instructed to fortify SQUARE FARM. A party consisting of 1 Section R.E. and 25 attached Infantry was sent up at dusk with wire, pickets and sandbags. They reached the site, but little work was possible owing to the continuous shelling and machine gun fire.

This Company was withdrawn next day to H.18.a.

Summary.

SUMMARY.

The only work achieved was that done by the 11th Hants Pioneers on Nos. 2 and 3 Tracks, in addition to a little maintenance work on the main FREZENBERG road.

The situation never admitted of the useful employment of the R.E. and their attached Infantry.

20th August, 1917.   Lieut-Colonel, R.E.
                                                 C. R. E. 16th Division.

16 Div. R.E Situation at Zero 16-8-17

H.7.c.8.6 D.H.Q   ○ 🚩 C.R.E.

47 Bde. HQ ○🚩 H.16.c.3.3. 156 Fld Coy RE

○ H.16.d.5.9 11th Hants (P) H.Q. & 1.Coy

H.18.a. ○ Transport 155 & 157 Fld Coys. R.E.

|← 7000 yards →|

YPRES

CRE's Adv. Report Centre ○🚩 Adv. D.H.Q   ○ 1 Section 155 Fld Coy
I.8.d.1.8.   1 Section 157 Fld Coy

Brigade Boundary

I.4.d.6.2. Jawes Farm
48th Bde HQ ○🚩
O.C. 155 Fld Coy RE

        🚩
    ○ 49 Bde H.Q. I.5.a.0.5. Mill Cott.
    O.C 157 Fld Coy RE

~~~~~ OLD BRITISH FRONT LINE ~~~~~
~~~~~ OLD GERMAN FRONT LINE ~~~~~

3 Sections 155 Fld Coy RE ○   ○   ○ 3 Sections, 157 Fld Coy RE
Wiring Party 7th Leinst. Reg. 11th Hants (P)   Wiring Party 6th C.R.
                                2 Coys

|← 3500 yards / 1500 yards →|

────────── BLACK LINE ──────────

R.J. Butterworth
Lt Col
20.8.17   C.R.E. 16 Div.

SECRET.   Copy No. 11

appendix 11

16th DIVISIONAL ENGINEERS OPERATION ORDER No.36.

24th August, 1917.

1. The 16th Division (less Artillery) is to relieve the 21st Division (less Artillery) in the Line in the VIth Corps Centre Sector.
   The relief to be completed by 10 a.m. 28th August.
   The Command of the Centre Sector will pass from G.O.C. 21st Division to G.O.C. 16th Division at 6.p.m. on 27th Aug., at which hour Div. H.Q. will close at ACHIET LE PETIT and reopen at MOYENNEVILLE.

2. BRIGADE RELIEFS.

   47th Inf. Bde. relieves 64th Inf. Bde. in Right Section on night 26th/27th August.

   48th Inf. Bde. relieves 62nd Inf. Bde. in Left Section on 27th August, at times to be arranged between Brigadiers.

   49th Inf. Bde. becomes Brigade in Reserve on 28th Aug. Brigade H.Q. at MOYENNEVILLE.

3. The reliefs of Technical personnel will take place as shewn on attached Table.
   Field Company Commanders will get in touch with the corresponding Officers of 21st Divisional Engineers at 9.30 am. on 25th August, and arrange to see round the work.

4. Field Company Commanders will send on an advance party of 1 Officer and 4 Cyclists to take over billets on evening of 26th August. Field Companies will march into their new billets early on morning of 27th August. The exact time is to be arranged with Field Company Commanders of 21st Div. Engr

5. PIONEERS.

   O.C. 11th Hants (P) will arrange direct with O.C. 14th Northumberland Fusiliers to take over work and billets.
   H.Q. 14th N.F. at BOYELLES. (S.12.d.9.2).

6. C.R.Es. Office will open at MOYENNEVILLE at 6 p.m. 27th August.

7. A C K N O W L E D G E.

Issued at 8.p.m.   R.E. Stradling
                                                           Captain, R.E.
                                                       for C. R. E. 16th Division.

Distribution:-

    1. C.R.E.   6. 16th Div. 'G'.
    2. 155th Fld. Coy.   7. 21st Div. Engrs.
    3. 156th Fld. Coy.   8. 16th Div. 'Q'.
    4. 157th Fld. Coy.   9. File.
    5. 11th Hants.(P)   10. War Diary.
                                11. "   "

SECRET.

Table to accompany 16th Div.Engrs. O.O. No. 36. 24th August,1917.

	Date.	Units.		Billets to be taken over by 16th Div.Engrs.		REMARKS.
		Relieving.	To be relieved.	From.	At.	
LEFT	Aug. 27th.	155th Field Coy. R.E.	98th Field Coy. R.E.	126th Fld Coy. R.E.	Behind ST.LEGER. B.2.d.5.8.	To take over work in Left Section, ROYAL DUMP at CROISILLES (T.18.c.8.2) and Company Dump at ST. LEGER STATION (T.28.b.05.15).
RIGHT	Aug. 27th.	156th Field Coy. R.E.	126th Field Coy. R.E.	98th Fld. Coy. R.E.	ST. LEGER. B.4.a.8.7.	To take over work in Right Section, GUINNESS DUMP at ECOUST and Company Dump at ST. LEGER STATION (B.3.a.4.5).
RESERVE	Aug. 27th.	157th Field Coy. R.E.			HAMELINCOURT. S.29.d.3.4.	To take over work of Reserve Company. All plans will be submitted to C.R.Es. Office prior to commencing work.

WAR DIARY.

FOR MONTH OF SEPTEMBER, 1917.

VOLUME 22

UNIT:- H.Q. 16th Div Engineers.

Army Form C. 2118.

ROYAL ENGINEERS,
H.Q.
16TH DIVISION.

No............
Date............

WAR DIARY
or
INTELLIGENCE SUMMARY.
(Erase heading not required.)

Instructions regarding War Diaries and Intelligence Summaries are contained in F. S. Regs., Part II. and the Staff Manual respectively. Title pages will be prepared in manuscript.

Place	Date	Hour	Summary of Events and Information	Remarks and references to Appendices
MOYENNEVILLE	1.9.17		Normal work. — Hutty Coy formed for mutually new experiences of application. — CRE's instructions re TECHNICAL ASSISTANCE for 16" D.W. Art. moved (334/9) appendix (1)	Appendix 1
	2.9.17		CRE's scheme for R.E. & Pioneer Work (Provisional) issued (appendix 2.)	Appendix 2
	3.9.17 to 9.9.17		Normal line work with distribution of technical duties as laid down in Appendix (1).	
	10.9.17 to 17.9.17		Normal line work.	
	18.9.17		HQ RE. moved to BIENVILLERS	
BIENVILLERS	19.9.17 to 25.9.17		Normal linework	
	26.9.17		CRE. gone on leave. — Major P.F. WHITE DSO: RE. acting CRE.	
	27.9.17 to 29.9.17		Normal line work.	
	30.9.17			R98 twenty copies forwarded

appendix (1)

ROYAL ENGINEERS,
H.Q.
16TH DIVISION.
No. 3334/9.
Date.

155th Field Company, R.E.
156th Field Company, R.E.
157th Field Company, R.E.
11th Hants (Pioneers).
16th Div. Arty.)
16th Div. 'G'.) For information.
16th Div. 'Q'.)

Technical assistance for 16th Div. Artillery.

The following technical personnel will be placed at the disposal of the G.O.C. R.A. to assist and supervise work in Artillery Positions:-

    R.E.   1 Officer and 12 O.R.
    11th Hants. 1 Officer and 20 O.R.

2.   The R.E. Officer will advise on all work, having regard to material available and suitability of design and lay-out on the ground. He will check all Indents for stores, and arrange direct with Adjutant, R.E. for the necessary chits, to enable units to draw their requirements expeditiously from the Divisional Dumps.

He will allot the labour to the various jobs, and arrange for supervision by himself and the Pioneer Officer, as may be convenient to the Brigade Groups, R.F.A.

3.   The R.E. personnel will be found as follows:-

    Lieut. G.R. ALLEN, 156th Field Company, R.E.

    4 Sappers. (to include 1 Carpenter and 1 Mason) from each Field Company.

    Officer and 20 men 11th Hants as detailed by O.C. 11th Hants (P).

4.   The above will be allotted to Brigades as follows:-

    Lieut. G.R. ALLEN.   177th Brigade R.F.A.
    4 Sappers 156th Fld. Co.   B.17.a.6.4.
    2 Sappers 157th Fld. Co.
    10 O.R. 11th Hants (P).

/Officer

Officer 11th Hants.　　　　　180th Brigade R.F.A.
4 Sappers 155th Fld. Co.　　T.8.c.4.2.
2 Sappers 157th Fld. Co.
10 O.R. 11th Hants (P)z

5.　　　　The two parties will report for duty before noon on 2nd September, taking unexpended portion of the day's rations and rations for the 3rd.　　They will be accommodated by the R.F.A., and rationed from the 4th Sept.

　　　　　　　　　　　　　　　　R.J.Butterworth

1st September, 1917.　　　　　　　　Lieut-Colonel, R.E.
　　　　　　　　　　　　　　　C. R. E. 16th Division.

SECRET.

Appendix (2)
Provisional
H.Q.
16TH DIVISION.
3334/12.

16th Division.

Scheme for R.E. and Pioneer Work.

1. **Sub-division of Trench System.**

    For the purposes of work in the line the 16th Division Sector will be divided into three Sub-sectors with the following boundaries:-

    Right Sub-sector.   PELICAN AVENUE (inclusive) to the Sap at U.14.c.25.90 (inclusive)

    Centre Sub-sector.   Sap at U.14.c.25.90 (exclusive) to SENSEE RIVER (exclusive).

    Left Sub-sector.   RIVER SENSEE (inclusive) to PUG AVENUE (inclusive).

    The Right Sub-sector corresponds with the Right Section held by the 47th Bde. and the Centre and Left Sub-Sectors with the left Section held alternately by the 48th and 49th Bdes.

2. **Responsibility for Work in Front and Support Lines.**

    Right Sub-sector.   156th Field Company, R.E.

    Centre Sub-Sector.   157th Field Company, R.E.

    Left Sub-sector.   155th Field Company, R.E.

3. **Responsibility for Work in Reserve Line and Second System.**

    155th Fld. Coy.   A6 - A15
    AS7 - AS14.

    Second System. C7 - C11.

    157th Fld. Coy.   A1 - A5.
    AS5 - CROISILLES PERIMETER DEFENCES.

    Second System. C1 - C6.

    156th Fld. Coy.   RAILWAY RESERVE.

    Second System. L'HOMME MORT - ST. LEGER LINE.

4. **Details of Work.**

    (1) **Front Line.**   This consists of a line of Posts connected by a Command Trench.

    (a) The Posts are for the most part too small, and require extending. Each should consist of not less than three firing bays.

/The

The trenches, including the boyaux from the Command Trench are to be revetted and trenchboarded. Blocks in the form of gates protected by barbed wire are to be erected at all entrances to the Post, and Rifle Racks, Bomb and S.A.A. cupboards will be fixed in each Post. Entrances will be safeguarded against bombing by rifle straights or bomb anchors, vide sketch.

(b) The Command Trench will be cut to uniform pattern i.e. 2' at bottom, and sides sloping at 4/1, with berm left on each side. Trenchboards laid on pickets, and drain under boards, vide Type C. This trench need only be revetted in wet or clayey spots, or where provided with a firestep.

(ii) Support Line.

Right.

(a) MANCHESTER TRENCH will be firestopped at intervals and extended later towards PELICAN AVENUE.

(b) STRANGEWAYS RESERVE will be revetted, traversed, and firestepped at selected points to form Supporting Points.

(c) ~~A fire trench from about U.26.b.6.4. to U.26.d.5.7 will be dug, revetted and firestepped to cover Right flank.~~

(d) Work will be continued on firesteps at upper end of PELICAN, QUEEN'S, KNUCKLE and STAFFORD AVENUE.

Centre.

(a) HUMP LANE - LINCOLN TRENCH will be cleared, and Supporting Points selected and prepared.

(b) BURG TRENCH will be similarly treated from U.13.4. to LUMP LANE.

Left.

(a) Work will be continued on revetting and forming firesteps at points in HIND TRENCH, HORN TRENCH, CLAW SUPPORT, PUG AVENUE.

(iii) Reserve Line.

Right. RAILWAY RESERVE.
The wire will be strengthened by another band, leaving gaps at 100 yards intervals for counter-attack.
Fire bays will be revetted at intervals, and steps provided for reaching them, where the railway embankment necessitates.

Centre and Left.

Line of small works, A1, A2, etc., with supporting works AS1, AS2.
These will be connected up later by a lateral Communication Trench to form a continuous Reserve Line with RAILWAY RESERVE.

The

The immediate work required is to trenchboard, revet and improve firebays and M.G. emplacements in the existing works. The wire should be made continuous along the whole line leaving the usual gaps for counter-attack, in addition to the complete wiring in of the works themselves.

(iv) Communication Trenches.

Right.   PELICAN, QUEEN'S, KNUCKLE and STAFFORD.

All require opening out and cutting to standard template, vide type C. Revetment will not be necessary in the chalk formation.

Drainage requires careful attention, and provision of sump-holes where water collects in a cup, and cannot be led away.

Centre.

FACTORY, JANET, NELLY.

These will be treated in the same way as for the Right.

Left.

HIND TRENCH.

Trenchboards require renewing, and drainage improved.

The following leading to SHAFT TRENCH will be trenchboarded, and revetted as may be necessary.

FOP, FUN, FARMER, FULDNER.

PGU AVENUE. This is in good order, but requires attention to drainage, and more revetting in parts.

(v) Tramlines.

The following new tram lines will be constructed:-

(a) A spur from GUINNESS DUMP. Tram to the upper end of PELICAN AVENUE.

(b) A line from Light Railway at about T.4.c.7.9. to STALEY BRIDGE on 16 lb. rail, and thence to FOP LANE on 9 lb. rail.

(c) A connection is projected between GUINNESS and ROYAL DUMP tramways, so that Right Sector can be supplied from either of these two dumps.

5. <u>Responsibility for work will be as follows:-</u>

<u>Front Line</u>.

    Wire.   Troops in the line.

    Posts.   R.E., attached Infantry and Garrison.

<u>Command Trench</u>. Troops in the line with R.E. supervision.

<u>Support Line</u>. R.E., attached Infantry and Garrison.

<u>Reserve Line and 2nd System</u>.

    R.E.   Special working parties from Reserve Battn.

<u>Communication Trenches. Tramway Construction and Maintenance</u>.

    11th Hants (Pioneers).

6. Weekly reports will be furnished by 1st D.R. or Orderly on Mondays.

    With the report will be sent a trench map corrected up-to-date, which will be returned the same evening.

    The following conventional signs will be used to show progress of work on trenches:-

    New trenches dug, or old trenches cleared and cut to standard section.

 Red.

Trenches revetted.

Green.

Trenches revetted and trenchboarded.

Yellow.

Trench drained

Blue.

Sump holes.

Blue.

New tram line.

 Red.

New wire.

× × × × × × × Red.

7. <u>Distribution and Reliefs of Field Companies</u>.

    Each Field Company will be organised for work as follows:-

　　　　　2 Sections.　　　Front Line and Support.

　　　　　1 Section.　　　Reserve Line.

　　　　　1 Section.　　　Hutting.

　　　Reliefs will take place, fortnightly, on Sundays, reliefs to be completed by sunset. 1st Relief Sunday 16th Sept.

　　　The personnel required for the Divisional Dump, BOYELLES will be found from the Hutting Sections.

8.　　　Distribution and Relief of 11th Hants (P).

　　　This will be in the hands of the O.C. 11th Hants, who will include in his Weekly Report the distribution of his Companies on the various items of work.

2nd September, 1917.

　　　　　　　　　　　　　　　　　R.H. Butterworth
　　　　　　　　　　　　　　　　　Lieut-Colonel, R.E.
　　　　　　　　　　　　　　　C. R. E. 16th Division.

155th Fld. Coy.
156th Fld. Coy.
157th Fld. Coy.
11th Hants (P).
16th Div. 'G'　　)
47th Inf. Bde.　) For information.
48th Inf. Bde.　)
49th Inf. Bde.　)

Drawing to accompany
C.R.E. No. 3334/12.

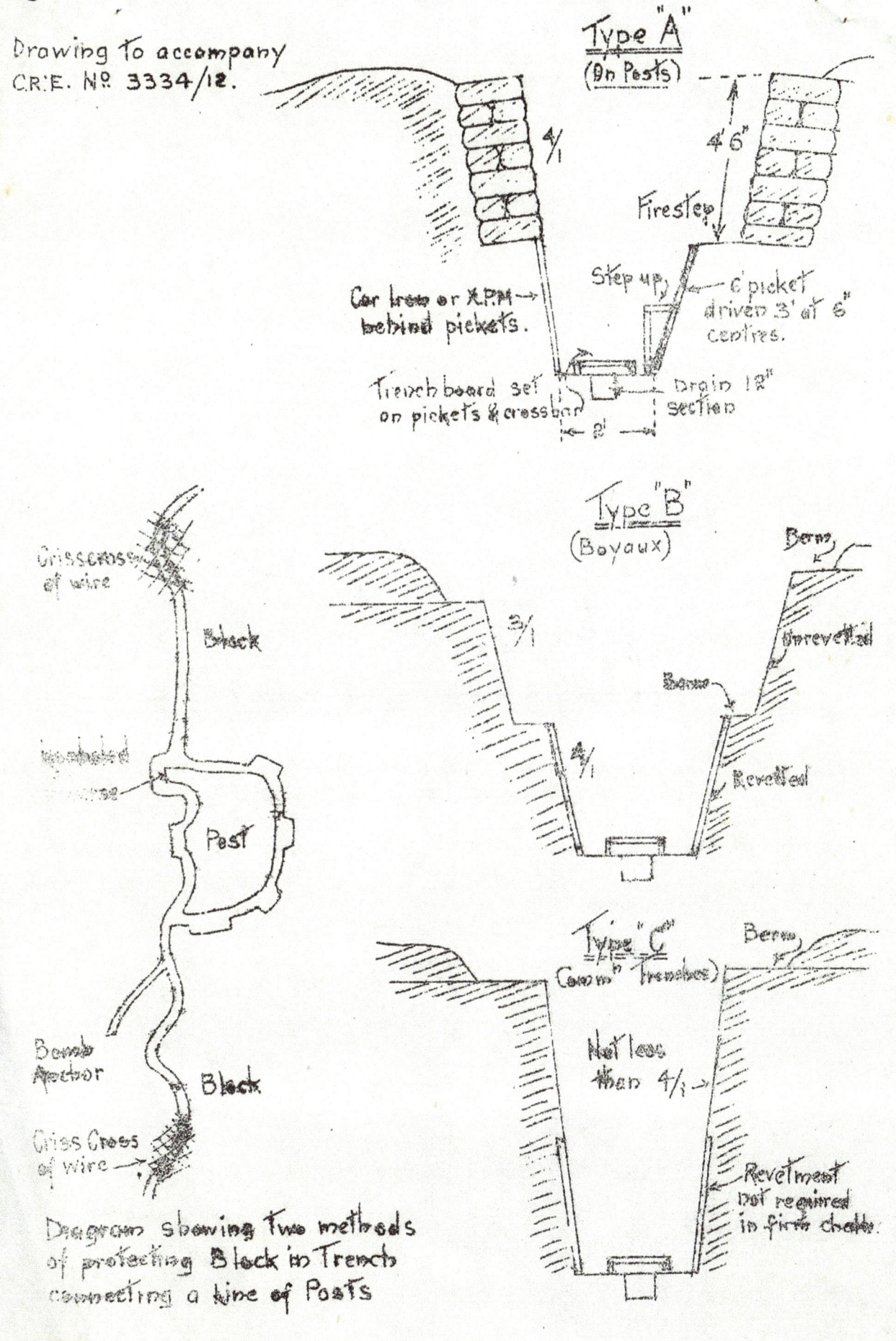

WAR DIARY

FOR MONTH OF OCTOBER, 1917.

UNIT H.Q. 16th Div Engineers

VOLUME NUMBER 23

Army Form C. 2118.

WAR DIARY
or
INTELLIGENCE SUMMARY.
(Erase heading not required.)

Instructions regarding War Diaries and Intelligence Summaries are contained in F. S. Regs., Part II. and the Staff Manual respectively. Title pages will be prepared in manuscript.

ROYAL ENGINEERS,
H.Q.
16th DIVISION.

Place	Date	Hour	Summary of Events and Information	Remarks and references to Appendices
REHAGNIES	1.9.17		Normal line work —	
	8.10.17			
	9.10.17		CRE. returns from leave — Major Whitnel rejoins his Coy —	
	10.10.17		Normal line work — 3rd Corps in line with 1 section 9 tank on hutting	
	31		Work at rear Divisional Areas — Right Rail-ways very short of timber — Tramways	
	12.10.17		dps. material very difficult to ward end of month — Preparation for minor operation commenced —	

R.B.S. Kashay
C.R.N.E.S
(Initialled)

T2134. Wt. W708—776. 5000000. 4/15. Sir J. C. & S.

WAR DIARY

FOR MONTH OF NOVEMBER, 1917.

VOLUME:- 24

UNIT:- H.Q. 16th Div. Engineers

Army Form C. 2118.

WAR DIARY
or
INTELLIGENCE SUMMARY.
(Erase heading not required.)

Instructions regarding War Diaries and Intelligence Summaries are contained in F.S. Regs., Part II. and the Staff Manual respectively. Title pages will be prepared in manuscript.

Place	Date	Hour	Summary of Events and Information	Remarks and references to Appendices
BERTRANCOURT	1.11.17 to 18.11.17		Reparations for Afternoon to TUNNEL TRENCH + TUNNEL SUPPORT carried with preparation to enemy withdrawal. – Tunnel chambers (as main in appendix 1) filed in + ifzs wing parties formed and all preparations completed for work in guns & the appending – Trestles slabs for road construction taken up for use on CROISILLES – FONTAINE ROAD –	Appendix 1
	19.11.17		155 + 157 Fd Coys installed forward HQ's. CROISILLES CAVES – 157 Cy at CHALK PIT (U.19 a 2.3) as given in CRE's operation Order No. FC. 7. (appendix 2.)	Appendix 2
	20.11.17 to 26.11.17		TUNNEL TRENCH taken and R.E. work carried out as given in F.C. 2 with the exception left Right Flank work (inf'ys infant's not gained – British JOUEMETZ U) the Strong point could not be made & the Right flank was moved round MARS MIETZ U later – on 23/24 – thie JOUEMETZ U S was taken and work completed to plan.	
			Casualties – R.E. Officers – R.E. O.R. Attached Officers O/Att'd Y. O.R.
			Killed – — 4 — 9
			Wounded 1 20 3 67
			— 5

Army Form C. 2118.

WAR DIARY
or
INTELLIGENCE SUMMARY.
(Erase heading not required.)

Place	Date	Hour	Summary of Events and Information	Remarks and references to Appendices
MESSINES	28.11.17		ee's bees 3340/4 ward (Appendix 4) giving detail of work proposed on TUNNEL TRENCH TUNNEL SUPPORT consolidation.	Appendix 4
	26.11.17 & 30.11.17		Work in consolidation continued — wiring of mine of division.	

R.E. Pickering
Capt.
для 16 Div

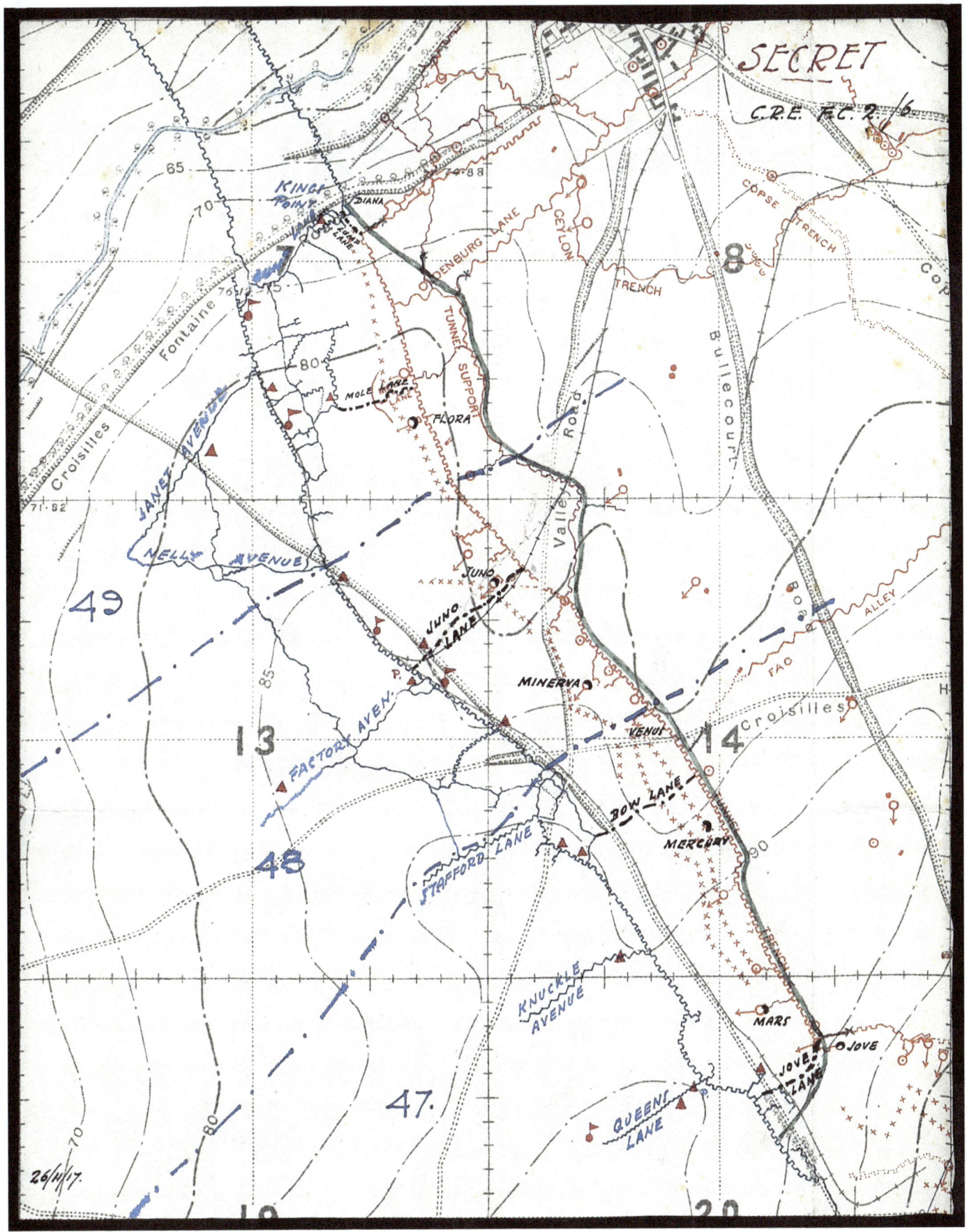

SECRET.   F.C.2.

SCHEME OF WORK (R.E. and Pioneers) after capture of
TUNNEL TRENCH and TUNNEL SUPPORT.

A. 47th BRIGADE.

   (1) WIRE.
         1 Section 156th Field Coy.R.E. assisted by Infantry
      Wiring and Carrying Parties will wire the front of
      TUNNEL TRENCH from JOVE to Sap at U.14.a.7.1., when they
      will connect with wire of 48th Brigade.
         They will also wire the right flank from JOVE for
      a distance of 50 yards South towards NOB SAP.
         Total distance = 950 yards.
         A four strand fence will be erected, to be
      afterwards reinforced.

   (2) BLOCKS.

      (a) Trench Blocks will be made in TUNNEL TRENCH E. of
          JOVE, and in FAG ALLEY by specially told off
          Bombing Parties assisted by details 156th Fld. Co.R.E.

      (b) A Tunnel Block will be made in TUNNEL TRENCH East
          of JOVE by No. 1 party 174th Tunn. Coy. R.E.

   (3) LEWIS GUN POSTS.

         4 L.G. Posts will be constructed in TUNNEL TRENCH
      by Lewis Gun Detachments assisted by details 156th Fld.
      Coy. R.E. as follows:-

         (1) N. of and close to JOVE.
         (2) N. of HANS at about U.14.d.21.05.
         (3) about U.14.d.1.5.
         (4) N. of FAG ALLEY at about U.14.a.75.05.

         The exact position of these will be determined by
      the Lewis Gun Commander on the spot.

   (4) COMMUNICATION TRENCHES.

      (1) JOVE LANE. This will be dug by 11th Hants (P).
          Route NOB SAP (U.20.b.2.5) to a point in TUNNEL
          TRENCH just N. of JOVE (U.20.b.43.70). Length 180 -
          200 yards.

             True bearing from NOB SAP = 49°

          Firebays will be constructed at intervals on the
          right or South Side of this Trench for Flank defence.

      (2) BOW LANE. This will be dug by special Infantry
          parties under 156th Fld. Coy.R.E. supervision.

             Route. S.E. corner of LAURAHS LOOP (U.14.c.
          46.57) to point in TUNNEL TRENCH 50 yards S. of
          FAG ALLEY (U.14.c.90.26). Length. 250 - 270 yards.
             True bearing from U.14.c.46.57. = 63°30'

                                                  (5)

(5) RECONNAISSANCE OF TUNNEL.

This will be undertaken by 2 parties 174th Tunn. Coy. R.E.
No. 1. JOVE HEBUS to Sap at U.14.d.05.39. (excl.), including forming Block in TUNNEL East of JOVE, vide 2(1).
No. 2. Sap at U.14.d.05.39 (incl) to U.14.a.7.1.
Each party will take explosives for blowing up steel doors or blocks met with in the TUNNEL Shafts.

(6) R.E. DUMPS.

(1) U.20.b.2.5. Wire, Pickets, 3 Scaling Ladders.
    (MARTIN ROAD).

(2) U.14.c.6.1. Wire, Pickets, 3 Scaling Ladders.
    (off KNUCKLE) Explosives, Picks and Shovels, Baby Elephant Sheeting.

(3) U.14.c.40.45. Wire, Pickets, Trenchboards.
    (off BAUMANS SUPPORT) 3 Scaling Ladders, Explosives.

(4) U.14.c.3.5. Trenchboards, "A" Frames, X.P.M.
    (off BAUMANS SUPPORT) Corrugated Iron Sheets.

(5) U.20.a.7.4. Wire, Trenchframes, revetting material.
    (QUEEN'S LANE).

PIONEER DUMPS.
    U.20.b.85.50.
    (QUEEN'S LANE). Trenchboards. "A" Frames. X.P.M.
                     Special for JOVE LANE.

(7) ACCOMMODATION. For working party Reliefs.

    Right. PELICAN AVENUE DUGOUT. U.21.c.00.22.

    Left.   BAUMAN LOOP DUGOUTS.   U.14.c.4.6.

(8) ADVANCED HEADQUARTERS, 156th Field Coy.R.E. U.19.a.2.3.

B. 48th Brigade.

(1) WIRE. Infantry Wiring and Carrying Parties assisted by 155th Fld. Coy.R.E. will wire TUNNEL TRENCH from U.14.a.7.1. (where they will connect with 47th Bde.) to junction of TUNNEL TRENCH and SUPPORT at U.14.a.32.57., and thence along TUNNEL SUPPORT to trench junction U.8.c.02.19. (where they will connect with 40th Bde. wire).
Total distance = 800 yards.

A single row of strengthened concertina wire will be erected, G.H.Q. Drill No. 2.

The remainder of TUNNEL TRENCH will be wired as a later operation from U.14.a.32.57. to connect with 40th Bde. at U.7.d.85.10.

(2) BLOCKS. Details 155th Fld. Coy.R.E. will be prepared to assist in making blocks, if tactical situation requires them.

(3) SUPPORTING POINTS.
Strong Points will be constructed and wired in by 155th Fld. Coy.R.E. and attached Infantry at the following points:-
    1. MINERVA HEBUS. U.14.a.4.3.
    2. JUNO HEBUS.   U.14.a.03.65.

(4) COMMUNICATION TRENCHES.

　　JUNO LANE. This will be dug by the 11th Hants (P).
　　Route. BURG TRENCH U.13.b.70.27. (just N. of FACTORY
　　AVENUE) to JUNO SAP U.14.a.10.63. and TUNNEL TRENCH.
　　　　Length. 300 - 350 yards.
　　　　True bearing from U.13.b.70.27. = 48°

(5) RECONNAISSANCE OF TUNNEL.

　　　　This will be undertaken by No.3 Party 174th Tunn.
　　Coy. within limits of Brigade U.14.a.7.1. to U.7.d.85.10.
　　　　This party will take explosives fo. blowing in steel
　　doors, and blocks in TUNNEL Shafts.

(6) R.E. DUMP.

　　　　FACTORY AVENUE.　U.13.d.15.75.
　　　　Concertinas, Barbed wire, Pickets, Sandbags, Pit-
　　Props, Scantling, X.P.M., and Corr. Iron. Sheets.
　　Explosives (with Mobile charges) 6 Escalading Ladders,
　　Picks and Shovels.

　　　　Wire and material for immediate work will be carried
　　up on Y/Z Night, and spaced in NO MAN'S LAND along the
　　line of MARTIN ROAD.

　　PIONEER DUMP.　　Head of FACTORY AVENUE.

　　　　Trenchboards, Frames, X.P.M.　Special for work
　　in JUNO LANE.

(7) ACCOMMODATION. For working party Reliefs.

　　　　In old German Dug-outs in front of U.13/1 by
　　arrangement with 48th Bde.

(8) ADVANCED HEADQUARTERS. 155th Field Company, R.E.

　　　　CROISILLES CAVES.　T.24.a.2.5.

C. 49th Brigade.

(1) WIRE.

　　　　One Section 157th Fld. Coy. R.E. assisted by Infantry
　　Wiring and Carrying Parties will wire TUNNEL SUPPORT from
　　junction with 48th Bde. (U.8.c.02.20) to OLDENBURG LANE,
　　thence diagonally across the front of TUNNEL TRENCH to
　　DIANA (U.7.b.38.18) and round the North Side of KING'S
　　POINT (U.7.b.32.25).　Length = 800 yards.

　　　　As a later operation a belt of wire will be run along
　　TUNNEL TRENCH from U.7.d.85.10 to DIANA. Length = 600 yards.

(2) BLOCKS.

　　　　Trench Blocks will be made by special Bombing Parties
　　assisted by details 157th Fld. Coy. R.E. in:-

　　　　(a) OLDENBURG LANE.
　　　　(b) Cross trench from U.7.d.72.90. to PRINCE TRENCH.
　　　　(c) PRINCE TRENCH.

(3) STRONG POINTS.

Strong Points will be made by R.E. and attached Infantry at :-

    (1) End of LUMP LANE.
    (2) End of SAP 1.

(4) COMMUNICATION TRENCHES.

    (1) MOLE LANE.
    Route. Head of No. 1 Sap (U.7.d.42.35) to connect with German Trench (MOLE LANE) and TUNNEL TRENCH at U.7.d.70.45. Length 150 - 175 yards (incl. German Trench)
    True bearing from No. 1 Sap 61°

    (2) LUMP LANE.
    Route. Point in LUMP LANE near right hand bombing post to TUNNEL TRENCH (U.7.d.45.10).
    Length. 80 - 100 yards.
    Approx. bearing. 135°.

(5) RECONNAISSANCE OF TUNNEL.

This will be undertaken by No. 4 Party 174th Tunn. Coy. R.E. within limits of Bde. U.7.d.85.10 to Northern extremity of Tunnel. Explosives will be taken to blow in steel doors, or any blocks met with.

(6) R.E. DUMPS.

1.	JANET AVENUE. (U.7.c.78.20)	Wire, Pickets, Concertinas, Revetting Material, Sandbags, Picks and Shovels, Baby Elephants.
2.	Sap. 1. (U.7.d.35.30)	Wire, Pickets, Concertinas, Picks and Shovels.
3.	HUMBER SUPPORT. (Old saps between CHERRY LANE and APPLE LANE)	Wire, pickets, Concertinas, Trenchboards.
4.	CRAGSIDE. (U.7/2).	Trenchboards.
5.	LUMP LANE. (old saps A.C. near head)	Wire, Pickets, Concertinas, Sandbags, Trenchboards, Picks and Shovels.

(7) ACCOMMODATION. For working party reliefs.

In dug-outs under Brigade arrangements.

(8) ADVANCED HEADQUARTERS. 157th Field Coy. R.E.

    CROISILLES CAVES. T.24.a.2.8.

R.A. Butterworth

5th Nov. 1917.

    Lieut-Colonel, R.E.
    C. R. E. 16th Division.

Distribution:-

    155th Fld. Coy.R.E.
    156th Fld. Coy.R.E.
    157th Fld. Coy.R.E.
    C. R. E.
    11th Hants (P).
    174th Tunn. Coy.R.E.
    16th Div. 'G'
    47th Inf. Bde.
    48th Inf. Bde.
    49th Inf. Bde.
    War Diary.
      "   "
    File.

Drawing No
F C. 2/1
2
3
4
5

SECRET. F. C. 2/1.

AMENDMENT TO F. C. 2 of 5th Nov. 1917.

1. Para: A. Sub para: 4.

    Map Reference following word FAG ALLEY should read U.14.c.10.86.

2. Para: A. PIONEER DUMPS.

    Map Reference U.20.b.85.50 should read U.20.a.85.50.

6th Nov. 1917. Lieut-Colonel, R.E.

C. R. E. 16th Division.

Copies to all recipients of F. C. 2.

appendix 2.

S E C R E T.

C.R.E's OPERATION ORDER NO. F. C. 7.

1. The following roadjustments of the Divisional Front have been ordered to take place on 18th/19th November:-

    (a) The 101st Inf. Bde., 34th Div. will take over the front held by the 49th Inf. Bde. from its present left at U.1.a.3.6. up to the point U.1.a.2.0.

    (b) The 9th Inf. Bde., 3rd Div. will take over from the 47th Inf. Bde. that portion of the front line between present Inter-Divisional Boundary, and point U.20.d.95.40.

    (c) The Inter-Brigade Boundaries will then become as shown on Secret Map issued with C.R.E's F. C. 2. on 5th Novr. 1917.

2. O.Cs. Field Companies R.E. will conform to the above, and establish their Advanced Headquarters by the evening of 19th Novr. as follows:-

    155th Field Coy.   CROISILLES CAVES.   T.24.a.2.8.
    156th Field Coy.   CHALK PIT.   U.19.a.4.3.
    157th Field Coy.   CROISILLES CAVES.   T.24.a.2.8.

    Completion to be reported to H.Q.R.E.

3. All Hutting details, and others, except those on permanent employ at H.Q.R.E., will rejoin their Units after work on 19th Novr.

4. Each Field Company will hold in readiness One Section, prepared in all respects to act as a Mobile Section in the case of a rapid withdrawal of the enemy.
    This Section may have to form part of a tactical advance guard, and must be ready to deal with obstructions, repair bridges and open up water supplies. (Explosives, wire rope and well buckets, blocks and tackles, cross-cut saws, felling axes, spikes and nails, are indispensable).

5. Apart from the Section mentioned in 4, O.Cs. will dispose of their personnel and arrange for reliefs to carry out the approved programme of work, vide F. C. 2.

6. Headquarters R.E. will remain at BEHAGNIES.

    Advanced Headquarters. CROISILLES CAVES,
    (Lieut. R.B. JENNINGS) from 19th inst.

7. **ORDERLIES.**

   Each Company will send 2 Cyclo Orderlies to report to H.Q.R.E. BEHAGNIES, on evening of 19th Novr.

8.   Reports during operations to Advanced R.E. Headquarters CROISILLES CAVES. A brief statement of work done, together with list of casualties, is required.

   This will be furnished daily by 9.a.m., report to include work done during previous night.

Issued at 8.0. p.m.

17th Novr. 1917.

RJ Mullensorth

Lieut-Colonel, R.E.

C. R. E. 16th Division.

Distribution:-

155th Fld. Coy.
156th Fld. Coy.
157th Fld. Coy.
16th Div. 'G'.
16th Div. 'Q'.
C.E. VI Corps.
11th Hants (P).
47th Inf. Bde.
48th Inf. Bde.
49th Inf. Bde.
174th Tun. Coy.R.E.
C. R. E.
War Diary (2).

Appendix 3.

S E C R E T.   3337/2.
===========

O.C. 155th Field Company, R.E.
O.C. 156th Field Company, R.E.
O.C. 157th Field Company, R.E.
O.C. 11th Hants (P).
O.C. 174th Tunnelling Coy. R.E.
16th Division 'G'.
16th Div. Artillery.
47th Inf. Bde.
48th Inf. Bde.
49th Inf. Bde.

C.R.E'S Instructions as to action in the Event
of an Enemy Withdrawal. No. 3.

1.   Para: 4 Provisional Instructions No. 1 is cancelled.

        For para:- 6 (a) and (b) substitute:-

        (a) Rapid construction of tracks for Infantry and
            Pack Animals.

        (b) Repairs to existing roads and tracks (except
            CROISILLES - FONTAINE road).

2.   O.C. 11th Hants (Pioneers) will be prepared to carry
out the following work:-

        (a) Hasty repairs to CROISILLES - FONTAINE road for
            immediate use of artillery and horse traffic.

        (b) Following (a), the constructional repair of same
            with soling and road-metal to take heavy guns and
            motor transport.

        (c) Assist in forward move of the guns of 177th and
            180th Brigades R.F.A., by bridging gaps, making ramps
            and improving tracks.

1st Nov. 1917.   Lieut-Colonel, R.E.

                                                  C. R. E. 16th Division.

SECRET.   3337/5.

C. R. E's Instructions as to Action in the event of an Enemy Withdrawal. No.4.

1. **TRANSPORT.**

    (a) Transport will be available on Mobilization Scale only.
    Any deficiencies in vehicles or animals will be at once made up and all outstanding indents completed.

    (b) Each Company will reform its Pack Section of 20 animals.
    Extra Pack-saddlery is available and will be issued on demand.

2. **KITS.**

    (a) All kits will be cut down to a minimum.

    (b) The Divisional Chaff Store, BOYELLES, will be used as a Divisional Store in which all Divisional property will be stored.
    All surplus kits will be stored in this place and receipts obtained from the Town Major.

3. **AREA STORES.**

    Area Stores, such as Chaff-cutters, Soyers Stoves, etc. will be handed over to the Town Major concerned, and receipts taken.

4. **WATER SUPPLY.**

    Special precautions will be taken with regard to all water supplies in enemy territory.
    The M.O. i/c R.E. will go forward to some point which will be notified day by day, and samples of water will be sent back to him by Units for Poison and Chloride test.   Water will not be taken into use, before passed by him.

5.   Special attention is drawn to attached Third Army Memo re "March Discipline"

15th Novr. 1917.   Lieut-Colonel, R.E.

                                                C. R. E. 16th Division.

Copies:-
  155th Fld.Coy.R.E.
  156th Fld. Coy.R.E.
  157th Fld. Coy.R.E.
  M.O. i/c R.E.
  C. R. E.
  File.

Third Army No.G.13/Z.

1. "The necessity for enforcing the strictest march discipline in all movements is brought to your notice."

2. Special attention is directed to the following points:-

   (a) Punctuality from the starting point - no main traffic routes to be blocked by troops waiting to march off.

   (b) Intervals of 200 yards will be maintained between Batteries, Sections of Divisional Ammunition Columns, Companies, Transport of Battalions, and similar Units. The units themselves must keep closed up.
   In bus or lorry movements a five minutes interval between each group of six vehicles will be maintained.

   (c) No "double banking."

   (d) All units, except a column consisting of entirely mechanically propelled vehicles, will observe the regulation clock hour halts.

   (e) In the event of a vehicle breaking down, it will at once be cleared from the road.

   (f) An Officer will march in rear of each Battery, Section D.A.C., Company, or similar Unit.

   (g) A free passage for traffic moving in the opposite direction will be kept.

   (h) On arrival at destination, main traffic routes will at once be cleared.

S E C R E T.

> ROYAL ENGINEERS,
> H.Q.
> 16TH DIVISION.
> No. 3337/6
> Date

C. R. E's Instructions as to Action in the event of an Enemy withdrawal. No.5

1. Para: 4 Instructions No. 1 is cancelled.

2. The special duties of the 2 Sections placed at the disposal of the Brigadiers in the Line are:-

   (1) To assist the Infantry to consolidate captured trenches and tactical points.

   (2) To mark out and prepare overland tracks, and improve existing roads and tracks with any material available on the site.

   (3) To remove obstructions from roads.

   (4) To repair existing bridges, and improvise Infantry bridges over streams and gaps.

   (5) To look for and improve temporary Command Posts (other than ruined dug-outs) for Brigade, Battalion and Company H.Q.

   (6) To reconnoitre Enemy dumps, and have lists made of Engineer material available generally in the area.

   (7) To reconnoitre and report on forward roads, tramways and railways.

   (8) Open up and improve water supplies.

   (9) General R.E. work or supervision of work required by the Brigade Commanders.

3. The special duties of the parties of the 174th Tunnelling Company, R.E. will be:-

   (1) To act as reconnaissance parties for mines and booby traps.

   (2) To repair and improve deep dug-outs selected for Command Posts and accommodation.

18th Novr. 1917.

RP Mutterwath
Lieut-Colonel, R.E.
C. R. E. 16th Division.

Copies to:-

155th Field Coy.R.E.	47th Inf. Bde.
156th Field Coy.R.E.	48th Inf. Bde.
157th Field Coy.R.E.	49th Inf. Bde.
174th Tunn. Coy.R.E.	C. R. E.
11th Hants (P)	(War Diary 2).
16th Div. 'G'	
16th Div. Arty.	

SECRET.　　　　　　　　　3340/14. appendix 4

CONSOLIDATION OF TUNNEL TRENCH AND TUNNEL SUPPORT.

Synopsis of proposed Work.

1. **WIRE.**

    All unwired portions of the front line to be wired at once, and additional wire to be erected to make the wire defence along the whole front and flanks thoroughly strong.

2. **FRONT AND SUPPORT LINES.**

    TUNNEL TRENCH. Dig out mud, and lay trenchboards on pickets. Select sites for 'T' heads, dig and revet (a good many 'T' heads exist, which will require deepening and revetting). Later, join two or more 'T' heads to form defensive posts. In Left and Cent Brigades it is proposed to site a post opposite each alternate Tunnel Entrance.

    TUNNEL SUPPORT. Dig out mud, and lay trenchboards. Construct posts as for TUNNEL TRENCH. Later, provide splinter-proof cover for garrison of each post.

    NOTE:- All posts to be provided with bomb and ammunition recesses.

3. **BLOCKS.** Construct solid blocks with bombing post and L.G. or T.M. Emplacements in:-

    (1) JOVE - PLUTO TRENCH.
    (2) VULCAN ALLEY.
    (3) FAG ALLEY.
    (4) OLDENBURG LANE.
    (5) OLDENBURG - PRINCE CROSS TRENCH.
    (6) PRINCE LANE.

4. **COMMUNICATION TRENCHES.(NEW).** Deepen, cutting sides to natural slope, and trenchboard.

    (1) JOVE LANE.
    (2) MARS LANE.
    (3) BOW LANE.
    (4) MINERVA LANE.
    (5) JUNO LANE.
    (6) MOLE LANE.

    COMMUNICATION TRENCHES (OLD). Clear blown places in QUEEN'S, NELLY and JANET LANES.

5. **BURG SUPPORT.** To be cleared where blown.

    CRAGSIDE.)　　To be dismantled, and stores used for work
    SAP 4.　　)　　elsewhere.

6. **THE TUNNEL.** (1) A Tunnelling reconnaissance to be made.

    (2) All mines to be removed from the shafts and gallery.

    (3) Repairs to entrances, and damaged places to be put in hand.

    (4) All entrances to be marked starting with No. 1 at LUMP LANE and running South.

7. GENERAL.

   (1) Notice Boards to be erected at junctions of new C.T's with old front line, and new Support and Front lines.

   (2) All MEBUS to be marked with notice boards.

   (3) Boards with coordinates to be erected in front line.

8. RESPONSIBILITY FOR WORK.

   1,2,3.   Infantry assisted by Field Companies, R.E.
   4, 5.   11th Hants (Pioneers).
   6.(1),(2),(3).   174th Tunnelling Coy. R.E.
   8 (4), 7.   Field Companies, R.E.

25th Novr. 1917.

R/M Butterworth
Lieut-Colonel, R.E.
C. R. E. 16th Division.

Distribution:-

G. O. C.
16th Div. 'G'.
47th Inf. Bde.
48th Inf. Bde.
49th Inf. Bde.
155th Fld. Coy. R.E.
156th Fld. Coy. R.E.
157th Fld. Coy. R.E.
174th Tunn. Coy. R.E.
11th Hants (P).
C.E. VI Corps.
C. R. E.
File (2).

WAR DIARY

FOR MONTH OF DECEMBER, 1917.

VOLUME : - 25.

UNIT :- Headquarters 16th Div. Engineers.

Army Form C. 2118.

WAR DIARY
or
INTELLIGENCE SUMMARY.
(Erase heading not required.)

DECEMBER 1917   HQ RE 16 DIV

Place	Date	Hour	Summary of Events and Information	Remarks and references to Appendices
BERAMIES	1.12.17		Water consolidation continued.	
"	2.12.17		ditto	
			- 16 Div Ey OO No 36 issued (appendix 1)	Appendix 1
" & YTRES	3.12.17		D.H.Q. (WINTER) moved to YTRES - 5" Corps Area.	
YTRES	4.12.17		Fd Coy. moved to Bde Groups in 5 Corps Area - 155 ROCQUIGNY - 158 - MEAULENCOURT - 157 BARASTRE.	
" & PERONNE	5.12.17		DHQ (WINTER) transferred to 7" Corps Area & visited at FLAMICOURT (PERONNE)	
			CRE visited HQ 55th Div - 155 + 157 Fd Coys move into 49" Bde	
			to TINCOURT AREA. - 155 - COURCELLES - 157 Fd Coy - BUIRE.	
	6.12.17		CRE visited CRE 55th Div to take over RE work - 155 + 157	
			Fd Coys move forward to relieve Commanding Coys of 55th Div.	
			Pioneers and Tunnellers reconnaissance parties	
			182nd Coy move to TIN COURT area under orders of 47 Inf Bde.	
VILLERS FAUCON	7/12/19		HQ RE to VILLERS FAUCON, 156 Fd Coy to VILLERS FAUCON relieving 423 Field Coy RE.	
" "	8/12/19		155 Fd Coy, 157 Fd Coy RE in TEMPURE defences 156 Telegraphs RMS Coy defences	

Army Form C. 2118.

WAR DIARY
or
INTELLIGENCE SUMMARY.
(Erase heading not required.)

HQ RE 16 DIV

DECEMBER 1917

Instructions regarding War Diaries and Intelligence Summaries are contained in F.S. Regs., Part II. and the Staff Manual respectively. Title pages will be prepared in manuscript.

Place	Date	Hour	Summary of Events and Information	Remarks and references to Appendices
VILLERS FAUCON	9/12/17		Work as above	
"	10/12/17		2 sections 157 relieving & relieved 1st Fld Coy forward Battalion Reserves at 1st Coy HQ at VILLERS FAUCON	
"	11/12/17		work as above	
"	12/12/17		work as above	
"	13/12/17		work as above	
"	14/12/17		work as above	
"	15/12/17		work as above	
"	16/12/17		work as above Capt RGTOTTENHAM ADC leave in accordance Adj RE	
"	17/12/17		work as above	
"	18/12/17		work as above Capt the RESPADLING 155 adj. to leave Lt ABSTENNINGS RE acting	
"	19/12/17		work as above	
"	20/12/17		work as above	
"	21/12/17		work as above	
"	22/12/17		work as above	
"	23/12/17		work as above CRES orders 155 to 40 Divn	
"	24/12/17		157 Fd Coy takes over RONSSOY defences from 155. 155 Kelly Bret & harvey to VILLERS FAUCON	Appendix 2

WAR DIARY
or
INTELLIGENCE SUMMARY. HQ RE 16 DIV

Army Form C. 2118.

DECEMBER 1917

Place	Date	Hour	Summary of Events and Information	Remarks and references to Appendices
	25/12/17		Lt Col Smith went O/1 cas w Coy W40 missed 155# 157 Field Coy went in line 15 & Field coy out	Appdcs 3
	26/12/17		under as above	Appendices
	27/12/17		CRE's orders No 41 relief of 156 & 157 Fd Coy Rengs missed, went as above	
	28/12/17		went as above	
	29/12/17		156 Fd Coy RE relieved 157 Fd Coy in the line. 157 Fd Coy in rear Appx	
	30/12/17		Appx issued for MM relieve by 157 Fd Coy 156 Fd Coy for grenelle CROISILLES went as above	
	31/12/17		went as above	

C. R. E'S ORDER NO. 40.

23rd December, 1917.

(1)   The following moves and reliefs will take place:-

156th Field Company, R.E. to billets at TINCOURT on 26th Decr. 1917, for rest and training.

(2) <u>Arrangements for Work.</u>

O.C. 155th Field Coy. R.E. will take over work in hand on LEMPIRE VILLAGE DEFENCES.

O.C. 11th Hants (P) will take over work on Battalion hutments in Railway cuttings W. of ST EMILIE.

Officers concerned will arrange to take over on 24th Decr.

(3)   156th Fld. Coy. will move at hour and by route selected by O.C.

Arrival and location in TINCOURT to be reported to this Office.

(4)   O.C. will arrange for his billets with TOWN MAJOR TINCOURT. Arrangements will be made with TOWN MAJOR VILLERS FAUCON to retain and safeguard the present billets during the Companies absence.

R.F.A. Butterworth
Lieut-Colonel, R.E.
C. R. E. 16th Division.

Distribution:-

155th Field Coy. R.E.
156th Field Coy. R.E.
157th Field Coy. R.E.
11th Hants (P).
16th Div 'G'.
47th Inf. Bde.
48th Inf. Bde.
49th Inf. Bde.
C. R. E.
War Diary (2)
File.

War diary

C. R. E'S ORDER No. 40/1.

26th December, 1917.

Amendments to C. R. E's Order No. 40 dated 23rd December, 1917.

(1) Para: (1). Owing to inadequate accommodation at TINCOURT 156th Field Coy. R.E. will remain in their present billets at VILLERS FAUCON. Coy. H.Q. at E.22.d.8.4.

(2) Para: (2) No change.

(3) Paras: (3) and (4). Cancelled.

Lieut, R.E.

for C. R. E. 18th Division.

Copies to all recipients of O. No.40.

SECRET.

C. R. E's ORDER No. 41.

27th December, 1917.

1. 156th Field Company, R.E. will relieve 157th Field Company, R.E. in the Line, Left Section, on 29th/30th December.

2. On completion of relief the Coy's will be disposed as follows:-

    156th Fld. Coy.   H.Q. and 2 Sections. VILLERS FAUCON.
                                       2 Sections RONSSOY.

    157th Fld. Coy.   VILLERS FAUCON.

3. Work will be taken over on 29th Decr., a statement being made out of all work in hand and proposed, with detail of working parties, and a copy sent to C.R.E. by evening of 30th Decr.

4. All trench maps, and air-photographs of the Left Section will be transferred.

R.J.F. Butterworth

Lieut-Colonel, R.E.

C. R. E. 16th Division.

Distribution:-

    155th Fld. Coy. R.E.
    156th Fld. Coy. R.E.
    157th Fld. Coy. R.E.
    16th Div. 'G'
    47th Inf. Bde.
    49th Inf. Bde.
    C.R.E.
    File.
    War Diary (2).

WAR DIARY,

FOR MONTH OF JANUARY, 1918.

VOLUME :- 26.

UNIT :- H.Q. 16th Div. Engineers.

Army Form C. 2118.

WAR DIARY
or
INTELLIGENCE SUMMARY.
(Erase heading not required.)

Instructions regarding War Diaries and Intelligence Summaries are contained in F. S. Regs., Part II. and the Staff Manual respectively. Title pages will be prepared in manuscript.

Place	Date	Hour	Summary of Events and Information	Remarks and references to Appendices
VILLERS FAUCON	1.1.18 to 3.1.18		{ Normal trench work — work in main forward defence line.	reg
	4.1.18		Cpl. STRAPPING returned from leave & took over duties of Orderly R.	reg
	5.1.18 to 12.1.18		{ as on 1.1.'18	reg
	12.1.18		Held R.F.A. BUTTERWORTH started for G.H.Q. conference & CRES.	reg
			Major P.F. WHITTALL took over duties of CRE.	reg
	13.1.18 to 21.1.18		{ as on 1.1.18 — Lieut JENNINGS went on leave 15.1.18.	reg
	22.1.18		RWR & HQ RE. moved into new camp near TINCOURT	reg
TINCOURT J.4.b.	23.1.18 to 31.1.18		{ Normal trench work —	

R.E. Stewart Capt R.E.
for CRE

WAR DIARY.

FOR MONTH OF FEBRUARY, 1918.

VOLUME:- 24

UNIT:- HQ 16th Div Engineers

Army Form C.

WAR DIARY
or
INTELLIGENCE SUMMARY. HQ RE 16 DN   February 1918
(Erase heading not required.)

Instructions regarding War Diaries and Intelligence Summaries are contained in F.S. Regs., Part II and the Staff Manual respectively. Title pages will be prepared in manuscript.

Place	Date	Hour	Summary of Events and Information	Remarks and references to Appendices
TINCOURT	1/2/18		155, 156 & 157 Fd Coys at VILLERS FAUCON CRE's orders No 4 & 5 issued. Lt/Col R.P.A. BUTTERWORTH proceeds from Appendix 1.	
J.17.b.9.6	2/2/18		Major WHITTALL RE q/CRE returned to 157 Fd Coy R/D	leave
"	3/2/18		155 Froops in left sector. 157 others in Reserve Area. 156 Fd Coy 7 Right sector R/D Capt WIVENDEN R/D R/D	
"	4/2/18		Work as above. Lt R B JENNINGS returned from leave. R/D	Noyes from leave R/D
"	5/2/18		Work as above R/D	
"	6/2/18		Work as above R/D	
"	7/2/18		Work as above R/D	
"	8/2/18		Work as above R/D	
"	9/2/18		Work as above R/D	
"	10/2/18		Work as above CRE's Instructions No 4 & 6 issued R/D	Appendix 2
"	11/2/18		CRE Order No 47 issued R/D	Appendix 3
"	12/2/18		Work as above. N.S.C.	
"	13/2/18		Work as above R/D	
"	14/2/18		Work as above (Continued Int) R/D	
"	15/2/18		157 Fd Coy to work in left sector (EPEHY) 155 centre sector & 156 right sector R/D	
"	16/2/18		Work as above R/D	
"	17/2/18		Work as above R/D	
"	18/2/18		Work as above R/D	
"	19/2/18		Work as above R/D	
"	20/2/18		Work as above R/D	
"	21/2/18		Work as above R/D	

Army Form C. 2118.

WAR DIARY
or
INTELLIGENCE SUMMARY.
(Erase heading not required.)

HQ RE 16 Div

Army Nyff / Johnny Nyff

Instructions regarding War Diaries and Intelligence Summaries are contained in F. S. Regs., Part II. and the Staff Manual respectively. Title pages will be prepared in manuscript.

Place	Date	Hour	Summary of Events and Information	Remarks and references to Appendices
TINCOURT J.17.b.9.b	22/3/18		Instructions RE	
	23/3/18		Instructions RE	
	24/3/18		CRE orders No 48 issued RE	Appendix F
	25/3/18		Work on line RE	
	26/3/18		CRE orders No 49 issued RE	Appendix G
	27/3/18		CRE orders No 50 issued RE	
	28/3/18		CRE orders S1A issued cancelling No 50. order No 52 also issued RE	

Signed for CRE 16 Div

SECRET.
==========

C. R. E'S ORDER No. 45.

1st February 1918.

1. 155th Field Company, R.E. will relieve 157th Field Company, R.E. in Left Sub-Sector on night 3rd/4th Feb. 1918.

   O.C. 155th Fld. Coy. will arrange to carry out work in back areas on 3rd February and O.C. 157th Fld. Coy. will arrange for work in line on night 3rd/4th.

   Work will be changed over on 4th February.

2. On completion of relief Companies will be disposed as follows:-

   157th Field Coy. R.E.   VILLERS FAUCON.

   155th Field Coy. R.E.
      H.Q. and 2 Sections.   VILLERS FAUCON.
      2 Sections.   RONSSOY.

3. A detail of work handed over, showing projected work and detail of working parties will be made out and a copy forwarded to C.R.E. by evening of 4th Feb.

4. All trench maps, and air photographs of areas will be handed over.

5. Completion of relief to be notified to this Office.

6. ACKNOWLEDGE.

                                   R.E. Stradling
                                   Captain, R.E.
                              for C. R. E. 16th Division.

   Distribution:-

       C. R. E.
       155th Field Coy. R.E.
       156th Field Coy. R.E.
       157th Field Coy. R.E.
       16th Div. 'G'.
       47th Inf. Bde.
       48th Inf. Bde.
       49th Inf. Bde.
       11th Hants (P).
       --   File.
       War Diary (2).

SECRET.

C. R. E'S INSTRUCTIONS No.46.

10th February, 1918.

ANTI-TANK DEFENCE.

Orders have been received for the Divisional Front to be defended by Minefields.

The minefields will be laid out, fences erected, and excavations made, under arrangements made by the C.R.E., the mines will be placed, fuzed and maintained under the C.R.A.

Secret Map "M"/____ showing the location of the minefields, counter-attack passages and gaps is being prepared, and will be issued later.
Drawing No. 293 shewing details of layout etc. is attached.

The minefields will be indicated by red-discs attached to the top strand of wire in each bay of the protective fence, and counter-attack passages and gaps marked with Camouflaged boards. The gaps will be normally at intervals of 110 yards, and across the usual tracks.

Minefields will be laid out in sections of 110 yards, requiring 110 mines. Extreme accuracy is essential to obviate future accidents in maintenance or removal of charges.

Officers Commanding Field Companies will be responsible for the laying out of the minefields on their Brigade Front, and will inform C.R.E. when a section is ready for charging.

R.F.A. Butterworth
Lieut.Colonel, R.E.
C. R. E. 16th Division.

Distribution:-

    155th Field Company, R.E.
    156th Field Company, R.E.
    157th Field Company, R.E.
    16th Div. 'G'.)
    16th Div. Arty.)
    47th Inf. Bde.) for information.
    48th Inf. Bde.)
    49th Inf. Bde.)
    11th Hants (P).)
    C.E. VII Corps.)
    C. R. E.
        File (2)

SECRET.

C. R. E'S ORDER No. 47.

11th February, 1918.

1. 49th Inf. Bde. (less M.G. Coy) will relieve 64th Div. (less M.G. Coy) in Left Section of 16th Div. Front from X.19.b.2.4. to X.26.d.50.45. on night 14th/15th February.

2. In connection with the above, the following reliefs of technical troops will take place:-

   (a) 157th Field Co.R.E. will relieve 126th Field Co. R.E. on 14th Feb. Details to be arranged direct between Field Company Commanders.
      126th Field Co.R.E. will work until evening of 14th/15th and 157th Field Co.R.E. will start on morning of 15th.
      There will be no work on night 14th/15th on account of reliefs.
      O.C. 157th Field Co.R.E. will arrange with 40th Inf. Bde. for working parties for 15th inst.
      There will be no change of billets.

   (b) O.C. 11th Hants (P) will detail 1 Company to take over work on RED LINE from 14th Northumberland Fusiliers (P), starting work on 15th inst. Details of reliefs should be arranged direct between Battalion Commanders.
      11th Hants (P) will also take over billets for 1 Company in PEIZIERE from 14th Northumberland Fus.

3. Completion of reliefs will be reported to this Office.

4. ACKNOWLEDGE.

R E Stradling

Captain, R.E.

for C. R. E. 16th Division.

Distribution:-

      155th Field Coy.R.E.
      156th Field Coy.R.E.
      157th Field Coy.R.E.
      11th Hants (P).
      16th Div. 'G'.
      16th Div. 'Q'.
      47th Inf. Bdo.
      48th Inf. Bde.
      49th Inf. Bdo.
   C.R.E. 21st Div.
      126th Field Co.R.E.
      14th Northumberland (P).
   File.
   W.D. (2).

SECRET.
============

C. R. E'S ORDER No. 48.

WARNING ORDER.

24th February, 1918.

1. The 21st Division will probably relieve the 16th Division in the line on or about 1st March.

2. The following reliefs of technical troops will probably take place and the respective Field Companies and pioneers 21st Division have been instructed to get into touch with Units they are relieving:-

16th Div. Unit.	21st Div. Unit.
155th Field Coy.	126th Field Coy.
156th Field Coy.	97th Field Coy.
157th Field Coy.	98th Field Coy.
11th Hants (P)	14th N. Fusrs (P).

3. Field Company Commanders and O.C. 11th Hants (P) will please forward to C.R.E. copy of handing over programme of work (in progress and proposed) together with tracing corrected to date of relief.

4. ACKNOWLEDGE.

R.E. Standing

Captain, R.E.

for C. R. E. 16th Division.

Copies:-
 155th Field Coy.R.E.
 156th Field Coy.R.E.
 157th Field Coy.R.E.
 11th Hants (P).
 C.R.E. 21st Div.
 File.
 W.D.

SECRET.

C. R. E's ORDER No. 49.

26th February, 1918.

1. C.Y.11 Dump will be taken over by 21st Division on morning of 3rd March.

2. The Workshops will not be handed over but will remain under charge of Sapper KEMP, who will keep the present Workshop personnel and in addition 6 of the Infantry working party with him.

3. The N.C.O. i/c 21st Div. Dump will visit C.Y.11 on 1st March for instruction in arrangements of Dump.

   The N.C.O. and party to relieve Sergeant McCLELLAN will report at ROISEL on 1st March and 16th Div. party will march out to TINCOURT on evening of same day.
   This party will report to C.R.E's Office for work on morning of 2nd March.

4. On relief the Dump party (less those mentioned in para:2) will march to TINCOURT for billets and will report to C.R.E's Office for work on the day following.

5. R.S.M. Green with the undermentioned will join H.Q.R.E. on relief:-

   Corpl. McLoughlan.
   Dr. Gray.
   Dr. Facey. (with Limbered G.S. wagon).

6. Telephone at present at C.Y. 11 will be handed in to C.R.E's Office.

7. ACKNOWLEDGE.

R.E. Stradling
Captain, R.E.
for C. R. E. 16th Division.

Distribution:-

W.O. i/c R.E. Dump.
C.R.E. 21st Div.
O i/c Roisel R.E. Dump.
16th Div. 'G'.
16th Div. 'Q'.
155th Fld. Co.R.E.
156th Fld. Co.R.E.
157th Fld. Co.R.E.

S E C R E T.

C. R. E'S ORDER NO. 50.

27th February, 1918.

Reference Warning Order No. 48.

The reliefs of technical troops will take place on 1st and 2nd March. Details as under.

2. **155th Field Coy.R.E.** Relieving Unit 126th Field Coy.R.E.
Forward billets at RONSSOY will be handed over on 1st, and work will cease in the line that afternoon.
The Company will remain in their present billet at VILLERS FAUCON, and work in the BATTLE ZONE.

3. **156th Field Coy.R.E.** Relieving Unit 97th Field Coy.R.E.
Company billets at ST. EMILIE, Transport Lines VILLERS FAUCON and Forward Billets in RONSSOY will be handed over on 1st, and the Company will proceed by route march to HAUTE ALLAINES for training. Work will cease in the line after nightwork 28th Feb/1st March.
Advance party will be sent forward on 1st March to take over billets from the Town Major HAUTE ALLAINES.

4. **157th Field Coy.R.E.** Relieving Unit 98th Field Coy.R.E.
Forward billets in EPEHY will be handed over on 2nd March, and work will cease in the line that afternoon.
Two Sections will start work on hutting at J.10.b. on the morning of 1st March, and the remainder of the Company on 3rd March.
The Company will remain in their present billets at VILLERS FAUCON.

5. **11th Hants (pioneers).** Relieving Unit 14th Northumberland Fus. (P).
Forward billets at RONSSOY will be handed over on 1st March, and work will cease that afternoon.
The Battalion will remain in its present billets at VILLERS FAUCON.
One Company will start work on 3rd March in the BATTLE ZONE. Details of work will be forwarded to O.C.

6. All details of reliefs will be arranged between O.C's concerned.

7. ACKNOWLEDGE.

RE Stradling

Captain, R.E.

for C. R. E. 16th Division.

Distribution:-

155th Field Coy.R.E.   File.
156th Field Coy.R.E.   W.D. (2).
157th Field Coy.R.E.
 11th Hants (P).
C.R.E. 21st Div.
16th Div. 'G'.
16th Div. 'Q'.
47th Inf. Bde.
48th Inf. Bde.
49th Inf. Bde.
16th Div. Signals.
C.R.E.

S E C R E T.

C. R. E's ORDER No. 51.A.

28th February, 1918.

1. C. R.E's order No. 50 of 27th February, is cancelled.

2. 157th Field Coy.R.E. will be relieved by 98th Field Coy.R.E. on 1st March and after handing over forward billets at RONSSOY, the forward Sections will proceed to Company H.Q. VILLERS FAUCON.

3. Company of 11th Hants (P) will be relieved in EPEHY by Company of 14th Northumberland Fusrs. (P) on 1st March.

4. Details of reliefs will be arranged between O.C's concerned.

R E Stradling
for
Lieut.Colonel, R.E.
C. R. E. 16th Division.

Distribution:-

    155th Field Coy.R.E.
    156th Field Coy.R.E.
    157th Field Coy.R.E.
    11th Hants (P).
    C.R.E. 21st Div.
    16th Div. 'G'.
    16th Div. 'Q'.
    47th Inf. Bde.
    48th Inf. Bde.
    49th Inf. Bde.
    16th Div.Signals.
    C.R.E.
    File.
    W.D. (2).

S E C R E T.

C. R. E'S ORDER NO. 52.

28th February, 1918.

1. The Fifth Army have issued orders for Divisions to hold their battle fronts with two Brigades in the Line.

2. Consequent on above the 47th and 48th Brigades remain in the line, while the 49th Bde. will be withdrawn into support.

3. All reliefs of Field Companies and 11th Hants (Pioneers) (with the exception of the relief of 157th Field Coy.R.E. by 98th Field Coy.R.E. and the EPEHY Company of 11th Hants by 14th Northumberland Fusiliers (P)) are cancelled.

4. The following will be the detail of work and distribution of technical troops:-

(1) 156th Field Coy.R.E.

Distribution.

 (a)   1 Section.   Front Line System.
 (b)   1 Section.   RED LINE.
 (c)   1 Section.   RED LINE SUPPORT.
 (d)   1 Section.   In Reserve.

Detail of Work.

 (a) Continue work on posts and firebays.- DUNCAN AVENU and CAUSEWAY. Prepare QUEUCHETTES COPSE for all round defence.

 (b) THISTLE and SHAMROCK. Dig and revet firebays, afterwards joining up with travel trench. Wire strongly front of SHAMROCK TRENCH from BASSE BOULOGNE SOUTH to ORCHARD POST.

 (c) SHAMROCK SUPPORT. Dig and revet firebays, join up with travel trench. Wire.

 (d) Put billets into state of defence.

  2 Companies will be detailed from Reserve Brigade for work on (b) and (c).

(2) 155th Field Coy.R.E.

Distribution.

 (a)   1 Section.   Front Line System.
 (b)   1 Section.   RED LINE and RED LINE SUPPORT.
 (c)   1 Section.   YELLOW LINE.
 (d)   1 Section.   In Reserve.

Detail of Work.

 (a) Continue work on BIRD - MULE - ROOME and OCKENDEN.

 (b) Continue work on RIDGE RESERVE NORTH, cut C.T. forward from TETARD WOOD to ROOME, and back to join 21st Div. RED LINE at F.2.a.1.2.
  Deepen and revet firebays in Support Line starting with DEELISH POST.

(c)

(c) put up wire entanglement (2 bands) from 21st Div. Boundary about F.7.a.Central to cross-road in F.8.a.6.3.
Construct and wire in small posts at:-

(1) F.8.a.16.05.   (2) F.7.d.83.83.
(3) F.7.d.50.62.   (4) F.7.d.10.73.

(d) place billets in state of defence, and assist generally in preparation of VILLERS FAUCON Defences.

NOTE:- 2 Companies from Reserve Brigade will be available for work on (c), and all available labour from Support Battalion of Brigade in the line on (b)

3. 157th Field Coy. R.E.

Distribution.

(a) 1 Section.   ST EMILIE Defences.
(b) 1 Section.   Switches.
(c) 1 Section.   BROWN LINE.
(d) 1 Section.   In Reserve.

Detail of Work.

(a) Continue work on Machine Gun emplacements, revetment of posts, and wiring.

(b) Join up RAPERIE SWITCH, deepen and revet firebays in BOIS SWITCH (starting at WOOD POST and working West).

(c) Join up posts S. of ST. EMILIE - RONSSOY ROAD, and improve wire.

(d) place billets in state of defence, and assist generally in preparation of VILLERS FAUCON Defences.

NOTE:- 1 Battalion will be available from Reserve Brigade for work on (a),(b), (c).

4. 11th Hants (P).

Distribution.

(a) 1 Company.   RONSSOY DEFENCES.
(b) 1 Company.   RED LINE (South)
(c) 1 Company.   RED LINE (Central).
(d) 1 Company.   In Reserve.

Detail of Work.

(a) Continue work according to programme, giving preference to provision of firebays, and deepening of retrenchment on East side of BELLICOURT - EPEHY road.

(b) Improve ROSE TRENCH, and provide Fire-bays. Strengthen wire with additional band, Construct Support Line to ROSE TRENCH connecting RIDGE RESERV SOUTH with THISTLE TRENCH, and wire.

(c) provide firebays, and deepen RED SUPPORT Line N.W. Corner of LEMPIRE to DEELISH POST (exclusive).

(d) place billets in state of defence, and assist generally in preparation of VILLERS FAUCON Defences.

NOTE:-

NOTE:- Two Companies from Reserve Brigade will be available for work on ROSE TRENCH, two Companies on RED LINE SUPPORT, while the Support Battalion in RONSSOY will provide working parties for its defences.

5. The Adjutant, R.E. will arrange for tool dumps (consisting of 50 Shovels and 10 picks) to be made at the following points:-

    (a) RAPERIE SWITCH.

        (1) RAPERIE.
        (2) CLIFF POST.
        (3) TEE POST.
        (4) QUARRY POST.
        (5) TEMPLE POST.

    (b) BOIS SWITCH.

        (1) WOOD POST.
        (2) MOON POST.
        (3) Firebay, F.14.c.5.2.
        (4) TWO WAYS POST.

    (c) MALASSISE SWITCH.

        (1) In quarry at F.13.b.5.7.
        (2) post F.13.b.5. 1.
        (3) post F.13.d.3.7.

    (d) BROWN LINE.

        (1) post F.19.b.1.6.
        (2) Post F.19.a.75.10.
        (3) post F.19.c.9.4.
        (4) Hollow Road F.25.a.8.8.
        (5) Bank at F.25.b.15.10.

The number of tools in each dump will be increased to 100 shovels and 20 picks when available. Each dump will be marked with a board " RESERVE DUMP - NOT TO BE TOUCHED"

6. Captain R.B. JENNINGS, R.E. will be responsible for preparation and keeping up to date of maps of defences, and will arrange for a constructive system of notice boards, direction boards and labels in the BATTLE ZONE, which will be prepared at the Dump, and erected under his orders and supervision.

7. Work on the Anti-Tank Minefields will be carried on by the Special parties of Infantry attached to Field Companies, under supervision of O.C. Field Coy. concerned.

8. ACKNOWLEDGE.

                                              R.J.A. Butterworth
                                              Lieut. Colonel, R.E.

                                              C. R. E. 16th Division.

Distribution over.

16th Divisional Engineers

C. R. E.

16th DIVISION

MARCH 1918

Appendices attached:-

Report on Operations 21st March to 3rd April.
Operation Orders.

Army Form C. 2118.

WAR DIARY
or
INTELLIGENCE SUMMARY.
(Erase heading not required.)

HQ RE 16 Div   MARCH 1918
Vol 28

Place	Date	Hour	Summary of Events and Information	Remarks and references to Appendices
TINCOURT T.1.b.4.b	1		157 Fd Coy provides left section (Wordoms) to Co Dfce Right sector 155 Central sector	
	2		work as above	RK9
	3		work as above	RK9
	4		work as above	RK9
	5		2/Lt PURNELL arrived on reinforcement to 155 Field Coy RE work as above	RK9
	6		4/Lt CORNALL transferred to 157 Fd Coy RE work as above	RK9
	7		work as above	RK9
	8		ORs wounded and onto section work as above	RK9
	9		work as above	RK9
	10		157 Fd Right sector 156 works on St SMAIT defences - Brown Line 155 Left sector	RK9
	11		work as above	RK9
	12		Capt J O'Sullivan 155 3mo leave	RK9
	13		Lt WEBSTER 15 Fd Coy RE from leave Capt O'Sullivan left troops 15.2.18 reports 1/55 Battle Station	RK9
	14		Capt RG MacLure 155 Fd Co to leave on Bologne 157 ordered to Fra DH tomp of emergency 1918	RK9
	15		Battle Stations for Fd Coys	RK9
	16		Battle Stations " " "	RK9

Army Form C. 2118.

WAR DIARY
or
INTELLIGENCE SUMMARY.
(Erase heading not required.)

HQ RE 16 Div

MARCH 1918

Place	Date	Hour	Summary of Events and Information	Remarks and references to Appendices
INCOURT J.17.b.9.6	17		Brute Stations working normal [R/B]	Batt
	18		" " " " [R/B]	
	19		" " " " [R/B]	
	20		" " " " [R/B]	
	21	4/40am	Heavy enemy bombardment commenced. Main Battle Station carried 5.40am. Telephones to ISS [R/B]	
			156 cut by 6.45am. The Corp ordered to withdraw transport to safer place 10.45am. [R/B]	
		10/45	CRE's Instruction for Defensive issued. 6 year Corps. [R/B]	
		11/3	Div HQ Shelled Shrapnel + 4.2 HE [R/B]	
		1/55 pm	Seven EA over camp. [R/B]	
		2/0 pm	Enemy reported holding RONSSOY & RAPERIE switch. Lt WEBSTER & Lt STEMMLER with others [R/B]	
			2 Forward OE sections of RONSSOY carried VILLERS FAUCON having fought their way back Lt BAXTER WIP CRE no 56 & 156 & 11 Hants[?] Appendix 1	
		4/15	wounded. Lt CORNELL killed shortly before arrival from RONSSOY [R/B]	
		6/15	Capt Penn MO retired from VILLERS FAUCON. Capt MacLaughlin arrived with the two lorries from [R/B]	
			RE dump VILLERS FAUCON	
		5.0 pm	CRE motors GOC [R/B]	
		8.15 pm	CRE's order via S7 received G/phone G.157+G.155 x withdrawal to Green Line [R/B]	Appendix 2

WAR DIARY
INTELLIGENCE SUMMARY
Army Form C. 2118.

HQ RE 16DIV
MARCH

Place	Date	Hour	Summary of Events and Information	Remarks and references to Appendices
TINCOURT J17.9.b	21/3/18	pm 2/45	K.1.C 155 Rd Regt/157 & 156 K.13.c. & J.18.b. 157's retro to fire BELLUMP Villa RRJ	appendix 3
			FAUCON cancelled 4/30pm 156 Rd Coy RE in BROWN LINE 3340/pls & various	
		9/10	All Villa FAUCON dump pacht carried except 14th HARNEY 1to injure arrive wounded RRJ	
	22/3/18 1/40		180 Tunnellis personnel at DHQ required their Coy in return from 6 "590" RRJ	
			St WHITEDOVE 156 Rd Coy reported killed RRJ	
		2.45am	ORE received instructions to O2 155/157 at DHQ to work in GREEN LINE RRJ	
		5/45-	Enemy bombardment began on our front, increasing in volume almost to 8am. Very misty RRJ	
		9.10-	VICE-BRIGADIER appears Capt Turner RAMC head up to Coy with ORE (ie GREEN LINE	RRJ
		10/30-	ORE returned from GREEN LINE 5000 rounds S.A.A. sent up to 155/157 midday 1/30 ORE 6 DOINET 1/45 RRJ
DOINGT I.36a advanced at TINCOURT J.17.9.b. 6		11.30pm	TINCOURT wood shelled 3/40pm DHQ shelled HE & shrapnel RRJ	
		4/30pm	5W0 shelling DHQ LT HAUCH 155 Reder & his section injured with instructions to return to DHQ RRJ	
		4/50	16 Div G move to advance 600 yds west of old DHQ 5 or 6 EA flying in DHQ bombing RRJ	
		4/15	+ machine gunning a previd GREEN LINE Support and small open Ko.C.1.1 heavily shelled RRJ
			Read instructions from CRE by telephone Houlette & Coy turn up to go to DOINET GREEN SUPPORT UA	
			continue shelling SP's 1 reported to G while on departure & left 7.10 pm	
	7/15		orders received 157 Rd Coy Greens in area 155 at COURCELLES isse 115 at DOINET I36a RRJ	

Army Form C. 2118.

WAR DIARY
or
INTELLIGENCE SUMMARY.
(Erase heading not required.)

MARCH 1918

16 Corps RE HQ

Place	Date	Hour	Summary of Events and Information	Remarks and references to Appendices
DOINGT T.36.a	22/3/18	6.45pm	155 ordered to reconcentrate at Gouzeaucourt T.32.c. 158 Gouzeaucourt T.36.c. RHQ	
		10.15p	Ordered by 'G' to be prepared to move at one minute's notice	
	23/3/18	3.0 am	Recent order to be ready to move off cancelled 10.30pm	
		6.40am	Orders arrived to move under orders 48 I. Bde 155 + 156 ordered to BIACHES	
BIACHES H.30.d.2.7		7.50am	HQ RE to H.30.d. Biaches. ORE by car Capt Jennings + Lt WEBSTER with transport. arrived BIACHES 10.50 am RHQ	
		2pm	Received orders to move an armoured portable to HERBECOURT. moved off ORE by car Capt Jennings 157 RHQ Lt WEBSTER with transport	
HERBECOURT H.25.d.		3.10pm	HQ RE arrived 155 + 156 + 157 Transport himself on roadside from H.25 & G.H.30.d. 157 RHQ	
			Dismounted with 48 I.B. on line	
		6.15pm	ORE sent down to 155 + 156. 6.45pm OC 157's position (report arrived say no he was	
			on west bank of Somme at I.31.a.1.2). 9pm ORE from the Coys. RHQ	
		8pm	ORE orders Capt Jennings + Lt WEBSTER with transport. Ord orders Coys 155 156 + 157 Transport ordered to proceed to East of CAPPY. RHQ	
CAPPY		11pm	HQ RE arrived CAPPY. 155 156 Coys & 157 Transport ordered to proceed to Ivrench	
E.24.c	24/3/18	8.50am	west of CAPPY Hq himself. 4.0 am 157 dismounted arrived	
E.23.d			Cappy bridge blown up for traffic RHQ	

Army Form C. 2118.

WAR DIARY
or
INTELLIGENCE SUMMARY.
(Erase heading not required.)

RE FR 16 DN

MARCH 1918

Place	Date	Hour	Summary of Events and Information	Remarks and references to Appendices
CAPPY E.24.c	24/3/18	AM 9/30	CRE went round Relays. Capt Turner RAMC returned [WB]	
	24	10/10	LT WEBSTER rode to ECLUSIER with C Sappers 156 [WB]	
	24	11/30 PM	LT WEBSTER returning heavily lorried ECLUSIER bridge for traffic PUB [see expenditure?]	
	24	4/10	LT WEBSTER with lorry to CHAULNES for tools [WB]	
	24	5/30	Recvd mem G.673 to be prepared to move at short notice [WB]	
	24	6/0	Transport pack attacks SP.R.I.T BULLEN to MORLANCOURT. CRE + Capt JENNINGS to FROISSY Bridge	
	24		along Canal bank to BRAY. CRE to MORLANCOURT. Capt Jennings & LT CAPPY to try truck	
	24		up extensive from 156 for 157. BRAY bombed by E.A. [WB]	
	24		CRE to bivouac 6.0 (escort to Relays). Tea boys asked to prepare demolition of	
	24	5/30pm	FROISSY, BRAY, CERISY, CHIPILLY bridges. (9:30pm All Motor transport moved to PONT NOYELLES [WB]) [WB]	
MORLANCOURT	24	9:30 pm	RSMR report BR [WB]	
KB.W.7.3	25/3/18	10 AM 11:30 pm	OC 157 arrived to accept send sappers for FROISSY Bridge [WB]	
			157 guard at BRAY 156. CHIPILLY first 157. ECLUSE - met then [impale?] groups [WB]	
		6:30 AM	Capt Jennings to CHIPILLY + ETINEHEM for tools (uncertain for BRAY bridge) [WB]	
		7:30 AM	LT WEBSTER took Cross appro for shrs Hutson LA FLAQUE [WB]	
		11. Am	CREI order no 60 issued to Relays [WB]	Appendices 9

Army Form C. 2118.

WAR DIARY
or
INTELLIGENCE SUMMARY.   C.E. 49 16 Div

(Erase heading not required.)

MARCH 1918

Place	Date	Hour	Summary of Events and Information	Remarks and references to Appendices
MERICOURT	25/3/18	2.30pm	CRE to OE. XIX Corps re car. MG9	
"	"	3.10 pm	LT WEBSTER with REHQ to LAMOTTE en SANTERRE MG9	
"	"	"	Capt Jennings arrived Zeneghi at BRAY ECLUSE & CHIPILLY with CRE's orders for moving to PROYART. 157 huds & one to MERICOURT with the Brigade (49) MG9	
"	"	4.30 pm	HQ arrived 4.30pm. 141 Fd Coy Transport to R2? A. 9.7. arrived 8.00pm MG9	
LAMOTTE en SANTERRE P.36.a	"	"	CRE & LT WEBSTER to 47 IBde MORCOURT. IIIame PROYART and 49 Me MESCHUGNOLLES MG9 Sent orders for construction of PROYART line to Fd Coys + 11/Hants MG9	
" "	26/3/18	"	CRE by car to PROYART. went round PROYART line MG9	
" "	"	"	Capt Jennings with lorry of tools to PROYART & CHUIGNOLLES OAS	
" "	"	"	LT WEBSTER with bus to HAMEL re line defences L PROYART & PROISSY MG4	
" "	"	4.10 pm	REHQ to HAMEL MG4	
HAMEL P.10.C	26/3/18	5.10 pm	CRE sent REHQ to Fd Corps on withdrawal from PROYART line. OAS	
"	"	5.15 pm	BEA orders very low.	
"	"	8.00 pm	Capt Jennings with HQ Roundabout Rd. Maj Dyson Lyston Whitechapel with this	
"	"	10 pm	Capt Jennings to SAILLY LAURETTE bridge. LT WEBSTER utho & to CERISY bridge MG9	

Army Form C. 2118.

WAR DIARY
~~INTELLIGENCE SUMMARY.~~
(Erase heading not required.)

HQ RE 16 DIV
MARCH 1918

Place	Date	Hour	Summary of Events and Information	Remarks and references to Appendices
HAMEL P.10.c	26/3/18		To ascertain the effects of bombardment. MO to ADS BAILLY. M59	
	27/3/18	3.15pm	Instructions received to have HQ transport cleared of Rly G.S. Wagon. M59	
		5am	Lt WEBSTER left with transport leaving officers horses & ambulance Waggon to VILLERS FAUCOURT. M59	
			~~Wednesday~~ Lt HALL 156 hrs met with his ambulance party, & various	
			stragglers from 2nd Corps arrived. Defense arrangement of HAMEL prepared.	
			Lt HALL put in charge of his party, all stragglers & RE dump personnel.	
			Capt Jennings to SAILLY LAURETTE Bridge & report on second demolition. M59	
		4pm	~~Mr Webster~~ Orders sent Lieut WEBSTER Transport to FOUILLOY & wait	
			transport. HAMEL shelled all day. 4/5 2nd Bn Transport returned to LIEUT RAINEY. M59	
		4pm	Found that DHQ had moved. HAMEL being shelled heavily during	
			morning. Much infantry retiring through HAMEL. M59	
FOUILLOY	4/30		Moved HQ RE 16 DIV to FOUILLOY R.S. 11 & F/5. in line in front of HAMEL. M59	
O.10.a	28/3	7/11pm	Situation reports from C. Robson to 16 Div. Counterattack in HAMEL (J.11.d.A). M59	
		8.30am	ORS Capt Jennings & MO motorcycle to BOIS DE VAIRES. M59	
		9/30	HQ RE established. M59	
BOIS de VAIRE P.14.d		10/30	Capt Jennings to HAMEL. Found RE dogs in Sunken Road P.10.c burning. M59	

WAR DIARY
or
INTELLIGENCE SUMMARY.
(Erase heading not required.)

Army Form C. 2118.

HQ RE 76 DIV

MARCH 1918

Place	Date	Hour	Summary of Events and Information	Remarks and references to Appendices
BOIS de VAIRE P.19.d	28/3/18	—	Moved the HQ from 1K school here HAMEL owing to shelling at later end P.10.a.6.3 HAMEL being shelled heavily. RAJ	
P.10.a.2.8		1pm	Move HQ RE to P.10.a.2.8 RAJ	
P.10.a.2.8		1/30	CRE & Capt Jenings to HAMEL 67th Coy. Heavy shelling about P.10.a Capt Jen-p wounded (at dump) MO left with orders for FOUILLOY. RAJ	
FOUILLOY O.10.a.		5pm	CRE + Capt Je-p arrive FOUILLOY RAJ	
		5pm	Major HOLBROW reported killed in action HAMEL RAJ	
		11pm	Capt SHELLEY sent up to take command of 156 Fd Co. RE RAJ	
	29/3/18	10am	Capt Je-p to 11 Field Ambulance transferred RAJ	
		11/0	Lt WEBSTER to CE XIX corps for 3 store RAJ	
		11/30	CRE + MO. to HAMEL & 76th Engrs. RAJ 4pm lub to DRAHOUNET from base	
			RE dumps established at O.13.a.7.8 & supplied by Corps. RAJ	
	30/3/18	10 am	20 & 30 RE dumps heavy bombardment in our front. RAJ	
			CRE to XIX corps about stores. In Epehrs DRAHOUNET L.57.Z.4.7.5 RAJ	
			Lt OSMOND reported wounded. Lt NORMAN (156) reported killed & Lt HALL (156) wounded RAJ	
			RE dumps attacked at HAMEL P.9.c.3.7 supplied by both dumps from O.12.a.7.8 RAJ	

Army Form C. 2118.

WAR DIARY
or
INTELLIGENCE SUMMARY
(Erase heading not required.)

HQ RE 16 DIV

MARCH 1918

Place	Date	Hour	Summary of Events and Information	Remarks and references to Appendices
FOUILLOY	30/3	7 pm	RE unnecessary transport worked back to FOURET VALLY re-camped 2 pm. Proceeded with LT CULVER (155) [RE]	
	31/3	9.15 am	OTTO returned preceding of Rly lop out on to STEPS. [RE]	
		10.0 am	OREB LT WEBSTER to HAMEL Arranging to have W/L BN 46	
			for immediate Relief of Op in Support (CO) [RE]	
		11.15	Bibling [?] W Op on way in AUBIGNY. Otty Kesley Davenport &	
			same from LE PETIT BLANGY & AUBIGNY [RE]	
		2 pm	ISS 200 cay ammunition pierres driven to AUBIGNY [RE]	
		3.30 pm	OREB LT WEBSTER returned from HAMEL [RE]	
			Stew asked to HAMEL & HAMEL LT WEBSTER CRE took horse & RE dump	
			back to HAMEL towine. [RE]	
			WATERVILLE - Traffic unmolested by RO Spencer Capt RE for CRE 16 DIV	

SECRET.   Appendix I.

C.R.E's OPERATION ORDER No. 56.

21st March, 1918.

1. Situation.   The enemy is reported to be in MALASSISE FARM, and RED LINE South of that point. The situation as regards RONSSOY is not clear, but it seems probable that it is either held by the enemy or masked, as the enemy is reported holding the West end of the RAPERIE SWITCH.

    The 47th Brigade is now moving up to occupy and hold the BROWN LINE.

2. The Divisional Commander expects to have to hold the enemy back on either (1) The MALASSISE SWITCH or (2) On a line from 21st Div. YELLOW LINE at about F.7.a.4.2. to BROWN LINE near its crossing by ST EMILIE - EPEHY Broad Guage Railway (E.18.b.9.4).

3. The O.C. 11th Hants (pioneers), assisted by O.C. 156th Field Coy.R.E., will arrange to connect up and deepen (1) or dig and wire (2), according to instructions which will be sent later.

    If (2) is dug, it will take the form of a traversed fire trench, dug as deep as circumstances will admit, the wire will be made double apron with gaps, or at any rate as strong as time and material will allow.

4. On receipt of these orders O.C. 156th Field Coy.R.E. will proceed to Headquarters 11th Hants (p) in Light Railway Cutting (ST EMILIE) F.24.a.6.7. and make preliminary arrangements for the night's work.

5. O.C. 156th Field Coy.R.E. will arrange for wire to be brought up from the R.E. Dump. Instructions have been, meanwhile, sent direct to Captain SHELLY, 156th Fld. Coy. Horse Lines to load up 2 pontoon wagons with wire and pickets, and await orders of O.C. 156th Field Coy.R.E. at R.E. Dump, VILLERS FAUCON.

6. Both O.C. 11th Hants (p) and O.C. 156th Field Coy.R.E. will send in a report on completion of work, stating what progress has been made.

    ACKNOWLEDGE.

                                    R.M.Butterworth
                                    Lieut-Colonel, R.E.
                                    C. R. E. 16th Division.

    Copies:-
            O.C. 11th Hants (p).
            O.C. 156th Field Coy.R.E.
            16th Div. 'G'.
            C.R.E.
            File.

SECRET.
============

Appendix 2

C. R. E's OPERATION ORDER No. 57.

21st March, 1918.

1. Situation.   We are now holding the BROWN LINE with the 47th Brigade and 2 Battalions 116th Brigade.
   11th Hants (Pioneers) and 156th Field Coy. R.E. are garrisoning ST EMILIE.

2. 155th and 157th Field Companies will move on receipt of these orders, and occupy the GREEN LINE as follows.

   155th Field Coy. R.E.   K.1.c.

   157th Field Coy. R.E.   K.13.c. and J.18.b.
                                (but to keep North of the village of HAMEL).

3. The existing posts will be improved as far as is possible, and the Sections organised to put up a stern fight in case of hostile attack.

4. The Officers Commanding will make all arrangements for an immediate move, sending their baggage and stores to their present horse-lines, and will then report to D.H.Q.

5. A Staff Officer will be waiting at D.H.Q. to point out the exact posts in the GREEN LINE, which are to be held.

6. O.C. 157th Field Coy. R.E. will send orders to Sergt. SMYTH and party at the R.E. Dump to march to Divisional H.Q.

7. ACKNOWLEDGE.

                                        Lieut. Colonel, R.E.
                                        C. R. E. 16th Division.

Copies:-
    155th Field Coy. R.E.
    157th Field Coy. R.E.
    16th Div. 'G'.
    C.R.E.
    File.

Appendix 3

3340/148

O.C. 156th Field Company, R.E.

    I have received your situation report, and have shewn it to the Divisional Commander, who expressed great satisfaction on receipt of such a useful and circumstantial report.

    You will be withdrawn from ST EMILIE as soon as the situation allows it. Meanwhile do what you can to assist the 47th Brigade.

    It is anticipated that no work can be done to-night in accordance with C.R.E's Order No.56, but the situation is not quite clear, so I am not sending out instructions to cancel.

    Please inform O.C. 11th Hants (pioneers).

    NOTE:- In case of withdrawal through VILLERS FAUCON, do your best to fire the R.E. Dump.

    Later:- 155th and 157th Coys. are being withdrawn to garrison GREEN LINE.

21-3-18.

                                        Lieut.Colonel, R.E.
                                    C. R. E. 16th Division.

SECRET.   Appendix 4

C. R. E.'s ORDER NO. 60.

25th March, 1918.

1. 16th Division has been transferred from VII Corps to XIX Corps. The River SOMME forms the dividing line between VII and XIX Corps, XIX Corps on Right, VII Corps on Left.

2. The role of the Division will now be to guard the line of the SOMME river and the canal on the left flank of XIX Corps from a possible attack from the North. Line to be protected extends from G.24.c.2.3. (exclusive) S.W. of FRISE to CERISY GAILLY (inclusive).

3. Responsibility for guarding above line will be as follows:-

    48th Inf. Bde. Crossing at G.24.c.2.3. (exclusive) to L.30.c.0.5.

    49th Inf. Bde. L.30.c.0.5. to L.25.c.0.7.

    47th Inf. Bde. L.25.c.0.7. to CERISY GAILLY (inclusive).

4. Inf. Bdes. will move at once on receipt of this order and will take up positions for the immediate defence of the crossings in their respective Sections. Main bodies are to be kept concentrated S. of the Canal with strong pickets at the crossings. Active patrolling is to be carried out between posts. 48th Inf. Bde. will be responsible for gaining touch with left of 39th Div.

5. Each O.C. will attach one Section to his Brigade and the remainder of the R.E. will move to PROYART in Div. Reserve. Units may take over accommodation in Village or in wood to North, whichever they prefer and report location.

6. O.C's will still be responsible for maintenance of charges on bridges etc. prepared for demolition. Small parties will be detailed to each to safeguard them. These parties may be found from attached Sections if a.O.C. Bde. concurs.

7. H.Q.R.E. will move to LAMOTTE en SANTERRE - P.30.c. Report centre will open at 6.0.pm.

8. ACKNOWLEDGE.

                                        [signature]
                                        Captain, R.E.
                                        for C. R. E. 16th Division.

Copies:-   155th Fld. Coy.R.E.
            156th Fld. Coy.R.E.
            157th Fld. Coy.R.E.
             47th Inf. Bde.)
             48th Inf. Bde.) for information.
             49th Inf. Bde.)
             16th Div. G.   )

NOT OFFICIAL

M. G. Taylor

P
with the
Royal Engineers
of the
Irish Division

21ˢᵗ MARCH 1918 – 4ᵗʰ APRIL

by C·R·G

FOREWORD.

The fighting troops of a Division are the Infantry, Artillery and Field Companies R.E. vide F.S. Regulations Part I (Operations).

In Trench Warfare this fact is often lost sight of, for, from the nature of things, the Field Company Sapper is looked upon as the builder of dugouts, provider of trenchboards and revetting material, and the handy man of all trades in and out of the line.

In the retreat, however, he comes into his own, and he both works and fights, laying down his shovel to pick up a rifle, and defending a bridge-head until it is his job to drop the bridge prior to retirement. In all phases of war it is his honourable task to assist the Infantry and Artillery in gaining and maintaining the advantage over the enemy, using, for this purpose, his technical skill and training as an Engineer. But when chance offers, as in a withdrawal he is happy to fight alongside the infantry, and great is his reward if he gains some mead of praise for his stout resistance in a village street, or for timely support, at a critical moment.

The withdrawal of the Allied Armies under the concentrated and well-prepared attacks of the German forces delivered on 21st. March 1918 may well be said to mark the turning point of the great Eurppean War. Then it was that the German General Staff - calculating on our big losses in the Ypres and Cambrai battles of 1917 - hoped to break the allied front, sever the British and French along the line of the Somme, and win the War before the Americans could effectively intervene.

Trench warfare was converted into open fighting and the change of tactics was destined to put into the hands of one or other of the opposing forces the opportunity of strategical combination hitherto impracticable.

The dogged retirement..............

- 2 -

The dogged retirement of the Third and Fifth Armies, the fine defence of the First Army at BETHUNE, and the gallant stand of the Second Army on the SCHERPENBERG-MONT DES CATS position, though yielding a few miles of territory, laid the foundation of a victorious counter-thrust.

Following close upon this the magnificent leading and fighting of the French about REIMS and CHATEAU THIERRY, enabled the Generalissimo of the Allied Forces, Field Marshal FOCH, to set in motion a strategical combination which was to have far-reaching and decisive results.

The share taken by the 16th. Irish Division in the March battles, their early and desperate defence of RONSSOY village, and their subsequent fighting withdrawal, and recovery on the HAMEL - MARCELCAVE line, find their place in the official records and war diaries. It is hhpeHope of the writer to place on record the work and action of the Royal Engineers of this Division during this period, both in appreciation of the work done, and gallantry shewn, and also as a possible help to future students of Engineer work in a retreat.

The order of Battle of the 16th. Division on 21st. March 1918 was as follows :-

Division Commander

Major General Sir C.P.A. HULL, K.C.B.

R.F.A.

G.O.C. R.A. Brigadier General C.E.C.G. CHARLTON, D.S.O.

177 - 180 - 189 - 277 Brigades R.F.A.

R.E.

C.R.E. Bt: Lt: Col: R.F.A. BUTTERWORTH, D.S.O., R.E.

155 - 156 - 157 Field Companies R.E.

49th. Brigade.

Brigadier General P. LEVESON GOWER, C.M.G., D.S.O.

2nd. Royal Irish Regiment,

7th. Royal Irish (South Irish Horse),

7/8th. Royal Iniskilling Fusiliers.

48th. Brigade.

Brigadier General F.W. RAMSAY, C.M.G., D.S.O.

1st. Royal Dublin Fusiliers,

2nd. Royal Dublin Fusiliers,

2nd. Royal Munster Fusiliers.

47th. Brigade.

Brigadier General H.G. GREGORIE, D.S.O.

6th. Connaught Rangers,

2nd. Leinster Regt.,

1st. Royal Munster Fusiliers.

16th. Machine Gun Battalion.

Lieut: Col: R. LE BUTT D.S.O.

11th. Hants Pioneers.

Lieut: Col: B.E. CROCKETT, D.S.O.

DETAIL AND DISPOSITION OF THE DIVISIONAL ENGINEERS 21st. MARCH.

155 Field Company - O.C. Major E.I. SCOTT, R.E., T.F.

    H.Q. & 3 Sections - VILLERS FAUCON.

        1 Section - RONSSOY.

Left Brigade Sector.

    157 Field Coy. - O.C. Major P.F. WHITTALL, D.S.O., R.E.

        H.Q. & 3 Sections - VILLERS FAUCON.

            1 Section - RONSSOY.

Right Brigade Sector.

    156 Field Coy. - O.C. Major T.L. HOLBROW, M.C., R.E.

        H.Q. & 2 Sections - ST. EMILIE.

            2 Sections - VILLERS FAUCON.

In reserve.

Orders in case of attack.

O's C. Field Companies were instructed to collect their units as far as the tactical situation allowed, and man the village defences under the orders of the commander designated in the Divisional Defence Scheme.

    155 Field Co. } VILLERS FAUCON.
    157 "   "   }

    156 Field Co.   ST. EMILIE.

Horse transport, with technical wagons and stores, were to be parked clear of the village, pending further orders.

The opening of the attack.

The attack in the early hours of the 21st. March came in the nature of a suprise - it had been long anticipated but there were no special signs or final warning on the night of 20/21 March that the blow would fall next day.

The enemy barrage came down with almost perfect synchronism at 4.15 a.m., the Battle Lines, Battery Positions, and villages of LEMPIRE, RONSSOY, ST. EMILIE and VILLERS FAUCON being heavily shelled with H.E..............

shelled with H.E. and Gas. All telephone communication forward of Brigade Headquarters was at once destroyed.

A thick fog enveloped the whole area - a grey white darkness of the consistency of steam. Advancing under its cover the enemy early reached the Southern edge of the LEMPIRE-RONSSOY defences, where hot fighting took place. The two forward sections of 155 and 157 could not for the moment be extricated and fought under the orders of the O.C. LEMPIRE defences. Later on they were withdrawn to VILLERS FAUCON by Lieut: F.H. KING (Royal Irish Regt., attached R.E.) - Lieut: G.H. BAXTER R.E. having been mortally wounded while engaged at close quarters in the defence of the citadel.

After a severe struggle in which the gallant battalion of South Irish Horse was practically annihilated and in which the 7/8 Inniskillings suffered very heavy xasualities, the villages of RONSSOY and LEMPIRE fell into the enemy's hands. This happened at approximately 11 a.m. and had the effect of turning our Battle Line from the South. A withdrawal to the Switch Line EPENY - ST. EMILIE became imperative.

Meanwhile the Left Brigade put up a fine fight and held on tenaciously to the MALASSISE Farm position where the gallant defence of the Dublin Fusiliers continued until late in the afternoon.

The 155 and 157 Field Companies, under the command of Major WHITTALL who became O.C. Village defences, manned the defences of VILLERS FAUCON. They suffered some casualities through shell-fire, including 2nd. Lieut: N.C. GORNALL who was killed while taking a message from the O.C. to one of his groups.

157 successfully evacuated their transport during a lull in the shelling, to the neighbourhood of MARQUAIX. Unluckily a big shell struck the harness room of 155 and a great part of the transport was consequently immobilized. However, by making several trips the greater number of the wagons were got clear of the village.

156 Field Coy., ...

156 Field Coy. not being immediately required for the defence of ST. EMILIE, the O.C. reported to the Brigadier 49th. Brigade, and was instructed to extend our line to the right and head off small parties of German scouts who were advancing, with light machine guns in order to work round the flank of the ST. EMILIE position from the South. This was a task dear to Major HOLBROW's heart, and he fought his company tile late in the afternoon on the right, and did most useful service. He was ably backed up by his senior subaltern, Lieut: W.B.G.WHITEHOUSE, and his C.S.M. H. GATES, until the former was unluckily killed by a machine gun bullet.

156 Company was relieved at 3 p.m. by the Munster Fusiliers and withdrew to a support position in rear of ST. EMILIE. Major HOLBROW sent off an excellent sketch and tactical report timed at 5.5.p.m. which was the first reliable information of the situation on our extreme right, to reach Division Headquarters.

The situation at nightfall of 21st. March was:- 16th. Division on Brown Line (Corps Line) just east of ST.EMILIE - touch on the right with the 66th. Division who had fallen back behind TEMPLEUX-GERRARD - 21st. Division still holding out in EPEHY.

As regards the R.E., 155 and 157 had been withdrawn to the Green Line just east of TINCOURT, having been relieved in VILLERS FAUCON by the 2nd. Leinsters - 156 remained in support at ST. EMILIE.

After dark Capt: J. SHELLY of 156 Field Coy. ran some transport into ST. EMILIE, the outskirts of which were occupied by the Germans and succeeded in removing all the Officers' and Mens' Kits and Mess Gear. Major HOLBORN turned out his Company again to assist the infantry to dig in, and succeeded in strengthening the railway cutting midway between ST. EMILIE and VILLERS FAUCON.

During the night 21/22 March orders were issued for the withdrawa of the Division on the Green Line (HINCOURT - TEMPLEUX - LA-FOSSE). The C.R.E. was instructed to improve the defences of the Green Line, using 155 and 157 Field Companies and any infantry that were available

The 7th. Corps Cyclist Coy........

The 7th. Corps Cyclist Coy. were sent up to strengthen the right flank of the line which rested on the COLOGNE River just South of TINCOURT.

At daylight, work was started on deepening the Green Line which, in our sector was a spit-locked trench protected by three belts of good wire. The Cyclist Coy. was employed in wiring the marsh from the TINCOURT → ROISELLE high road up to the river. Meanwhile the infantry withdrew from the ST. EMILIE position and came into line by noon on the Green Line.

This line had a fine field of fire, and the further advance of the enemy was held up during the day. 155 and 157 remained in line and assisted in the defensive action.

Earlier in the day 156 had a difficult retreat through VILLERS FAUCON and were withdrawn to DOINGT.

Divisional Headquarters moved that afternoon to DOINGT, and during the night 155 was withdrawn from the line and joined 156.

22nd. MARCH.

Divisional Headquarters moved at 7-a.m. via PERONNE to BIACHES, where Divisional Headquarters were established.

155 and 156 Field Companies marched to BIACHES and remained during the day in Div: Reserve. The infantry fell back, stubbornly resisting, from TINCOURT via DOINGT to PERONNE, reaching the latter town in the late afternoon. Fighting took place throughout the day and many tactical points were resolutely held, while the general retrograde movement conformed to the movement of the Division on the left flank.

Here 157 Field Company distinguished itself, in acting as part of the rearguard for the 49th. Brigade. On approaching DOINGT, which is a small village in the main road about 3 miles from PERONNE, the enemy pressed the 49th. Brigade very hard with the intention of making the passage of the SOMME at PERONNE a difficult operation.

157 Field Coy............

157th. Field Coy. under Major WHITTALL, and two Companies of 11th Hants Pioneers under Major HAZARD fought a valuable delaying action in the village. It was realized that, by taking cover in the houses and enclosures, a stout fight could be put up against the enemy, whose principal wepons at the moment were rifles and machine guns.

A house to house fight took place, and valuable time was gained for the extrication of the infantry. Major WHITTALL received a bar to his D.S.O. f r this action, and there is little doubt that Major HAZARD would have been similarly rewarded if he had had the luck to survive the retreat.

Capt: G. HOWSON of the Pioneers shewed great initiative in the same action but, holding too long on to a building, was surrounded and captured. However, he eluded his captors and rejoined his company later in PERONNE.

The infantry crossed the SOMME just before dusk, and took up a position covering the river approaches in and about BIACHES. The Bristol Bridge on the PERONNE - AMIENS Road was blown at 6 p.m.

The road between BIACHES and HERBECOURT was now much congested with horse traffic and transport and three enemy aeroplanes came over and machine-gunned it. It was, however, a timorous effort from a great height, and three or four men only, were wounded.

During the night the infantry were withdrawn on relief by the 39th. Division, and marched into bivouac between HERBECOURT and CAPPY, and Divisional Headquarters moved to CAPPY.

157 was ordered to rejoin 155 and 156 Field Cos. west of CAPPY and reached that village at 3 a.m. on the 23rd. The men were in splendid spirits, and were singing as they went through, in spite of having continuously marched and fought since 7 a.m. on the 22nd.

23rd. MARCH.

A most brilliant day of sunshine. The division spent the day in support. The Field Cos. were ordered to fill up with S.A.A. and

be ready to move............

be ready to move at half an hour's notice. News was very scarce but the general impression was that the Fifth Army were standing on the line of the SOMME, and that the Division would soon be on its way again into line East or North East.

Towards the afternoon, however, it was evident that the enemy was pressing forward on the North Bank of the SOMME, as the Artillery fire was increasing momentarily in that direction.

At about 3 p.m. the Divisional Commander issued orders that bridgeheads were to be prepared at FROISSY, CERISY, and MERICOURT, each of which would be held by a brigade. The C.R.E. was instructed to arrange for the necessary work at each bridgehead, in co-operation with the Brigadier concerned, and to prepare the bridges at those places for demolition. For this purpose 155 Field Coy. was told off for FROISSY - 156 for CERISY - and 157 for MERICOURT.

Lieut: WEBSTER was sent off with two lorries to fetch picks and shovels from the Army Dump at CHAULNES; he got there at 8 p.m. to find the place in flames. He then went on to LA FLAQUE which was deserted and picked up the necessary tools. These he delivered at each of the Bridgeheads, and reached H.Q., R.E. at 7 a.m. on the 25th., having covered a distance of nearly 70 miles in the dark over absolutely strange roads, and been within an ace of being captured near CHAULNES.

Divisional Headquarters moved that evening to MORLANCOURT. The C.R.E. arranged work and demolition at the three bridgeheads, and reached D.H.Q. via BRAY at midnight. The latter town was seriously blocked with transport, and was bombed by the enemy, though luckily no hit was obtained in the main traffic thoroughfare.

25th. MARCH.

The Division was transferred from the VII to the XIX Corps H.Q. HARBONNIERES. D.H.Q. moved to WARFUSEE-LAMOTTE about 3 miles from VILLERS-BRETONNEUX.

The Field Coys...............

The Field Cos. worked all day in preparing bridges at FROISSY, MERICOURT, and CERISY for demolition, and in fortifying bridgeheads at these places. 10 bridges in all were got ready, including the railway bridge at FROISSY which carried a line of rail, and double width railway on a 4' brick-arch span. Capt: JENNINGS, acting adjutant scoured the country for gun-cotton and fuse, and sufficient was obtained to supplement that carried to make up the necessary charges.

The enemy was now developing a strong attack on the North of the SOMME on the line CURLU - MONTAUBAN - LONGUEVAL.

The Brigades were moved up to a preparatory position west of PROYART with a view to holding up an advance on the South of the river. The Field Coys. were instructed to move into the village of PROYART, leaving a small detail at each group of bridges to carry out the demolition when ordered.

At 8 p.m. that evening information was received that the Fifth Army was falling back on the line CHAULNES - BRAY - ALBERT, and the 16th. Division was ordered to prepare and occupy the section of this general line between PROYART and the River SOMME at FROISSY - connecting on the right with the 39th. Division.

The C.R.E. visited Brigade H.Q. at M.NCOURT and MERICOURT, and the Field Coys. at PROYART, and made arrangements to start work at daybreak next morning.

26th. MARCH.

So n after daylight the C.R.E. met the three Brigadiers at PROYART, and arranged the siting of the line, and details of work to be done. The Defences of PROYART and line joining up with the 39th. Division was given to the 11th. Hants Pioneers - the remainder, a distance of about 6,000 yards, was sub-divided among the three Field Coys. each working on a Brigade Sector, with infantry parties provided by the Brigade.

A supply of wire was found at LA FLAQUE and FROISSY Dumps and there were plenty of picks and shovels at the former.

The line selected............

The line selected had a good field of fire into, and across, the small valley running from PROYART via CHIGNOLLES to the SOMME at FROISSY and was not under observation from the high ground further east, except on the left where it was overlooked from the north bank of the river. The line passed just in rear of CHIGNOLLES which was at the bottom of the valley, and it was intended to deny the occupation of this to the enemy by rifle and Stokes Mortar fire.

At about 1 p.m. Germans appeared on the South of the SOMME, pushing in the advanced line of infantry scouts. Our half completed line was soon under erratic but fairly brisk machine and Field Gun fire. The R.E. and Pioneers with the infantry working parties stood to arms, and lined the trenches and banks. The attack was not driven home and at 3 p.m. the R.E. were relieved and went back into support in MORCOURT wood just west of PROYART.

In the meantime the 10 bridges had been blown up by the R.E. detachments - a good job was made of the big FROISSY bridge in which the crown was attacked, making a wide gap up to the abutment on each side.

At 4 p.m. the C.R.E was ordered to reconnoitre a position covering MORCOURT, to be garrisoned by the Field Cos. in the event of the PROYART line being forced back, and to dispose of the three Field Cos. for its defence.

The Field Cos. were accordingly moved back to a preparatory position close to MORCOURT village. They had however very little rest that night, for at 2 a.m. on the 27th. they were called upon to extend the left flank of the Divisional front, and guard the crossings of the SOMME on the flank of the 49th. Brigade. They marched off under the command of Major P.F. WHITTALL towards FROISSY, and, based in the FROISSY - MERICOURT road, pushed out an outpost line on the river bank from FROISSY to ETINEHEM and CERISY.

27th. March. . . . .

27th. MARCH.

The enemy attacked the PROYART Line at 9 a.m. and after severe fighting captured the village of PROYART, forcing the 47th. Brigade south-west, thus leaving the 48th. and 49th. Brigades in a precarious position. The 11th. Hants Pioneers formed a defensive flank on the right of the 48th. Brigade, and, being well handled by Lieut: Col: CROCKETT, facilitated the withdrawal of the 48th. Brigade to the MORCOURT Line. The 49th. Brigade held on to the left flank, and commenced to withdraw at about 2 p.m. It was then reported that the Germans had crossed the SOMME at CHIPILLY about 1½ miles in rear of the MORCOURT Line.

The three Field Companies who were on the extreme left guarding the crossings of the SOMME, retired slowly and protected the left flank of the 49th. Brigade in their withdrawal. The MORCOURT Line was, by this time, turned by the enemy crossing at CHIPILLY south-west on LAMOTTE. The position was extremely critical as a rapid advance by the enemy on the CERISY - LAMOTTE road would have endangered the retreat of the 48th. and 49th. Brigades - on LAMOTTE.

The R.E. and Pioneers did useful work at this juncture, for, advancing towards CERISY, they opened heavy rifle fire on the advancing infantry, and gained valuable time for our Brigades. The 155th. Field Company under Major SCOTT, especially distinguished itself. The Company was led forward to gain touch with the advancing infantry and Lieut: A.C. ATOCK bravely charged and destroyed a machine-gun detachment.

This counter-attack had, undoubtedly, great effect on the hostile troops who had forced the CHIPILLY crossing, and took the pressure temporarily off the flanks of our retreating Brigades who successfully passed through LAMOTTE to the MARCELCAVE - HAMEL Line.

In their left-flank action the Pioneers fought splendidly, and Major HAZARD, who did so well at DOINGT on the 23rd., and Captains THYNE and MACONOCHIE were all missing.

155 Field Coy...............

155 Field Company were the last British Troops to pass through the village of LAMOTTE, and they fought wonderfully for men who had had so little infantry training. Each section supported the other in its retirement, and the value of the left side of the street was fully realised and made use of. Lieutenants J.P. HAUGH and C.V. BROOK, and Company Sergt: Major W. ARGYLE especially distinguished themselves.

For their brave and excellent work on this afternoon, Major SCOTT and Lieutenant ATOCK were awarded the M.C.

At nightfall the 48th. and 49th. Brigades were holding the old French line running in rear of LAMOTTE village - as far as the village of HAMEL - the Field Companies and Pioneers holding the extreme right on the main PERONNE - AMIENS high road.

Divisional Headquarters remained at HAMEL throughout this critical day. Meanwhile the Employment Coy. and all batmen and spare clerks were organised for its immediate defence by the A.Q.M.G. Lieut: Colonel G.A.C. WEBB. The village was heavily shelled, but not attacked, and towards the evening Headquarters was moved to the Convent at FOUILLOY - just clear of the town of CORBIE.

28th. MARCH.

Advanced Divisional Headquarters was formed on the west edge of the BOIS DE VARIE. The Division was relieved in the MARCELCAVE - HAMEL Line by a mixed force of Tunnellers, A.T. Companies, Instruction Staffs, etc. raised and organised by Major-General P.G. GRANT, Chief Engineer, Fifth Army. This Unit afterwards came under the command of Major-General CAREY, R.A. and became known as Carey's force.

156th. Field Company R.E. had suffered heavily during the retreat and its O.C. Major HOLBROW was only able to muster 20 Sappers. The Company was reinforced by the addition of some twenty infantry and a few Sappers (the original Dump Party) from H.Q., R.E. under 2nd. Lieutenant S.A. HALL.

All three Field Companies........

All three Field Companies were placed in close support at HAMEL and dug themselves into the side of a hollow road at the Southern exit of the village. The men looked, and were, very tired, but their spirits and moral remained unimpaired. Major WHITTALL, who was a splendid example of cheerfulness to everyone, told me that afternoon that the men were fit and willing for any job of work or fighting, but it was useless to expect any rapid movement out of them.

I found Major HOLDROW in a cottage at the edge of the village helping his Company cook to make stew. His first thought, at all times, was the care and comfort of his men, and it was only a little later in the same afternoon that, in leaving his billet during a bombardment to look after three of his men, he was killed by a shell. And so passed away a fine young Officer "sans peur et sans reproche".

Captain JENNINGS who accompanied the C.R.E. that afternoon, was wounded in the leg by a shell splinter, but remained at duty.

The 48th. and 49th. Brigades, together with the R.E. and Pioneers were now formed into a mixed Brigade under Brigadier General F.W. RAMSAY.

Total Strength		700 rifles.
Infantry - as 2 battalions	...	380.
Pioneers - as 1 battalion	,,,	200.
R.E. - as 1 battalion	...	120.
		700.

Captain TILLY was in command of the Pioneer Battalion, and Major WHITTALL of the R.E. Battalion.

29th. MARCH.

The fine spell of weather howkbroke and during the night there was a very heavy fall of rain which continued off and on all day.

The British line covering CORBIE and VILLERS-BRETONNEUX was strengthened by the arrival of the 1st. Cavalry Division at FOUILLY and two Australian Divisions on the west bank of the SOMME.

The C.R.E. went up to HAMEL and selected sites for an advanced dump at north-west edge of HAMELET. Meanwhile Lieutenant WEBSTER went off to XIX Corps Headquarters and obtained a supply of wire and pickets and some tools, which were taken forward by him after dark to the HAMEL Dump.

30th. MARCH.

The weather cleared somewhat, and there was much enemy aerial activity. Two big flights of Fokkers were operating for an hour over our lines, until engaged in a heavy air battle by our scouts, and chased away. A very heavy barrage was put down at 11 a.m. by the enemy on the front line (held by Carey's force) and HAMEL, followed up by an infantry attack. The enemy succeeded in entering the front line just east of HAMEL, and the R.E. and Pioneers were called upon by the Brigadier, 48th. Brigade, to counter-attack. The R.E. counter attack was delivered in three lines - 157th. leading under Lieutenants J.R. OSMOND and E.H. BANCROFT, supported by the 156th. in two lines, led by Captain J. SHELLY and 2nd. Lieutenant S.A. HALL. It was a gallant little effort and was completely successful in driving the enemy out of the part of the front line and support lines occupied. Various infantry Officers told me that it was an inspiring sight to see those three thin lines going ahead at a steady double over the open. Three out of the four Officers became casualties - Lieutenant. HALL and BANCROFT being killed, and Lieutenant OSMOND wounded. Also Sergt. HUGHES and 2nd./Cpl. FRYER, D.C.M., M.M. - a brilliant young N.C.O. - were killed.

The Sappers remained in the line until relieved next morning and excellent work was done by Lieutenant ATOCK 155th. Company R.E. who worked backwards and forwards with a small party of Sappers, carrying up rations, water, and ammunition. One of the party, Sapper FINLAYSON, afterwards received the D.C.M.

During the night a squad of infantry were taken up by Lieutenant WEBSTER, and some useful wiring done.

31st. March............

31st. MARCH.

A brilliant day of sunshine. Orders were issued that Carey's Force was to be relieved by the 1st. Cavalry Division, and that the 16th. Division would take over the portion of the line between HAMEL and the SOMME. The C.R.E. reconnoitred the front line with Lieut: WEBSTER, with a view to improving the defences in the 16th. Division Sector. The German dead were lying about in heaps, showing how heavily the 228th. Bavarian Division had suffered in their attempt to wrest HAMEL from our possession, on the previous day.

The line held by our troops was an old French defence trench - much fallen in and shallow - but with very fair wire in front. With a little work it seemed easily capable of strengthening and improvement

The opportunity was taken by the C.R.E. of inspecting the bridge across the SOMME at BOUZENCOURT. This was partially blown but quite passable for infantry. It had been apparently struck by a shell which caused one charge to detonate, cutting the girder on one side only. As the bridge was just in rear of our front line it was a bit of luck that the demolition had not been more complete. Captain HUGHES, 155th. Field Company took a limber with explosives up to GOUZENCOURT after dark, and prepared this bridge for demolition in case of further retirement.

During the night 31st. March/1st. April, the Field Companies were withdrawn from the line to AUBIGNY and the Hants Pioneers to VAIRE.

1st. APRIL.

Work was organised for improving our front line, and for preparing a Switch Line from the village of VAIRE to meet the main road near VILLERS BRETONNEUX. The latter was sited in conjunction with the 1st. Cavalry Division, and work was started by our R.Es. the same evening.

The 11th. Hants under Captain HOWSON commenced deepening and revetting the shallow parts of the front line and in strengthening the wire.

2nd. April.................

2nd. APRIL.

Very heavy German bombardment to the South of VILLERS BRETONNEUX but quiet on our front. The weather was fine and some useful work was done on our defensive system and the switch line.

3rd. APRIL.

16th. Division was relieved by the 14th. Division, and the Field Companies were moved by 'bus to SALLEUX late that afternoon.

-o-o-o-o-o-o-o-o-o-o-

This brings to a conclusion these few notes on the work and fighting of the Royal Engineers 16th. Division during the critical period 21st. March to 4th. April.

It is an interesting fact that each Field Company learnt the use of Lewis Machine Guns on the retreat, and, finally, between 30 and 40 of these weapons were handed over to the Infantry, after having done excellent service.

In the form of an appendix are added a Special Order of the Day issued by General Sir H.P. GOUGH, commanding the Fifth Army, and three letters received from the Divisional Commander and Brigadiers of the 16th. Division in kind appreciation of the efforts of the R.Es.

I think it can be fairly said that the Sappers, under difficult and unusual conditions, did their best to worthily uphold the traditions of the Corps, and that they have, perchance, also earned the right to say with their brothers of the infantry

"Et militavi non sine gloria".

-o-o-o-o-o-o-o-o-o-

APPENDIX.

SPECIAL ORDER OF THE DAY
BY
General Sir H. de la P. GOUGH, K.C.B., K.C.V.O.,
Commanding Fifth Army, Dated 26th. March, 1918.

I wish to express to all Officers and men of the Fifth Army my immense admiration for the truly magnificent way all ranks have fought in this desperate struggle against immense odds. The very grandest traditions of British Soldiers and of the British race have been maintained. We are fighting for our lives, our existence, our honour and in your hands all these are safe. It is a matter now only for a few days before reinforcements arrive to alter the situation.

          sd/ H.P. GOUGH   General.

Major-General Sir C.P.A. HULL, K.C.B.

G.O.C. 16th. (Irish) Division.

                    2/9/18.

My dear Butterworth,

  Your letter reached me just as we were starting the fighting in these parts, hence the delay in answering.

  I am very glad to hear that the deeds of the Field Companies of the 16th. Division during last March and April are to be brought to light. Their fighting qualities were beyong praise, and they helped the remains of the infantry in many a tight corner by their dash and grasp of the situation.

  Notably the 156th. Company on March 21st. at ST. EMILIE where the fighting was hard and the situation at the moment decidely mixed. On March 23rd. the 157th. Company attached to the 49th. Infantry Brigade put up a stout resistance on the extreme right of our line, and when the order to withdraw was sent, gave material assistance to the Brigade when passing through DOINCT.

  I think one of their best actions was when the three Companies were ordered to move from MORCOURT to MERICOURT during the night of the 26th/27th. March, in order to guard the crossings at the latter place and probably the left of the 49th. Infantry Brigade. Owing to the enemy pressure forward on the north of the river and eventually crossing at CHIPILLY on the 27th., our left was under heavy fire from its flank and rear, the way the Engineers held their ground and eventually fought their way back, was splendid.

  The 155th. Company I remember expecially did good work there. I have no doubt there are other instances but these shewed what stuff they were made of, and how they proved themselves first class fighters in a first class fighting division. You yourself deserve every credit for this and I am glad to have the opportunity of again thanking you for all you did during those strenuous times.

            Yours very sincerely,

               AMYATT HULL.

16th (IRISH) DIVISION
LINE OF RETREAT. 21ST – 27TH MARCH, 1918.

21st. Barrage came down, 4.45 a.m. Infantry attack in dense fog, 8 a.m. Attack on St. Emilie, 3 p.m. R.E. forward Sections withdrawn from Ronssoy, 11 a.m. 155th and 157th took up battle positions for defence of Villers Faucon. 166th formed defensive flank on right of 49th Brigade. Situation at nightfall:—155th and 157th ordered to withdraw from Villers Faucon to green line; 158th in outpost position, guarding right flank, south of St. Emilie. Ronssoy encircled and captured, 12 noon.

22nd. Enemy advanced on green line; 156th being rearguard for 49th Bde. with 2 companies of Hants (Pioneers), under Major Hazard. Fought a gallant action at Doingt, where they held the enemy for 2 hours while the Brigade was extricated. 155th and 157th worked on green line. Wired gap across marsh on south. Defended green line. 155th withdrawn 7 p.m. Joined 156th at new D.H.Q. Doingt.

23rd. D.H.Q. moved at daybreak, via Peronne, to Biaches. 155th and 156th followed D.H.Q. 157th formed rearguard for 49th Bde. with 2 companies of Hants (Pioneers), under Major Hazard. Our infantry cleared Bristol bridge at 6.0 p.m., when the bridge was blown. Peronne was then in flames. D.H.Q. moved after dusk to Cappy, via Herbecourt.

24th. 157th reached Cappy at 3.0 a.m., having marched and fought continuously for 24 hours, the men singing. A brilliant day of sunshine. No news. 6.0 p.m.—R.E. proceeded to form bridgeheads at Froissy (155), Cerisy (156), and Méricourt (157). Lt. Webster took 2 lorries to Chaulnes for tools and materials, found it in flames. Went on to La Flacque, re-crossed the Somme and delivered tools to Field Companies. D.H.Q. moved to Morlancourt. Bray seriously blocked with traffic, military and civil, and bombed.

25th. 16th Div. placed under XIX Corps. D.H.Q. moved to Lamotte. R.E. completed bridgeheads; prepared 10 bridges for demolition. 4 p.m. 155th, 156th and 157th to Proyart, leaving sections to blow up bridges. Froissy bridge and Méricourt bridges (6) demolished. Enemy advanced on N. bank of Somme. A quiet night.

26th. C.R.E. ordered to construct defensive line, Proyart to Somme. Right, left—Hants, 158th, 155th and 157th. Worked until 3.0 p.m., when enemy attacked. R.E. and Hants relieved at 6.0 p.m. Placed in support on Proyart—Méricourt road; dug in. D.H.Q. to Hamel.

27th. Position of 48th and 49th Brigades precarious. 2 a.m.—R.E. ordered up to extend left flank. 10 a.m.—Heavy attack on Méricourt position. 48th and 49th withdrawn to Méricourt line. R.E. moved along river as flank guard. 3 p.m.—Enemy appeared on south bank at Cerisy. 49th Bde. saved from being outflanked by action of 155th and 157th, and 1 Coy. Hants. 5 p.m.—48th and 49th withdrawn to Hamel—Marcelcave line. 6 p.m.—155th Coy. fought their way through Lamotte closely pressed. 8 p.m.—155th and 157th in support near Lamotte. No news of 156th or 47th Bde. D.H.Q. to Fouilloy.

28th. Adv. D.H.Q., Bois de Vaire. Carey's force took over H-M line. 48th and 49th Hants and R.E. in close support. Remnants of 156th Coy. with O.C. reached Hamel.

29th. 1st. Cav. Div. with 16th Div. took over H-M line from V-B rd. to Somme. R.E. and Hants wired & deepened front line.

30th. 11 a.m.—Heavy bombardment followed by infantry attack (228th Div.). 156th. & 157th took part in counter-attack driving enemy back to his trenches.

31st. Quiet day.

1st. "Field Coy's." relieved by R.E., 1st Cav. Div. and withdrawn to Aubigny.

2nd & 3rd. Worked on new switch line in rear of Hamel. 16th Division relieved by 14th Division. Moved back to Sailleux.

SCALE.
AMIENS—CORBIE ... 10 MILES.
CORBIE—PERONNE ... 19 "
AMIENS—PERONNE ... 29 "
PERONNE—RONSSOY ... 10 "

16th DIV. R.E. – 21st MARCH, 1918.

HEADQUARTERS.
Bt. Lt.-Col. R. F. A. Butterworth, D.S.O.   Capt. R. B. Jennings, M.C.
Lieut. F. Webster.

155th COY., R.E.
Major E. I. Scott.
Capt. A. E. Hughes.
Lieut. J. P. Haugh.
2nd-Lt. C. Baines.
2nd-Lt. C. V. Brook.
2nd-Lt. A. G. Alock.

156th COY., R.E.
Major T. L. S. Holbrow, M.C.
Capt. J. Shelley, M.C.
Lieut. A. Culver.
2nd-Lt. J. W. G. Whitehouse.
2nd-Lt. E. J. Norman.
2nd-Lt. S. A. Hall.

157th COY., R.E.
Major P. F. Whittall, D.S.O.
Lieut. J. C. Black.
2nd-Lt. G. H. Baxter.
2nd-Lt. E. H. Bancroft.
2nd-Lt. J. R. Osmond.
2nd-Lt. N. C. Gornall.

Attached.
Lieut. F. J. King
Lieut. J. J. Rodgers (Royal Irish Regt.)

Attached.
Lieut. J. A. Stanistreet (2nd Leinsters).
Lieut. A. Gorman (Royal Irish Regt.)

KILLED IN ACTION.
Major T. L. S. Holbrow, M.C.
Lieut. J. W. G. Whitehouse.
2nd-Lt. E. J. Norman.
2nd-Lt. N. C. Gornall.
Lieut. J. J. Rodgers (Royal Dublin Fusiliers).

DIED OF WOUNDS.
2nd-Lt. S. A. Hall.
2nd-Lt. G. H. Baxter.

WOUNDED.
Capt. R. B. Jennings, M.C.
2nd-Lieut. J. R. Osmond.

AWARDS.
Major P. F. Whittall ... Bar to D.S.O.
Major E. I. Scott ... Military Cross.
2nd-Lt. A. G. Alock ... Military Cross.
Lieut. J. A. Stanistreet ... Military Cross.
Distinguished Conduct Medals, 2.
Military Medals, 9.

Army Form A. 2007.

CENTRAL REGISTRY.

Central Registry No. and Date.

RE/1952/16 NARRATIVES

Attached Files.

M

SUBJECT, AND OFFICE OF ORIGIN.

16th Division. — 155th, 156th, & 157th Field Coys. March & April 1918.

Referred to	Date	Referred to	Date	Referred to	Date
				1/13	
				P. A.	Date

Schedule of Correspondence.

B.

Narrative [?] - 16th Div

                                                  D. E. S.
                                            9th Nov. 1918.

Dear Mackintosh,

    I have at length written the yarn about the Divl. R.E. in the retreat, and send herewith 2 copies.

        Yrs. sincerely,

            (Sgd) R.J.W. Butterworth.

                      (2)

Dear Butterworth,

    Very many thanks for the narrative of the 16th Divn. Sappers - a very good record of some fine companies. I'm glad you've sent a copy to Records.

        Yrs. sincerely,

9.11.18.   (Sgd) E.E.B. Mackintosh.

P.

Brigadier General P. Leveson-Gower, C.M.G., D.S.O.

Commanding 49th Inf. Brigade.

1B

My dear Butterworth,

I am very glad to hear that you are putting on record the extraordinarily fine work performed by the R.E. Coys of the 16th Division during the operations of the 21st March - 3rd April.

It was towards the evening of the 21st and during the following days when the whole of the Infantry of the Division were engaged, and losses had been very heavy, that the fighting and steadiness of the R.E. Coys were of invaluable assistance. Especially noticeable was the gallantry displayed by the 156th Coy at St Emelie on the 21st, by the 157th Coy at Doigt on the 23rd and by the 155th Coy who covered the retirement on the 27th. On the morning of the 30th, when the Divisional front was attacked and partially penetrated the bravery of all three companies in the counter attack was worthy of the highest traditions of the Army.

The R.E. Coys of the 16th Division have at all times been held in high esteem by the Infantry for their personal fearlessness and the high standard of their technical work in the line, but during these operations they demonstrated that in addition their morale and fighting qualities as a formed body, acting as Infantry, left nothing to be desired.

Yours ever,

29 Aug 1918.

R. Leveson-Gower.

Brigadier-General (now Major-General) F.W. Ramsay, C.M.G., D.S.O.

Commanding 48th Inf. Brigade.

Headquarters,
58th Division.

Dear Butterworth,

I am anxious that my appreciation of the good work of the R.E. Companies during the operations 21st March - to April 3rd when attached to my Brigade should be conveyed to all ranks.

I may specially mention the fighting work of the 156th Company on the right flank at St Emilie on the 21st November, of the 157th Coy in passing through Doingt on the 23rd: and in the withdrawal from Morcourt on 27th, on which day the 155th also did good work in holding up the enemy's advance at Warfusee la Motte: and of all these companies in the counter attack against the Bavarians on the morning of the 30th March.

They worked well and in good formation under shell fire and though not trained as infantry they were equal to the best and shewed great determination and pluck throughout the operations

Yours Sincerely

3 April 1918.

Frank Ramsay.

P.

Major-General Sir. C.P.A. Hull. K.C.B.
G.O.C. 16th (Irish) Division.

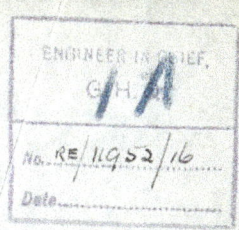

2/9/18.

My dear Butterworth.

Your letter reached me just as we were starting the fighting in these parts, hence the delay in answering.

I am very glad to hear that the deeds of the Field Coys of the 16th Divn during last March and April are to be brought to light. Their fighting qualities were beyond praise and they helped the remains of the infantry in many a tight corner by their dash and grasp of the situation.

Notably the 156th Coy on March 21st at St Emilie where the fighting was hard and the situation at the moment decidedly mixed. On March 23rd the 157th Coy attached to the 48th Inf. Bde, put up a stout resistance on the extreme right of our line and when the order to withdraw was sent, gave material assistance to the Brigade when passing through Doignt.

I think one of their best actions was when the three Coys were ordered to move from Morcourt to Mericourt during the night of the 26th/27th March, in order to guard the crossings at the latter place and probably the left of the 49th Inf. Bde., Owing to the enemy pressing forward on the north of the river and eventually crossing at Chipilly on the 27th, our left was under heavy fire from its flank and rear, the way the Engineers held their ground and eventually fought their way back was splendid

The 155th Coy I remember especially did good work there. I have no doubt there are other instances but these showed what stuff they were made of and how they proved themselves first class fighters in a first class fighting division. You yourself deserve every credit for this and I am glad to have the opportunity of again thanking you for all you did during those strenuous times.

Yours very sincerely

Amyatt Hull.

If you want to use this I should think it would be better as an appendix. I'm afraid the effort is poor, I'm not good with the pen, but anyhow it is sincere.
A.H.

FOREWORD.

The fighting troops of a Division are the Infantry, Artillery and Field Companies R.E. vide F.S. Regulations Part I (Operations).

In Trench Warfare this fact is often lost sight of, for, from the nature of things, the Field Company Sapper is looked upon as the builder of dugouts, provider of trenchboards and revetting material, and the handy man of all trades in and out of the line.

In the retreat, however, he comes into his own, and he both works and fights, laying down his shovel to pick up a rifle, and defending a bridge-head until it is his job to drop the bridge prior to retirement. In all phases of war it is his honourable task to assist the Infantry and Artillery in gaining and maintaining the advantage over the enemy, using, for this purpose, his technical skill and training as an Engineer. But when chance offers, as in a withdrawal he is happy to fight alongside the infantry, and great is his reward if he gains some mead of praise for his stout resistance in a village street, or for timely support at a critical moment.

The withdrawal of the Allied Armies under the concentrated and well-prepared attacks of the German forces delivered on 21st. March 1918 may well be said to mark the turning point of the great Eurppean War. Then it was that the German General Staff - calculating on our big losses in the Ypres and Cambrai battles of 1917 - hoped to break the allied front, sever the British and French along the line of the Somme, and win the War before the Americans could effectively intervene.

Trench warfare was converted into open fighting and the change of tactics was destined to put into the hands of one or other of the opposing forces the opportunity of strategical combination hitherto impracticable.

The dogged retirement..............

The dogged retirement of the Third and Fifth Armies, the fine defence of the First Army at BETHUNE, and the gallant stand of the Second Army on the SCHERPENBERG-MONT DES CATS position, though yielding a few miles of territory, laid the foundation of a victorious counter-thrust.

Following close upon this the magnificent leading and fighting of the French about REIMS and CHATEAU THIERRY, enabled the Generalissimo of the Allied Forces, Field Marshal FOCH, to set in motion a strategical combination which was to have far-reaching and decisive results.

The share taken by the 16th. Irish Division in the March battles, their early and desperate defence of RONSSOY village, and their subsequent fighting withdrawal, and recovery on the HAMEL - MARCELCAVE line, find their place in the official records and war diaries. It is hhpeHope of the writer to place on record the work and action of the Royal Engineers of this Division during this period, both in appreciation of the work done, and gallantry shewn, and also as a possible help to future students of Engineer work in a retreat.

- 3 -

The order of Battle of the 16th. Division on 21st. March 1918 was as follows :-

Division Commander

Major General Sir C.P.A. HULL, K.C.B.

R.F.A.

G.O.C. R.A. Brigadier General C.E.C.G. CHARLTON, D.S.O.

177 - 180 - 189 - 277 Brigades R.F.A.

R.E.

C.R.E. Bt: Lt: Col: R.F.A. BUTTERWORTH, D.S.O., R.E.

155 - 156 - 157 Field Companies R.E.

49th. Brigade.

Brigadier General P. LEVESON GOWER, C.M.G., D.S.O.

2nd. Royal Irish Regiment,

7th. Royal Irish (South Irish Horse),

7/8th. Royal Iniskilling Fusiliers.

48th. Brigade.

Brigadier General F.W. RAMSAY, C.M.G., D.S.O.

1st. Royal Dublin Fusiliers,

2nd. Royal Dublin Fusiliers,

2nd. Royal Munster Fusiliers.

47th. Brigade.

Brigadier General H.G. GREGORIE, D.S.O.

6th. Connaught Rangers,

2nd. Leinster Regt.,

1st. Royal Munster Fusiliers.

16th. Machine Gun Battalion.

Lieut: Col: R. LE BUTT D.S.O.

11th. Hants Pioneers.

Lieut: Col: B.E. CROCKETT, D.S.O.

DETAIL AND DISPOSITION OF THE DIVISIONAL ENGINEERS 21st. MARCH.

155 Field Company - O.C. Major E.I. SCOTT, R.E., T.F.

    H.Q. & 3 Sections - VILLERS FAUCON.

        1 Section - RONSSOY.

Left Brigade Sector.

    157 Field Coy. - O.C. Major P.F. WHITTALL, D.S.O., R.E.

    H.Q. & 3 Sections - VILLERS FAUCON.

        1 Section - RONSSOY.

Right Brigade Sector.

    156 Field Coy. - O.C. Major T.L. HOLBROW, M.C., R.E.

    H.Q. & 2 Sections - ST. EMILIE.

        2 Sections - VILLERS FAUCON.

    In reserve.

Orders in case of attack.

O's C. Field Companies were instructed to collect their units as far as the tactical situation allowed, and man the village defences under the orders of the commander designated in the Divisional Defence Scheme.

    155 Field Co. } VILLERS FAUCON.
    157 "   "

    156 Field Co.   ST. EMILIE.

Horse transport, with technical wagons and stores, were to be parked clear of the village, pending further orders.

The opening of the attack.

The attack in the early hours of the 21st. March came in the nature of a suprice - it had been long anticipated but there were no special signs or final warning on the night of 20/21 March that the blow would fall next day.

The enemy barrage came down with almost perfect synchronism at 4.15 a.m., the Battle Lines, Battery Positions, and villages of LEMPIRE, RONSSOY, ST. EMILIE and VILLERS FAUCON being heavily shelled with H.E..............

- 5 -

shelled with H.E. and Gas. All telephone communication forward of Brigade Headquarters was at once destroyed.

A thick fog enveloped the whole area - a grey white darkness of the consistency of steam. Advancing under its cover the enemy early reached the Southern edge of the LEMPIRE-RONSSOY defences, where hot fighting took place. The two forward sections of 155 and 157 could not for the moment be extricated and fought under the orders of the O.C. LEMPIRE defences. Later on they were withdrawn to VILLERS FAUCON by Lieut: F.H. KING (Royal Irish Regt., attached R.E.) - Lieut: G.H. BAXTER R.E. having been mortally wounded while engaged at close quarters in the defence of the citadel.

After a severe struggle in which the gallant battalion of South Irish Horse was practically annihilated and in which the 7/8 Inniskillings suffered very heavy xasualities, the villages of RONSSOY and LEMPIRE fell into the enemy's hands. This happened at approximately 11 a.m. and had the effect of turning our Battle Line from the South. A withdrawal to the Switch Line EPENY - ST. EMILIE became imperative.

Meanwhile the Left Brigade put up a fine fight and held on tenaciously to the MALASSISE Farm position where the gallant defence of the Dublin Fusiliers continued until late in the afternoon.

The 155 and 157 Field Companies, under the command of Major WHITTALL who became O.C. Village defences, manned the defences of VILLERS FAUCON. They suffered some casualities through shell-fire, including 2nd. Lieut: N.C. GORNALL who was killed while taking a message from the O.C. to one of his groups.

157 successfully evacuated their transport during a lull in the shelling, to the neighbourhood of MARQUAIX. Unluckily a big shell struck the harness room of 155 and a great part of the transport was consequently immobilized. However, by making several trips the greater number of the wagons were got clear of the village.

155 Field Coy.,

156 Field Coy. not being immediately required for the defence of ST. EMILIE, the O.C. reported to the Brigadier 49th. Brigade, and was instructed to extend our line to the right and head off small parties of German scouts who were advancing, with light machine guns in order to work round the flank of the ST. EMILIE position from the South. This was a task dear to Major HOLBROW's heart, and he fought his company tile late in the afternoon on the right, and did most useful service. He was ably backed up by his senior subaltern, Lieut: W.B.G.WHITEHOUSE, and his C.S.M. H. GATES, until the former was unluckily killed by a machine gun bullet.

156 Company was relieved at 3 p.m. by the Munster Fusiliers and withdrew to a support position in rear of ST. EMILIE. Major HOLBROW sent off an excellent sketch and tactical report timed at 5.5.p.m. which was the first reliable information of the situation on our extreme right, to reach Division Headquarters.

The situation at nightfall of 21st. March was:- 16th. Division on Brown Line (Corps Line) just east of ST.EMILIE - touch on the right with the 66th. Division who had fallen back behind TEMPLEUX-GERRARD - 21st. Division still holding out in EPEHY.

As regards the R.E., 155 and 157 had been withdrawn to the Green Line just east of TINCOURT, having been relieved in VILLERS FAUCON by the 2nd. Leinsters - 156 remained in support at ST. EMILIE.

After dark Capt: J. SHELLY of 156 Field Coy. ran some transport into ST. EMILIE, the outskirts of which were occupied by the Germans and succeeded in removing all the Officers' and Mens' Kits and Mess Gear. Major HOLBORN turned out his Company again to assist the infantry to dig in, and succeeded in strengthening the railway cutting midway between ST. EMILIE and VILLERS FAUCON.

During the night 21/22 March orders were issued for the withdrawal of the Division on the Green Line (HINCOURT - TEMPLEUX - LA-FOSSE). The C.R.E. was instructed to improve the defences of the Green Line, using 155 and 157 Field Companies and any infantry that were available

The 7th. Corps Cyclist Coy.........

The 7th. Corps Cyclist Coy. were sent up to strengthen the right flank of the line which rested on the COLOGNE River just South of TINCOURT.

At daylight, work was started on deepening the Green Line which, in our sector was a spit-locked trench protected by three belts of good wire. The Cyclist Coy. was employed in wiring the marsh from the TINCOURT & ROISELLE high road up to the river. Meanwhile the infantry withdrew from the ST. EMILIE position and came into line by noon on the Green Line.

This line had a fine field of fire, and the further advance of the enemy was held up during the day. 155 and 157 remained in line and assisted in the defensive action.

Earlier in the day 156 had a difficult retreat through VILLERS FAUCON and were withdrawn to DOINGT.

Divisional Headquarters moved that afternoon to DOINGT, and during the night 155 was withdrawn from the line and joined 156.

22nd. MARCH.

Divisional Headquarters moved at 7-a.m. via PERONNE to BIACHES, where Divisional Headquarters were established.

155 and 156 Field Companies marched to BIACHES and remained during the day in Div: Reserve. The infantry fell back, stubbornly resisting, from TINCOURT via DOINGT to PERONNE, reaching the latter town in the late afternoon. Fighting took place throughout the day and many tactical points were resolutely held, while the general retrograde movement conformed to the movement of the Division on the left flank.

Here 157 Field Company distinguished itself, in acting as part of the rearguard for the 49th. Brigade. On approaching DOINGT, which is a small village in the main road about 3 miles from PERONNE, the enemy pressed the 49th. Brigade very hard with the intention of making the passage of the SOMME at PERONNE a difficult operation.

157 Field Coy..............

- 8 -

157th. Field Coy. under Major WHITTALL, and two Companies of 11th Hants Pioneers under Major HAZARD fought a valuable delaying action in the village. It was realized that, by taking cover in the houses and enclosures, a stout fight could be put up against the enemy, whose principal wepons at the moment were rifles and machine guns.

A house to house fight took place, and valuable time was gained for the extrication of the infantry. Major WHITTALL received a bar to his D.S.O. f r this action, and there is little doubt that Major HAZARD whould have been similarly rewarded if he had had the luck to survive the retreat.

Capt: G. HOWSON of the Pioneers shewed great initiative in the same action but, holding too long on to a building, was surrounded and captured. However, he eluded his captors and rejoined his company later in PERONNE.

The infantry crossed the SOMME just before dusk, and took up a position covering the river approaches in and about BIACHES. The Bristol Bridge on BRACHBEONNE - AMIENS Road was blown at 6 p.m.

The road between BIACHES and HERBECOURT was now much congested with horse traffic and transport and three enemy aeroplanes came over and machine-gunned it. It was, however, a timorous effort from a great height, and three or four men only, were wounded.

During the night the infantry were withdrawn on relief by the 39th. Division, and marched into bivouac between HERBECOURT and CAPPY, and Divisional Headquarters moved to CAPPY.

157 was ordered to rejoin 155 and 156 Field Cos. west of CAPPY and reached that village at 3 a.m. on the 23rd. The men were in splendid spirits, and were singing as they went through, in spite of having continuously marched and fought since 7 a.m. on the 22nd.

23rd. MARCH.

A most brilliant day of sunshine. The division spent the day in support. The Field Cos. were ordered to fill up with S.A.A. and be ready to move...............

be ready to move at half an hour's notice. News was very scarce but the general impression was that the Fifth Army were standing on the line of the SOMME, and that the Division would soon be on its way again into line East or North East.

Towards the afternoon, however, it was evident that the enemy was pressing forward on the North Bank of the SOMME, as the Artillery fire was increasing momentarily in that direction.

At about 3 p.m. the Divisional Commander issued orders that bridgeheads were to be prepared at FROISSY, CERISY, and MERICOURT, each of which would be held by a brigade. The C.R.E. was instructed to arrange for the necessary work at each bridgehead, in co-operation with the Brigadier concerned, and to prepare the bridges at those places for demolition. For this purpose 155 Field Coy. was told off for FROISSY - 156 for CERISY - and 157 for MERICOURT.

Lieut: WEBSTER was sent off with two lorries to fetch picks and shovels from the Army Dump at CHAULNES; he got there at 8 p.m. to find the place in flames. He then went on to LA FLAQUE which was deserted and picked up the necessary tools. These he delivered at each of the Bridgeheads, and reached H.Q., R.E. at 7 a.m. on the 25th., having covered a distance of nearly 70 miles in the dark over absolutely strange roads, and been within an ace of being captured near CHAULNES.

Divisional Headquarters moved that evening to MORLANCOURT. The C.R.E. arranged work and demolition at the three bridgeheads, and reached D.H.Q. via BRAY at midnight. The latter town was seriously blocked with transport, and was bombed by the enemy, though luckily no hit was obtained in the main traffic thoroughfare.

25th. MARCH.

The Division was transferred from the VII to the XIX Corps H.Q. HARBONNIERES. D.H.Q. moved to WARFUSEE-LAMOTTE about 3 miles from VILLERS-BRETONNEUX.

The Field Coys....................

The Field Cos. worked all day in preparing bridges at FROISSY, MERICOURT, and CERISY for demolition, and in fortifying bridgeheads at these places. 10 bridges in all were got ready, including the railway bridge at FROISSY which carried a line of rail, and double width railway on a 4' brick-arch span. Capt: JENNINGS, acting adjutant scoured the country for gun-cotton and fuse, and sufficient was obtained to supplement that carried to make up the necessary charges.

The enemy was now developing a strong attack on the North of the SOMME on the line CURLU - MONTAUBAN - LONGUEVAL.

The Brigades were moved up to a preparatory position west of PROYART with a view to holding up an advance on the South of the river The Field Coys. were instructed to move into the village of PROYART, leaving a small detail at each group of bridges to carry out the demolition when ordered.

At 8 p.m. that evening information was received that the Fifth Army was falling back on the line CHAULNES - BRAY - ALBERT, and the 16th. Division was ordered to prepare and occupy the section of this general line between PROYART and the River SOMME at FROISSY - connecting on the right with the 39th. Division.

The C.R.E. visited Brigade H.Q. at M NCOURT and MERICOURT, and the Field Coys. at PROYART, and made arrangements to start work at daybreak next morning.

26th. MARCH.

Soon after daylight the C.R.E. met the three Brigadiers at PROYART, and arranged the siting of the line, and details of work to be done. The Defences of PROYART and line joining up with the 39th. Division was given to the 11th. Hants Pioneers - the remainder, a distance of about 6,000 yards, was sub-divided among the three Field Coys. each working on a Brigade Sector, with infantry parties provided by the Brigade.

A supply of wire was found at LA FLAQUE and FROISSY Dumps and there were plenty of picks and shovels at the former.

The line selected........ ....

The line selected had a good field of fire into, and across, the small valley running from PROYART via CHIGNOLLES to the SOMME at FROISSY and was not under observation from the high ground further east, except on the left where it was overlooked from the north bank of the river. The line passed just in rear of CHIGNOLLES which was at the bottom of the valley, and it was intended to deny the occupation of this to the enemy by rifle and Stokes Mortar fire.

At about 1 p.m. Germans appeared on the South of the SOMME, pushing in the advanced line of infantry scouts. Our half completed line was soon under erratic but fairly brisk machine and Field Gun fire. The R.E. and Pioneers with the infantry working parties stood to arms, and lined the trenches and banks. The attack was not driven home and at 3 p.m. the R.E. were relieved and went back into support in MORCOURT wood just west of PROYART.

In the meantime the 10 bridges had been blown up by the R.E. detachments - a good job was made of the big FROISSY bridge in which the crown was attacked, making a wide gap up to the abutment on each side.

At 4 p.m. the C.R.E was ordered to reconnoitre a position covering MORCOURT, to be garrisoned by the Field Cos. in the event of the PROYART line being forced back, and to dispose of the three Field Cos. for its defence.

The Field Cos. were accordingly moved back to a preparatory position close to MORCOURT village. They had however very little rest that night, for at 2 a.m. on the 27th. they were called upon to extend the left flank of the Divisional front, and guard the crossings of the SOMME on the flank of the 49th. Brigade. They marched off under the command of Major P.F. WHITTALL towards FROISSY, and, based in the FROISSY - MERICOURT road, pushed out an outpost line on the river bank from FROISSY to ETINEHEM and CERISY.

27th. March. ....

27th. MARCH.

The enemy attacked the PROYART Line at 9 a.m. and after severe fighting captured the village of PROYART, forcing the 47th. Brigade south-west, thus leaving the 48th. and 49th. Brigades in a precarious position. The 11th. Hants Pioneers formed a defensive flank on the right of the 48th. Brigade, and, being well handled by Lieut: Col: CROCKETT, facilitated the withdrawal of the 48th. Brigade to the MORCOURT Line. The 49th. Brigade held on to the left flank, and commenced to withdraw at about 2 p.m. It was then reported that the Germans had crossed the SOMME at CHIPILLY about 1½ miles in rear of the MORCOURT Line.

The three Field Companies who were on the extreme left guarding the crossings of the SOMME, retired slowly and protected the left flank of the 49th. Brigade in their withdrawal. The MORCOURT Line was, by this time, turned by the enemy crossing at CHIPILLY south-west on LAMOTTE. The position was extremely critical as a rapid advance by the enemy on the CERISY - LAMOTTE road would have endangered the retreat of the 48th. and 49th. Brigades - on LAMOTTE.

The R.E. and Pioneers did useful work at this juncture, for, advancing towards CERISY, they opened heavy rifle fire on the advancing infantry, and gained valuable time for our Brigades. The 155th. Field Company under Major SCOTT, especially distinguished itself. The Company was led forward to gain touch with the advancing infantry and Lieut: A.G. ATOCK bravely charged and destroyed a machine-gun detachment.

This counter-attack had, undoubtedly, great effect on the hostile troops who had forced the CHIPILLY crossing, and took the pressure temporarily off the flanks of our retreating Brigades who successfully passed through LAMOTTE to the MARCELCAVE - HAMEL Line.

In their left-flank action the Pioneers fought splendidly, and Major HAZARD, who did so well at DOINGT on the 23rd., and Captains THYNE and MACONOCHIE were all missing.

155 Field Coy...............

155 Field Company were the last British Troops to pass through the village of LAMOTTE, and they fought wonderfully for men who had had so little infantry training. Each section supported the other in its retirement, and the value of the left side of the street was fully realised and made use of. Lieutenants J.P. HAUGH and C.V. BROOK, and Company Sergt: Major W. ARGYLE especially distinguished themselves.

For their brave and excellent work on this afternoon, Major SCOTT and Lieutenant ATOCK were awarded the M.C.

At nightfall the 48th. and 49th. Brigades were holding the old French line running in rear of LAMOTTE village - as far as the village of HAMEL - the Field Companies and Pioneers holding the extreme right on the main PERONNE - AMIENS high road.

Divisional Headquarters remained at HAMEL throughout this critical day. Meanwhile the Employment Coy. and all batmen and spare clerks were organised for its immediate defence by the A.Q.M.G. Lieut: Colonel G.A.C. WEBB. The village was heavily shelled, but not attacked, and towards the evening Headquarters was moved to the Convent at FOUILLOY - just clear of the town of CORBIE.

28th. MARCH.

Advanced Divisional Headquarters was formed on the west edge of the BOIS DE VARIE. The Division was relieved in the MARCELCAVE - HAMEL Line by a mixed force of Tunnellers, A.T. Companies, Instruction Staffs, etc. raised and organised by Major-General P.G. GRANT, Chief Engineer, Fifth Army. This Unit afterwards came under the command of Major-General CAREY, R.A. and became known as Carey's force.

156th. Field Company R.E. had suffered heavily during the retreat and its O.C. Major HOLBROW was only able to muster 20 Sappers. The Company was reinforced by the addition of some twenty infantry and a few Sappers (the original Dump Party) from H.Q., R.E. under 2nd. Lieutenant S.A. HALL.

All three Field Companies.........

- 14 -

All three Field Companies were placed in close support at HAMEL and dug themselves into the side of a hollow road at the Southern exit of the village. The men looked, and were, very tired, but their spirits and moral remained unimpaired. Major WHITTALL, who was a splendid example of cheerfulness to everyone, told me that afternoon that the men were fit and willing for any job of work or fighting, but it was useless to expect any rapid movement out of them.

I found Major HOLEROY in a cottage at the edge of the village helping his Company cook to make stew. His first thought, at all times, was the care and comfort of his men, and it was only a little later in the same afternoon that, in leaving his billet during a bombardment to look after three of his men, he was killed by a shell. And so passed away a fine young Officer "sans peur et sans reproche".

Captain JENNINGS who accompanied the C.R.E. that afternoon, was wounded in the leg by a shell splinter, but remained at duty.

The 48th. and 49th. Brigades, together with the R.E. and Pioneers were now formed into a mixed Brigade under Brigadier General F.W. RAMSAY.

```
Total Strength        ...    ...   700 rifles.
Infantry - as 2 battalions    ...   380.
Pioneers - as 1 battalion     ...   200.
R.E.     - as 1 battalion     ...   120.
                                    ----
                                    700.
```

Captain TILLY was in command of the Pioneer Battalion, and Major WHITTALL of the R.E. Battalion.

28th. MARCH.

The fine spell of weather now broke and during the night there was a very heavy fall of rain which continued off and on all day.

The British line covering CORBIE and VILLERS-BRETONNEUX was strengthened by the arrival of the 1st. Cavalry Division at POUILLY and two Australian Divisions on the west bank of the SOMME.

The C.R.E. went up to HAMEL and selected sites for an advanced dump at north-west edge of HAMLET. Meanwhile Lieutenant WEBSTER went off to XIX Corps Headquarters and obtained a supply of wire and pickets and some tools, which were taken forward by him after dark to the HAMEL Dump.

30th. MARCH.

The weather cleared somewhat, and there was much enemy aerial activity. Two big flights of Fokkers were operating for an hour over our lines, until engaged in a heavy air battle by our scouts, and chased away. A very heavy barrage was put down at 11 a.m. by the enemy on the front line (held by Carey's force) and HAMEL, followed up by an infantry attack. The enemy succeeded in entering the front line just east of HAMEL, and the R.E. and Pioneers were called upon by the Brigadier, 48th. Brigade, to counter-attack. The R.E. counter-attack was delivered in three lines - 157th. leading under Lieutenants J.R. OSMOND and E.H. BANCROFT, supported by the 156th. in two lines, led by Captain J. SHELLY and 2nd. Lieutenant S.A. HALL. It was a gallant little effort and was completely successful in driving the enemy out of the part of the front line and support lines occupied. Various infantry Officers told me that it was an inspiring sight to see those three thin lines going ahead at a steady double over the open. Three out of the four Officers became casualties - Lieutenant HALL and BANCROFT being killed, and Lieutenant OSMOND wounded. Also Sergt. HUGHES and 2nd./Cpl: FRYER, D.C.M., M.M. - a brilliant young N.C.O. - were killed.

The Sappers remained in the line until relieved next morning and excellent work was done by Lieutenant ATOCK 155th. Company R.E. who worked backwards and forwards with a small party of Sappers, carrying up rations, water, and ammunition. One of the party, Sapper FINLAYSON, afterwards received the D.C.M.

During the night a squad of infantry were taken up by Lieutenant WEBSTER, and some useful wiring done.

31st. March............

31st. MARCH.

A brilliant day of sunshine. Orders were issued that Carey's Force was to be relieved by the 1st. Cavalry Division, and that the 16th. Division would take over the portion of the line between HAMEL and the SOMME. The C.R.E. reconnoitred the front line with Lieut: WEBSTER, with a view to improving the defences in the 16th. Division Sector. The German dead were lying about in heaps, shewing how heavily the 228th. Bavarian Division had suffered in their attempt to wrest HAMEL from our possession, on the previous day.

The line held by our troops was an old French defence trench - much fallen in and shallow - but with very fair wire in front. With a little work it seemed easily capable of strengthening and improvement.

The opportunity was taken by the C.R.E. of inspecting the bridge across the SOMME at BOUZENCOURT. This was partially blown but quite passable for infantry. It had been apparently struck by a shell which caused one charge to detonate, cutting the girder on one side only. As the bridge was just in rear of our front line it was a bit of luck that the demolition had not been more complete. Captain HUGHES, 155th. Field Company took a limber with explosives up to GOUZENCOURT after dark, and prepared this bridge for demolition in case of further retirement.

During the night 31st. March/1st. April, the Field Companies were withdrawn from the line to AUBIGNY and the Hants Pioneers to VAIRE.

1st. APRIL.

Work was organised for improving our front line, and for preparing a Switch Line from the village of VAIRE to meet the main road near VILLERS BRETONNEUX. The latter was sited in conjunction with the 1st. Cavalry Division, and work was started by our R.Es. the same evening.

The 11th. Hants under Captain HOWSON commenced deepening and revetting the shallow parts of the front line and in strengthening the wire.

2nd. April..................

2nd. APRIL.

Very heavy German bombardment to the South of VILLERS BRETONNEUX but quiet on our front. The weather was fine and some useful work was done on our defensive system and the switch line.

3rd. APRIL.

16th. Division was relieved by the 14th. Division, and the Field Companies were moved by 'bus to SALEUX late that afternoon.

-o-o-o-o-o-o-o-o-o-o-

This brings to a conclusion these few notes on the work and fighting of the Royal Engineers 16th. Division during the critical period 21st. March to 4th. April.

It is an interesting fact that each Field Company learnt the use of Lewis Machine Guns on the retreat, and, finally, between 30 and 40 of these weapons were handed over to the Infantry, after having done excellent service.

In the form of an appendix are added a Special Order of the Day issued by General Sir H.P. GOUGH, commanding the Fifth Army, and three letters received from the Divisional Commander and Brigadiers of the 16th. Division in kind appreciation of the efforts of the R.Es.

I think it can be fairly said that the Sappers, under difficult and unusual conditions, did their best to worthily uphold the traditions of the Corps, and that they have, perchance, also earned the right to say with their brothers of the infantry

"Et militavi non sine gloria".

-o-o-o-o-o-o-o-o-

APPENDIX.

SPECIAL ORDER OF THE DAY
BY
General Sir H. de la P. GOUGH, K.C.B., K.C.V.O.,
Commanding Fifth Army, Dated 26th. March, 1918.

I wish to express to all Officers and men of the Fifth Army my immense admiration for the truly magnificent way all ranks have fough in this desperate struggle against immense odds. The very greatest traditions of British Soldiers and of the British race have been maintained. We are fighting for our lives, our existence, our honou and in your hands all these are safe. It is a matter now only for a few days before reinforcements arrive to alter the situation.

sd/ H.P. GOUGH   General.

Major-General Sir C.P.A. HULL, K.C.B.

G.O.C. 16th. (Irish) Division.

2/9/18.

My dear Butterworth,

Your letter reached me just as we were starting the fighting in these parts, hence the delay in answering.

I am very glad to hear that the deeds of the Field Companies of the 16th. Division during last March and April are to be brought to light. Their fighting qualities were beyond praise, and they helped the remains of the infantry in many a tight corner by their dash and grasp of the situation.

Notably the 156th. Company on March 21st. at ST. EMILIE where the fighting was hard and the situation at the moment decidely mixed. On March 23rd. the 157th. Company attached to the 49th. Infantry Brig put up a stout resistance on the extreme right of our line, and when the order to withdraw was sent, gave material assistance to the Brigade when passing through DOINGT.

I think one of their best actions was when the three Companies were ordered to move from MORCOURT to MERICOURT during the night of th 26th/27th. March, in order to guard the crossings at the latter place and probably the left of the 49th. Infantry Brigade. Owing to the enemy pressure forward on the north of the river and eventually crossing at CHIPILLY on the 27th., our left was under heavy fire from its flank and rear, the way the Engineers held their ground and eventually fought their way back, was splendid.

The 155th. Company I remember expecially did good work there. I have no doubt there are other instances but these shewed what stuff they were made of, and how they proved themselves first class fighters in a first class fighting division. You yourself deserve every credi for this and I am glad to have the opportunity of again thanking you for all you did during those strenuous times.

Yours very sincerely,

AMYATT HULL.

II.

Brigadier-General P. LEVESON-GOWER, C.M.G., D.S.O.

Commanding 49th. Infantry Brigade.

1/9/18.

My dear Butterworth,

I am very glad to hear that you are putting on record the extraordinarily fine work performed by the R.E. Companies of the 16th. Division during the operations of the 21st. March to 3rd. April.

It was towards the evening of the 21st. and during the following days when the whole of the infantry of the Division were engaged, and losses had been very heavy, that the fighting and steadiness of the R.E. Companies were of invaluable assistance. Especially noticeable was the gallantry displayed by the 156th. Company at ST. EMILIE on the 21st., by the 157th. Company at DOINGT on the 23rd., and by the 155th. Company who covered the retirement on the 27th. On the morning of the 30th. when the Divisional Front was attacked and partially penetrated the bravery of all three Companies in the counter-attack was worthy of the highest traditions of the Army.

The R.E. Companies of the 16th. Division have at all times been held in high esteem by the Infantry for their personal fearlessness, and the high standard of their technical work in the line, but during those operations they demonstrated that in addition their morale and fighting qualities as a formed body, acting as Infantry, left nothing to be desired.

Yours ever,

P. LEVESON-GOWER.

Brigadier-General F.W. RAMSAY, C.M.G., D.S.O.

Commanding 48th. Infantry Brigade.

Headquarters,
58th. Division,
6/4/1918.

Dear Butterworth,

I am anxious that my appreciation of the good work of the R.E. Companies during the operations 21st. March to April 3rd. when attached to my Brigade should be conveyed to all ranks.

I may especially mention the fighting work of the 156th. Company on the right flank at ST. EMILIE on the 21st. March, of the 157th. Company in passing through DOINGT on the 23rd., and in the withdrawal from MORCOURT on 27th., on which day the 155th. also did good work in holding up the enemy's advance at WARFUSEE LA MOTTE ; and of all these Companies in the counter-attack against the Bavarians on the morning of the 30th. March.

They worked well and in good formation under shell fire, and though not trained as infantry they were equal to the best and shewed great determination and pluck throughout the operations.

Yours sincerely,

FRANK RAMSAY.

16th (IRISH) DIVISION
LINE OF RETREAT, 21ST – 27TH MARCH, 1918

1st.
Field Co'ys. withdrawn to R.E. Ist Corps Div. and with drawn to Aubigny.

2nd & 3rd.
Worked on "switch" rd. in rear of Hamel.

16th Division relieved by 39th Div. & moved back to Saileux.

30th.
11 a.m. Heavy bombardment followed by infantry attack (2/28 Bav. Div.).

156th & 157th took part in counter-attack, enemy driven back to his trenches.

31st.
Quiet day

28th.
Adv. D.H.Q. Blanqi de Vert. Cachy's force took over H-M line. 48th and 49th Maintained R.E. effort. Remnants of 156th Co'y. with O.C. reached Hamel.

27th.
Position of 48th and 49th Brigades precarious.
2 a.m. R.E. ordered up to extend to left flank.
10 a.m. Heavy attack on Mericourt drove R.E. back to Morcourt. 156th R.E. moved along river as flank guard.
3 p.m. Enemy appeared on south bank at Cerisy, 49th Bde. saved from being outflanked by action of 156th and 157th, and 1 Coy. Hants.
5 p.m.–48th and 49th withdrawn to Hamel–Marcelcave line.
6 p.m.–155th Coy. fought their way through Lamotte closely pressed near Lamotte.
8 p.m.–156th and 157th in support near Lamotte.
No news of 156th or 47th Bde. D.H.Q. to Fouilloy.

26th.
C.R.E. ordered to construct advanced line, Proyart to Somme. Right to left–Hants, 156th, 155th and 157th.
R.E. completed bridgeheads, prepared bridges for demolition.
Worked until 3.0 p.m. when enemy attacked.
4 p.m.–155th, 156th and 157th to Proyart, leaving sections to blow up bridges. Proyart bridge and Mericourt bridges (6) demolished.
Enemy pressed on N. bank of Somme. A quiet night.

25th.
16th Div. placed under XIX Corps. D.H.Q. moved to Lamotte.

24th.
157th reached Cappy at 2.0 a.m., having marched and fought continuously for 24 hours.
A brilliant day of sunshine. No news.
6.0 p.m. R.E. proceeded to form bridge heads at Froissy (155), Cerisy (156), and Mericourt (157).
Lt. Webster took 2 lorries to Chaulnes for tools and materials, found it blazing West end with Field units. Recovered some tools and delivered tools to Field Companies.
D.H.Q. moved to Moracourt.
Bray seriously blocked with traffic, military and civil, and bombed.

23rd.
D.H.Q. moved at daybreak via Peronne, to Buire. 155th and 156th followed D.H.Q.
157th formed rearguard for 49th Bde. with 2 companies of Hants (Pioneers) under Major Hazard. Fought a gallant action at Doingt, where Brigade was extricated.
One battery covered Bristol bridge at 6.0 p.m. when the last regulated convoy, Peronne was then in flames.
D.H.Q. moved after dusk to Cappy via Neslecourt.

22nd.
Enemy advancing on Epervans green line. 156th holding infantry attack to South East by 9 a.m. fell back through Villers-Faucon to Tincourt.
Attack on St. Emilie, 12 noon.
R.E. forward Section withdrawn from Ronssoy, 11 a.m. 155th and 157th took full fighting positions for defence of Villers Faucon.
156th formed defensive flank to right of 49th Brigade.
Situation at nightfall – 155th and 157th holding right flank East of Villers Faucon, 155th in green line, 156th refused flank south of St. Emilie.

21st.
Enemy opened at 4.45 a.m. intensive artillery bombardment followed at 9.30 by large infantry attack aided by gas and mist, 3/4 mile visibility.

16th DIV. R.E. HEADQUARTERS 21st MARCH, 1918
B.G.O.C. R.F.A. Brigworth. D.S.O.   Capt. R.B. Jameson, M.C.
                                          Lieut. F. Webster

155th Co'y., R.E.
Major F.E. Cowley
Capt. M.A. Eager
Lieut. J.C. Clarke, M.C.
Lieut. W.G.V. Whitehead
2nd Lieut. A.G. Allen

156th Co'y., R.E.
Major T.L.S. Holbrow, M.C.
Capt. J.C. Shirley, M.C.
Lieut. J.W.G. Whitehead
2nd Lieut. S.E.L.

Attached
Lieut. F.J. King
Lieut. J.J. Rodgers

157th Co'y., R.E.
Major E.J. Haberton, M.C.
Lieut. J.W.G. Whitehead
2nd Lieut. N.C. Garner
2nd Lieut. A.G. Allen

Attached
Lieut. J. Stevenson
Lieut. A. Cory

KILLED IN ACTION
Major J.A.G. Holbrow, M.C.
Lieut. J.W.G. Whitehead
2nd Lieut. V.J. Norton
2nd Lieut. N.C. Garner
Lieut. J.J. Rodgers

DIED OF WOUNDS
2nd Lieut. J.A. Innes
2nd Lieut. G.H. Baker

WOUNDED
Capt. R.B. Jameson, M.C.
2nd Lieut. J.R. Grimwood

AWARDS
Major P.J. Whetsall   B.– in D.S.O.
Major A.G. Aves   Military Cross
2nd Lieut. A.G. Aves   Military Cross
Lieut. J.A. Stevenson   Military Cross

Distinguished Conduct Medals, 2
Military Medals, 9

SCALE
AMIENS—CORBIE .... 10 MILES
CORBIE—PERONNE 19   "
AMIENS—PERONNE 28   "
PERONNE—RONSSOY .... 10 "

MQR816
Job 29
April 1918

Army Form C. 2118.

A.Q.Q.3. 16 Div.

WAR DIARY
or
INTELLIGENCE SUMMARY.
(Erase heading not required.)

Instructions regarding War Diaries and Intelligence Summaries are contained in F.S. Regs., Part II. and the Staff Manual respectively. Title pages will be prepared in manuscript.

Place	Date	Hour	Summary of Events and Information	Remarks and references to Appendices
FOUILLOY	1/8/16	3 a.m.	156th Fd. C.R.E and 157th Fd. C.R.E. relieved from line E. of HAMEL by Cavalry Squadron of 1st Cav. Div.	
		9 a.m.	C.R.E. gave orders to prepare defence line in front of HAMELET and VAIRE-SOUS- CORBIE. Arranged with the Detachment of Sqdn. A.I.F. to continue wiring and commenced by Lt WEBSTER previous evening into the wood in J.32.D (Sheet 62D). Proceeded to HAMEL before that of cleaning these and visits G.O.C. 16 Bde. Afternoon proceeded to J.153 - 152.7757 5th Corps redoubt at MARICOURT. Capt JENNINGS reconnoitre the dumps of wire material and R.S. stores in FOUILLOY.	
		4.30 p.m.		
		7.30 p.m.	Lt. WEBSTER and HORE R.E. Army personnel together with few details of 48? S.M.Y. Fd. Coys to prepare defence line in front of VAIRE - near CORBIE - continues wire commenced 31/7/16.	
	2/8/16	9 a.m.	C.R.E. reconnoitre line at request of G.O.C. 16 Bn. in front of HAMELET running from S. E. of B.2.a.o.G. thence to P.13. central along J.33.a, J.32.d - P.2.a following road running. Sheet 62.D	
		9.30 a.m.	Capt. JENNINGS to CORBIE to look for boards for bridging.	
		12 noon	Lt. WEBSTER at request of G.S.O.I. 16 Div. accompanies Staff of 1st Cav. Division. Reconnoitre line from P.30.B to VAIRE - ran. - CORBIE (Sheet 62 D).	
		2 p.m.	C.R.E. visit field companies at MARICOURT.	
		7 p.m.	Lt. WEBSTER taken Hq. A.E. Army Group personnel to deepen old French Trenches	

Army Form C. 2118.

H.Q. R.E. 16 Div.

WAR DIARY
or
INTELLIGENCE SUMMARY.
(Erase heading not required.)

Instructions regarding War Diaries and Intelligence Summaries are contained in F. S. Regs., Part II. and the Staff Manual respectively. Title pages will be prepared in manuscript.

Place	Date	Hour	Summary of Events and Information	Remarks and references to Appendices
FOUILLOY	2/6		at P.S. A.L.5 (Sheet 62D).	
"	3/6	11 am	Orders received for relief of Division and move to SAZEUX.	
		12.15 pm	LT WEBSTER carries orders to 157, 158 Field Coys. Arrange MATEUX - Transport immediately and dismounted personnel by bus from Corps reserve.	
			S-D BLANGY - TRONVILLE at 8.30 pm.	
		2.30 pm	LT WEBSTER leaves FOUILLOY for SAZEUX with HQ R.E. Transport.	
		3.15 pm	Dismounted personnel returns to HQ R.E. leave by bus.	
		4 pm	Capt. JENNINGS & M.O. leave by the mounted Coys by bus.	
JAZEUX		8 pm	arrive SAZEUX. 8 pm. Orders received to move to CERISY on L. Report Stn Coys.	
SAZEUX	4/6	11 am	HQ R.E. move to CERISY. LT WEBSTER & M.O. with personnel & Transport returns by lorry. Capt. JENNINGS with three Officers & 72 other ranks remained return with Div HQ Transport by lorry. HQ RE Transport by march route with Div HQ Transport. 153 Fd Coy. at GREBAULT MESNIL, 156, 157 Field Coys. at ANICOURT.	
CERISY	5		Calls to Field Coys. at GREBAULT etc.	
"	6		Do.	

Army Form C. 2118.

WAR DIARY
or
~~INTELLIGENCE~~ SUMMARY.
(Erase heading not required.)

H.Q. R.E. 16 Div.

Instructions regarding War Diaries and Intelligence Summaries are contained in F.S. Regs., Part II. and the Staff Manual respectively. Title pages will be prepared in manuscript.

Place	Date	Hour	Summary of Events and Information	Remarks and references to Appendices
CERISY	7		Capt. G.E. GRIMSDALE R.E. reported from 3rd Field Squadron to take over command of 156 Field Company R.E.	
	8		Capt. R.E. STRADLING (Capt. R.E.) and Capt. GREENHOW (157 Field Coys.) report from leave.	
			C.R.E. goes by car to see E-in-C G.H.Q.	
			Capt. GREENHOW reports his unit. Orders received from G. re move of D.H.Q. & G.H.Q. and entrainment to FAUQUEMBERGUES on 10th.	
	9		CRES; ordered 153, 155 & 157 Field Coys. 155 Field Coys. to move north Donnes, 153 and 157 Field Companies to remain behind Brigade in G.H.Q. line of defence.	Appendix No. 1
			C.R.E. accompanied by Adjutant R.E., inspects 156 Field Co. and 157 Field Coys.	
			Move of H.Q.R.E. to GAMACHES. LT WEBSTER arrives GAMACHES to open office at 10 a.m. Capt. JENNINGS takes transport.	
		4 p.m	C.R.E. and Adjutant R.E. arrive GAMACHES.	
GAMACHES	10		Move of H.Q.R.E. to FAUQUEMBERGUES. 1st Field Coy at DARGNIES	
		7 a.m	LT. WEBSTER with transport and a few dismounted personnel and details entrain.	

T2134. Wt. W708—776. 500000. 4/15. Sir J C. & S.

Army Form C. 2118.

WAR DIARY
or
INTELLIGENCE SUMMARY.
(Erase heading not required.)

H.Q. R.E. 16 Div

Place	Date	Hour	Summary of Events and Information	Remarks and references to Appendices
FAUQUEMBERGUES	11.		at MERICOURT, detrain at WIZERNES 11 p.m. and complete journey by march route. Capt JENNINGS with remainder of personnel trained by lorry by day with stores. C.R.E. and Adjutant R.E. travel by car. 155 Field Coy. R.E. at BOUT-DE-LA-VILLE N of FAUQUEMBERGUES	
do.	12.		C.R.E. and Adjutant R.E. to C.E. XIII Corps by car. re work and stores. C.R.E. and Adjutant to 155 Field Coy R.E. - Adjutant R.E. afterwards proceeded and arranged Div. area re work the close on Rifle Range in the area. Capt. JENNINGS goes round D.H.Q. billets re camp services. C.R.E. and Adjutant R.E. accompanied by G.S.O.(1) 16 Div. and O.C. 155 Field Coys. go round Div. area re Rifle Range and work thereon.	
		2 p.m.	Orders received from "G" to be ready to move at an hours notice trench in night defence 155 Field Coys and 11 Hants. (Pioneer) informed / stand down order	
		7.30 p.m.	O.C. 155 Field Coys. sends C.R.E. FAUQUEMBERGUES bombed by E.A	

Army Form C. 2118.

WAR DIARY
or
~~INTELLIGENCE~~ SUMMARY.
(Erase heading not required.)

H.Q. R.E. 16th Divn

Place	Date	Hour	Summary of Events and Information	Remarks and references to Appendices
FAUQUEMBERGUES	13		C.R.E. Adjutant R.E. and Lt. WEBSTER goes to AIRE and meet Brig Gen McINNES G.H.Q. re new line near defences. Adjutant arranges about stations. C.R.E. and Lt. WEBSTER accompanied by Lt. Col. DAWFORD R.E. G.H.Q. reconnoitre new line from MOLINGHEM to STEENBECQUE.	Appendix No. 4
		3.30pm	Adjutant R.E. goes to R.E. ST OMER re left decamp to the formed stone	
			re 155 Field Coys R.E. and Capt HANSON A/O.C. H. HANTS (Pioneers) visit C.R.S. C.R.E.'s Order No. 62 re move of 155 Field Coy R.E. issued (Sector MOLINGHEM 25xxx BOSSINGHEM H.Q. THIEDOUANE etc.)	Appendix No. 2
do	14		Draft of 5 officers (Capt. McInnes, 2. Lts 2anfrs 16 December-23 January for 155 R.H.G. "Lt. BOYES, "Lt. WORSLEY for 157 Field Coy) and 112 other ranks for 16 Div. R.E. arrive AIRE	Appendix No. 4
			C.R.E., Capt. JENNINGS and G.S.O.11 16 Div. meet Corps Commander (XIII Corps) for further reconnaissance of new line.	
		11.25am	C.R.E. order No. 62/1 issued to 155 Field Coy. R.E. and transport with draft to move to ENGUINEGATTE	Appendix No. 3
		5 pm	Move of 155 Field Coy. R.E. complete.	
			of Capt CLARKE R.E. (O/C R.E. Draft) instructed by phone to report with draft to H.Q. 155 Field Coys. at ENGUINEGATTE for accommodation and rations	
			Adjutant R.E. goes to vie draft and make arrangement for rations	
		8 pm	C.R.E. v Capt. JENNINGS return.	JM

Army Form C. 2118.

H.Q. R.E. 16th Div.

WAR DIARY
or
~~INTELLIGENCE~~ SUMMARY
(Erase heading not required.)

Instructions regarding War Diaries and Intelligence Summaries are contained in F.S. Regs., Part II. and the Staff Manual respectively. Title pages will be prepared in manuscript.

Place	Date	Hour	Summary of Events and Information	Remarks and references to Appendices
AUGUEMBERGUES	14		Party of 1 N.C.O. and 5 sappers of 16 Div. Artillery Coy. report at H.Q.R.E., having failed to find their company after relief of 16 Div. in line. Also 6 stragglers from R.E. Draft. All sent on to ENGUINEGATTE to join 155 Field Coy R.E.	
do.	15	9.15am	C.R.E. away to view line to meet officer of 153rd Field Coy. and O.C. 11th Hants Pioneers to work on new line. Flagging and Capture out of new lines commenced. Capt. JENNINGS away with horses to AIRE for picks and shovels for work on new line.	Appendix No. 4.
		11am	Move of H.Q.R.E. to AIRE. Adjutant by car. Lt. WEBSTER and M.O. & with stores and personnel. H.Q. 153 Field Co. R.E. 1 Section and R.E. Draft move to LA ROUPIE	
AIRE		2½ pm	Capt. DAVID R.E., Lts. DAVIDSON, PATERSON, CHRISTISON, and LYNE, with 153 Co. R.E. join from leave. to be attached to 16 Div. R.E. Employed for work on new line. Capt. JENNINGS formed 1st draught out for working parties at MOLINGHEM O.P.d.5.6. CHAPEL O.3.c.8.2. LA ROUPIE I.32.d.5 & HOUVERRON I.27.a. THIENNES STN. I.23.6. STEENBECQUE I.5.d.7.6. MORBECQUE D.25.d.9.6.	Sheet 36(A).

JW

Army Form C. 2118.

WAR DIARY
or
~~INTELLIGENCE SUMMARY.~~
(Erase heading not required.)

H.Q. R.E. 16 Div.

Place	Date	Hour	Summary of Events and Information	Remarks and references to Appendices
AIRE	15		Information received that Lt-Col FALCON R.E. will be sent to act as assistant to C.E. 16 Div. for work.	
			C.R.E's Instructions for work on Reserve line No 1 cement ("La peripherie front line alluded into 3 sectors viz. NORTH (MORBECQUE St. to CAMP DE LA LYS exclusive) SOUTH (Camp de la Lys inclusive to HOLINGHEN O.9.d.6.0 (Sheet 36a))	Appendix No 3
			ISBERGUES STEEL WORKS Defence.	
			Labour allotted as follows :— Composite Brigade 16 Div. for North. Portugese Infantry Brigade for South. 11th Hants Pioneers for Isbergues R.E.	Appendix No. 5
			Each to have inspector of works appointed for each sector viz. Major E.T. SCOTT R.E. for 133 Field Coys.) C.R.E. North, Lt-Col FALCON R.E. C.R.E. South, and Lt-Col B.G. CROCKETT D.S.O. O.C. 11th Hants Pioneers C.R.E. Isbergues. H.Q. as follows	
			H.Q.R.E. Corante factory AIRE C.R.E. North THIENNES C.R.E. South LA ROUPIE C.R.E. ISBergues Camp I.26.a (Sheet 16t).	

Army Form C. 2118.

H.Q. Q.E. 16 DN

WAR DIARY
or
~~INTELLIGENCE SUMMARY~~
(Erase heading not required.)

Instructions regarding War Diaries and Intelligence Summaries are contained in F.S. Regs., Part II. and the Staff Manual respectively. Title pages will be prepared in manuscript.

Place	Date	Hour	Summary of Events and Information	Remarks and references to Appendices
AIRE	16.		153 Sect Co (One 1 Officer & a return.) At THIENNES together with all details C.R.E. around the time new reserve line barrage work. Capt. JENNINGS and Lt. WEBSTER forming dumps as mentioned in Appendix 5. Of tools and mining stores.	Appendix No 4.
		2 p.m.	Made arrangement on new Meteren line. Pending arrival of 1st Coy. FAZER, "Lt. BROOK and Lt. WEBSTER set out PORTUGUESE BRIGADE trench on South Sector. 21st, 22nd and 34th Battns of PORTUGUESE BRIGADE work in South sector. Cinquante Anglais on N. Sector and 1st HANTS PIONEERS in ISBERGUES. Capt. DAVID R.E. and "Lt. DAVIDSON with 3rd O.R. attached to PIONEERS for work.	Appendix No 6
		4 p.m.	C.R.E. instructions for work on Reserve line No 2 viewed given details of lines and sections etc. Trenches and also tasks to be allotted for 3 days work.	
		5.30 p.m.	C.R.E.; instructions for work on Reserve line, No 3 sector given, distribution of R.E. personnel between the three sectors also method of rationing the R.E. Personnel.	Appendix No 7
			Capt. JENNINGS arranges billets at ISBERGUES for the R.E. personnel under 3.	

JW

Army Form C. 2118.

H.Q. R.E. 1ST DIV.

WAR DIARY
or
INTELLIGENCE SUMMARY.
(Erase heading not required.)

Instructions regarding War Diaries and Intelligence Summaries are contained in F. S. Regs., Part II. and the Staff Manual respectively. Title pages will be prepared in manuscript.

Place	Date	Hour	Summary of Events and Information	Remarks and references to Appendices
			Work on South Section.	
	17		Capt. CLARKE, Lt. LAW, and Lt. DUCKWORTH move from THIENNES with 100 O.R., R.E. and occupy billets at ISBERGUES.	
		9 pm	CRE's Instructions for Work on Reserve Line No.4 issued re preparing roadway & Embankment from PONT D'ISBERGUES from left boundary at MORBECQUE of defences.	Appendix N.
AIRE	18		Work continued as above. Lt. Col. FALCON R.E. reports to CRE 16" Div. for duty. C.R.E. around South and ISBERGOES areas. Lt. WEBSTER and Capt. JENNINGS staying overnights to assist in destruction of strive closer to the lorries with further loads to allotted to a.m. by 1st Army. Also 6 lorries from S.M.E.X.D. Cpl. L. MORSEY to hospital sick. Work as above. Lt. Col. FALCON visits our huts on CRS South Section. CRE. 1st Div. arrived with CRS South in morning, and with CRE walk & Spr. Campbell &c. in afternoon selecting tactical position.	Appendix No. A.
	19		Capt. JENNINGS and Lt. WEBSTER to BETHUNE for transportable return from Front control. CRE's Instructions for Work on RESERVE LINE N°5 issued, giving various details of how work can be afforded thereto. NOTE on SECTORS & LEBTS. Lt. WEBB to FORET DE CLAIRMARAIS for stores.	Appendix 9.

Army Form C. 2118.

HQ RE 16 DN

WAR DIARY
or
INTELLIGENCE SUMMARY.
(Erase heading not required.)

Instructions regarding War Diaries and Intelligence Summaries are contained in F. S. Regs., Part II. and the Staff Manual respectively. Title pages will be prepared in manuscript.

Place	Date	Hour	Summary of Events and Information	Remarks and references to Appendices
AIRE	19		CRE. Instructions for Work on Reserve Line No. 6 issued for trenches on low water beyond present	Appendix No. 10.
"	20		Work as usual	
"	21		As above. 2nd R. Munst. Fus. leave Div. then deflecting CR.E. North of labourer. 155th Field H.Q. v 156th #STEENBECQE.	
"	22		Work as above. Capt Jennings with CRE tracing out new width line (Le Bas switch) from I.G. O. P.S. No. 6 to KEMMEL-NORBECQ RD C.R.E. goes to see E-in-C. afterwards went to 156th + 157th Fd. Comps. Appendix No. 2 "LT. LN." transported (wounded) CR.E. Instructions for Work on Reserve Line No. 7. Appendix No. 7	
"	23		2nd R. G. Regt. v 2nd Leic. Regt. leave Division and CRE. Instructions for Work on Reserve Line No. 8 issued. re Readjustment of Labour. Work on Mesri continued.	No. 11
"			Capt Jennings completes the laying out of LE BAS SWITCH and Reserve HARE -6 appointed O/C to be consulted — taken of position in STEENBECQUE. O/C Le Bas Switch joined by Capt. DAVID & Lt. DAVIDSON R.E. v 6 other members R.E. from C.R.E. South.	
AIRE	24		Work in Le Bas North Commenced. New Reserve line in N.W. Sector visited by C.R.E. 16 Div. TCols. W. H.	Appendix No. 14
			CRE. Instructions No. 8 issued as amendment to Instruction No. 2 CRE Instructions No. 9 issued re Reserves de finiscrolls North	Appendix No. 12 Appendix No. 13
"	25		Work on Line continued. 2nd R.D. Fus. leave the Div. All Labour now found by R.S. + 2N.T.S. Pioneers.	
			Portuguese CRE's Instruction for Work on Reserve Line No. 10 issued. 1st Irish Pioneers at Hazebrouck	Appendix No. 14
"	26		Work as usual. CRE 16 Div. + LT. WEBSTER see Capt. HOWSON 11"Hants Pioneers at Hazebrouck. projects on Canal d'Aire at O.11.6.5.3 (Sheet 36N) + demolition of houses at O.11.a.70.93. very demolition of work on canal of present enemy bridges + clearation of houses before field of fire	

T2134. Wt. W708—776. 500000. 4/15. Sir J.C. & S.

Army Form C. 2118.

H.Q. R.E. 16 Div.

WAR DIARY
or
INTELLIGENCE SUMMARY.
(Erase heading not required.)

Place	Date	Hour	Summary of Events and Information	Remarks and references to Appendices
HAZEBROUCK	26-0-77		The Method Defences & present escarp. for enemy. CRE. over CRA. roads & shewing new support line trench works. Support line traced out. MAJ. R.E. move to Command Section MRE both 26-0-77. C.E. XI Corps in attendance.	Appendix No 4.
	27		Work as usual. New reserve line North/East commenced. Informed that 153 T.S.T. Field Coys. Tyneries Division from Reserve Army extension on 28th August.	Appendix No 4.
	28		Work as usual. 2 groups Heavy Artillery (Belgian) commence work with CRE. Night. CRE's Instructions for Work in Reserve Line No. 11 issued as memo. Reserve defences in emergency. Position allotted to Field Coys of 16 Div No. 15 XI Corps.	Appendix No. 15
			Mister P. F. WHITTAR D.S.O. (O.C. 157 Field Coys) appointed CRE II Corps. Capt. R.B. JENNINGS (153 Field Coys) now attached R.E./Army will now to command 157 Field Coys vice Major P. F. Whittar S.S.O. R.A.	
	29		Work as usual. 153 & 157 Field Coys. arrive THENNES. 153 Rabbitous move to billets at PECQUES & 157 Field Coys. R.E. to ISBEAGUES.	
			CRE's Instructions for Work in Reserve Line No 12 issued re schedule of arrangements.	Appendix No. 16.

Army Form C. 2118.

WAR DIARY
or
INTELLIGENCE SUMMARY.
(Erase heading not required.)

H.Q.R.E. 16 Div.

Place	Date	Hour	Summary of Events and Information	Remarks and references to Appendices
AIRE	28		Of labour responsible for work in reward of 157 & 75? Field CoyRS.	Appendix No. 16.
	29		CRE's Instructions for work in Reserve Area No. 13 issued to more of field Coys on the allotment of the reinforcements to their respective units	Appendix No. 17.
AIRE	30		157 Field Co. R.E. move to STEENBECQUE, 75? to PECQUEUR ment rate over with execution of CRE's Instruction No. 12 (Appendix No. 16) CRE. Webb later over work on letter hand off from Capt. R.B. JENNINGS. Information received that 11th Hants (Pioneers) leaves the Division. CRE's Instruction No. 12 consequent upon withdrawal of 11th Hants (P).	Appendix No. 18

J. Webb, Lt. R.E.
for .... Lieut.-Col. R.E.
C. R. E. 16th Division.

Appendix No. 1   H.Q. R.E.
                     War Diary
SECRET.   April 1918

C. R. E's ORDER No. 61.

8th April 1918.

1. On being transferred to another Army the 18th Div. (less Artillery, 156 and 157th Field Coys and M.G. Battn) will move by road to the GAMACHES Area on 9th April and entrain at WOINCOURT and EU on 10th April.

2. 155th Field Coy. will move from GREBAULT-MESNIL at 11.30 a.m. on 9th April via VISMES AUVAL - MAISNIERES following behind 11th Hants (P) as far as DARGNIES where Field Coy. will billet for the night.
   O.C. 155th Field Coy. R.E. will arrange to send forward billeting party to DARGNIES

3. 155th Field Coy. R.E. will entrain at WOINCOURT by No. 10 train on 10th instant and detrain at WISERNES.
   Train leaves WOINCOURT at 16.04 and Company should arrive at entraining station 3 hours before departure of train.

4. A billeting party composed as follows should report at EU Station at 8.19 a.m. on 9th instant and should be provided with bicycles.
   Parties will report to Billeting Officer of 47th Bde. H.Q. at the station one hour before departure of train. (7.19)

   1 Officer per Brigade H.Q.
   1 Officer and 2 N.C.Os. per Battalion.
   1 N.C.O. per Field Ambulance.
   1   "   per Div. Train Coy.
   1   "   for Div. Train H.Q.
   1   "   155th Field Coy. R.E.
   1   "   Mob. Vet Section.
   2 N.C.O's for Divnl Headquarter.

   They will be met by an Officer of the Divisional Staff at Detraining Station, ARCQUES.

5. All the trains consist of 1 Officers' coach (capacity 32 Officers) 17 flat trucks, 30 covered trucks.
   Each flat truck will take an average of four axles; each covered truck will take 40 men, or 6 H.D. Horses, or 8 L.D. Horses or Mules.
   No personnel or stores will be allowed in the break-vans at each end of the train, or on the roofs of the trucks. No covered truck should be used for baggage, as it restricts the space available for personnel.
   Supply and baggage wagons will join their own Units prior to entrainment and will accompany them in every case.
   The entrainment of all Units must be completed half-an-hour before the time of departure of the train, when it will be moved from the loading station.
   Breast ropes for horse trucks must be provided by units themselves. Ropes for lashing vehicles on to flat trucks will be provided by the Railway Authorities.

P.T.O.

6. The journey will take approximately eight hours.

7. 156th and 157th Field Coys. will remain in their present billets pending further instructions.

8. Supply arrangements will be as follows:-

Refilling at present Refilling point on the morning of 9th instant for all Units including 156 and 157 Field Cos R.E. and 16 M.G. Battn. Supplies being delivered to Units by Train Wagons for consumption 10th inst.

In afternoon of 9th inst. there will be a second refilling for consumption 11th inst. for all Units, less 156 and 157 Field Cos. R.E. and 16th M.G. Bn., supplies being conveyed by 16th M.T. Coy. to places as selected by O.C. 16th Divnl Train in the neighbourhood of EU and WOINCOURT, supplies being loaded on train wagons which, when loaded, will park in vicinity of Railway Stations. O.C. Train will be responsible in each case that wagons are on platform in sufficient time to allow of entraining with 1st line transport of their respective Units.

Rations for consumption 12th instant will be drawn by 16th M.T. Coy. and will be refilled on to train wagons in new areas near detraining stations. Arrangements have been made for 156 and 157th Field Coys.R.E. and 16th M.G. Battn to draw as details from ABBEVILLE, No. 9 Detail Issue Store. - O.C. 16th M.T. Coy. arranging to leave two lorries for this purpose. These lorries will report on 10th instant to O.C. 157th Field Coy.R.E. at GREBAULT-MESNIL, who will be responsible for the rationing of drivers and upkeep of lorries.

Supply Officers and Supply Details will in each case proceed by first train of their respective Brigade Groups.

It is absolutely necessary that all Units accept the rations and forage delivered to them on morning of 9th inst. for consumption 10th inst. in order to free the supply wagons for the second refilling on afternoon of 9th instant.

9. H.Q.R.E. will close at CERISY at 10 a.m. and will reopen at same hour at GAMACHES.

10. ACKNOWLEDGE.

RESTAVL ?

Captain, R.E.

for C. R. E. 16th Division.

Distribution:-

155th Field Coy.R.E.
156th Field Coy.R.E.
157th Field Coy.R.E.
16th Div. 'G'
16th Div. 'Q'
11th Hants (p).
16th Div. Sigs.
C.R.E.
File.
W.D. (2)

Appendix No 2
HQ RE War Diary April 1918.

SECRET.
==========

C. R. E's ORDER No. 62.

v 13th April 1918.

1. The Division is moving to-morrow to the THEROUANNE Area.

2. 155th Field Coy.R.E. will move as follows:-

   Headquarters and Transport.   THEROUANNE AREA.

   1 Section.   MOLINGHEM.

   2 Sections.   ~~LE BAS.~~ BOESINGHEM

3. The three detached Sections will move by motor lorry, and will carry one day's rations, and blankets.
   3 Lorries will parade at 155th Coy. H.Q. at 6.30 am. They will rendezvous as follows:-

   1 Section (with O.C.)   MOLINGHEM CHURCH 9. a.m.

   1 Section (with O.C.)   THIENNES STATION 10.a.m.

   1 Section (with O.C.)   Railway Crossing 500 yards N.W. of LE BAS. 10.30 a.m.

   C.R.E. will visit each rendezvous and issue instructions. Subsequently O.C. Sections will arrange their own billets.

4. Headquarters and 155th Fld. Coy. and Transport will move by march route to THEROUANNE AREA, sending on an Officer in advance to obtain allotment of billets from 16th Division 'Q' Staff Officer. Time of March will be notified later.

5. ~~H.Q.R.E. will move to THEROUANNE, and open at at   p.m.~~ RKJ

6. Acknowledge.

R B Jennings
Captain, R.E.
for C. R. E. 16th Division.

Distribution:-
   155th Field Coy.R.E.
   16th Div. 'G'.
   16th Div. 'Q'.
   C.R.E.
   File.
   War Diary.

Appendix No. 3.

H.Q. R.E.
War Diary
April 1918

SECRET.

C.R.E's ORDER No. 62/1.

14th April 1918.

Reference para: 4 C.R.E's Order No. 62.

1. 155th Field Coy. R.E. (less 3 Sections) will move to ENGUINEGATTE via FAUQUEMBERGUE and COYECQUE. Head of column must cross the FAUQUEMBERGUE - ST OMER road at 2.40 p.m.

2. Completion of move and location of 155th Fld. Coy. H.Q. to be reported to C.R.E's Office.

3. Acknowledge.

Issued at 11.25 a.m.

R. Strady
Captain, R.E.

for C.R.E. 16th Division.

Addressed all recipients of ...

Appendix No 4

W.D. April 1916

H.Q. R.E.

Appendix No. 5.   *W.D. April 1918*

C.R.E's INSTRUCTIONS FOR WORK ON RESERVE LINE. No.1.

Reference. Sheet 36A.

1. Reference 16th Div. No. G.28/1 of 15th April.
16th Division is responsible for the line from MOLINGHEM (road inclusive) to MORBECQUE Station (inclusive).

2. For works purposes the line will be divided into three Sectors:-

   North Sector.   MORBECQUE STATION to CANAL DE LA LYS (exclusive).

   South Sector.   CANAL DE LA LYS (inclusive) to MOLINGHEM (O.9.d.6.0).

   ISBERGUES STEEL WORKS DEFENCES.

3. The Composite Brigade will work on the North Sector, and the Portuguese Brigade in the South Sector. A proportion of R.E. and Pioneers will be alloted to each Sector for supervision.

4. Lieut-Colonel C.G.FALCON,R.E. will act as C.R.E. SOUTH Sector, Major E.I. SCOTT, 155th Field Coy.R.E. as C.R.E. NORTH Sector, and Lieut.Colonel B.E. CROCKETT, D.S.O., as C.R.E. ISBERGUES.

5. The C.R.E. of each Sector will be responsible for the actual siting of the trenches, the distribution of stores, the co-ordination of work between the Sub-Sectors, and the distribution of the technical personnel for supervision of the infantry, or any special R.E. or skilled work (such as construction of bridges, M.G. emplacements, etc.).

6. Each Sector will be divided into 4 Sub-Sectors, numbered 1 to 8, commencing on the right of the line.

7. Each Sub-Sector will be worked on by a Battalion, the Commander of which will be responsible for carrying out all the work including digging, wiring, clearing field of fire and communications. He will be assisted by the R.E. Subaltern detailed to his Sub-Sector, who will hand over full details of the work to be done, and assist with technical labour and supervision.

8. Lieut.Colonel B.E. CROCKETT,D.SO., 11th Hants (with 11th Hants (P) and a proportion of R.E.) will be responsible for the construction of the defences of ISBERGUES STEEL WORKS from road at O.11.c.2.6. (inclusive) to PONT D'ISBERGUES.

9. The normal supply of tools and material will be from Divisional Dump, CONCRETE FACTORY, AIRE (H.23.c.9.8) by arrangements made by Adjutant,R.E. Requirements will be sent in by C.R.E's as early as possible during the day for the following day.

10. Dumps of tools are being formed at:-

		Shovels.	Picks.
MOLINGHEM.	O.8.d.5.6.	500	150
CHAPEL.	O.3.c.8.2.	600	200
LA ROUPIE.	I.32.d.5.8.	500	150
HOULERON STATION.	I.27.d.	1000	300
THIENNES STATION.	I.23.b.	1200	400
STEENBECQUE.	I.5.d.7.6.	600	200
MORBECQUE STATION.	D.35.d.9.6.	600	200

11. Headquarters.

H.Q.R.E.	CONCRETE FACTORY, AIRE.
C.R.E. SOUTH.	LA ROUPIE.
C.R.E. NORTH.	THIENNES.
C.R.E. ISBERGUES.	CAMP. I.26.c.

15th April, 1918.

Sd. R.F.A. BUTTERWORTH,
Lieut-Colonel, R.E.
C. R. E. 16th Division.

Distribution:-

Divisional Commander.	1.
C.R.E. North.	10.
C.R.E. South.	10.
C.R.E. ISBERGUES.	4.
16th Div. 'G'	1.
16th Div. 'Q'	1.
16th Div. Sigs.	1.
G.O.C. Composite Bde.	4.
G.O.C. 1st Portuguese I.B.	5.
Major GLOVER.	1.
C.R.E.	6.
File.	2.
War Diary.	2.

Appendix No. 6.

C.R.E's INSTRUCTIONS FOR WORK ON RESERVE LINES. No.2.

Preparation of Line of Resistance.

1. _Trace._   Irregular, with bastions for cross-fire and enfilade fire.

Traversed.

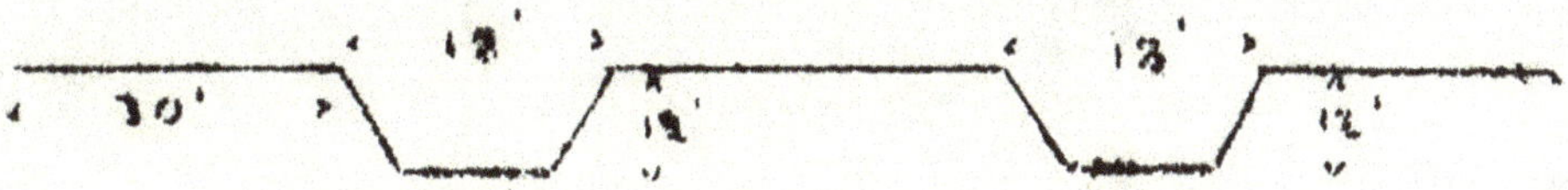

[trench cross-section diagram: 10', 12', 12', 12']

Dogleg.

[diagram: 18'-30']

Waved.

[diagram: 70'-100', 16'-30']

2. _Profile._ Fire Trench.

1st Task.

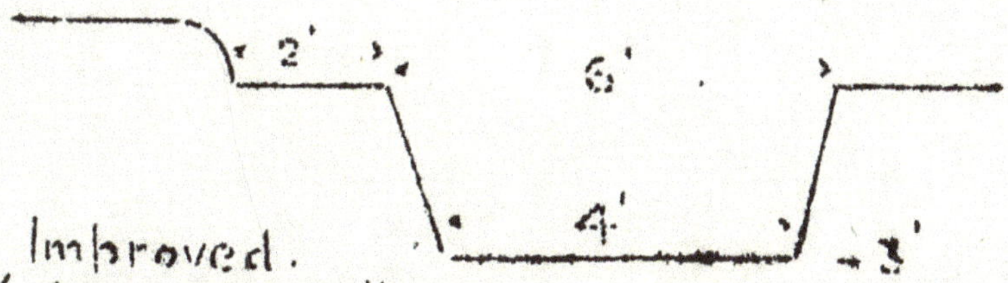

[diagram: 2', 6', 4', 3']

Improved.
(if ground admits.)

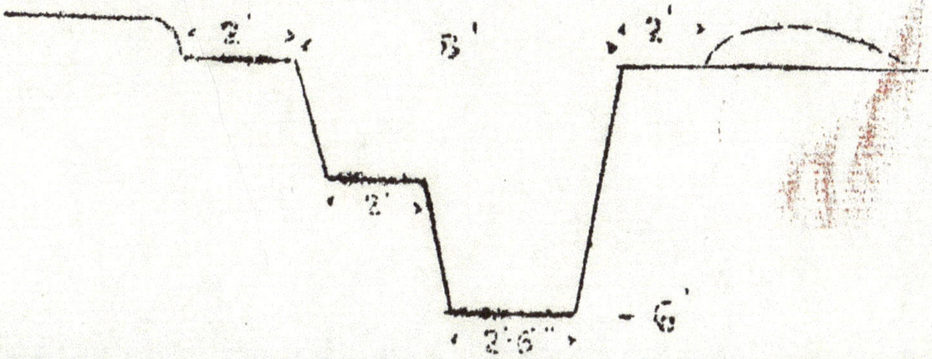

[diagram: 2', 5', 2', 2', 2'6", 6']

Travel Trench.

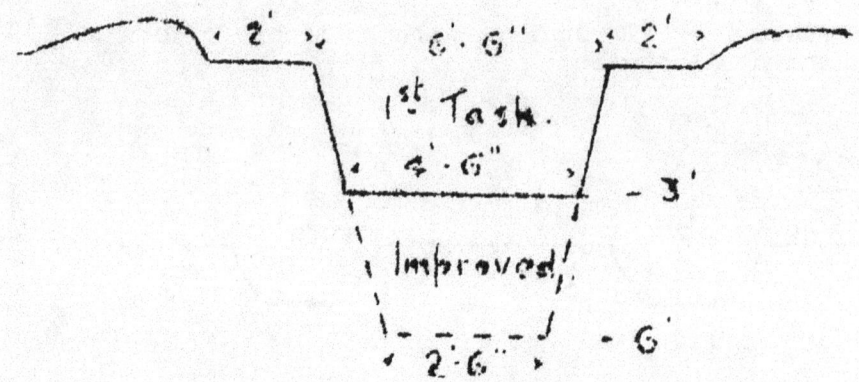

3. Wire.

Double Apron Fence with two bays of low wire in front, the latter concealed if possible. Distance from trench not less than 60 yards. Wire to be very irregular, and existing fences and hedgerows to be entangled.
Gaps at every hundred yards, marked by small white cross on a picket.

Gaps in wire thus ───── ─────

Not ─────────

Wire to run obliquely to front line and assist enfilade fire from firebays or machine guns.

4. Clearance of Foreground.

Thin lower part of hedges, when close to fire trench, cut down and entangle more distant hedges. Leave standing all parallel hedges.

5. Communications.

Provide bridges over dykes and streams. Cut gaps in parallel hedges in rear of trench line. Communications to Outpost Line and to Reserve Line (or covered ground in rear) will be blazed or marked by signboards and dug when labour is available.

Sd. R.F.A. BUTTERWORTH,

16th April, 1918.
Lieut-Colonel, R.E.

C. R. E. 16th Division.

Distribution as for No.1.

Appendix No. 7.   *W.D. April 1918.*

C.R.E's INSTRUCTIONS FOR WORK ON RESERVE LINES. NO.3.

Distribution of R.E.

The following will be the distribution of R.E. to work Sectors vide C.R.E's Instructions No.1.

1. C.R.E. NORTH.

   155th Field Company, R.E.
   2nd Lieut. WORSLEY, R.E.
   2nd Lieut. BOYCE, R.E.

2. C.R.E. SOUTH.

   Captain CLARK, R.E.
   Lieut.   H.D.L. PATERSON, R.E.
   "   R.A. CHRISTISON, R.E.
   "   D.R. LYNE, R.E.
   2/Lt.   LAW, R.E.
   "   DUCKWORTH, R.E.

   100 Other Ranks.

3. C.R.E. ISBERGUES.

   Captain   DAVID.
   2nd Lieut.   C.E. DAVIDSON.

   50 Other Ranks.

In addition 2 portuguese Field Coys. and pioneer Battn. are allotted to C.R.E. South.

Rationing of R.E. personnel.

1. All R.E. Personnel attached C.R.E's North, South and ISBERGUES will be rationed by 155th Field Coy. R.E. until further orders.

2. Rations will be distributed by lorry now attached 155th Field Coy. in accordance with strength shown above.

3. Later the party attached to C.R.E. ISBERGUES will be rationed by 11th Hants (P).

16th April, 1918.   Sd. R.F.A. BUTTERWORTH, Lieut. Col. R.E.

C. R. E. 16th Division.

Distribution:-

Divisional Commander.	16th Div. Sigs.
C.R.E. North.	G.O.C. Composite Bde.
C.R.E. South.	G.O.C. 1st portuguese Bde.
C.R.E. ISBERGUES.	Major GLOVER.
16th Div. 'G'.	C.R.E. 16th Div.
16th Div. 'Q'.	Capt. CLARKE.
16th Div. Train.	Capt. DAVID.
C.E. XIII Corps.	Capt. Merriot, att. portuguese Bde.

Appendix No. 8.   W.D. April 1918.

C.R.E's INSTRUCTIONS FOR WORK ON RESERVE LINES. No. 4.

PICQUET LINE.

1. The Corps Commander directs that the Railway Embankment from PONT D'ISBERGUES to our Left boundary at MORBECQUE STATION shall be prepared for defence.

2. Firebays are to be dug where the bank is suitable, and machine gun emplacements constructed.

3. The whole line is to be wired.

4. Small localities in front of the railway line are to be selected, and developped to form points d'appui.

   NOTE:- No digging is to be carried out, which will weaken or obstruct the permanent way, as the line is used for heavy traffic.

16th April, 1918.   Sd. R.F.A. BUTTERWORTH, Lieut.Col.

                         C. R. E. 16th Division.

Distribution:-

   Divisional Commander.
   C.R.E. North.
   C.R.E. South.
   C.R.E. ISBERGUES.
   16th Div. 'G'.
   16th Div. 'Q'
   G.O.C. Composite Bde.
   G.O.C. 1st Portuguese Bde.
   Major GLOVER.
   C.E. XIII Corps.
   C.R.E.
   File.
   W.D. (2).

Appendix No. 9   W.D. April 1918

C.R.E's INSTRUCTIONS FOR WORK ON RESERVE LINES.   No. 5.

Wire Entanglements.

1. As already notified, the entanglements will take the form of a double-apron fence. Central pickets 9' apart, with two bays of medium wire in front. No loose wire will be added.

2. All fences covered by fire should be made into obstacles by intertwining wire, and adding an apron on our side of the fence.

3. Gaps will be made in a right handed direction, and marked with a cross erected two feet above highest picket vide sketch.

Crosses are available at R.E. Dump CONCRETE FACTORY.

18th April 1918.   Sd. R.F.A. BUTTERWORTH,
                                            Lieut-Colonel, R.E.

                                    C.R.E. 16th Division.

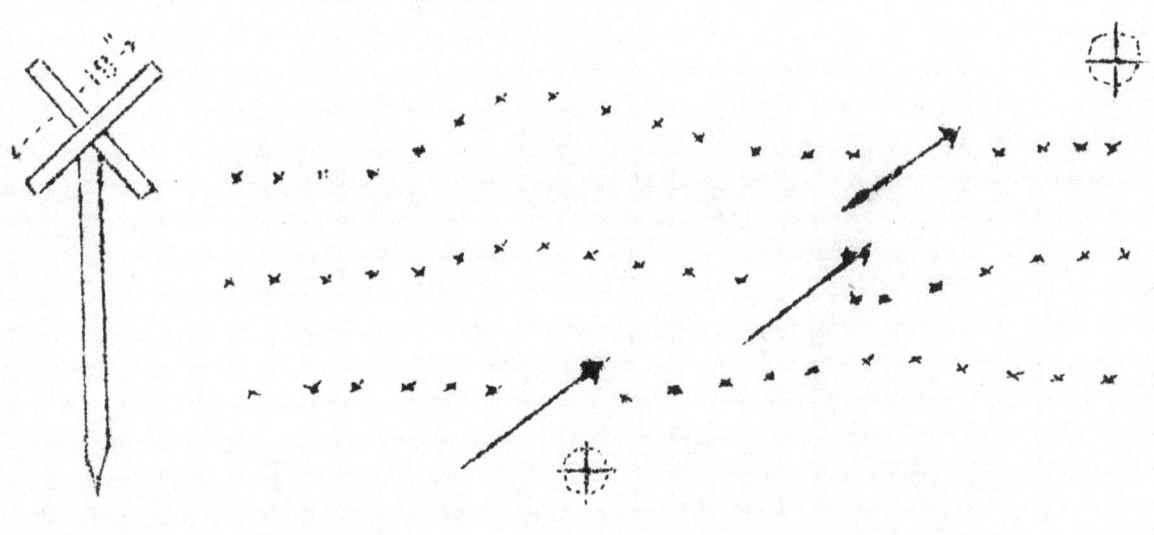

Signboard.

Distribution:-
    C.R.E. North   6.   G.O.C. Composite Bde.   5.
    C.R.E. South   6.   File.   2.
    C.R.E. ISBERGUES   4.

Appendix No. 10. W.D. April 1918.

C.R.E's INSTRUCTIONS FOR WORK ON RESERVE LINES. No.6.

TRENCHES ON LOW GROUND.

Reference C.R.E's Instructions No.2, the Army profile of Trench is unsuitable for low-lying ground.

1. A trench 3' wide should be dug to start with, and carried down to a safe depth above water level (say 1'6" or 2').

2. Breastwork must then be built up to form a parapet and traverses, and later a parados, but this will be built to cover the backs of the firebays first.

3. It is of the greatest importance that the borrow pit for the breastwork should be dug 20 feet from the cutting line of the trench, or in the end the earth from the breastwork will eventually slide back into the borrow pit.

4. In very wet ground grouse butts will be built up at intervals, and the front, which will be strongly wired, defended by cross-fire from these.

19th April, 1918.   Sd. R.F.A. BUTTERWORTH, Lieut.Col.R.E.
                                   C. R. E. 16th Division.

Distribution:-

Divisional Commander.	1.
C.R.E. NORTH.	10.
C.R.E. SOUTH.	10.
C.R.E. ISBERGUES.	4.
16th Div 'G'	1.
G.O.C. Composite Bde.	5.
G.O.C. Portuguese Bde.	4.
Major GLOVER.	1.
Lieut. MARRIOT.	1.
C.R.E.	2.
File.	2.
War Diary.	2.

Appendix No. 11   W.D. April 1918.

C.R.E's INSTRUCTIONS FOR WORK ON RESERVE LINES. No.7.

READJUSTMENT OF LABOUR.

1. In consequence of the posting of 2 battalions of the Composite Brigade, 16th Division to other Divisions, the following readjustments will take place -

    Nos. 21 and 28 Battalions and 2 Groups of pioneers, 1st Portuguese Inf. Bde. will move from South Sector, and come under C.R.E. NORTH for work from to-morrow 24th April.

2. 16th Division 'Q' are arranging for the move and billeting in STEENBECQUE AREA.

3. Necessary alterations in work will be made by C.R.E's on the following basis:-

C.R.E. SOUTH.

   (a) Complete No. 2 Sub-Sector, including wire.

   (b) Lay out - dig and wire Locality - O.9.Central.

   (c) Carry on with work in Nos. 3 and 4 Sub-Sectors including wiring of the railway line.

   (d) Construct breastwork switch CHAPEL to O.3.b.9.0.

Troops available.

   Nos 21 and 34 Battalions, Portuguese Inf.Bde.
   2 Companies Portuguese pioneers.
   1 Portuguese Field Company.

C.R.E. NORTH.

   (a) Make line fightable on edge of STEENBECQUE Village (No.7 Sub-sector).

   (b) Complete work in No.5 Sub-Sector, including LOCK POST.

   (c) Carry on wiring line of railway.

   (d) Complete work (including wire) in localities LE BAS and STEENBECQUE Station.

Troops available.

   1st Battalion Rl. Dublin Fusrs.
   No. 22 Battalion 1st Portuguese Infantry Bde.
   2 Companies Portuguese pioneers.

C.R.E. ISBERGUES.

   (a) Complete work on ISBERGUES Defences.

   (b) Reconnoitre for Reserve Line - MOLINGHEM - behind Windmill O.8.b.4.1. - LA ROUPIE.   Flag out for approval by 'G'.

Troops available.

   11th Hants (pioneers).
   1 Battalion Portuguese Inf. Bde. - to be allotted when available.

O i/c LE BAS SWITCH.

    (a)   Start work on LE BAS SWITCH commencing at road I.6.a.0.5.

Troops available.

    No. 28 Battalion 1st portuguese Inf.Bde.

4.   All troops on the work - including 1st Rl.Dublin Fusrs - 1st protuguese Infantry Brigade and pioneers - will turn out at full strength for work, the only exceptions being cooks and necessary fatigue men.

5.   ACKNOWLEDGE.

23rd April, 1918.

R.F.A. Butterworth
Lieut-Colonel, R.E.
C. R. E. 16th Division.

Distribution:-

    Divisional Commander.
    C.R.E. NORTH.
    C.R.E. SOUTH.
    C.R.E. ISBERGUES.
    O i/c LE BAS Switch.
    16th Div. 'G'.
    G.O.C. Composite Bde.
    G.O.C. 1st portuguese Inf.Bde.
    Major GLOVER.
    Lieut. MARRIOTT, R.E.
    16th Div. 'Q'.
    C.R.E.
    File.
    War Diary (2)

Appendix No. 12   W.D. April 1918.

C.R.E's INSTRUCTIONS FOR WORK ON RESERVE LINES.   NO. 8.

Profile and Trace.

In amendment to C.R.E's Instructions No. 2. the following profile and Trace will be adopted :-

1. Localities suitable for Digging.

   Trace.

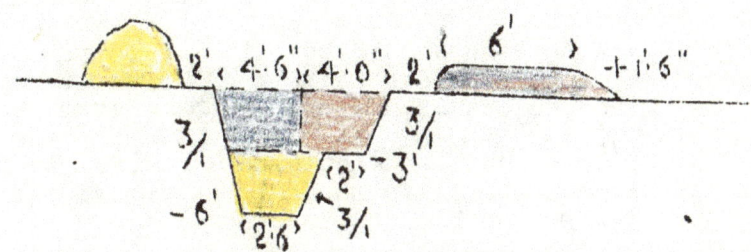

   Profile. (Fire Bay).

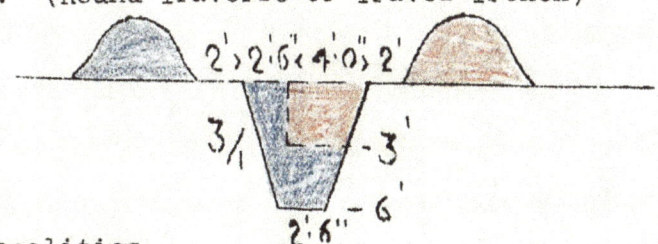

   Profile. (Round Traverse or Travel Trench)

2. Wet Localities.

   (Fire Bay)

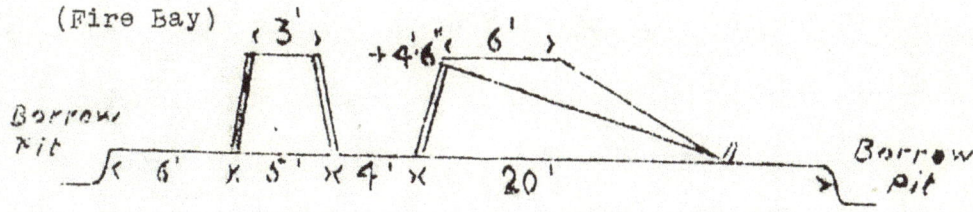

   Travel Trench.

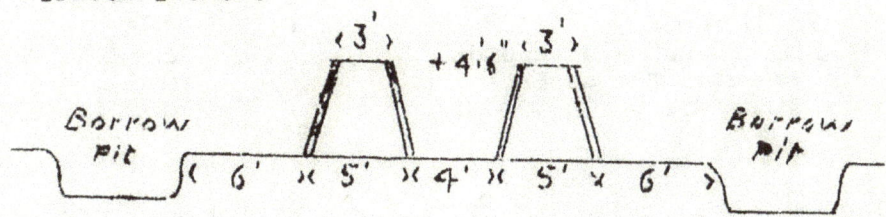

Distribution as for No.1.   (sd) R.P.A. BUTTERWORTH,
                                    Lieut-Colonel, R.E.
                               C.R.E. 16th Division.

Appendix No. 13   W.D. April 1918.

C.R.E's INSTRUCTIONS FOR WORK ON RESERVE LINES. NO.9.

The Divisional Commander directs that immediate attention shall be paid to

(1) The Blocking of all forward roads.
(2) Preparation of Important Localities.
(3) Erection of Notice Boards.

1. The following work is required:-

(a) Wire entanglements parallel to the road for a distance of 50 - 100 yards, in front and to the rear of point where main wire defence crosses the road.

(b) Machine gun emplacements for guns firing straight up the road.

(c) A large supply of chevaux-de-frise to form one or more formidable blocks across the road.

As regards -

(a) The entanglements should be close up to the road, so as to deny to the enemy the use of the ditch or bank.

(b) Machine guns should be sited in convenient houses or outhouses, or dug in behind a heap of road-metal, or other object affording natural cover from view.

(c) Chevaux-de-frise should be placed close alongside roads, where block is to be made, and provided with loose ends of wire for binding together.

Roads affected.

C.R.E. SOUTH.

MOLINGHEM - BERGUETTES STATION.	O.9.c.
ISBERGUES - BERGUETTE. (2 roads)	O.9.a.
ISBERGUES - PONT D'ISBERGUES.	O.3.a.
LE BRAY - LA LACQUE.	I.34.c.
HOULERON - ST VENANT.	I.34.b.

C.R.E. ISBERGUES.

BERGUETTES STATION - CANAL.	O.11.c.

C.R.E. NORTH.

THIENNES - TANNAY.	I.28.b.
LE BAS - FORET.	J.7.d.
MORBECQUE - CROIX MARRAISE.	J.1.b.
STEENBECQUE - STATION.	D.25.d.

O i/c LE BAS SWITCH.

STEENBECQUE - STATION.	I.6.b.
STEENBECQUE - MORBECQUE.	C.30.d.
Bye-Road from LE HAUT.	C.30.b.
LE ROMARIN - MORBECQUE.	C.24.b.

2.

(a) Full use should be made of strong buildings - Machine Guns well sited, for which platforms are prepared, and sandbag cover against rifle fire provided, will be most valuable for defence.

In out-buildings or deserted farms this work can be put into execution, in tenanted buildings work can be done to a limited extent only, but in the latter case a description can be painted on the house M.G. post No. 1 and 2 or

FORTIFIED HOUSE as the case may be.

(b) Hedges should be defended by enfilade fire, cruciform posts at re-entrants are very useful, trenches should be concealed as far as possible.

IMPORTANT LOCALITIES.

C.R.E. SOUTH.

1. MOLINGHEM.   O.9. c. d.
2. HOULERON.

C.R.E. NORTH.

1. STEENBECQUE STATION.
2. LE BAS.
3. LOCK POST.
4. MOATED FARM.

O i/c LE BAS SWITCH.

LE HAUT.   D.30.c.

C.R.E. ISBERGUES.

STEEL WORKS.

3. NOTICE BOARDS.

(a) Notice Boards are required at all posts, M.G. posts, Fortified Houses, etc., or the lettering can be marked in black or white on the house or building affected - vide para: (2)

(b) Direction boards TO No. 1 POST

TO MOATED FARM should be placed on roads or

tracks to facilitate the location of the various machine gun emplacements, and strong points, etc.

These will be prepared at Divisional Dump on requisition by C.R.E's.

Boards marked M.G. POST and X

for wire gaps are ready for issue.

R.F.A. Butterworth

Lieut-Colonel, R.E.

24th April, 1918.   C.R.E. 16th Division.

Distribution:-

    C.R.E. NORTH.
    C.R.E. SOUTH.
    C.R.E. ISBERGUES.
    O i/c Le Bas Switch.
    Divisional Commander.   )
    16th Div 'G'.   )
    G.O.C. Composite Bde.   ) for
    G.O.C. 1st Portuguese Bde.) information.
    Major GLOVER.   )
    Lieut. Marriott, R.E.   )
    C. R. E.
    File.
    W.D. (2).

Appendix N°. 14.   W.D. April 1918.

C.R.E's INSTRUCTIONS FOR WORK ON DEFENCE LINES. NO. 10.

DOG LEG.

    This type of "Dog Leg" is to be used where switches or C.T's come into the main line.

    Attention is directed to kink at "A" – which should be left handed.

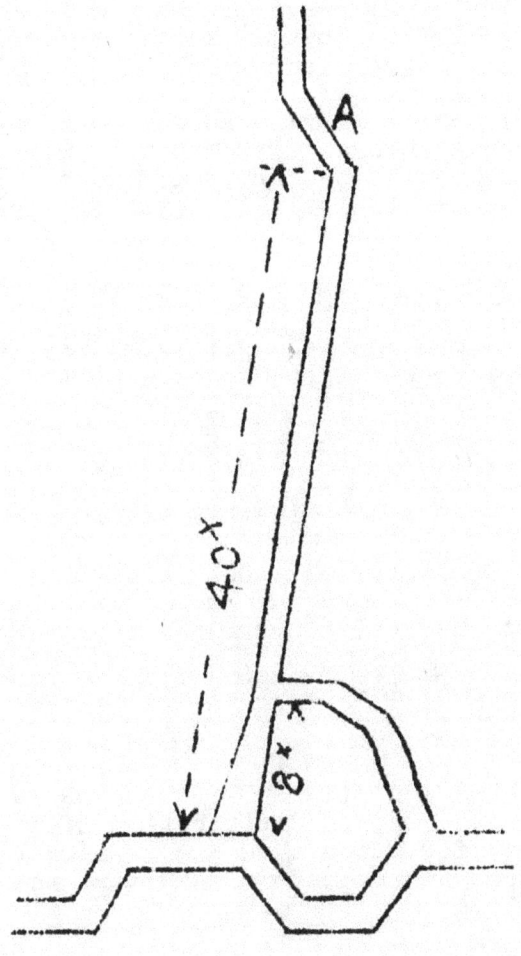

25th April 1918.   (sd) R.F.A. LUTTERWORTH,
                                                 Lieut-Colonel, R.E.
                                         C. R. E. 16th Division.

Distribution as for No. 8.

Appendix No. 15   W.D. April 1918

SECRET.

C.R.E's INSTRUCTIONS FOR WORK ON RESERVE LINES. No.11.

1. Instructions have been received for all rearward systems of defence to be manned in case of emergency by nucleus garrisons. The troops selected to form these nucleus garrisons must be permanently detailed, must be quartered in the vicinity of the system and must be acquainted with the lines of trenches, machine gun emplacements and all details of the system.

   Their chief duty will be to form a nucleus garrison and to act as guides to troops withdrawing, so that in no case may such troops pass through prepared positions without halting to defend them. The smaller the numbers available for this duty, the better must be their acquaintance with the details of the system.

2. The 16th Division is to find nucleus garrisons as above for that portion of the LILLERS - STEENBECQUE Line on which it is working. No Portuguese troops are being used for this purpose, so that only troops available will be the three Field Coys and the
   11th Hants pioneers.
   All available personnel of these units is to be used.

3. The points at which nucleus garrisons are to be formed and the allotment of responsibility for forming the garrisons will be as follows:-

   (a) THIENNES.   157th Field Coy. R.E.

   (b) LE BAS.   156th Field Coy. R.E.

   (c) STEENBECQUÉ STATION. 155th Field Coy. R.E.

   O.C. 11th Hants (Pioneers) is garrisoning the line

   MOLINGH. STATION.
   STEEL WORKS.
   ISBERGUES DEFENCES.

4. O.C. Field Companies will submit schemes as soon as possible showing the proposed distribution of troops to the various localities for which they are responsible. These schemes will include an estimate of the time that it will take to man the localities.

   (a) When the units are in billets at the time of receiving the order to do so.

   (b) When they are at work.

5. The unit told off to each locality will at once carry out a through reconnaissance of the defences for which it is responsible so as not only to be able to go into position without loss of time should the emergency arise, but also to be capable of guiding retiring or reinforcing troops to their positions as ordered in para: 1.

6. ACKNOWLEDGE.

                                          R.F. Butterworth

28th April, 1918.   Lieut-Colonel, R.E.
                                          C. R. E. 16th Division.

Appendix No. 16 *W.D. April 1918*

SECRET.

C. R. E's INSTRUCTIONS FOR WORK ON RESERVE LINES. No.12.

1. Reference C.R.E's Instructions No. 1 and Special Map 1/20,000 (Drawing No.305) issued therewith, the following reorganisation of Works Sectors, responsibility for work, and allotment of troops for work, will come into effect from 1st May.

SCHEDULE OF REORGANISATION.

Officer i/c Work.	Works Sector.	Troops for Work.	Billet Locality.
Lieut-Colonel B.E. CROCKETT.	Localities STEEL WORKS - MOLINGHEM.	11th Hants (P). 2 Groups Portuguese Pioneers.	ISBERGUES.
C.R.E. SOUTH. (Lieut-Colonel C.G. FALCON,R.E.)	Sub-Sectors 1 and 2. MOLINGHEM (excl) to CANAL D'AIRE (incl). Locality. PONT D'ISBERGUES.	5 Officers 55 O.R.,R.E. 1 Battalion Portuguese Infantry.	ISBERGUES.
O.C. 157th Fld.Coy. (Captain R.B. JENNINGS,R.E.)	Sub-Sectors 3, 4 and 5. CANAL D'AIRE (excl) to THIENNES (incl) Localities. LOCK POST and HOULERON.	157 Fld. Co.R.E. 1 Battalion Portuguese Inf. 1 Portuguese Field Company.	PECQUEUR.
O.C. 156th Fld.Coy. (Major G.E. GRIMSDALE,R.E.)	Sub-Sectors 6 and 7. THIENNES (excl) to LE BAS (incl) Localities. LE BAS and MOATED FARM. PLAINE HAUTE Switch.	156 Fld Co.R.E. 1 Battalion Portuguese Inf. 1 Group Portuguese Pioneers.	STEENBECQUE.
C.R.E. NORTH. (Major E.I. SCOTT,R.E.)	Sub-Sector 8. LE BAS (excl) to STEENBECQUE STATION (incl). Locality. STEENBECQUE STATION. LE BAS - LE CRINCHON Switch.	155 Fld. Co.R.E. 1 Battalion Portuguese Inf. 1 Group Portuguese Pioneers.	STEENBECQUE.

2. All taking over and readjustment of work between Officers will take place on 30th April.

3.   The necessary moves and arrangements for billets are being arranged, and will take place under the orders of 16th Division 'Q'.

4.   ACKNOWLEDGE.

                                        SD. R.F.A. BUTTERWORTH.
29th April, 1918.   Lieut-Colonel, R.E.
                                        C. R. E. 16th Division.

Distribution:- C.R.E. NORTH.
                C.R.E. SOUTH.
                O.C. 156th Field Coy. R.E.
                O.C. 157th Field Coy. R.E.
                O.C. 11th Hants (P).
                Divisional Commander.   )
                16th Div. 'G'.   )
                16th Div. 'Q'   )
                16th Div. Sigs.   ) For information.
                G.O.C. 1st Portuguese Bde)
                Major GLOVER.   )
                Lieut. MARRIOTT, R.E.   )
                C.R.E.
                War Diary.(2)
                File.

Appendix No. 17   *W.D. April 1918.*

SECRET.

C.R.E's INSTRUCTIONS FOR WORK ON RESERVE LINES. NO.13.

(1) Reference C.R.E's Instructions No. 12. The following moves of Field Companies will take place to-morrow 30th inst.

    (a) 156th Field Coy.R.E. will move from PECQUEUR to STEENBECQUE. Billeting Officer to report to Staff Captain, 49th Infantry Bde. at 9.0 a.m. at Bde. H.Q. BOESEGHEM. Present billets will be handed over to 157th Field Coy.R.E.
        Handing over party will be left behind if necessary.

    (b) 157th Field Coy.R.E. will move from ISBERGUES to PECQUEUR and take over billets from 156th Field Coy.R.E. Time will be arranged by O.C. 157th Field Coy.R.E.

(2) **REINFORCEMENTS.**

    (a) All reinforcements for 157th Field Coy. now attached to C.R.E. SOUTH will rejoin their Company before it leaves ISBERGUES in the morning.

    (b) Details of 157th Field Coy.R.E. now attached 155th Field Coy.R.E. will rejoin their Unit after work to-morrow.

    (c) All reinforcements (under Lieut. DUCKWORTH, R.E.) for 156th Field Coy.R.E. now attached C.R.E. SOUTH will rejoin their Company after work to-morrow.

    (d) Lieut. DAVIDSON, R.E. and R.E. Base personnel now in NORTH Sector will proceed to ISBERGUES after work to-morrow and report to C.R.E. SOUTH.
        Captain DAVID, R.E. will remain at STEENBECQUE and work under O.C. 155th Field Coy.R.E.

    (e) Nominal rolls should be sent with these parties.

(3)   A C K N O W L E D G E.

29th April, 1918.

Captain, R.E.
for C. R. E. 16th Division.

Distribution:-

155th Field Coy.R.E.	S.C. 49 Bde.)
156th Field Coy.R.E.	16th Div 'G')
157th Field Coy.R.E.	16th Div 'Q') for
O i/c LE BAS SWITCH.	16th Div Sigs.) informa-
C.R.E. SOUTH.	16th Div. Train) tion.
File.	C.R.E.
	War Diary (2).

Appendix No. 18   *W.D. April 1918.*

SECRET.

C.R.E's INSTRUCTIONS FOR WORK ON RESERVE LINES. No.14.

The following are amendments to C.R.E's Instructions No. 12 consequent upon withdrawal of 11th Hants (P).

1. C.R.E. SOUTH will now take over responsibility for all work South of CANAL D'AIRE including STEEL WORKS and HOLINGHEM LOCALITIES.

   Captain HOWSON, 11th Hants (P) and 1 complete Section 157th Field Company, R.E. will come under his orders from this date in addition to Portuguese Battalion and 2 Groups Portuguese Pioneers mentioned.

2. Portuguese Heavy Artillery will continue to work under C.R.E. NORTH.

3. The 2 Groups Portuguese Pioneers working in NORTH Sector will now both work under O.C. 156th Field Coy. R.E. (and not one with 156th Fld. Coy and one with C.R.E. NORTH, as stated).

4. No change of billets will take place in the case of the Portuguese Field Coy. and Portuguese Infantry Battn. working under 157th Field Coy. R.E.

   They will march daily from their billets at ISBERGUES.

5. On arrival the Portuguese Machine Gun Company will work in the Southern Sector under C.R.E. SOUTH.

6. ACKNOWLEDGE.

R.E. Stradling
Capt. R.E.

30th April, 1918.

for Lieut-Colonel, R.E.
C. R. E. 16th Division.

Distribution:-

C.R.E. NORTH. (O.C. 155 Fld Coy).
C.R.E. SOUTH.
O.C. 156th Field Coy. R.E.
O.C. 157th Field Coy. R.E.
O.C. 11th Hants (P).
Divisional Commander.
16th Div 'G'.
16th Div 'Q'.
G.O.C. 1st Portuguese Bde.
Major GLOVER.
Capt. SELLARS.
Lieut. MARRIOTT, R.E.
C.R.E.
War Diary (2)
File.

} For Information.

Army Form C. 2118.

H.Q.R.E. 16 Div.

Vol 30

WAR DIARY
or
INTELLIGENCE SUMMARY.
(Erase heading not required.)

Instructions regarding War Diaries and Intelligence Summaries are contained in F.S. Regs., Part II. and the Staff Manual respectively. Title pages will be prepared in manuscript.

Place	Date	Hour	Summary of Events and Information	Remarks and references to Appendices
AIRE. Sheet 36ᵃ H.2.k.e. 7.9	1/5/15	9.30am	C.R.E arrived South maker [?] line afterwards proceeding to 156 & 157 Field Coys and HQ Scots. Work carried on as usual. Weather – fine.	
do	2 do	9.45am	C.R.E. received G.H.Q. line visit G.O.C. 1 Army. C.R.E./ Army and G.O.C. 16 D.V. Major D.E. Maurice 154 Coy. C.R.E. of Administrative CMLS. II Corps. 40 Officers & 157ʳᵈ R.E. Speed Infantry covered in care for work on G.H.Q. line. Divided into 2 Batt^s one on STEENBECQUE and one on PERY U.S.U.K. allotted of work as follows. STEENBECQUE Batt^n = ½ Batt^n to 157 Fd Cy & 1 Batt^n to 157 Fd Cy. PERYUNT Batt^n to 157 Fd Cy. Work on G.H.Q. line as usual. Weather – fine.	
do	3/5/15		C.R.E. to TSBERGUES, THIENNES and STEENBECQUE opened the G.H.Q. divn. C.R.E. XI Corps visited office rep. problem of bridging and road metalling. Irish Infantry commence work. 1 p.m. Work on usual in GHQ later. ISBERGUES stalled during morning. 1 on / R.E. 13. Details covered. Weather – fine. Work on G.H.Q. lines as usual.	
do	4/5/15		C.R.E. + Adjt. G. Ischerques. C.R.E. G.O.C. 16 D.D.R.M. afternoon procuring covered to DD + GF his work. Major General SKINNER G.O.C. 14 Div. Weather – fine. Work on G.H.Q. line as usual.	
do	5/5/15		C.R.E. O'See G.H.E. 14 Div. afternoon procrues officers C.H.Q. of present BR harvesters and R. Nolan. accepted for further under XIV Corps in 1 Corps area (2½/1₅ – 5/5). Offer to Corps in afternoon. C.R.E. to no C.R.E. (South) weaver. Work on GHQ line as usual. Weather – very cost.	
do	6/5/15		C.R.E. to STEENBECQUE & Morbecque re G.H.Q. line in morning. Three G.O.C. 16 D.V. evening. Work on G.H.Q. line as usual. Weather fine.	[signature]

Army Form C. 2118.

WAR DIARY
or
~~INTELLIGENCE SUMMARY.~~
(Erase heading not required.)

H.Q. R.E. 16 DIV

Place	Date	Hour	Summary of Events and Information	Remarks and references to Appendices
HRS Sheet 36 H.28.c.7.6.	7/5/16		CRE annual G.H.Q. lines with G.O.C. 16 Div. Orders to 15 Bn Coy & CRE 16 Div. to put position No. 10 of 16 Div. 17 metres anneyan at Istapeque to put hands of probable Hendicare by direction of Brit. Engineer. Made on G.H.Q as arranged. Weather not in pressure. Fine shower afternoon.	
do.	8/5/16		CRE around MOERINGHEM & G.H.Q. line with G.S.O.1. 16 Div. Lt. WEBSTER & Isbergues. CRE Instructions for Works in Reserve Area No. 15 issued (Appendix 1.) Work on G.H.Q. line as usual. Weather - fine.	Appendix No. 1
do.	9/5/16		CRE to THIENNES and STEENBECQUE. CRE 16 Div. called as junction. 1st & 16th Div G.H.Q line. Weather fine. Wire Obstacles finished by R.E. 11.50 p.m.	
do.	10/5/16		CRE to Isbergues & Morbecque and Steenbecque around G.H.Q lines. Obs to B.XI Corps re allotted work on G.H.Q line around Wallen fin.	
do.	11/5/16		CRE to & Belle Motieus to meet C.E. VIII Corps re position of lines. Wet & Work on G.H.Q lines around Wallen - fine.	
do.	12/5/16		Sunday. Work on G.H.Q. line until mid-day. Weather wet in morning - fine afternoon.	
do.	13/5/16		CRE to Isbergues and Morbecque. Mayor E.J. Scott 2nd Lt. A.S.C. "Attached 153 Field Coy. Receive substitute general of M.C. for junction from 2 N.Z. - 6 Yr. Work on G.H.Q line as usual. Weather fine during day - very wet evening.	
do.	14/5/16	6:30 p.m.	CRE around G.H.Q. line. Andrews Steenbecque. Work on G.H.Q. line as usual. CRE's Instructions for work in Reserve lines No. 16 issued (Appendix No. 2) him marching orders for move of 153 to Mean Self Train Amerine and on SAINT OMER AREA. y - 153 Fld Co Globa and 153 Fld C. lodies on G.H.Q line.	Appendix No. 2
do.	15/5/16	11.45 V.M.	CRE's Instructions No. 17 issued Confirm 10^n 16 regrouping for moves 153 Fld Co Xhoukeysmurch at 155 (Appendix N°. 3). Work on G.H.Q. lines as usual. Weather - fine.	Appendix No. 3

Army Form C. 2118.

H.Q.R.E 16 D N

WAR DIARY
or
~~INTELLIGENCE SUMMARY~~
(Erase heading not required.)

Instructions regarding War Diaries and Intelligence Summaries are contained in F. S. Regs., Part II. and the Staff Manual respectively. Title pages will be prepared in manuscript.

Place	Date	Hour	Summary of Events and Information	Remarks and references to Appendices
Arr.	15/5/16	9 am	Personnel of 153rd Fd. Co. R.E. move to Desvres (same area) as G.H.Q Det. 1st Field C.R.E. C.R.E. b/w Etaples & Boulogne to meet O.C. 153rd & 152nd Co's afterwards proceeding to H.Q. 14 Div. Adjt. & Det. 1 R.S. calls to see Adjt. & takes over with all C.R.E. records. G.H.Q. Coy now with G.O.C. 14 Div. & Adjt. 14 Div. Reconnaissance work on G.H.Q. line.	
"	16/5/16		Lieut. Webb proceeds to Samer to arrange for a place for H.Q. at Samer. Personnel of 1st Fd. Co. R.E. leave here for Samer. Stops at midnight.	
Arr. Samer	17/5/16	10.30 pm 12 noon	Aire. Wire wounded J.E.A. C.R.E. Adjt. leave Aire for Boulogne. Personnel of 1st Fd. Co. R.S. leave by motor lorry.	
"	"	6.30 pm	H.Q.R.E. established at Samer. Adjt. to leave arrived on Boulogne Division shortly to arrange, and to do R.E. Recce. in 15 Div. Administration Area.	
"	18/5/16		C.R.E. to O.E. 1st Army and GOCRA to arrange in we return for R.E. personnel. One section 153rd Fd Co R.E. move into Samer for R.E. Services of Field Camps, Samer, newly made for reception of 7 Army Div. Troops at Samer.	
"	19/5/16		C.R.E. & 6758 Fd. C.R.E. of Desvres & around Administrative Area. M. 153 Fd C.R.E. instructed to make reconnaissance of immediate area for R.E. services especially Water Supply - Baths for pioneers area should not for this reason one section 153 is each when returned	

T2134. Wt. W708—776. 500000. 4/15. Sir J. C. & S.

Army Form C. 2118.

WAR DIARY
or
~~INTELLIGENCE SUMMARY~~
(Erase heading not required.)

1 6 D iv. H.Q. R.E.

Place	Date	Hour	Summary of Events and Information	Remarks and references to Appendices
Sunes	19/5/16		Parents (Donchivonville Aux - Sect A) - one section to Sucrey (Halayhun Aux - Sect B) - one section at Sunes (Deurnes Aux N - Sect C) - H.Q. 153rd West at Deurnes (Deurnes Aux E - Sect D). These section conformed to Left Side Area of 16 Div.	
"	20/5/16		After work began, March of 153rd Section to assume as above. CRE and Adjt to Habyshun and Parents area to arrange supplies in those districts. Reconnaissance of the area being finished with by Technical Officer. Reed Camp at dawn completed.	
"	21/5/16		Adjt. Red. to Calais for R.E. stores. Lt. White to No. 1 Rd Coll at Igny St Machel for return. Temporary dump formed at Calou Sheet 13 5 D 16. R.S. Lennie's in billets are commenced.	
"	22/5/16		4" Austrian Engineer Regt. Arrived. Several Surveyed Wiltshire Area. CRE rode C.E. 4th Arm Div. CRE Wiltshire to see CE 4" Arm Div to gives circumstances with him to arrange Rifle Range site, afterwards pr M.G. School at Mont Tonpin. To prepare foundation work to accompany that 10 Officers 4" Armee Engineer Regt attached to get section 153 H. CRE, & to be introduced to Officer 4" Armee Engineer Regt. A." Aur. Engrs attached to HQ R.E to perform service HQ R.Q.	
"	23/5/16		Manu a above ; one Officer 1 Officer v. Under 20 Carpenters, 2 Blacksmith, to proceed from 4 Aurer Engrs. as attached to HQ R.E. Marce a above, circuit out Inspection lorry. Adjt. to Deurnes with O.S. material. CRE around Administration Area with Col. Skinner ad Almer. Div.	

T2134. Wt. W708-776. 500000. 4/15. Str J. C. & S.

Army Form C. 2118.

WAR DIARY
or
~~INTELLIGENCE SUMMARY~~
(Erase heading not required.)

H.Q. R.E. 16 Div.

Instructions regarding War Diaries and Intelligence Summaries are contained in F. S. Regs., Part II. and the Staff Manual respectively. Title pages will be prepared in manuscript.

Place	Date	Hour	Summary of Events and Information	Remarks and references to Appendices
Scorm	23/5/16		Arrangements made with Major S. Conyers Engineer from 4 Armee Engineers to permit of work in Divn. area. Work on R.E. services in all areas much concerned.	
"	24/5/16		Move as above completed — transport hypoth: heavy. The noise below reorganised into four groups as Divn. area R.Q. (2) Doulieuville area R.W. (3) Hoplinghem Area R.P.W. (5) Jerzeus Area. Each of these areas represented by one Deutd. R.E. office in one area Dn. office (CRE; Imolaten A. 3. Appendix No 4. CRE; Imolaten A. 4 united. Military of chaplain slain. C.E. 4 Armee Divn. arranges some conference between Armee Engineer for work in R.E. services completed to Carly for work in Dvensin area W. Work on R.E. services until divisym. CRE's M.S.O. arrangements as usual refly. Move of two companies in advance by motor lorry. CRE Carly area. CRE to Perenchies chaps. noté J 500′ Range. 500′ rifle range set out by Lt. Weller RE etc. CRE to 16th Fld Ams at Denain, which annex R.E. services made & munitions map afternoon proceeding to 500′ Range set at Eryzghem (Perenchies area) & afterwards to Middelen to see GOC 4.⁰ Armee Div. Work refs. services presents.	Appendix 4. Appendix 5.
	25/5/16			
	26/5/16			
"	27/5/16			

Army Form C. 2118.

WAR DIARY
or
INTELLIGENCE SUMMARY.
(Erase heading not required.)

Place	Date	Hour	Summary of Events and Information	Remarks and references to Appendices
Somme	28/5		CRE. & 118 & 157 Fld Coys. reconnoitred 14 Div. and G.H.Q reserve line in front of Aire - Cohen with him. CE. 1 Anzac Div. Major Wheeler knew Eyres. to see modern heavy defences. Work on R.E. reserves.	
	29/5		CRE. & CRE. Morgan to Proventy & Beures area. Work on R.E. schemes & proceeded.	
	30/5		Div. R.E. dump established at railhead Samer. Work on R.E. schemes, rifle range.	
	31/5		CRE. arranged Box-Car administration area - Halinghen & Derms. [initial]	

[signature]
for Lieut Col CRE 15 D[?]

Appendix. N°1

H.Q. R.E.
W.D. May.1918.

C.R.E's INSTRUCTIONS FOR WORK ON RESERVE LINES. No.15.

SIGN POSTS and DIRECTION BOARDS.

In view of the necessity to facilitate the location of trenches, grouse butts, fortified houses, and M.G. posts, the following steps should be taken.

(1) At all points, where a trench crosses a road, a board should be erected as follows -

| RESERVE LINE | or | MILL SWITCH |
| G.5.d.4.3. | | C.15.c.1.5 | etc.

or same painted on house or wall.

(2) At each Grouse Butt 2 arrow notices

and a white stake driven at the gap in the hedge etc. between butts.

(3) Board | FORTIFIED HOUSE | or | M.G. POST |
         | B.7.d.1.2. | | B.7.d.1.2.| or same

painted in bold letters on the house.

(4) For M.G. Emplacements in the Line Board | M.G. | or | L.G. |

(5) Direction boards in roads, lanes, etc.

| TO FORTIFIED HOUSE → | | TO M.G. POST → |

or same painted on wall or house.

Necessary boards will be prepared at Divisional R.E. Dump, AIRE, on requisition from C.R.Es. and Officers i/c Sectors.

8th May, 1918.

Sd. R.F.A. BUTTERWORTH,
Lieut-Colonel, R.E.
C. R. E. 16th Division.

Distribution:-
C.R.E. SOUTH.   16th Div. 'G'.   )
155th Fld. Coy.   G.O.C. Composite Bd.   )
156th Fld. Coy.   G.O.C. port. Bde.   )
157th Fld. Coy.   Major Glover.   ) For
Div. Commander.   Capt. SELLARS.   ) information.
                       Lieut. Marriott.   )

H.Q.R.E. 16đⁿ
W.D. May '18

Appendix No. 2

SECRET.

C.R.E's INSTRUCTIONS FOR WORK ON RESERVE LINES. No. 16.

WARNING ORDER.

Reference. HAZEBROUCK 5.A. and CALAIS. Sh.13.

1. The 16th Div. will move very shortly to the SAMER AREA to train an American Division arriving there.

2. D.H.Q., Bde. H.Q. and Battalion Training Staffs, 155th Field Coy.R.E. and Div. Signal Coy.R.E. will move to-morrow to new area.

   Details will be issued later.

3. Billeting party from 155th Field Coy.R.E. of 1 Officer and 2 N.C.Os. will be held in readiness to proceed to-night. This party will probably be required to pick up a lorry at BOESINGHEM.

4. O.C. 155th Field Coy.R.E. will arrange to hand over all work to O.C. 156th Field Coy.R.E. to-morrow morning early.

   The necessary readjustment of work between the various Officers i/c Sectors will be made later.

5. ACKNOWLEDGE.

R E Stradling

14th May, 1918.   Captain, R.E.

                                       for C. R. E. 16th Division.

Distribution:-

   C.R.E. SOUTH.
   155th Field Coy.R.E.
   156th Field Coy.R.E.
   157th Field Coy.R.E.
   16th Div 'G'.   )
   16th Div. 'Q'.   )
   Major GLOVER.   ) for information.
   1st Portuguese Inf.Bde.   )

H.Q. R.E. 16 Div.
W.D. May '18

Appendix No. 3.

S E C R E T.

C.R.E's INSTRUCTIONS FOR WORK ON RESERVE LINES, No. 17.

Reference. HAZEBROUCK 5.A. and CALAIS. Sh. 13.

1. Reference C.R.E's warning order of today (Inst.No.16.)
Para 3 of this order is cancelled - No billetting party will be sent ahead.

2. Eight Motor Lorries will report to O.C. 155th Field Company R.E. at 9 a.m. at STEENBECQUE CHURCH to convey dismounted personnel to new billeting area at DESVRES (Calais. Sh.13. 4.E.O.½.). Officer i/c this portion to report to Major GREENWOOD, D.A.A.G., for billets on arrival.

3. Mounted portion of Company will proceed under 2nd in Command, at time to be fixed by Field Coy. Commander, to DOHEM (Sh. Hazebrouck 5.a. - 5.C.2½.7.) to billet for night 15/16th inst. Billets will be obtained from Area Commandant THEROUANNE.
Transport will move on to DESVRES the next morning (16th inst.) under arrangements made by Capt. Hughes, R.E.

4. O.C. 155th Field Coy. R.E. will hand over all work to O.C. 156th Field Coy. R.E. and he himself and handing over Officers will proceed later in the day.
One Lorry will be detained to convoy the handing over party and will not proceed until orders are received from C.R.E.

5. C.R.E. will meet O.C. 155th Field Coy. R.E. and O.C. 156th Field Coy. R.E. at 155th Coy. billets at 10 a.m. tomorrow.

6. ACKNOWLEDGE.

R.E.Stradbrxxx

14th May, 1918.   Captain, R.E.

Issued at 11.50 p.m.   for C. R. E. 16th Division.

Distribution:-

    155th Field Coy. R.E. (3Copies)
    156th Field Coy. R.E.
    157th Field Coy. R.E.
    16th Div. "G".)
    16th Div. "Q".) for information.

HQ RE 16 Div.
W.D. May 1918

Appendix No 4.

C.R.E's. INSTRUCTIONS. A.3.

ENGINEER STORES.   SAMER AREA.

1. For purposes of Engineer Stores the Area is divided into five Groups, each under the charge of one R.E. Officer and one American Engineer Officer.

These Groups are :-
(1) DESVRES AREA (48th Bde.)

    (a) E. of Bde.H.   BILLETED AT.

        Major SCOTT, M.C., R.E.)
        Lieut. HAMMOND, 4th Regt. Engineers.)   DESVRES.

    (b) Lieut. ATOCK, M.C., R.E.)
        " HILL, 4th Regt. Engineers.)   SAMER.

(2) HALINGHEN AREA. (49th Bde.)

    Lieut. HAUGH, R.E.)
    " LYON, 4th Regt. Engineers.)   FRENCQ.

(3) DOUDEAUVILLE AREA (47th Bde.)

    Lieut. BROOK, R.E.)
    " GORDON, 4th Regt. Engineers.)   PARENTY.

(4) SAMER AREA (D.H.Q.)

    Adjutant, R.E.   ) C/O. C.R.E. 16th Div.
    Lieut. STAFFORD, 4th Regt. Engineers) SAMER.

2. Engineer Stores will be issued under two categories.

    (1) Issues to British Troops.
    (2) Issues to American Troops.

Units will submit Indents to the Engineer Representative for their Area, who will visit site of work, check quantities and forward to C.R.E. 16th Division on C.R.E's Form No.2., together with a duplicate copy of stores required.

C.R.E. will wire to Unit when to draw.

(P.T.C.

- 2 -

If any special store is very urgently required, the Engineer Officer will wire to C.R.E. and then send in by next D.R. the C.R.E's Form No.2.

Every Indent must be clearly marked whether for American or British Troops.

For large items of work (e.g. Rifle Ranges, etc.) the estimate of stores required will be submitted direct to C.R.E. 16th Division by Engineer Officer in charge.

In the case of American Troops without transport, stores will be sent to Unit by C.R.E. if this is asked for on stores indent.

Stores are very difficult to obtain in this area and it is specially requested that every effort be made to apply for exactly the amount of material required, and that when issued for a specific work, shall not be used on another without sanction from C.C. 4th American Engineers or C.R.E. 16th Division.

R E Stradling

Captain, R.E.
for C.R.E. 16th Division.

Copies to all Units in
16th Division and 4th
American Division.

H.Q.R.E. 16 D^n
W.D. May 1918.
Appendix P.5

C.R.E's INSTRUCTIONS NO.A./4.

ENGINEER STORES.

Details of arrangements re issue to 4th American Division.

Reference C.R.E's Instructions No. A./3.

On receipt of C.R.E's Form No.2 at H.Q.R.E. 16th Div., the following will be the procedure:-

The estimate will be given a Job number, examined by Adjutant, R.E. and Lieut. STAFFORD, Amer. Engrs. and the issue of the Stores (or their equivalent) authorised on duplicate Stores Indent (sent in by Unit with Form No.2). This duplicate will be sent to 16th Divisional R.E. Dump. The R.S.M., R.E. will make out A.F. 108 in triplicate and will pass these stores to American Engineer Officer (Lieut. GIRLICK) who will sign receipt on A.F. 108.

A.F. 108 will be marked with job number in right hand top corner.

The original of this receipt will be kept in Book, duplicate to C.R.E's Office and triplicate with lorry or other transport conveying the Stores from Dump.

The duplicate sent to C.R.E's Office will form American Officers receipt for stores as required by D.W. Circular Memorandum No.66.E. dated 21-9-17.

24th May, 1918.   Lieut.Colonel,R.E.

                                              C. R. E. 16th Division.

    Distribution:-

            O.C. 155th Field Coy.R.E.
            Lieut. HAUGH, R.E.
            Lieut. BROOK, R.E.
            Lieut. ATOCK, R.E.
            Lieut. HAMMOND, Amer.Engrs.
            Lieut. HILL,   "   "
            Lieut. LYON,   "   "
            Lieut. GORDON,   "   "
            Lieut. STAFFORD, "   "
            Lieut. GIRLICK,   "   "
                W.O. i/c 16th Div.Dump.
            O.C. 4th Amer. Engrs. (for information.
            16th Div. 'Q'.   "   "
            C.E. First Army.   "   "

ORIGINAL
Army Form C. 2118.

H.Q. R.E. 16 DN

WAR DIARY
or
INTELLIGENCE SUMMARY
(Erase heading not required.)

Place	Date	Hour	Summary of Events and Information	Remarks and references to Appendices
Donnel Rue de Paquet	1/6/16		CRE to Devises Caley Annex. met CRE Harrow. OE 1st Anzac Div. - afternoon proceeded G.Bantz in morning. 157 Field arrive at Neuf Berquin Div. Mother 2nd Z' arrive by 12.45 till 17 and Eng. Weather fine	
	2/6		CRE G.Bantz. Thur 7 Engine transp. work with regard to railway for 5th Anz. Div. about 3 armies. etc. Work as above. Fine.	
	3/6		CRE arranged Rifle Range with C.E. 1st Anzac Div. Work as usual. Fine	
	4/6		Work as usual. fine	
	5/6		1st Anzac Div. Eng Companies roll personnel encephalic attached to HQ.A.E. in Flanders 1st A.E. at Meteren on account of wagons [...] for move of 1st Anzac Eng. Select Officers 157 Fld. E.RS returned to carry on R.E. services with HQ of Famine stops 7 16 Div. Fine	
	6/6		Work as above. Inch [?] transport personnel, horseshoe work. CRE to [...] VII Corps school P.	Appendix No 1
	7/6		CRE 157 HdCRS. 1st. C. Schall. Copt. 157 Flanders as instructor. S. Donegan. CRE.Amer 24/6 S.	
	8/6		157 Ann. Ord CRS [...] return name 7/15. H.C. GZARES. Fine Jeannie.	
			157 Mine GZARES. 1st Anz. Eng. attached HdQRS. with return to Melehun. Weather Fine.	Appendix No 2
	9/6		CRE's order OB 6 2/ (Appendix N°2) enrued natur re-enforcements 7th N. Dist. Between 155-157 7th Anz. Div. have area. Cafer R.S. Heading R.S. adj. about 16 Div. R.S. accidently injured	

Army Form C. 2118.

H.Q. R.E. 16 D N.S.

WAR DIARY
~~INTELLIGENCE SUMMARY~~
(Erase heading not required.)

Instructions regarding War Diaries and Intelligence Summaries are contained in F.S. Regs., Part II. and the Staff Manual respectively. Title pages will be prepared in manuscript.

Place	Date	Hour	Summary of Events and Information	Remarks and references to Appendices
Suvla	10/8/15		G. landed Lala Baba Kereunli. L.T. Wighton acting. Capt. Rafe late on Staff at Walker-ridge.	
"	11/8/15		C.R.E. around Southern area with Major V.C. 157 Field Coys. Weather fine.	
"	12/8/15		C.R.E. around Northern area with O.C. "A" Anzac Div. and O.C. 155 Field Coy. Weather fine.	
"	13/8/15		Lt. Hough 153 Field Coy R.E. attached to H.Q. R.E. Work as usual on R.E. sources @ 75/- same. Work in advance.	
"	14/8/15		C.R.E. unwell confined to room — Work in advance — Same.	
"	15/8/15		C.R.E. away ill — Work in advance — Same. P'/109 Artl — reconnoissance — From Div.H.Qrs. + various staffs trips to England benefit or division. Div.Engr. to Lt. Left behind and report when Div. comes across again. Lt. Hough ever ill.	
"	16/8/15		C.R.E. away ill. Work in advance. Lt. Hough ill.	
"	17/8/15		C.R.E. away ill. Work in advance. More in rearward in P'/109 arrived out. 6th Armoured Bde. to come under 30 Inf. Div. for administration & transport. 16 D N.S bde alike ad Tomm recently on such as usual — Same. Lt. Hough ill.	
"	18/8/15		Work as usual but rate sources of 30° D.N.	
"	19/8/15		C.R.E. to see G.S. 30 Army Div. afterwards proceeds to Westburn Green C.E. 30 Army Div. - fine.	
"	20/8/15		L Col. Bell move to Beyrufier H.Q Aug to Devon transmit 157. 1783 Coys. respect-Turk air work.	

Army Form C. 2118.

WAR DIARY
or
INTELLIGENCE SUMMARY
(Erase heading not required.)

H.Q. R.E. 16 Div.

Instructions regarding War Diaries and Intelligence Summaries are contained in F. S. Regs., Part II. and the Staff Manual respectively. Title pages will be prepared in manuscript.

Place	Date	Hour	Summary of Events and Information	Remarks and references to Appendices
Neuvry	21/6/18		Army Rays. Work as usual.	
"	22/6/18		C.R.E. arrived. Meeting & transport with Major F. Field & 1st Lt H.N.S. to choose site of proposed School Hqrs also for 305 Engr. Regt. (20 Annex. 011). Site chosen at Neuvy grit. Work as usual.	
"	23/6/18		1 Coy. 305 Eng. Regt. Here to Neuvrygut to do reconn work, moves in evening. met proposed Engineer School. Work as usual. Just Chief Engr School accepts - 7 Hay Course 18th Officers 20 O.R.'s. Conquered Major S. Scott Dr. 1st Lt W. E. Alspaut. At Neuvy. A.O. - L.N.C.O. Instructors. Work Continued.	
"	24/6/18		Work as usual. Eng. School function.	
"	25/6/18		Work as usual.	
"	26/6/18		Work as usual.	
"	27/6/18		Work as usual.	
"	28/6/18		Work as usual. 34 Div liqr area - Train in flames. D.D handed over to 117 Bde. (39th Div).	
"	29/6/18		Work as usual.	
"	30/6/18		Work as usual.	

M White Capt R.E.
Act. in present ADW

W.D. June.
H.Q. R.E. 16 Div.

Appendix No. 1

C.R.E's ORDER No. 63.
=======================

1. For purposes of work on R.E. Services in 16th Div. Administrative Area the following move will take place tomorrow 8th instant.

2. 157th Field Company R.E., less personnel working at ENQUIN, will move from present billets to LACRES. CALAIS Sheet 13. 5.D.

3. O.C. 157th Field Company R.E. will arrange to send an Officer forward to meet representative from H.Q., R.E., at cross roads 5.D.04.18. at 11.30 a.m. to take over billets.

4. Move to be complete by 6 p.m.

5. ACKNOWLEDGE.

7th June, 1918.   M. Webster Lieut
                                   Lt. Captain, R.E.
                           for C.R.E. 16th Division.

Distribution:-

       157th Field Coy. R.E.
       155th Field Coy. R.E.)
       16th Div. "G".   )
       16th Div. "Q".   ) for information.
       16th Div. Signal Coy.)
       S.S.O., 16th Div.   )
       C.R.E.
       War Diary.
       File.

Army Form C. 2118.

H.Q.R.E. 16 Div.

VOL 32

WAR DIARY

or ~~INTELLIGENCE SUMMARY~~

(Erase heading not required.)

Instructions regarding War Diaries and Intelligence Summaries are contained in F. S. Regs., Part II. and the Staff Manual respectively. Title pages will be prepared in manuscript.

Place	Date	Hour	Summary of Events and Information	Remarks and references to Appendices
Samer	1/7/18		C.R.E. goes on leave. Work on G'reuxcic practically finished except refreshments. Work on d'reuxcic preparation. Major E.J Scott M.C. R.E. acting C.R.E.	
	2/7/18		Work on above	
	3/7/18		Work on above	
	4/7/18		Work on above	
	5/7/18		do	
	6/7/18		do	
	7/7/18		do	
	8/7/18		do	
	9/7/18		do	
	10/7/18		do. "Sir White" arrive in reinforcement 6757 Fld Coy. Strength procedure above	
	11/7/18		Work on d'reuxcic	
	12/7/18		Work on above	
	13/7/18		Work on above	
	14/7/18		Work on above	
	15/7/18		C.R.E. return from leave. Work on above.	

Army Form C. 2118.

WAR DIARY
or
~~INTELLIGENCE SUMMARY~~
(Erase heading not required.)

Instructions regarding War Diaries and Intelligence Summaries are contained in F.S. Regs., Part II. and the Staff Manual respectively. Title pages will be prepared in manuscript.

Place	Date	Hour	Summary of Events and Information	Remarks and references to Appendices
Samer	16/7/16	—	Work as usual — Thursday returns	
	17/7/16	—	Ditto. CRE's Orders No. 87 (W.D. Appendix No. 1)	Appendix No. 1
	18/7/16	—	Major Gen. Heath E-in-C visited 157 & 157 Field Coys.	
			CRE's order No. 68 (W.D. Appen No. 2) ref. E-in-C's inspection - & instructions re Training	Appendix No. 2
			Field Coys.	
	19/7/16		Work as usual on G'HQ. Scheme. Lt. McIntosh 157 Fd Coy. joins H.Q.R.E.	
	20/7/16		Work as usual.	
	21/7/16		Work as usual.	
	22/7/16		Lt.-Col. Rutherford CRE leaves for Cambridge returns Staff. Duties — afterwards to general. Major E.J. Brett MC Actg. CRE	
	23/7/16		H. G.H.Q. filled up new appointment.	Appendix No. 3
	24/7/16		Work as usual.	
			CRE's order No. 69 (W.D. Appen. No. 3) re preliminary canvass for Field Coys (155-157) re preparation & keeping training. 157th Field Company	
	25/7/16	—	155th told off man to HARDELOT RIFLE for practice & work as usual.	
	26/7/16		Work & training as usual above. Lt. Col. Simmons F.M.C.R.E. joins to take	
	3		up appointment as C.R.E.	

Army Form C. 2118.

WAR DIARY
or
INTELLIGENCE SUMMARY.
(Erase heading not required.)

Instructions regarding War Diaries and Intelligence Summaries are contained in F. S. Regs., Part II. and the Staff Manual respectively. Title pages will be prepared in manuscript.

Place	Date	Hour	Summary of Events and Information	Remarks and references to Appendices
Samer	27/8	—	C.R.E's Order No 70. (W.O. Appendices No 4) in addition to Order No 69.	Appendices No 4
	28/8	—	Work & training as usual	
	29/8	—	165th Field Coy returned from HARDELOT PLAGE to SAMER. The 167th Field Coy proceeded from LACRES to HARDELOT PLAGE for Pontoon & Bridging training. C.R.E's Order No 72 (W.O. Appendix No 5) in detached Section 156th Coy at CARLY regarding Carrying ad DESIRES	Appendices No 5
	30/8	—	C.R.E's Order No 73 (W.O. Appendix No 6) in move of 157th Field Coy from HARDELOT to FRENCQ	Appendices No 6
	31/8	—	Work & training as usual	

J. Cameron Black.
Lieut. R.E.
for C.R.E. 16th Div.

H.Q. R.E. 16th Div.　　　　　　　　　　　　　　Appendix No 1.
W.D. July 1918

C. R. E.'s ORDER NO. 66.

17th July, 1918.

1. The Engineer-in-Chief has expressed his intention of inspecting the 155th and 157th Field Companies R.E. at an early date.

2. The inspection of the 155th Field Coy. R.E. will take place on the WIERRE - DESVRES Road, N.W. of LONG FOSSE (figure 80) - That of 157th Field Coy. R.E. at junction of 5 Roads LACRES.

3. The Companies will be drawn up in Column of Route, i.e. O.C. and Trumpeter leading, No. 1. Section complete with Transport, No. 2, No. 3, No. 4, Captain, Headquarter Transport and personnel. Column to face Engineer-in-Chief on arrival.

4. Dress. - Light Marching Order. Special attention that Officers, Sappers and Drivers are turned out precisely in all details, and there is no variation whatever in dress and what is carried in the case of Officers, Sappers and Drivers respectively.

5. O.C. Companies will be notified of the hour of the inspection, and they will arrange all details to have their Commands drawn up $\frac{3}{4}$ hour earlier, so that any mistakes etc. may be rectified, and dust or dirt collected on the march removed.

6. Each Section etc. will be brought to attention as the Engineer-in-Chief approaches, but no salute will be given except by Officers, all of whom will salute on the approach of the Engineer-in-Chief.

7. The packing of Tool Carts, Limbers, Pontoon Wagons, etc. and Pack Animals will be absolutely correct.

8. The C.R.E. looks to all ranks to do credit to the Division on this very special occasion.

R.F.A. Butterworth

17th July, 1918.　　　　　　　　　　　　　　Lieut-Colonel, R.E.
　　　　　　　　　　　　　　　　　　　C. R. E. 16th Division.

Distribution.:-
　　155th Field Coy. R.E.
　　157th Field Coy. R.E.
　　117th Inf. Bde. (for information)
　　File, (2)
　　War Diary.
　　C. R. E.

H.Q. R.E. 16th Div.
W.D. July 1918.

Appendix No. 1

C.R.E's ORDER NO. 67.

17th July, 1918.

Reference C.R.E's Order No. 66.

1.   Inspection of 157th Field Company R.E. will take place at 11 a.m., 18th instant, and 155th Field Company R.E. at 12 noon.

      Assembly parades will take place ¾ hour earlier in each case.

2.   Field Company Commanders will send out Cyclist guides on main road to look out for and direct Engineer-in-Chief's Car.

17th July, 1918.   Captain, R.E.

                                        for C. R. E. 16th Division.

Distribution :-

      155th Field Coy. R.E.
      157th Field Coy. R.E.
      117th Inf. Bde. (for information).
      File.
      War Diary.
      C. R. E.

H.Q. R.E. 16th Div.
W.D. July 1918.

Appendix
No 2

C. R. E's ORDER NO. 68.

18th July, 1918.

1. The Engineer-in-Chief expressed his satisfaction at the smartness and physical condition of all ranks of both 155th Field Company R.E. and 157th Field Company R.E. at his inspection today.

    The C.R.E. received his congratulations on behalf of the Field Companies on the fine recovery made after the trying times during the operations on the Somme Front on March 21st and onwards.

2. The Engineer-in-Chief expressed a wish that the Field Companies should now take every opportunity to train, especially in work connected with mobile operations.

    Field Company Commanders will therefore make every endeavour to give Officers and men under their command a thorough training under the following sub-heads.

    (a) Musketry.
    (b) Close and extended order drill.
    (c) Outpost duties.
    (d) Rear-guard Actions.
    (e) Demolitions.
    (f) Pontoon and other hasty Bridging.
    (g) Smart turnout of personnel, horses and vehicles.
    (h) Small schemes for Sections, to include writing orders - rapid turnout and movement with some definite object in view, such as a demolition - defence of a tactical point, etc.

18th July, 1918.

Captain, R.E.
for C. R. E. 16th Division.

Distribution :-

155th Field Coy. R.E.
157th Field Coy. R.E.
File.
War Diary.
C.R.E.

H.Q. R.E.
W.D. July 1918

Appendix
No 5

C.R.E's ORDER No. 69.

24th July, 1918.

PONTOON BRIDGING.

1. The 155th Field Company R.E. will proceed to the Lake at HARDELOT in S.E. (Calais Sh. 1S.) on Thursday 25th July, and carry out a course of pontoon & trestle bridge training.

    This Unit will return to DESVRES on Tuesday 30th July, 1918.

2. The 157th Field Company R.E. will proceed to the above training ground on Tuesday 30th July, returning on Saturday 3rd. August, 1918.

3. In order that more effective practice may be carried out, the bridging equipment of both Companies will proceed on Thursday 25th July, and remain during the whole period of training of both Companies.

4. A small personnel will be left behind by Field Coys., to look after billets and dumps whilst the units are away training.

5. Units will be accommodated under Canvas. Each Unit should take with them what Canvas they have on charge.

    The remainder required will be made up as far as possible from the Divisional R.E. Dump, SAMER.

24th July, 1918.

Major, R.E.
A / C. R. E. 16th Division.

Distribution :-
    155th Field Coy. R.E.
    157th Field Coy. R.E.
    117th Inf. Bde.
    O.C. 16th Div. Details.
    File.
    War Diary.

H.Q. R.E. 16th Div
W.D. July 1918.

Appendix No 4

C. R. E's ORDER NO. 70.

27th July, 1918.

Pontoon Bridging.

1. The arrangements for return of 155th Field Company R.E. to DESVRES, contained in para 1. of C.R.E's Order No. 69. are cancelled.

2. Para 2. of C.R.E's Order No. 69. is cancelled.

3. 155th Field Company R.E. will now return to billets at DESVRES, from the Training grounds at HARDELOT on Monday 29th July, 1918.

4. The 157th Field Company R.E. will proceed to the Training Ground at HARDELOT (CALAIS Sh. 13. S.E.) on Monday 29th July, 1918, and return to billets at LACRES on Friday 2nd. August 1918.

5. ACKNOWLEDGE.

Captain, R.E.

for C. R. E. 16th Division.

Distribution :-

155th Field Coy. R.E.
157th Field Coy. R.E.
O.C. 16th Div. Details.
File.
War Diary.

H.Q.R.E. 16th Div.
W.D. July 1918

Appendix
No 5

C. R. E'S ORDER NO. 72.

30th July, 1918.

On return of 16th Division to HAMEL AREA, the 156th Field Company R.E. will remain at DERNANCOURT, and the following move will take place on Tuesday 30th instant.

1. The Section 155th Field Company R.E. at present at CARLY will move to DERNANCOURT and will be accommodated in the 155th Field company R.E. billeting area.

2. All R.E. stores in the Area Dump at CARLY will be returned to the Divisional R.E. Dump.

One Motor Lorry will report at CARLY at 8.30 a.m. 30th instant, for this purpose. Officer i/c Section 155th Field Company R.E. will provide loading personnel.

3. Move to be completed by 5 p.m.

4. ACKNOWLEDGE.

Captain, R.E.

for C.R.E. 16th Division.

Distribution:-
155th Field Company R.E.
O. i/c Section, 155th Fld. Coy. R.E.
16th Div. "Q".)
Area Group Comdt.) For information.
File.
War Diary.

H.Q. R.E. 16th Div.
W.D. July 1918

Appendix No 6

C. R. E's ORDER NO. 73.

30th July, 1918.

On the return of the 16th Division to BAPAUME AREA, the 48th Infantry Brigade will be stationed in FREMICQ Area and the following moves will consequently take place.

1.   157th Field Company R.E. will move into billets in FREMICQ on return from training at BANDICOT on 2nd. August 1918.

2.   O.C. 157th Field Company R.E. will arrange to send forward a small advance party in charge of an Officer to arrange billets with Sub Area Commandant at FREMICQ.
        This party to proceed to FREMICQ on 1st. August, 1918.

3.   O.C. 157th Field Company R.E. will move stores from LACHEF to FREMICQ under his own arrangements.

4.   ACKNOWLEDGE.

                                        Captain, R.E.
                                  for C.R.E. 16th Division.

Distribution:-
        157th Field Company R.E.
        158th Field Company R.E.
        D.A.A.G., 16th Div.
        G.S.O., 16th Div.
        Sub Area Commdt, FREMICQ.
        File.
        War Diary.

Army Form C. 2118.

WAR DIARY
or
INTELLIGENCE SUMMARY.

H.Q. R.E. 15th Division.

WR 3

Place	Date	Hour	Summary of Events and Information	Remarks and references to Appendices
SAMER	1/8/18	—	C.R.E.'s Order No 74. (W.D. Appendix No 1.) re movement of 154th Field Company from Ofekin din. N21.	N21.
	2/8/18	—	HARDELOT PLAGE to FRENCQ. 9/8	
	3/8/18	—	154th Field Coy. move from HARDELOT PLAGE to FRENCQ. 9/8	
	4/8/18	—	C.R.E. visits 166th Field Coy. at STEENBECQUE. 9/8	
	5/8/18	—	Work as usual. 9/8	
	6/8/18	—	Ditto 9/8	
	7/8/18	—	C.R.E. inspects transport & mounted Personnel of 155th Field Coy. 9/8	
			157th Field Coy. 9/8	
			Ditto	
	8/8/18	—	Capt (A/Major) A.E. HUGHES, M.C., R.E. taken over command of 154th Field Coy. vice Capt (A/Major) G.E. GRIMSDALE, R.E. Lieut (A/Capt) J.R. HAIGH, R.E. takes over duties of 2nd in Command 155th Field Coy. vice Capt (A/Major) A.E. HUGHES, M.C., R.E. 9/8	
	9/8/18	—	Training of 155 & 156 Coys commences according to programme issued by C.R.E. 9/8	
	10/8/18	—	Training as above. C.R.E. inspects Dismounted Personnel of 154th Coy. 9/8	
			157th Coy. 9/8	
	11/8/18	—	Ditto 9/8	
			Training as per previous programme.	

Army Form C. 2118.

WAR DIARY
or
INTELLIGENCE SUMMARY.
(Erase heading not required.)

Instructions regarding War Diaries and Intelligence Summaries are contained in F. S. Regs., Part II. and the Staff Manual respectively. Title pages will be prepared in manuscript.

Place	Date	Hour	Summary of Events and Information	Remarks and references to Appendices
	12/8/18	—	C.R.E.'s Order No 75. (W.D. Appendix No 2.) ref. reforming new of 156th Field Coy to upper Division. JB	Appendix No 2.
	13/8/18	—	156th Field Coy move from STEENBECQUE to BLEQUIN under orders of XI Corps (5th Army). JB	
	14/8/18	—	156th Field Coy move from BLEQUIN to LACRES under orders of C.R.E. 15th Div. (and No 75. W.D. Appendix No 2.) JB	
	15/8/18	—	Forming up per programme. JB	
	16/8/18	—	C.R.E.'s Order No 76. (W.D. Appendix No 3.) Warning order to concentrate of Division from XVII Corps to I Corps. JB	Appendix No 3.
	17/8/18	—	C.R.E.'s Order No 77. (W.D. Appendix No 4.) Detailed orders of move to I Corps area. JB	Appendix No 4.
			2nd Lieut. Roberts, R.E. (157th Coy) leaves for course at I Corps Gas School.	
			2nd Lieut. Auchmuty, R.E. (156th Coy) leaves for course at I Corps Sch. School. JB	
	18/8/18	—	156th Coy transport move from DENNEBROEUCQ to QUILEN and under 4th Div arrangements. JB	
	19/8/18	—	156th Coy Dismounted men from LACRES to SAILLY LABOURSE by bus & march via FRENCQ " " " to QUILEN area under 49th Bde arrangements. 157th Coy transport " " " to QUILEN and under 49th Bde arrangements. 156th Coy transport " " " QUILEN area to ANVIN area under 4th Div arrangements. H.Q. R.E. move from SAMER to ANVIN JB	

A 5834 Wt. W4973/M687 750,000 8/16 D.D. & L. Ltd. Forms/C.2118/13

Army Form C. 2118.

WAR DIARY
or
INTELLIGENCE SUMMARY.
(Erase heading not required.)

Instructions regarding War Diaries and Intelligence Summaries are contained in F. S. Regs., Part II. and the Staff Manual respectively. Title pages will be prepared in manuscript.

Place	Date	Hour	Summary of Events and Information	Remarks and references to Appendices
ANVIN	20/5	—	159th Field Coy move from FRENCQ to NEVAL area	
			156th " " " transport move from ANVIN area to MAISNIL-LES-RUITZ	
			157th " " " transport " " QUILEN area " ANVIN area	
			C.R.E. & Lieut BLACK, R.E. move from ANVIN to RUITZ to take over area	
	21/5	—	C.R.E., 1st Div JB	
			156th Field Coy move from SAILLY LABOURSE to ANNEQUIN & take over billets	
			& move in line from 2nd Field Coy	
			157th Field Coy move from DIEVAL area to SAILLY LABOURSE	
			157th " " " transport move from ANVIN area to MAISNIL-LES-RUITZ	
			155th " " " " " " DESURES area " QUILEN area JB	
	22/5	—	157th " " " move from SAILLY LABOURSE to ANNEQUIN & take over	
			billets & work of 409 Field Coy	
			155th Field Coy move from DESURES to SAILLY LABOURSE & take over	
			Reserve work from 2 3rd Field Coy	
			156th Field Coy transport move from QUILEN area to ANVIN area	
			H.Q. R.E. & Walker and company from 1st Div R.E. JB	
			155th Field Coy transport move from ANVIN area to MAISNIL-LES-RUITZ JB	
RUITZ	23/5	—	Work as usual JB	
	24/5	—	— ditto — JB	
	25/5	—	— ditto —	
	26/5	—	Lieut CULVER, R.E. admitted to Hospital (accidentally injured) JB	

Army Form C. 2118.

WAR DIARY
or
INTELLIGENCE SUMMARY.
(Erase heading not required.)

Instructions regarding War Diaries and Intelligence Summaries are contained in F. S. Regs., Part II. and the Staff Manual respectively. Title pages will be prepared in manuscript.

Place	Date	Hour	Summary of Events and Information	Remarks and references to Appendices
RUITZ	27/9	—	C.R.E.'s Orders No 78 (W.D. Appendix No 5.) of move of 155 Coy transport from MAISNIL-LES-RUITZ to NOEUX-LES-MINES	Appendix No 5.
	28/9	—	155th Field Coy transport moves from MAISNIL-LES-RUITZ to NŒUX-LES-MINES. C.R.E.'s Orders No 79 (W.D. Appendix No 6.) of intercompany relief between 155 Coy & 166 Coy R.E.	Appendix No 6.
	29/9	—	Work as usual. 2/Lieut. OTOCK, R.E. admitted to hospital N.Y.A.	
	30/9	—	Work as usual.	
	31/9	—	Nil.	

J Champ Shah Lieut R.E.
for C.R.E. 1st Division

H.Q. R.E.   W. D. Appendix No 1
16th Div.

C. R. E's ORDER NO. 74.

1st August, 1918.

On departure of 157th Field Coy. R.E. for FRENCQ on 2nd inst. the following arrangements will be made re bridging stores at HARDELOT.

1. O.C. 157th Field Coy. R.E. will leave behind a Loading party of 1 N.C.O. and 16 men to work under orders of Lieut. BLACK, R.E. attached to H.Q.R.E. This party will be taken to FRENCQ on completion of duty by motor lorry.

2. Lieut. BLACK will report to O.C. 157th Field Coy. R.E. at 8.30 a.m. to take over all equipment belonging to R.E. Dump, SAMER.

3. O.C. 157th Field Coy. R.E. will arrange to have all tents held on charge from R.E. Dump struck before handed over, and all bridging stores such as spars, lashings, Artillery Bridges, Casks, and stores on charge to 155th Field Coy. R.E. will be parked ready for easy and quick removal.

4. All latrine pits must be properly filled in, and Administrative Stores, latrine seats, latrine screens, Cookhouses, etc. stacked ready for removal.

5. O.C. 155th Field Company, R.E. will arrange to send pontoon wagons for the pontoon equipment of his Company to the training ground at HARDELOT, to arrive at this place at 9.0. a.m. 2nd inst.

6. ACKNOWLEDGE.

Captain, R.E.
for C. R. E. 16th Division.

Distribution:-

155th Field Coy. R.E.
157th Field Coy. R.E.
Lieut. BLACK, R.E.
File (2).

H.Q.R.E. 16th Div.   W.D. Appendix N°2

SECRET.

C.R.E's. ORDER No. 75.

12th August 1918.

156th Field Company R.E., will rejoin the 16th Division in the DOUDEAVILLE AREA on 14th August, and in consequence the following move will take place.

1. 156th Field Coy., R.E. will move from billets at BLEQUIN to billets at LACRES (CALAIS Sh.13. 5.D.) on morning of 14th August 1918.

2. For transportation of dismounted personnel, six motor lorries will report at the Area Commandant's Office, BLEQUIN, at 8.45 a.m. 14th August, to meet guide provided by O.C. 156th Field Company R.E.

3. Billets at BLEQUIN will be clear by 9.0 a.m. 14th August, and a certificate obtained from Area Commandant that they have been left clean and in good order.

4. Horse transport will move by march-route. No restrictions as to routes but they must be previously reconnoitred. The strictest march discipline will be maintained throughout - the usual halts being observed.

5. Billets at LACRES will be arranged by C.R.E. 16th Div., For this purpose O.C. 157th Field Company R.E. will arrange to send a guide to meet Lieut. BLACK R.E. at LACRES at 9.0 a.m. 14th August, to point out billets, watering facilities etc., at this village.

6. Completion of move to be reported immediately to this Office.

7. 156th Field Coy., R.E., and 157th Field Coy., R.E. to acknowledge.

12th August 1918.

                                              Captain R.E.
                                for C.R.E. 16th Division.

DISTRIBUTION.

156th Field Company R.E.	16th Division "G".)
157th Field Company R.E.	16th Division "Q".) For
C. R. E.	16th Division Sigs.)
File. (2)	16th Divisional Train.) Information
W. D. (2)	155th Field Company R.E.)

H.Q.R.E.
16th Div.

W.A. Appendix No 3.

S E C R E T.

C. R. E's ORDER No.78.

16th August, 1918.

W A R N I N G   O R D E R.

1. The 16th Division (less Artillery) will be transferred from XXII Corps to I Corps on 19th August and will relieve the 1st Division (less Artillery) in the line commencing 20th August.

2. The move of the 16th Division to 1st Corps area will take place by bus/road commencing 19th August and proceeding at the rate of one Brigade Group per day.

3. Brigade Groups will probably move in the following order

  (a) 47th Inf. Bde. Group.
  (b) 49th   "   "   "
  (c) 48th   "   "   "

4. Detailed orders as to the above moves and reliefs will be issued later.

5. ACKNOWLEDGE.

           Captain, R.E.
    for   16th Division.

Distribution:-
 O.C. 155th Fld.Coy.R.E.
 O.C. 156th Fld.Coy.R.E.
 O.C. 157th Fld.Coy.R.E.
 File.
 War Diary (2).

H.Q. R.E. 16th Div.   W.D. Appendix N° 4

SECRET.   Copy No. 9

C.R.E's ORDER NO. 77.

Reference:-   17th August, 1918.
1/100,000 Map, CALAIS,
HAZEBROUCK & LENS Sheets.

1. For the purpose of the move to the 1st Corps Area Inf. Bde. Groups will be constituted as follows:-

   <u>47th Inf. Bde. Group.</u>   47th Inf. Bde.
                                    156 Fld. Coy. R.E.
                                    77 Fld. Amb.
                                    16 M.G. Bn. (less 2 Coys).
                                    Advance parties 49 Inf. Bde.
                                    143 Co. A.S.C.

   <u>48th Inf. Bde. Group.</u>   48 Inf. Bde.
                                    155 Fld. Coy. R.E.
                                    112 Fld. Amb.
                                    11 Hants (Pioneers)
                                    145 Co. A.S.C.

   <u>49th Inf. Bde. Group.</u>   49th Inf. Bde.
                                    157 Fld. Coy. R.E.
                                    2 Coys. 16 M.G. Bn.
                                    Advance parties of 48 Inf. Bde.
                                    144 Co. A.S.C.

2. (a) Moves by bus and lorry will take place in accordance with attached Table A.

   (b) Moves by road in accordance with Table B.

   (c) Reliefs will be carried out in accordance with Table A and are to be completed by 6 a.m., August, 23rd 1918. Reliefs in the line will commence on 21st August and not as stated in para: 1 of C.R.E's Order No. 76, which should be amended accordingly.

3. On arrival in 1st Division Area the various formations will come under the command of G.O.C. 1st Division, by whom all further orders for debusment and reliefs are being issued, and under whose orders they will remain until the command passes.

4. The Command of the CENTRE SECTOR 1st Corps will pass from G.O.C. 1st Division to G.O.C. 16th Division on completion of relief night 22nd/23rd August.

5. (a) Reports to SAMER until 11 a.m. 19th August. After that hour to MONCHY CAYEUX.
   (b) Time on 22nd August at which report centre will close at MONCHY CAYEUX and reopen in BARLIN area will be notified later.

6. ACKNOWLEDGE.

Issued at 8.0. p.m.   J Webster Captain, R.E.
                                        for C.R.E. 16th Division.

Distribution overleaf.

Distribution:-

No. 1.   155th Fld.Coy.R.E.
    2.   156th Fld.Coy......
    3.   157th Fld.Coy.R.E.
    4.   C. R. E.
    5.   16th Div. 'G')
    6.   16th Div. 'Q') f r information.
    7.)
    8.)   File.
    9.   W.J.
    10.

SECRET.   Table 'A'.   (Moves by bus and lorry) to accompany C.R.E's Order No.77.

Serial No.	Date	Formation	From	To	Relieving	Remarks
A	August 18	Advance parties from 47 Inf.Bde.	DOUDEAUVILLE Area.	NOEUX-LES-MINES Area.	—	By lorry under arrangements already notified, separately to all concerned.
B	19	47 Inf.Bde.Group & advance parties from 49 Inf.Bde.	DOUDEAUVILLE Area.	NOEUX-LES-MINES Area.	'A' Inf.Bde.Group 1st Div. in reserve	Embus 7.30 a.m. Buses facing N.E. on PARENTY-DOUDEAUVILLE Road. Leading bus opposite final E in DOUDEAUVILLE. These buses will take back 'A' Inf.Bde.Group 1st Div.
C	19	Div.H.Q. Group	SAMER Area	MONCHY CAYEUX	—	Embus 9 a.m. Buses facing E on SAMER-BEAUCORRY Road. Leading bus 50 yds. W. of Level crossing 500 yds. S. of E in SAMER.
D	20	49 Inf.Bde.Group & advance parties from 43 Inf.Bde.	HALINGHEM Area.	DIEVAL Area (BEUGIN-DIEVAL-BAJUS-BOURS)	—	Embus 9 a.m. Buses facing N. on main SAMER-MONTREUIL Road. Leading bus just short of the cross roads half mile E of the G in BOIS DE TINGRY. Billets from Area Comdt.DIEVAL, except for Bours where application will be made to Area Comdt. TANGRY.
E	21	47 Inf.Bde.Group	NOEUX LES MINES Area	LINE	'B' Inf.Bde.Group 1st Div.	Under orders to be issued by 1st Div.
F	21	49 Inf.Bde.Group	DIEVAL Area	NOEUX-LES-MINES Area	47 Inf.Bde.Group in reserve.	Embus 1 p.m. at debussing point for Serial D under arrangements to be made by G.O.C. 49th Inf. Bde. These buses will take back 'B' Inf.Bde.Group 1st Div.

Table 'A' (contd).

Serial No	Date	Formation	From	To	Relieving	Remarks
G	August 22	49 Inf.Bde.Group	NOEUX-LES-MINES Area	LINE	'G' Inf.Bde.Group 1st Div.	Under orders to be u/d by 1st Div.
H	22	48 Inf.Bde.Group	DESVRES Area	NOEUX-LES-MINES Area	49 Inf.Bde.Group in reserve	Embus 7.30 a.m. Buses facing S.E. on WIRWIGNES-COURSET Road. Leading bus just short of level crossing half mile due S. of D in DESVRES. These buses will take back 'G' Inf.Bde.Group 1st Div.
J	22	11 Hants (P)	GRANDAL-BEAUCORRY Area	SAILLY LABOURSE	Pioneer Bn. 1st Div.	Move to GRANDAL-BEAUCORRY Are. on 20 Aug. Billets on application to Area Comdt. DOUDEAUVILLE. Embus and move to 1st Div. Area wit 48th Inf.Bde.Group.
K	22	Div.H.Q.	MONCHY CAYEUX	BABLIN Area	H.Q. 1st Div.	Under arrangements to be made by 'Q' 18th Div.

S E C R E T.   TABLE B (TRANSPORT).

Serial No.	Date.	Formation.	From	To	Starting Point	Time	Remarks.
1	August 18th	47 Inf. Bde. Group	DOUDEAUVILLE Area	QUILEN.	Cross Roads 500x N.W. of E in ENQUIN.	5.0 pm.	
2.	19th	47th Inf. Bde. Group	QUILEN.	OREQUY.	As ordered by O.C. Group	5.B am.	
3.	19th	47th Inf. Bde. Group	CREQUY	ANVIN	- do -	5.0.pm.	
4.	19th	49th Inf. Bde. Group	HALINGHEM Area	QUILEN	As arranged by 49 Inf. Bde.	-	Not to enter QUILEN before 7 pm
5.	20th	47th Inf.Bde. Group	ANVIN	PERNES Area	As ordered by O.C. Group	5.0 am.	Ground for midday halt to be reconnoitred previously.
6.	20th	47 Inf. Bde. Group	PERNES Area	BARLIN Area	- do -	5.0 pm.	Guides from each unit in 47 Inf.Bde. Group to await Transport at RNITZ CHURCH from 7:30 p.m.
7.	20th	49th Inf.Bde. Group and H.Q. Group	QUILEN	CREQUY	- do -	5.0 a.m.	
8.	20th	do	CREQUY	ANVIN	- do -	5.0 p.m.	Div. H.Q. Group to join H.Q. at MONCHY CAYEUX
9.	21st	49th Inf.Bde. Group	ANVIN	PERNES Area	As ordered by O.C. Group	5.0.am.	As for Serial 5.
10	21st	49th Inf.Bde. Group	PERNES Area	BARLIN Area	- do -	5.0.pm.	Guides from each Unit of 49th Inf.Bde. Group to await Transport at RUITZ CHURCH from 7.30 p.m.

TABLE "B" (contd).

Serial No	Date	Formation	From	To	Starting Point	Time	Remarks
11	August 21st	48 Inf Bde Group	DESVRES Area	QUILEN	As arranged by 48 Inf. Bde.	—	Not to enter QUILEN before 7.0.pm.
12	21st 22nd	48 Inf. Bde. Group and 11 Hants.	QUILEN	ORBEQUY	As ordered by O.C. Group	5.a.m.	
13	22nd	- do -	ORBEQUY	ANVIN	- do -	5.p.m.	
14	23rd	- do -	ANVIN	PERNES Area	- do -	5.a.m.	As for Serial 5.
15	23rd	- do -	PERNES Area	BARLIN Area	- do -	5.p.m.	Guide from each unit of 48 I.B. Group to await transport at RUITZ CHURCH from 7.50 p.m.

NOTE:- In every case the O.C. Group will be the Officer Commanding the Coy.A.S.C. with that Group.

H.Q.R.E.
16th Div.

SECRET   N.A. Appendix No 5

C. R. E's. ORDER   No. 78.

27th August 1918.

1. The transport of 155th Field Company R.E. will move from its present Lines in J.36.b. to the standings allotted by the 48th Infantry brigade in K.&18.b.

2. The transport lines in J.36.b. will be clear by 7.0 a.m. 28th August 1918.

3. The shelters at present on the Lines in J.36.b. must be left standing, and no material whatever will be taken away from these.

4. Horse Standings and Billets will be left scrupulously clean, and in good order.

5. Completion of move to be reported to this Office.

6. Captain J.P. HAUGH R.E. to acknowledge.

27th August 1918.   F Summer... Lieut. Colonel R.E.
C.R.E. 16th Division.

DISTRIBUTION.
=============

O.C. 155th Field Coy., R.E.
Captain J.P.HAUGH, Transport Lines, 155th Field Coy., R.E.
16th Div. "A".)
16th Div. "G".)   For information.
D.A.D.V.S.   )
War Diary. (2).
File. (2).

****

H.Q. RE
16th Div.

N.A. Appendix No 6

SECRET.
==========

C. R. E's ORDER No. 79.

28th August, 1918.

1. The following inter-Company relief will take place on the 1st September, 1918.
   155th Field Coy.R.E. will relieve 156th Field Coy.R.E. in the HOHENZOLLERN Sector and will be responsible for Engineering work in that Sector from 5.0.p.m. on the 1st September, 1918.

2. O.C. 155th Field Coy.R.E. should at once get into touch with O.C. 156th Field Coy.R.E. and have the necessary Officer reconnaissance made, so as to ensure that there is no break of any kind in the continuity of work in the Sector.

3. O.C. 156th Field Coy.R.E. will detail two Officers to take over from 155th Field Coy.R.E. on 31st August, 1918, all work which that Company has now in hand.
   Special attention must be directed to the demolition scheme.

4. Arrangements for relief will be made directly between Company Commanders concerned, subject to the following restrictions:-

   (a) No undue movement will be shown during the relief.
       Movement between ANNEQUIN and SAILLY LABOURSE will be in parties of six or less, at 5 minutes intervals.

   (b) Transport will not be employed until after dusk.

5. ACKNOWLEDGE.

F. .... Lieut.Colonel, R.E.

C. R. E. 16th Division.

Distribution:-

    155th Field Coy.R.E.
    156th Field Coy.R.E.
    16th Div. 'G')
    47th Inf.Bde.) for information.
    48th Inf.Bde.)
    War Diary (2)
    File   (2).

WAR DIARY
or
INTELLIGENCE SUMMARY.
(Erase heading not required.)

Army Form C. 2118.

H.Q.R.E. XI Div N/8 34

Place	Date	Hour	Summary of Events and Information	Remarks and references to Appendices
RUITZ	1/9/18	—	Work as usual. C.R.E's Instructions as to action in the event of withdrawal given. (Appendix N°1) 155 Coy N2 relieved 155 Fellers as at Aix-Noulette Sector	Appendix N°1
	2/9/16	—	Work in breast.	
	3/9/18	—	Work as usual. 156 Have been moved to NOEUX-LES-MINES (C.R.E Order N°60)	Appendix N°2
	4/9/18	—	Work as usual. Lt Blad defends Sarleun	
	5/9/18		Work as usual in Holm of the Canadian Section. 155 Hd Co. pulled bridge across Vendelle-Auchel Rd.	
	6/9/18		157 Held Transport moves to NOEUX-les-mines (C.R.E) Order N°61) Appendix N°3	Appendix N°3
	7/9/18		Work as usual. 157 Held Co consolidating Auburn Trench. C.R.E Order N°62 (Appendix N°4) orders formation of Forward Dumps in Brigade Areas.	Appendix N°4
	8/9/18		Work as above	
	9/9/18		Work as above	
	10/9/18		Work as above	
	11/9/18		Work as above	
	12/9/18		Work as above — 157 Held Co. Consolidate Auburn Triangle	
	13/9/18		Work as above. Steps withdrawn from bridges prepared for demolition Lt Arch RE 155 Fiell Coy to Lille in effect (North End)	
	14/9/18			

WAR DIARY
or
INTELLIGENCE SUMMARY.
(Erase heading not required.)

Army Form C. 2118.

A.Q. R.E. 16 Div

Place	Date	Hour	Summary of Events and Information	Remarks and references to Appendices
RUITZ	15/9/16	—	Work as usual. C.R.E. Order N° 83 — Re Conveyance of Forse 8 — LESBRIQUES — and Railway Triangle into defended localities (Appendix N° 5)	Appendix N° 5
	16/9/16		Work as usual.	
	17/9/16		Work as usual	
	18/9/16		Work as usual.	
	19/9/16		Work as above. 2nd Lieut. R.S. returned from leave. Capt. Thomson M.O.R.	
	20/9/16		Work as above. 16 Div R.E. defaults for leave.	
	21/9/16		C.R.E. Order N° 85 issued (Appendix N°6) — Command theatre re assigned — Forse 8 and Railway Triangle handed over to 153rd & 155th Div respectively. Appendix of Village Line, 157 & London Divisions defence — Area of Village Line. 156 Div Pioneers Batt. and Wilson Siths Wooden Trams — G.R.8.'s Order N° 86 — move of Field Co Transport consequent upon re-organization of Divisional area. (Appendix N° 7)	Appendix N° 6 Appendix N°7
	22/9/16		Work as above. Major Smith 1st Fld Coy from 2nd R.E. 155 relieves 157 Hdly	
	23/9/16		H.Q. R.E. moves to DEBERIM. Move of Transport as in C.R.E. Order N° 86 Lt. Col. Commands C.R.E. departs for leave.	

Army Form C. 2118.

WAR DIARY
or
INTELLIGENCE SUMMARY.
(Erase heading not required.)

HQ 2nd ReDiv

Place	Date	Hour	Summary of Events and Information	Remarks and references to Appendices
DROUVIN	24/9/16	—	Lt Black RE upon leave (187 Fielder), W. Culver 187 Field Coy RE proceeded on instruction adjutant	
	25/9/16	—	Work as above	
	26/9/16	—	Work as above – 152 Fld Coy commence new post at station Cott.	
	27/9/16	—	Work as above	
	28/9/16	—	Work as above	
	29/9/16	—	Work as above – Motor rept commenced at Drouvin by 157	
	30/9/16	—	Work as above	

Culver
Fowler Major

H.Q. R.E.
16th Division

W.D. Appendix No 1
Sept 1918

SECRET.   3346/51.

PRELIMINARY INSTRUCTIONS AS TO ACTION IN THE EVENT OF
AN ENEMY RETIREMENT.

(1)   The following preliminary instructions are issued for guidance as to the lines on which an enemy withdrawal will be followed up and on which preliminary reconnaissances should be carried out.

(2)   Immediately the advance commences one Section of each Field Coy. in the line will be placed at the disposal of the Infantry Brigade to which it is affiliated. This Section should be detailed at once.

The most energetic and capable Subaltern should command this Section and C.R.E. and Brigades informed at once who has been detailed. Liaison methods should be arranged with Brigades for calling on this Section and C.R.E. informed what these are.

(3)   The remainder of the R.E. and 11th Hants (Pioneers) will remain at the disposal of the C.R.E. for work on improvement of roads and tracks across NO MAN'S LAND.

The following roads have been selected as the main roads to be made good in the event of an advance. -

    (i) ANNEQUIN - CAMBRIN - LE FAUBOURG - LA BASSEE road.

    (ii) VERMELLES - AUCHY - DOUVRIN road.

    (iii) Road connecting the above through A.23.a. and c.

    (iv) LA BASSEE - CITE STE. ELIE road.

The Division will be responsible for making the above roads passable for horse transport.

As far as can be seen at present the first work of R.E. and Pioneers will be -

    (a) Making good the four roads above for horse transport including field guns.

    (b) Making good for first line transport -

        (i) Alternative roads.

        (ii) Dry-weather tracks.

In this connection the Reserve Field Company and the 11th Hants will supply most of the road-making labour and supervision, therefore O.C. 156th Field Coy. R.E. and O.C. 11th Hants will each detail an Officer to reconnoitre the CAMBRIN - LA BASSEE Road and the VERMELLES - AUCHY Road as far forward as possible.

The reconnaissance and report of these two Officers should be combined, copies being kept by 156th Field Coy. R.E. and 11th Hants and a copy forwarded to C.R.E.

In

In accordance with orders from C.R.E. 155th and 156th Field Companies are reconnoitring alternative roads. When these are completed copies of their reports with tracings will be sent to each Field Company and to the Pioneers who will all detail Officers to check these on the ground.

All three Field Companies and 11th Hants should have at least two Officers who are well acquainted with all tracks and roads in the Divisional Area East of a true N. and S. line through L.6.Central.

Further, O.C. 11th Hants will please have a special reconnaissance made of the following tracks with a view to their being made good as fair-weather tracks for first line transport, Routes 3, 5, 7 and 10.
Copies of these reports will be sent to C.R.E.

O.C. 11th Hants will also be prepared to extend two of the CAMBRIN Tramways towards AUCHY if required.
He will please report which two of the following four he considers it best to extend -

        HERTFORD STREET.
        WILSON'S WAY.
        MAISON ROUGE.
        LEWIS ALLEY.

All reports should reach C.R.E. before 8.0. p.m. 4th Sept. 1918.

1st Sept. 1918.   F. Summers, Lieut.Colonel, R.E.

                                    C. R. E. 16th Division.

Distribution.

        155th Field Coy.R.E.
        156th Field Coy.R.E.
        157th Field Coy.R.E.
        11th Hants (Pioneers).
        16th Div. 'G'.   )
        47th Inf. Bde.) for information.
        49th Inf. Bde.)
        C.R.E.
        War Diary (2).

Appendix No 2 H.D. Hare Sept 2

SECRET.

C. R. E's ORDER No. 80.

2nd September 1918.

1. Transport of 156th Field Coy. R.E. will move from present standings in J.13.b. to new standings in 48th Inf. Bde. Lines in K.18.b. on morning 3rd Sept.

2. Lines in J.13.b. will be clear by 8.30 a.m. 3rd Sept.

3. Present billets must be left scrupulously clean and in good order, and no material whatever will be taken away.

4. Completion of move to be notified to this office.

5. Capt. SHELLY to acknowledge.

Webster Captain, R.E.
for C. R. E. 16th Division.

Distribution:-

Capt. SHELLY.
O.C. 156th Fld. Coy. R.E.
48th Inf. Bde.)
16th Div. 'Q'.)
16th Div. 'G'.)
16th Div. Train.) For information.
16th Div. Signals.)
D.A.D.V.S.)
Town Major, NOEUX-)
    LES-MINES.)
File (2)
War Diary (2).

Appendix No. 3   W.O
                  AQ.R.E
                  16 Div
                  Sept

SECRET.

C.R.E's ORDER No. 81.

6th Sept. 1918.

1.   The following moves of transport will take place on 6th Sept.1918.

   Transport of 156th Field Coy.R.E. will move to site on NOEUX - LES - MINES - BETHUNE Road about K.18.c.3.7. previously reconnoitred by O.C. 156th Field Coy.R.E.

   Transport of 157th Field Coy.R.E. will move to lines in K.18.c. vacated by 156th Field Coy.R.E.

2.   Both Companies will be clear of lines occupied at present by 3.0. p.m., but 157th Field Coy.R.E. will not march out before 2.30 p.m.

3.   Horse standings, billets and shelters will be left scrupulously clean. Adjutant R.E. will inspect those of 157th Field Coy.R.E. at 2.30 pm. if C.R.E. is unable to do so.

4.   Capt.'s GREENHOW and SHELLY to acknowledge.

Issued at 9.0. a.m.

                        J. Webster Capt
                        for. Lieut.Colonel,R.E.
                        C.R.E. 16th Division.

   Distribution:-

      Capt. GREENHOW.
      Capt. SHELLY.
      O.C. 156th Field Coy.R.E.
      O.C. 157th Field Coy.R.E.
      16th Div.'G'.   )
      16th Div.'Q'.   )
      48th Inf.Bde.   ) for information.
      16th Div.Train.)
      D.A.D.V.S.   )
      Town Major,NOEUX-)
        LES-MINES.   )
      16th Div.Sigs.   )
      File (2).
      W.D. (2).

SECRET.

Appendix No. 4   U.D.
                  HQ.R.E. 16 Div

C. R. E's. ORDER No. 82.

1. Three Forward Dumps of R.E. Stores essential for consolidation will be formed forthwith in each Brigade Area, somewhere in the vicinity of the RESERVE LINE of the present British Trench System.

2. Places suggested are :-

   RIGHT BRIGADE

      Junction with RESERVE LINE of (1) LEWIS ALLEY.
                   (2) RAILWAY ALLEY.
                   (3) BART'S ALLEY.

   LEFT BRIGADE.

      Junction with RESERVE LINE of (1) BERKSHIRE ROAD.
                   (2) CAMBRIN-LA BASSEE ROAD.
                   (3) WILSON'S WAY.

   The actual site of these Forward Dumps is, however, left to the O.C. Company concerned.
   Map References of places selected will be reported to this Office before 9.0 p.m., 8th instant, and repeated to Brigade.

3. Each Dump should contain :-

      1,500 Sandbags.
      Wiring materials for 250 yards of double apron
                       (fence.
      Enough Concertina wire for 500 yards.

4. All stores must be carefully camouflaged and labelled "RESERVE R.E. STORES".

5. A start should be made at once with the formation of these Dumps, and the necessary carrying or pushing parties demanded from Brigade.

7th September 1918.   F. Simmons. Lieut. Colonel R.E.

              C. R. E. 16th Division.

      D I S T R I B U T I O N.

155th Field Coy., R.E.
157th Field Coy., R.E.
16th Div. "G".   )
47th Inf. Bde.   )
48th Inf. Bde.   ) For information.
49th Inf. Bde.   )
156th Field Coy., R.E.)

   War Diary (2).
   File (2).

Appendix N° 5   H.Q.R.E. 16 Div
                 W.D.

SECRET.

C.R.E's ORDER No. 83.

15th Sept. 1918.

The following are to be converted into defended localities to form an Outpost Line of Resistance:-

(1) FOSSE 8 and CORONS de MAROC and PEKIN. (Garrison 2 Companies).

(2) The vicinity of LES BRIQUES and DIAMOND DOOR Cottage. (Garrison 1 Company).

(3) The RAILWAY TRIANGLE. (Garrison 1 Company).

The conversion of these localities will be undertaken as follows:-

No.1 by 155th Field Coy.R.E.
No.2 by 156th Field Coy.R.E.
No.3 by 157th Field Coy.R.E.

Os.C. Field Companies will reconnoitre their respective localities, if possible in conjunction with Brigade representative, and submit a report with sketches embodying their proposals to this Office before 8.0. p.m. 16th inst.

For all localities provision will be made for the following:-

(1) Fire positions for all round defence, special attention being given to the flanks and to the field of fire. Where possible use will be made of the existing old German trenches. Where these are too wide, trench slits will be dug in front, connected up and camouflaged.

(2) Command Posts.

(3) M.G. positions for flanking fire.

(4) Trench blocks and straight shoots in all old German trenches on the flanks of these localities.

(5) A continuous belt of wire surrounding the locality.

(6) The command by M.G. fire of the exits from AUCHY Village.

When completed all the localities will be mutually supporting.

Issued at 7.30 a.m.

F. Stannard, Lieut.Colonel, R.E.

C. R. E. 16th Division.

Distribution:-
155th Fld.Coy.R.E.
156th Fld.Coy.R.E.
157th Fld.Coy.R.E.
C. R. E.
File (2).
War Diary (2).

Appendix No 6   HQ RE
                16 Div.

DRAFT.

C. R. E's. ORDER No. 85.

21st September 1918.

In consequence of the reorganisation of the Divisional Area, the following readjustments of R.E. work will take place.

(1) The 157th Field Coy., R.E. will cease work on the RAILWAY TRIANGLE Defended Locality on the night 21st/22nd September 1918, on relief by 55th Divisional R.E.
At the same time all work will be relinquished North of the following boundary :- CAMBRIN DEFENCES (to 16th Division) - GRAFTON STREET - SPOTTED DOG - AZIMUTH ALLEY (the three latter to 55th Division.)

(2) The 157th Field Coy., R.E. will cease work on the extension of the WILSON ALLEY - AUCHY Tramway after the night shift on the 22nd September 1918.
This work will be taken over on the 23rd instant by the 156th Field Coy., R.E., who will reconnoitre the work on the 22nd September 1918. The current arrangements for Working Parties and provision of stores will be maintained after relief.

(3) The 156th Field Coy., R.E. will continue to work on the LES BRIQUES Defended Locality as before.

(4) The 155th Field Coy., R.E. will cease work on the FOSSE 8 Defended Locality after the night shift on 22nd September 1918, on relief by the 15th Divisional R.E.

(5) From the night 22nd/23rd September, exclusive, the 155th Field Coy., R.E. will be responsible for all Brigade work in the reorganised Divisional Sector forward of and including the VILLAGE LINE, with the exception of items enumerated in this Order as the work of other Units.
Work for the Brigade must include consolidation of the Infantry Posts in the Outpost Line.

(6) From midnight on the 22nd September 1918, the 157th Field Coy., R.E. will be responsible for work on the CAMBRIN and ANNEQUIN Defences, and all Back Area work behind the VILLAGE LINE.

(7) The 156th Field Coy., R.E. will relieve the 157th Field Coy., R.E. in billets in the afternoon of the 23rd September 1918.
Details of relief to be arranged between Os.C. Companies.
The minimum of Transport must be employed between SAILLY LABOURSE and ANNEQUIN before dusk.

(8) Completion of this relief to be reported to C.R.E. by wire.

(9) ACKNOWLEDGE.

21st September 1918.   F. Summers, Lieut. Colonel R.E.
                                        C. R. E. 16th Division.

(DISTRIBUTION overleaf.

DISTRIBUTION.
****

155th Field Coy., R.E.   16th Div. "G".
156th Field Coy., R.E.   48th Inf. Bde.
157th Field Coy., R.E.   49th Inf. Bde.
C.R.E. 15th Division.   11th Hants. (P).
C.R.E. 55th Division.   War Diary (2).
                              File (2).

****

SECRET.

Appendix N° 7

C. R. E's. ORDER NO. 58.

21st September 1915.

With reference to C.R.E's. Order No. 58 and 18th Div. No. A.955/1 dated 21-9-15 (attached), the following moves of transport will take place.

(1) 158th Field Coy., R.E. will take over Transport Lines of 419th Field Coy., R.E., 55th Division, at K.3.d.6.7., and will march out from present lines at 2.30 p.m. 23rd September 1915.

(2) 156th Field Coy., R.E. will take over Transport Lines of 422nd Field Coy., R.E., 55th Division, at K.3.d.6.7., and will march out from present lines at 3.0 p.m. 23rd September 1915.

(3) 197th Field Coy., R.E. will take over Transport Lines of 423rd Field Coy., R.E., 55th Division, K.3.d.6.7., and will march out from present lines at 3.30 p.m. 23rd September 1915.

(4) Officers in charge of transport will visit the 55th Divisional R.E. Lines during the morning of 23rd September 1915, for the purpose of taking over accommodation and reconnoitring routes.

(5) There will be no restrictions as to route, but Transport will not enter Lines in K.3.d. before 3.0 p.m. 23rd instant.

(6) ACKNOWLEDGE.

21st September 1915.   Lieut. Colonel R.E.

                                               C. R. E. 18th Division.

Distribution.

        158th Field Coy., R.E.
        156th Field Coy., R.E.
        197th Field Coy., R.E.
        18th Div. "Q". for information.
        War Diary (2).
        File (2).

Army Form C. 2118.

WAR DIARY
or
INTELLIGENCE SUMMARY
(Erase heading not required.)

H.Q. R.E.
W.D. Oct. 1918
Vol 35

Place	Date	Hour	Summary of Events and Information	Remarks and references to Appendices
DROUVIN	1/10/18	—	157 Field Coy. R.E. completed outposts of 156 Field R.M.E. Consolidates defended localities – 157 Coy. a received – lunch area.	
	2/10/18	—	Work as above. Report eving return. In afternoon 155 at defence of 146 role for forward reconnaissance; 1630 am routes. 157 stand to for Benefit	
	3/18		As above	
	4/10/18		155 Minor obstruction forward, 156 on roads. 157 standing to. Forward divity of 4.9. notified and Minelp alone then formed by all Coys.	
	5/10/18		As above. Reconnaissance for bridges. Bridge attempted at B.15.b.0.7. but could not be proceeded with on account of hostile M.G. then front Reconnaissance of Canal between Canal Anglois + Jct of La Bassée + Haute Deule Canals indicates demit at entrances with access to Valencia. CR.E Order No. 67 (Appendix No 1) - Relief of 153 Fld C. by 157 Fld C. on 7/10. 155 Mor C. on Forward arro A.V.Q.H. No 1.	
TAILLY LABOURSE	6/10/18		Footbridge completed over Canal at B.12.c.0.5. by 155. Work continues on A.V.C.H (— Billy Trak by 156. 157 store to assist pontoons & search Major Trapain A.V.C.H. sipped timber etc. during night of 5-7/10.	
	7/10/18		155 Relieved by 157. 155 worked on billets. 156 formed dredging dump at B.17.C. 157 relieves 155 & worked on A.V.C.H. billets.	Forestry 7/10/18

WAR DIARY
INTELLIGENCE SUMMARY
(Erase heading not required.)

Army Form C. 2118.

Instructions regarding War Diaries and Intelligence Summaries are contained in F.S. Regs., Part II. and the Staff Manual respectively. Title pages will be prepared in manuscript.

Place	Date	Hour	Summary of Events and Information	Remarks and references to Appendices
SAILLY LA BOURSE	8/10/18		155. 2 sections on pontooning drill. Gas masters inspected & stencilled for names. Gas work at D.H.Q. 2 L.Cpls horsley reported for duty with C.R.E. 156 Camouflaging DOUVRIN – BILLY Road. 2 sections moved into forward billets in AUCHY. R.E.H.Q. moved from DROUVIN to SAILLY LABOURSE.	
	9/10/18		167 Gas sentries arrived R.E.A. to make 18ft. pile salvaging R.E. material.	
			155 made 3 tarpaulin rafts. erected Armstrong Hut & for Appx Boz at AMMEQUIN FOSSE.	
			156 made 7 20' light infy. bridges & 2 x 24' do. 157 as above.	
	10/10/18		155 as above. 156 made petrol can rafts. 157 reconnoitred breach in HAUTE DEULE Canal at A.19.C.2.8. Do Black went to 10th Corps as adjutant.	
	11/10/18		155 as above. 156 ramrod working to LA BASSÉE road. 157 tried to dam breach as above, but did not succeed. LA BASSÉE canal bridges at B.18.B.45.60.	
	12/10/18		155 as above and erected horse trough at AMMEQUIN. 156 made a Pontoon Pocket B.20.a. J.E.	
			157 made new O.P. at BILLY. Ferried infy. across canal. Fired to dam above breach without success. Reconnaissances.	
	13/10/18		155. Training and engineer reviews. 156. Ladies. camouflage. 157. Reached canal. Forward. U.S.	
	14/10/18		155 Built 4 trestle Engineer reviews. 156 Ladders. C.R.E.s Orders cross formed 12/10/18 157 Prepared footbridge HAUTE-DEULE. F.W.S.	[Appendix] 2
	15/10/18		155 Two medium Pontoon Bridges 1. 156. Pontoon train, footbridge, Roads. 157 Found Pitols two foot bridge C.R.E.s over No 66 Found 15'.0".F.	[Appendix] 3
	16/10/18		155 Moved to Auchy. Two trestle bridges. 156. Trestle Bridge between Rd. Foot Bridge. 157 Moved to BAUVIN	
BILLY	17/10/18		155 Moved pontoon bridge (50 yds 26 min.) 156. Moved to PROVIN roads. 157 F.W.B. Over water 40'. Bde.	
BERCLAU	18/10/18		155. Moved to BERCLAU, ½Coy Trestle Bridge. 156. Trestle bridge HAUTE DEULE. 157 Mobr Pont AMACQ, roads, bodytype.	
PHALEMPIN	19/10/18	1700	155. 1. CAMPHIN, roads, 156 PHALEMPIN, roads, 157, moved TEMPLEUVE, roads, bodytype.	

WAR DIARY
or
INTELLIGENCE SUMMARY.
(Erase heading not required.)

Army Form C. 2118.

Place	Date	Hour	Summary of Events and Information	Remarks and references to Appendices
TEMPLEUVE	20/10/18		155 Coy Roads, 156 Coy Repairs, 157 Coy Roads and Booby Traps.	
	21/10/18		155 Coy moved to PONT'A MARCQ, 156 Coy Roads, Trestles for SCHELDT, 157 Coy Moved TRAINTIGNIES roads	
	22/10/18		155 Moved FLORENT, 156 Coy Moved LA POSTERIE, formed Pontoon Park FLORENT, 157 Coy 12 roads	
	23/10/18		155 Coy Roads, 156 Coy Roads and Trestles, 157 Coy Roads and making light bridges	
	24/10/18		155 Coy Roads, 156 Coy Roads and Trestles, 157 Coy Forward roads	
	25/10/18		155 Coy Roads, 156 Coy Roads, 157 Coy forward roads. C.R.E's Order No 90 issued	Appendix 1
	26/10/18		155 Coy Roads, 156 Coy Roads and Trestles, 157 Roads established light Bridges dump MERLIN	
	27/10/18		155 Coy Roads, 156 Coy Roads and Trestles, 157 Coy Roads	
	28/10/18		156 Coy Roads, 156 Coy Roads and Bridges for SCHELDT, forward Bridges dump FLORENT, 157 Coy Roads	
	29/10/18		155 Coy Roads, 156 Coy as above, 157 Coy Roads	
	30/10/18		155 Coy Roads, 156 Coy as above, 157 Coy Roads, and forward dump TRAINTIGNIES	
	31/10/18		155 Coy Roads, 156 Coy as above, 157 Coy as above. C.R.E's Order No 91 Relay of Engineers	Appendix 5

Stanhope Begg
for Lieut Col
C.R.E. 16 Div

Appendix No 1 H.Q.R.E.
W.D Oct 1918

SECRET.

C. R. Es ORDER No. 87.

5th October, 1918.

1. 157th Field Coy.R.E. will relieve 155th Field Coy.R.E. in forward area on morning of 7th October 1918. O.C. 157th Field Coy.R.E. will be responsible for Engineer work in Forward Brigade Area from 1200 hours 7th Oct.

2. Lieut. ROBERTS, 157th Field Coy.R.E. and 1 Section 157th Field Coy.R.E. will remain on duties connected with forward water supplies.

3. On completion of relief Companies will be disposed as follows:-

   155th Field Coy.R.E.   ANNEQUIN.

   157th Field Coy.R.E.
      3 Sections.   AUCHY.
      1 Section.   ANNEQUIN.

4. A detail of all work handed over, including reconnaissances - on hand and projected - will be made out and copy forwarded to this Office by evening of 7th inst.

5. 155th Field Coy.R.E. will be responsible for any projected pontoon bridges from 1200 hours 7th.Oct.

6. Completion of relief to be notified to this office by wire.

7. Field Coy's to ACKNOWLEDGE.

                                    Webster Captain, R.E.
                                 for C. R. E. 16th Division.

Distribution:-
   C. R. E.
   155th Fld. Co.
   156th Fld. Co.
   157th Fld. Co.
   16th Div. 'G'   )
   47th Inf. Bde.   )
   48th Inf. Bde.   ) for information.
   49th Inf. Bde.   )
   11th Hants (P)   )
   War Diary (2).
   File.   (2).

C. R. E's. O R D E R No. 88.

14th October 1918.

1. In the event of the enemy evacuating the line of the HAUTE DEULE CANAL and retiring a considerable distance it may become necessary for the Division to advance as a whole, covered by an advanced guard.
    In this case three Brigade Groups will be formed :-

    (a) Leading Brigade (47th Inf. Bde.) Group, including
        (156th Field Coy., R.E.

    (b) Support Brigade (48th Inf. Bde.) Group, including
        (155th Field Coy., R.E.

    (c) Reserve Brigade (49th Inf. Bde.) Group, including
        (157th Field Coy., R.E.

2. This Order applies simply to the march forward, and has nothing to do with work.
    At the end of the march, when work is required, the Field Companies R.E. will be withdrawn from the Brigade Groups, and a proportion of R.E. assistance allotted to Brigades according to the needs of the moment.

3. The formation of Groups will not come into being until ordered by the Division.

14th October 1918.   F. Summers, Lieut. Colonel R.E.
                                  C. R. E. 16th Division.

DISTRIBUTION.
=============

155th Field Coy., R.E.
156th Field Coy., R.E.
157th Field Coy., R.E.
War Diary (2).
File (2).

SECRET.

C. R. E's. ORDER No. 89.

15th October 1918.

1. 47th Inf. Bde. has reached a line running approximately N. and S. through East edge of PROVIN. 15th Division on our right is reported to have reached the line I.15. - I.9. - I.3. all central. 55th Division on our left is reported to have been held up on the West bank of the HAUTE DEULE CANAL.

2. 15th and 16th Divisions will advance to second Objective at dawn tomorrow, 16th instant.

3. 47th Inf. Bde. will reconnoitre ANNOEULLIN and if enemy is not holding it will advance at dawn to second Objective on whole Divisional front, viz, general line D.25.central - D.19.central - Road junction D.13.c.9.8. - D.7.a.1.3.

4. 157th Field Coy., R.E. will move to BILLY BERCLAU by 0600, 16th October, and will report to and be placed under the orders of B.G.C. 47th Inf. Bde. from that hour.
155th Field Coy., R.E. will move to the billets vacated by 157th Field Coy., R.E. at AUCHY tomorrow, move to be completed by 1000, 16th October.
O.C. 155th Field Coy., R.E. will send an advance party to take over the billets of 157th Field Coy., R.E. by 0630 16th October.
O.C. 157th Field Coy., R.E. will send a billetting party in advance to BILLY BERCLAU.

5. An Officer and half-section of 157th Field Coy., R.E. will be detailed for work on water supply of forward area, under Corps Water Supply Officer. Name of Officer to be wired to C.R.E. before 1800, 16th October.
Reconnaissance of forward water supply to be commenced on 16th instant. Reports to be rendered daily to Corps W.S.O. and repeated to C.R.E..

6. As soon as sites for horse lines have been reconnoitred in the AUCHY-HAISNES district, 155th and 157th Field Coys. R.E. will move their transport there.
Moves should be completed by 1700, 16th October.

7. Completion of moves, and locations of Headquarters and transport lines to be wired to C.R.E. as early as possible.

8. Supply Railhead will be at CUINCHY from 17th instant.

9. A C K N O W L E D G E   by   w i r e.

15th October 1918.
Issued at 0100

F. Summers Lieut. Colonel R.E.
C. R. E. 16th Division.

/Distribution over.

DISTRIBUTION.
****

155th Field Coy., R.E.
156th Field Coy., R.E.
157th Field Coy., R.E.
16th Division "Q".)
A.D.V.S.   )   For
16th Div. Train.   ) information.
11th Hants. (P).   )
C. R. E.
War Diary (2).
File. (2).

Appendix 4.

SECRET.

C.R.E'S ORDER No.90.

28th October, 1918.

The following will be the distribution of R.E. and Pioneers for work after the relief ordered in 16th Div. Order No.292.

1. 197th Field Coy.R.E. attached to 49th Bde. Group.

2. 155th and 156th Field Coy's R.E. and 11th Bn. Hants Regt. (P) will continue as at present unattached to any Group for work under C.R.E.

F. Summers Lieut.Colonel,R.E.

C. R. E. 16th Division.

Distribution:-
      155th Fld. Coy.R.E.
      156th Fld. Coy.R.E.
      197th Fld. Coy.R.E.
      11th Hants (P).
      File.
      War (S).

Appendix 5

S E C R E T.

C. R. E's ORDER No. 91.

31st October, 1918.

Reliefs and readjustments of work between Field Companies, R.E. will be carried out as follows:-

(1) 155th Field Company, R.E. will relieve 157th Field Company, R.E. of work on Front Line Posts, Main Line of Resistance and the gas-proofing of cellars in Forward Area. Work will be taken over by 155th Field Coy.R.E. at 0600 hours 2nd November.

155th Field Coy.R.E. will send Officers and N.C.O's on 1st November to reconnoitre and take over the above-mentioned work. In addition O.C. 155th Field Coy.R.E. will get into touch with 49th Inf. Bde. and ensure that there is no break in continuity so far as the requirements of 49th Bde. are concerned.

(2) 155th Field Coy.R.E. will retain their present billets but will take over and maintain the forward R.E. Dump at U.26.d.0.7.

(3) 156th Field Company, R.E. will take over from 155th Fld.Coy.R.E. all work on forward roads from 1200 hours on Novr.2nd. O.C. 156th Fld. Coy.R.E. will arrange to reconnoitre this work on Novr.1st.

In addition he will detail one Section to assist 155th Fld.Coy.R.E. in work on gas-proofing. This work will be allotted by C.R.E. on Nov.1st after consultation with O.C. 155th Fld.Coy.R.E.

The formation of an Advanced Bridging Dump will also be retained by 156th Field Coy.R.E.

(4) 156th Fld.Coy.R.E. will vacate their present billets at LA POSTERIE by 0700 on Nov.2nd and move to billets at present occupied by 157th Field Coy.R.E. at TAINTIGNIES. One Officer and three N.C.O's will remain behind to hand over work on rear roads to 157th Field Coy.R.E. and ensure continuity in this work. This Officer will remain attached to 157th Fld.Coy.R.E. for work until further orders, the N.C.O's will rejoin their Company on completion of the day's work.

(5) 157th Field Company, R.E. will take over work on roads from 156th Field Coy.R.E. at 1200 hours on Nov.2nd. This work will be handed over by the Officer left behind by 156th Field Coy.R.E.

C.R.E. will show O.C. 157th Fld.Coy.R.E. the work on these roads at 1400 hours on Nov.2nd.

(6) 157th Field Coy.R.E. will vacate their present billets at 0800 on No.2nd and move to the billets at LA POSTERIE now occupied by 156th Fld.Coy.R.E.

(7) Advance parties, as small as possible, will be sent forward by 156th and 157th Fld. Coy's.

The strictest march discipline will be maintained en route by both these Units and the proper intervals between Sections and vehicles observed.

(8) The traffic routes laid down in D.R.O's 624 and 630 will be closely studied.

(9). Field Coy's to acknowledge.

F. S........ Lieut.Colonel,R.E.
C.R.E. 16th Division.

Distribution:-

    155th Fld.Coy.R.E.
    156th Fld.Coy.R.E.
    157th Fld.Coy.R.E.
    16th Div. 'G'.   )
    16th Div. 'Q'.   )
    47th Inf. Bde.   )
    48th Inf. Bde.   ) for information.
    49th Inf. Bde.   )
    16th Div. Train   )
    D.A.D.V.S.   )
    File (2).
    W.D. (2).

WAR DIARY
INTELLIGENCE SUMMARY

Army Form C. 2118.

H.Q. R.E. 16th DIVISION
NOVEMBER 1918

Place	Date	Hour	Summary of Events and Information	Remarks and references to Appendices
TEMPLEUVE	1/11/18		155 Fld Coy. Roads. 156 Fld Coy. Roads & preparing material for trestle trc, bridge. 157 " C. 2 Section on Gas Curtains in ST MAUR & LONGUE SAULT. 1 Section on front posts + 1 sec on advance of resistance.	
	2/11/18		155 Fld Coy. relieved. 157 Fld Coy in line work & landed over road work 156 Fld Cy. Sec on Battle Zone road LONGUE SAULT. 1 Sec on forward outposts. 1 Sec preparing material for a new bridge. 156 Fld Coy moved to TAINTIGNIES took over headquarters Hon. 155 Fld Cy Hd 12 pln/120 Vdy Landed plan G.S.4/11/18. 157 Fld Coy handed over line work to 155 Fld Coy & took over rear front work from 156 Fld Coy. Coy moved to LA POSTERIE.	
	3/11/18		155 Coy as above. 156 Coy. 2 Sec on roads. 1 Sec on gas curtains TAINTIGNIES & LONGUE SAULT. 1 Sec on trestle bridge as above. 15 Cfy 2 Sec on roads. 1 Sec on pony trestle bridge etc.	
	4/11/18		155 Cy as above. 156 Coy as above at 2. 120.0 starting foot bridges made & transported to BRUXELLES. 157 Cy. 2 Section on foot roads floating pieces cut up into, one pont transported to BRUXELLES. 1 Sec roads. 1 Sec cleaning place for Div Loads at TEMPLEUVE	C.R.E. rode No.22 received 3/11/18 Offensive No.1
	5/11/18		155 Cy as above. 156 Cy as above but a 2nd floating bridge made & transported to BRUXELLES. 157 Cy as above. ... foot etc. transported to BRUXELLES	
	6/11/18		155 Cy Major E.J. Lott R.O.B.E. having been appointed C.I. ROUEN lands over to Major R. Ellison R.E. Offr. assumes Command (late 4/6 Fd F.O. Coy R.E. (1st Div) AUT. SAG. 55/554). AUT. SAg. Eo ary 55/591. Work as above. 156 Cy. As above but at 4 set floating bridge made + erected at G.H.Q. 157 Coy as above.	
	7/11/18		155 Cy. 2 Sec on rear Line of Resistance. 1 Sec on forward outposts. 1 Sec on bridge as before 156 Cy as above. 157 Cy by 3 Sec as before. One Sec eating the cavalry to cavalry track at TEMPLEUVE. (Lieut. N.A. Hickson reports to H.Q. for duty.)	6/11 C.R.E. Instructions No 13 received Appendix Pt 2
	8/11/18		155 Coy. 4 Sec rest at BRUYELLES formed distinct dump to stand by with wire for bridging PECANT. 156 Coy. At same on enquiries one unsuccessful attempts made to track canal. Cy about 5.11 157 Coy moved to FLORENT D tract to bridges camp BRUYELLES.	Offensive Pt 2

Army Form C. 2118.

WAR DIARY
or
INTELLIGENCE SUMMARY.
(Erase heading not required.)

Instructions regarding War Diaries and Intelligence Summaries are contained in F. S. Regs., Part II. and the Staff Manual respectively. Title pages will be prepared in manuscript.

(2.)

Place	Date	Hour	Summary of Events and Information	Remarks and references to Appendices
FLORENT	9/11/18		C.R.E. H.Q. moved to FLORENT. 155 Fd Coy. Two floating footbridges made across ESCAUT & certainly finished areas in strats. 156 Coy made of roadway & bridge across ANTOING & roadway completed. Coy moved to ANTOING. 156 Coy. Canal road at ANTOING V.15. a, y. made one flying fr. traffic. Bridge transports from TAINTIGNIES. Bridge commenced across ESCAUT & commenced repair material for tow of the Lock bridge near ANTOING. V.15.a.12. Coy moved to ANTOING. (see 155 Coy)	App
	10/11		155 Coy. As before. Commence 2 heavy trestle road bridges over Road. Sweney. Prepared material for repairing the TAINTIGNIES. Coy moved to ANTOING. 156 Coy. trestle bridge commenced & completed fit for traffic. 154 Coy. moved to newly allotted billets in ANTOING & Carnival made a 2 bridges at Road Camp	App
	11/11		155 Coy as above. 156 Coy as trestle bridge as above on side footwalk &c. 154 Coy as above.	App
	12/11		155 Coy as above. 156 Coy as above & completion of bridge. 154 Coy as above	App
	13/11		155 Coy as above. 1st bridge completed. 156 Coy moved to ATH. 154 Coy as above.	App
	14/11		155 Coy as above. 2nd bridge completed. 156 Coy Chateau demolished bridges at ATH 154 Coy 3 Ludos as before. 1 Coy occupy trestle bridge made by 156 Coy	App
	15/11		155 Coy work over 3rd & 4th bridges from 154 Coy & completion came. 156 Coy. as above Commenced bridges 2 culverts at ATH Station. 154 Coy handed over 2 trestle bridges to 155 Coy & moved to PETIT RUMES.	App
	16/11		155 Coy moved to PLACE COMPTE 156 Coy as above. 154 Coy moved to PLACE COMPTE	App
ATTICHES	17/11/18		C.R.E. H.Q. moved to ATTICHES. 155 Coy moved to MONCHEAUX. 156 Coy Anstowe 154 Coy moved to RUE-DE-MONCHEAUX.	App
	18/11		155 Coy Repairs to batts. MONCHEAUX. Sainry & Implessins. 156 Coy work as above. 154 Coy Clearing Attiches Village.	App

WAR DIARY or INTELLIGENCE SUMMARY.

(Erase heading not required.)

Army Form C. 2118.

(3.)

Instructions regarding War Diaries and Intelligence Summaries are contained in F. S. Regs., Part II. and the Staff Manual respectively. Title pages will be prepared in manuscript.

Place	Date	Hour	Summary of Events and Information	Remarks and references to Appendices
ATTICHES	19/8		155 Coy as for 18th. 156 Coy as laying track. 157 RE Services & training.	
	20/8		155 Coy RE Services & training. 156 Coys as above. 157 Coy RE Services & training.	
	21/8		155 Coy as above. 156 Coy as above. A bridge at LIGNE commenced also coke bridge near (3) autre. 157 Coy as above. Off ATH Station.	
	22/8		155 Coy as above. 156 Coy as above. 1 Brd pier nearly complete. 157 Coy as above. Calcaire of Cruche No. 1 road nearly commenced.	
	23/8		155 Coy 2 Sec moved to PONT-A-MARC, north of Sir. Charta & reo Facilities for 49th & 49th place, etc Chart as above. 156 Coy as above. 157 Coy as above no Coy moved to BERSEE & workshop 49 Inf Bde. remainder as above.	
	24/8		155 Coy 2 Section at PONT-A-MARC as before. remainder Church parade etc. 156 as above. A Brd bridge Church Colours commenced & Roman Channel to allow of plaring Baulks. 157 Coy Sec. at BERSEE as above. Repr. remainder as above.	
	25/8		155 Coy 2 Sec @ PONT-A-MARC as above Coy HQ. remainder moved to CHOIST 36.X28.B. 156 Coy as above. 157 Coy as above as colours.	
	26/8		155 Coy. 2 Sec @ PONT-A-MARC as above. Coy Sunday billets etc. 156 Coy as above. 157 Coy as above. 26th CCJC/1; also no. 93 General (Rep 2)	Appendix 3
	27/8		155 Coy 2 Sec @ PONT-A-MARC as above. Material attached for two trussed bridges 1 at ATH & 1 at LIGNE. 156 Coys as above. Leo. Upper BERSEE.	
	28/8		155 Coy as above. 156 Coy as above. 1 Trussed bridge at ATH in position. 157 Coy as Sec at BERSEE as now, all Sec. formed & removed back to R.E. field workshop ATTICHES. Remainder R.E. Services & training.	

A.5834 Wt.W4973/M687 750,000 8/16 D. D. & L. Ltd. Forms/C.2118/13

Army Form C. 2118.

WAR DIARY
or
~~INTELLIGENCE SUMMARY~~

(A.)

(Erase heading not required.)

Instructions regarding War Diaries and Intelligence Summaries are contained in F. S. Regs., Part II. and the Staff Manual respectively. Title pages will be prepared in manuscript.

Place	Date	Hour	Summary of Events and Information	Remarks and references to Appendices
ATTICHES.	29/1/8		155 Coy as on 28st. 156 Coy as on 28st. 157 Coy. Hos. at VERSEE as before, Cos. at 28 Ko to worksite, the R.E. huttings stages at MONCHIN-PEVELLE. The Lo. twenty-pdr. A.R. & Class bridge.	
	30/8		155 Coy. One Sec. moved from GUY-A-MARC to ATTICHES for work under C.R.E. Remainder of Coy awaiting orders. 156 Coy. work as above. 157 Coy. as after. Le Sinocca bridges completed ready for traffic.	

E.A. Hockley
for C.R.E. 1st Division

SECRET.

Appendix No. 1.

C.R.E's ORDER No.92.

3rd Novr. 1918.

1. 156th Field Company, R.E. and 157th Field Company, R.E. will each construct two footbridges of 120 ft. span using pairs of tin floats and trussed trench-boards of the type used in previous Divisional Operations.

2. 156th Field Coy. R.E. will construct their two bridges at TAINTIGNIES, C.R.E. supplying material.

3. 157th Field Coy. R.E. will construct their two at TEMPLEUVE Dump. C.R.E. will supply lorry transport and 157th Field Coy. R.E. will provide loading party and guide to take them to H.Qrs. of 156th Field Coy. R.E.

4. All four bridges must be finished by 1600 hours on 4th inst. and each Company will deliver its bridges at the Advanced Bridging Dump, Billet 38 BRUYELLES, on the night 4th/5th Nov. using Company transport.

5. C.R.E. will provide two extra G.S. wagons for each Company on the evening of Nov. 4th at Headquarters 156th Field Coy. R.E. Time of rendezvous will be notified by wire.

6. 155th Field Company, R.E. will furnish 156th and 157th Field Coy's each with a wagon and team on request of these two Companies. The Officer in charge of the transport will be responsible for the safe return to 155th Field Coy. R.E. of the wagon borrowed.

7. Acknowledge before 08.30 Nov. 4th.

F. Summons Lieut.Colonel, R.E.

C.R.E. 16th Division.

Distribution:-

    156th Field Coy.
    157th Field Coy.
    155th Field Coy. (for information).
    File.
    W.D. (2).

Inst. 4/1.

Reference C.R.E's Instructions No.4

(1) In para:6 for V.21.c.9.4 read
V.21.a.9.4. for position of No.2
footbridge.

(2) The location of the bridging dump
is now V.26.a.4.3.

6th Nov.'18.   P.Summers   Lieut.Col.R.E.

                         C. R. E. 16th Divn.

W.D
Appendix 2.

SECRET.

C.R.E's INSTRUCTIONS No.4.

6th Nov. 1918.

1.   The following instructions for the crossing of the ESCAUT are issued for the guidance of R.E. and Pioneers. All previous orders on this subject are cancelled.

2.   The crossing will be made between the CHATEAU DE BRUYELLES and V.9.d.0.3. by the Brigade in Line at the time the attack is ordered to be carried out.

3.   C.R.E. is responsible for dumping at BRUYELLES by Nov.5th 12 boats or rafts and 4 light "Single File" footbridges which will be at the disposal of the B.G.C. Brigade for crossing, but as there is a second stream to be crossed S. of ANTOING and as there may be considerable wastage, extra equipment will have to be provided. Separate orders on this point have been issued to 156th and 157th Field Companies,R.E.,who between them will construct 24 boats and six bridges.

5.   The boats and rafts are intended as a means of filtering patrols across the river to form small bridgeheads to cover the erection of the light footbridges, but it must be borne in mind that there are at present, at least six German footbridges existing and that, in all probability these will not be totally destroyed. 156th Field Coy.R.E. will therefore transport to BRUYELLES forthwith sufficient light timber and nails to effect emergency repairs to those bridges.

6.   The personnel employed in making the preliminary crossing will be:-

    155th Field Company,R.E. and
    2 Sections 157th Field Company,R.E.
    1 Company 11th Hants (P).

Work will be divided as follows:-

No. 1 Party.

2 Sections 155th Field Coy.R.E. will assist the two loading battalions in ferrying their men across, one Section to each Battalion.

No. 2 Party.

2 Sections 155th Field Coy. will construct

No. 1 Floating Footbridge near V.21.c.6.9.

No. 2 Floating Footbridge near V.21.c.9.4.

No. 3 Party.

2 Sections 157th Field Coy. will construct

No. 3 Floating Footbridge near V.15.d.0.8.

No. 4 Floating Footbridge near V.15.b.0.6.

For

2.

For carrying material down to the sites the following parties will be detailed by 11th Hants (P):-

(a) ½ Coy. to assist 155th Field Coy.R.E.

(b) ½ Coy. to assist 157th Field Coy.R.E.

All these parties will assemble at the Bridging Dump BRUYELLES at an hour ordered by Brigade.

Liaison will be maintained between 155th Field Coy. R.E. and the forward Companies of the front Battalions for the purpose of ferrying the latter across.

7. As soon as the Infantry reach the Canal a runner will be sent to the Bridging Dump to order forward the boats. No. 1 Party will then carry forward the boats to the places selected by the Company Commanders in front.

The Sappers will give every possible assistance in ferrying the infantry across the Canal and the need for energy, determination and speed is emphasized. It must be clearly understood that the R.E. and not the Infantry are responsible for the success of the crossing.

8. Similar liaison methods will be adopted by 155th and 157th Field Coy's for the construction of the four footbridges, which will be put across by No. 2 and 3 parties will all possible speed.

9. For the transport of material for these footbridges from the Dump to the sites the transport of the Divisional Bridging Train will be used.

To form this train the following units will contribute:-

155th Fld.Coy. 3 bridging wagons, 3 limbered G.S. wagons and 1 G.S. wagon.

157th Fld.Coy. 3 bridging wagons, 1 limber and 1 G.S.

11th Hants. 2 G.S. wagons and 2 limbers.

The train will be under the Command of Captain HAUGH, 155th Field Coy.R.E., who will have at his disposal one Officer to be detailed by O.C. 157th Field Coy.R.E. Name of the latter Officer to be reported to C.R.E. before 20.00 hours Nov.6th.

O.C. Bridging Train will be responsible for the delivery to each Bridging Party the material it requires and for the safe return of all wagons to their units on completion of the operation.

10. The B.G.C. Brigade in the Line will notify C.R.E., as soon as orders are issued ordering the crossing to be forced, when and where he wishes this transport to be assembled. C.R.E. will then order these wagons to report to Capt. HAUGH at TAINTIGNIES in time to reach the rendezvous.

/11

11. Strict attention must be paid to reports. A report will be made for each bridge by the Officer i/c immediately on completion direct to C.R.E. and repeated to his O.C. Coy.

C.R.E. will most probably be at the CHATEAU TAINTIGNIES.

12. The instructions for the construction of a heavy bridge across the canal, contained in my C.12/6 of 23rd ult. will be modified to this extent:-

    (a) 155th Field Coy. will take no part in its construction.

    (b) Only half a Company of 11th Hants will work on the bridge itself.

13. O.C. 156th Field Coy. will have at his disposal from Zero plus 2 hours on the day of the operation, ton lorries, remainder of company transport, and C.R.E's Box Car.

14. ACKNOWLEDGE.

S. Parker Beggs
Lieut.R.E.
for Lieut.Colonel.,R.E.
C. R. E. 16th Divn.

Distribution:-

155th Fld. Coy.R.E.
156th Fld. Coy.R.E.
157th Fld. Coy.R.E.
11th Hants (P).
16th Div. 'G')
C.E. I Corps.) for information.
48th Inf.Bde.)

DUPLICATE.

C.R.E's. ORDER No. 93.

28th November 1918.

Appendix 23.

1. 17th Field Coy., R.E. less the Section at BERSEE will move from RUE DE MONCHEAUX to ATTICHES and MARTINSART on November 27th 1918.

2. Company will be clear of MONCHEAUX by 0915 hours and will not enter ATTICHES before 1100 hours.

3. Billets will be left scrupulously clean and tidy and the strictest march discipline maintained en route.

4. An advance Party of one Officer and the Company Cyclists will report at C.R.E's. Office at 0900 hours November 27th. A Tool-cart will report at the same place and time, as some of the advance party will be required for work on arrival.

26th November 1918.   Lieut. Colonel R.E.

C. R. E. 16th Division.

DISTRIBUTION.

```
167th Field Coy., R.E.
16th Div. "G".          )
16th Div. "Q".          )   For
185th Field Coy., R.E.  )   Information.
16th Div. Train.        )
```

WAR DIARY or INTELLIGENCE SUMMARY.

Army Form C. 2118.

H.Q. R.E.
16th DIVISION.

Place	Date	Hour	Summary of Events and Information	Remarks and references to Appendices
ATTICHES	1/12/18		Three Companies resting – no work. Reconnaissance of bridge at COURRIERES made.	F/S
	2/12/18		155 Field Coy engaged on work for 47 & 48 Inf Brigades	SP/S
	3/12/18		156 " " " " " on Railway Bridges & Station at ATH	
	4/12/18		157 " " " " " "	
	5/12/18		" Stated. 16 Div workshops and for 49 Inf Bde EMBARQs	
	6/12/18		155 " " " " for 47 & 48 Inf Bde and Salvage Dumps at POINT-A.	
			156 " " " " in Railway Bridges & station at ATH & LYRE	
			157 " " " " to work for 16 Div ARTY. 1section in B.D. work –	
			" Two Sections detached to work for 49 Inf Bde	
			Shops & one section on work for 6th	
	7/12/18		155 & 157 Field Coys work as for 6th 156 Field Coy rest day	SP/S
	8/12/18		155 & 157 Field Coys Rest day 156 Field Coy working on Bridges at LYRE & ATH OK	
	9/12/18		O Colonel Summers (CRE) took over duties of A/CE 1st Corps & Major Shelley OC 157	SP/S
			Field Coy assumed duties of A/CRE 16 Div on 9/12	
	10/12/18		155 Field Coy 128 one Section detached for work on heavy bridge at COURRIERES	
			Remdr of Coy engaged on work for 47 & 48 Inf Bdes & Salvage	
			dumps at POINT-A MARCQ. Lieut C V BROOK struck off strength	
	14/12/18		of unit and effect from 2/12/18 (authority AG 55/602/1(0) dated 3/12	
			2nd Lieut MONTEITH joined for duty 11/12	
	15/12/18		155 " " " engaged on work on Railway Bridges & Station at ATH.	SP/S
			156 Field Coy Rg " " " " "	
			157 Field Coy Rg work as for 7/12	
			all three Coys rest day	

Sparkes Reg R.E. 16 Div
Capt & adj

Army Form C. 2118.

WAR DIARY
or
INTELLIGENCE SUMMARY.
(Erase heading not required.)

HORE
16th DIVISION

Instructions regarding War Diaries and Intelligence Summaries are contained in F. S. Regs., Part II. and the Staff Manual respectively. Title pages will be prepared in manuscript.

Place	Date	Hour	Summary of Events and Information	Remarks and references to Appendices
ATTICHES	16/12/78 to 21/12/78		153 Field Coy R.E. Workshop started for 47 & 48 Inf Bdes at X28b59. Remds of Coy working on Company Billets. Reconnaissance work.	SPS
			156 " " " continued on electric lighting at TEMPLEUVE	SPS
			157 " " " work continued on Railway Bridges station at ATH	SPS
	22/12/78		" " work ao for 7/12/78 CRE returned from COURSE/proceeded on leave to NICE on 19 R?	SPS
	23/12/78		153 Field Coy R.E. work ao for 21/12/78	SPS
			156 " " " work ao for 21/12/78	SPS
			157 " " " work ao for 21/12/78 Train load of R.E. stores unloaded at FRETIN	SPS
	24/12/78		Three Coys on work ao for 23/12/78	SPS
	25/12/78		Holiday – no work done	SPS
	26/12/78		do	SPS
	27/12/78 28/12/78		Three Coys on work ao for 24/12/78	SPS
	29/12/78		SUNDAY 155 & 157 Coys Rest day 156 Field Coy Laying pipe line for water supply	SPS
			at ATH	
	30/12/78 31/12/78		Three Coys on work ao for 28/12/78	

S Parker Begg? Lt Col
Comd?g? ? 6 Div SP13
Capt & Adjt

WAR DIARY
OF THE
16th DIVISIONAL ENGINEERS.

from January 1st. to January 31st. 1919.

Army Form C. 2118.

WAR DIARY

INTELLIGENCE SUMMARY

(I.) H.Q. R.E. 16th DIVISION
JANUARY 1919

(Erase heading not required.)

Instructions regarding War Diaries and Intelligence Summaries are contained in F. S. Regs., Part II. and the Staff Manual respectively. Title pages will be prepared in manuscript.

Place	Date	Hour	Summary of Events and Information	Remarks and references to Appendices
ATTICHES	1/1/19		155 Fld Cy R.E. Engaged on work for 47th & 48th Inf Bdes, & Bn. Fatigue Stands. 4th Coy Workshops. Section detached at ATTICHES engaged on Hqrs. Bridge at COURIERES.	
			156 Fld Cy R.E. Rest day.	
			157 Fld Cy R.E.	
	2/1/19		Lectures and work. Sec Artillery re-borer & to R.E. Workshops. Re Lectres & Riflework & its Coy Workshop.	Ap. 28
			155 Fld Cy R.E. Work as for 1st	App 28
			156 Fld Cy R.E. Engaged on bayer poles, gas water supply & furnishing of electricity at 47th	App 28
			157 Fld Cy R.E. Work as for 1st.	
	3/1/19		155, 156 & 157 Fld Cys R.E. All work as for 2nd.	App 28
	4/1/19		155 Fld Cy R.E. Work as for 2nd	App 40
			156 Fld Cy R.E. Work as for 2nd, & Bridge Carpenters	
			157 Fld Cy R.E. Work as for 2nd	
	5/1/19		155, 156, 157 Fld Cys R.E. Work as for 2nd	App 40
	6/1/19		155 Fld Cy R.E. As per Rueil Quarter-Masters charge commenced at LIGNE	App 40
			156 " " " 2nd	
			157 " " " 2nd	
	7/1/19		155 " " " 2nd Coys working parties for 70th Inf Bde	App 45
			156 " " " " " R.E.	
			157 " " " " " Bde	
	8/1/19		155, 156 & 157 Fld Cys " "	App 45
	9/1/19		155 Coy repairing hut, refuse	
			156 " Parade for service of	
			157 " as per regt report	App 46

WAR DIARY
INTELLIGENCE SUMMARY.

(Erase heading not required.)

Army Form C. 2118.

H.Q. R.E. 6th Divn.
JANUARY 1919

Place	Date	Hour	Summary of Events and Information	Remarks and references to Appendices
ATTICHES.	10/1/9	1555	HQ arrived Attiches a/m 9th	1/1/3
	11/1/9	1556	Coy. HEATH @ SEUS, no ceremony. BARRY @ 1300 hrs	
		1557	Work as for 9th	1/1/4
		1555	Work as for 9th	
	12/1/9	1556	Lieut. BARRY @ 0900 hrs. arrived NEZ-VELVAIN @ 1230 hrs	1/1/5
		1554	Work as for 9th	
		1555	Cert. Ser. Church Parade 11th	
	13/1/9	1556	Coy NEZ-VELVAIN @ 0900 hrs. arrived GENECH @ 1245 hrs	1/1/6
		1555	Work as for 9th. Kaile for 67 Inf. Bde V-B-VT-A-MARC commenced	
		1556	Coy GENECH @ 0900 hrs. arrived MARTINSART @ 1245 hrs	
		15/7	As for 9th	
	14/1/9	1555	Work at 9th 13th	1/1/5
		1556	Picture Parade Willies.	
		15/7	As for 9th	
	15/1/9	1555	Reef. Ch. Pde. at CURGIES. Conf. by CofE. Audience at R.E. HQ the Gen. Sub-a. Gen.	1/1/6
			8 (R.E.) took the Confirmation Class for Canadian R.E. desire & Coy. no. of the working	
		1556	Batches of Wire Obstacles issued to O.A. for investigation to U.A.	
		1557	Wire as for 9th. Conf. by Gen. Court for signal to U.A.	
	16/1/9	1555	Lt. ATTABUS, S.O.B., left. by motor for Beyfield & HQ LEGHAM/SOM 12	1/1/7
			...no doubt Comd. Ch. ... Ref. North Coast...	
		1556	Do Do As work at BMT-A-MARC arranged	
	17/1/9	1557	As for 9th	1/1/8
		1556	As for 9th	
		1557	Puppy camp for Coy. arrived from BMT-A-MARC camouflets etc.	1/1/9

WAR DIARY

INTELLIGENCE SUMMARY.

Army Form C. 2118.

T.O.C. 1st Division
January 1915

(Erase heading not required.)

Place	Date	Hour	Summary of Events and Information	Remarks and references to Appendices
ATTICHES	18/1/9	155 Fld Coy R.E.	Work as for 13th Jany. @ PONT-A-MARCQ on the Electric lighting installation	
		156 "	" 14th. Remounting of by washing races fitted 6d5	N/6
		15th " "	"	
	19/1/9	155 " "	"	
		156 " "	Rest day for Church Parade Divine Service E.R.E. on Sewd 2C.	N/6
		15th " "	test day	
		15th " "	" do	
	20/1/9	15th " "	The section on Cy works on the Electric Lt. PD FOETIN, & Lt 63 on Baths & Stg lights, set at PONT-A-MARCQ. No. 2 village Sect & closing the Py (large) for the day role at TEMPLEUVE.	N/3
	21/1/9	156 " "	Work as for 18th	
		157 " "	" " "	
		15th " "	do " 20th	
		15th " "	do " "	MN/6
	22/1/9	15th " "	do " 18th	
		155 " "	do " 20th	
		156 " "	do " 18th	
		157 " "	do " 22nd	
	23/1/9	155 " "	Church Parade (C) 65 -- RE Leo Garage for Forge & Carps. being fitted.	N/6
		156 " "	do " 20th R.E.	
		157 " "	do " "	
	24/1/9	155 " "	do " 23rd	
		156 " "	do " 20th 1st Cdn Cav Canada FGOC inf on paint of Coys	N/6
		157 " "	do " R.E.	
		15th " "	do " 22nd	
	25/1/9	15th " "	do " 20th Set Rt " " "	N/9
		15th " "	do " " Park Command to stand for 88th Cd at BREUZE	N/6
		15th " "	do " 23rd	

WAR DIARY

INTELLIGENCE SUMMARY

Army Form C. 2118.

(Erase heading not required.)

Place	Date	Hour	Summary of Events and Information	Remarks and references to Appendices
ATTACHED.	26/7	155 Th Ing. Bde.	New Inf. Batt. etc.	
		157 " "	do	
		154 " "	do	
	27/7	155 " "	do. No Co. make 2 can flungh for AEC	
		156 " "	do	
		154 " "	do	
		155 " "	1st in 20th	and no strong Offices + ten to a Bart a more impalet
		156 " "	do, or 12th. Gun Plays on Dog-out	
	28/7	154 " "	do to 22nd	1620
		155 " "	do " 20th	
		156 " "	do " 17th	
		154 " "	do " 22nd	
	29/7	155 " "	do " 22nd	The color 6. Sergt R. Grand Cross CSM R'm 1776
		156 " "	do " 20th	
		154 " "	do " R.R. 16 "	
			do " 22nd 17 an	
	30/7	155 " "	" " 18th "	
			do to 22nd	
		156 " "	do " 20th	
		154 " "	do " 18th	
	31/7	155 " "	do " 18th	
		156 " "	do " 22nd	1 am its for for 1778

Confidential.

War Diary

of the

16th DIVISIONAL ENGINEERS.

from February 1st. 1919 to
February 28th 1919.

WAR DIARY
INTELLIGENCE SUMMARY
(Erase heading not required.)

Army Form C. 2118.

H.Q. R.E. 16th DIVISION.

February 1919

Place	Date	Hour	Summary of Events and Information	Remarks and references to Appendices
ATTICHES	1/2/19	155 Fd. Coy. R.E.	Col. engaged on work for R.Ey. Bdge at TERGNIER & FRETIN & Instructions of Chief Engineer in probility of Col.	
		156 " "	Position of Ry Bdge reports to Chief Engineer (Sect. 36.C. 1.35.d.1.8) poor Riviery commenced.	
		157 " "	4 men sent out on Chaussiérlos	
			Coy on forced march at CANAL (HAUTE DEULE) at COMMEREAS (NAP. 36.C. 1.35.N.)	
2/2/19		155	Working in canals at for my Coys	
		156	Elles For Chaussiéristrade FRETIN	
3/2/19		157	do do 4 O.R. to Church	fig 6.
		155	do do do	fig 2.
4/2/19		156	do do Divit for R.ECH Pany of Sub 9 to M.E.	
		157	Work as for 1st.	
		155	Work as for 1st with 4 men doing 134 Coy on Kenzer forbes in Rouvalaly	fig 8.
5/2/19		156	Work as for 1st	
		157	do do 1st	
		155	do do 3rd	
6/2/19		156	do do 1st	fig.
		157	do do 3rd	
7/2/19		155	do do 1st	
		156	do do 3rd	44 O.R. left mail for Southerton
		157	do tel.	30 " " "
8/2/19		155	do 1st	31/5 " " "
		156	do do 3rd	Half debate for whole
		157	do do 1st	" " "

Army Form C. 2118.

WAR DIARY
INTELLIGENCE SUMMARY
(Erase heading not required.)

H.Q. R.E. 16th Division
February 1919 (2)

Place	Date	Hour	Summary of Events and Information	Remarks and references to Appendices
ATTICHES	9/2/19		[illegible handwritten entries]	
	10/2/19			
	11/2/19			
	12/2/19			
	13/2/19			
	14/2/19			
	15/2/19			
	16/2/19			
	17/2/19			

Army Form C. 2118.

WAR DIARY
or
INTELLIGENCE SUMMARY.
(Erase heading not required.)

(3) H.Q. R.E. 16th DIVISION
February 1919

Instructions regarding War Diaries and Intelligence Summaries are contained in F. S. Regs., Part II. and the Staff Manual respectively. Title pages will be prepared in manuscript.

Place	Date	Hour	Summary of Events and Information	Remarks and references to Appendices
ATTICHES	18/2/19	1st Fld. Coy. R.E.	Work on Rwy. line	N.S
		2nd " " "	do do do	
		3rd " " "	do do do	
	19/2/19	1st " " "	do do do	N.S
		2nd " " "	do do do	
		3rd " " "	do do do	
			No wire to cable C.L. on Rwy cars at Bruges	
			work a.m. 15/2	
	20/2/19	1st " " "	do do do	N.S
		2nd " " "	do do do	
		3rd " " "	do do do	
	21/2/19	1st " " "	do do do	N.S
		2nd " " "	do do do	Work Commenced on Rwy curve in by-pass
		3rd " " "	do do do	
	22/2/19	1st " " "	do do do	N.S
		2nd " " "	do do do	4 Officers leave to England & overseas
		3rd " " "	do do do	(1 O.R. tpt for five seconds)
	23/2/19	1st " " "	do do do	N.S
		2nd " " "	do do do	(1 O.R. leaves for officer & cadets)
		3rd " " "	do do do	
	24/2/19	1st " " "	do do do	N.S
		2nd " " "	do do do	No. Battery clerc (Corpls. Dr. work on F.N.D.
		3rd " " "	do do do	do do
	25/2/19	1st " " "	do do do	N.S
		2nd " " "	do do do	No O.R.s 1 N.O. left for home.
		3rd " " "	do do do	10 men to agric'lt. Coy. on Rwy Curve re-arised
				by 2nd Fld. Coys but is not in place & is at time to set.

Army Form C. 2118.

WAR DIARY
or
INTELLIGENCE SUMMARY.
(Erase heading not required.)

H.Q.R.E. 16th DIVISION
February 1919

(4.)

Place	Date	Hour	Summary of Events and Information	Remarks and references to Appendices
ATTICHES	26/2/19	1st Fd Coy RE	March as /s 25th	
		2nd "	do	
		3rd "	do	
	27/2/19	1st "	do	
		2nd "	do 25th	
		3rd "	do W post Reconnaissances	
			" " "	
			Holiday in place of Sunday	
	28/2/19	1st "	do	
		2nd "	do	
		3rd "	as per last "10 men working on bridge at COURRIÈRE	

D.A.G. 3rd Echelon.

C.R.E. 12/136.

    Herewith War Diary of the 16th Brigade Group Engineers for the month of March.

3/4/18.

F. Summers
Lieut. Col. R.E.
C.R.E. 16th Brigade Group.

Confidential

War Diary
H.Q. 16th Divisional Engineers.
1stto 31st March. 1919.

Army Form C. 2118.

WAR DIARY
or
INTELLIGENCE SUMMARY.
(Erase heading not required.)

(1) H.Q. R.E. 4th Division. March 1917.

Instructions regarding War Diaries and Intelligence Summaries are contained in F. S. Regs., Part II. and the Staff Manual respectively. Title pages will be prepared in manuscript.

Place	Date	Hour	Summary of Events and Information	Remarks and references to Appendices
ATTICHES	1/3/19		1st, 5th, 7th Fd. Co. R.E. ... (illegible)	
	2/3/19		1st " "	
	3/3/19		1st " & 2nd Sn. ...	
	4/3/19		All Coys ...	
	5/3/19		do ...	
	6/3/19		do ...	
	7/3/19		do ...	
	8/3/19		do ...	
	9/3/19		do ...	
	10/3/19		do ...	
	11/3/19		do ...	
	12/3/19		do ...	
	13/3/19		do ...	
	14/3/19		do ...	
	15/3/19		do ...	
	16/3/19		do ...	
	17/3/19		do ...	
	18/3/19		do ...	
	19/3/19		do ...	
	20/3/19		do ...	

WAR DIARY
or
INTELLIGENCE SUMMARY.

Army Form C. 2118.

16th Division
March 1919

Place	Date	Hour	Summary of Events and Information	Remarks and references to Appendices
ATTICHY	21/3/19			
	22/3/19			
	23/3/19			
	24/3/19			
	25/3/19			
	26/3/19			
	27/3/19			
	28/3/19			
	29/3/19			
	30/3/19			
	31/3/19			

DUPLICATE   Appendix 1

C.R.E's ORDER No.94
================================

= WARNING ORDER.
==================
                                              28th March 1919.

(1)   The 157th Field Company R.E. will entrain at Seclin on March
      29th and arrive Cologne on March 31st.

(2)   5 days rations will be taken on the train. 16th Brigade Group
      are arranging to deliver these to Seclin Station on the 29th inst.

(3)   Company transport will be used. C.R.E. will lend one lorry to
      assist. O.C. 157th Field Company R.E. to make necessary
      arrangements with Adjutant R.E.

                                                    Lieut Col. R.E.
                                           C.R.E. 16th Brigade Group.

WAR DIARY.

H.Q. 16th DIVISIONAL ENGINEERS.

April. 1919.

Army Form C. 2118.

WAR DIARY
of
INTELLIGENCE SUMMARY.

(Erase heading not required.)

H.Q. C.O. 152 Division
(D). April 1919

Instructions regarding War Diaries and Intelligence Summaries are contained in F. S. Regs., Part II. and the Staff Manual respectively. Title pages will be prepared in manuscript.

Place	Date	Hour	Summary of Events and Information	Remarks and references to Appendices
ATTICHES	1/4/19		155 Fld Coy RE took over 4 bav. at TEMPLEUVE Stn.	
			156 " " " " " Cleaning Wagons etc	
AVELIN	2/4/19		H.Q. R.E. moved to AVELIN.	
	3/4/19		155 Cy RE do on ret. work. Eng. & Cof.	
	4/4/19			
	5/4/19		work in Camp	
	6/4/19		do on ret work at TEMPLEUVE on forests system	
	7/4/19		do on ret work in Camp	
	8/4/19		Sunday no work	
	9/4/19		work in Camp	
	10/4/19		do on ret	
	11/4/19		do " "	
	12/4/19		do " "	
	13/4/19		Sunday no work	
	14/4/19		do on ret	
	15/4/19		Working in Camp	

Army Form C. 2118.

WAR DIARY
or
INTELLIGENCE SUMMARY.
(Erase heading not required.)

H.Q. E.S. 16th Division
April 1919

Instructions regarding War Diaries and Intelligence Summaries are contained in F.S. Regs., Part II. and the Staff Manual respectively. Title pages will be prepared in manuscript.

Place	Date	Hour	Summary of Events and Information	Remarks and references to Appendices
AVELIN	16/4/19	1st Feb at D.O.	Units in Camp	
	17/4/19	25/	Units in Camp	do
	18/4/19	25/	do	do
	19/4/19	25/	do	do
	20/4/19	25/	Sunday no work	do
	21/4/19	25/	Units in camp	do
	22/4/19	25/	Parade is had at (EMPLOYEE)	do
	23/4/19	25/	Parade in Camp	do
	24/4/19	25/	" " "	do
	25/4/19	25/	" " "	do
	26/4/19	25/	W.C. Campbell at TEMPLEUVE (on march to Calais) off to E.S	do
	27/4/19	25/	Units in Camp	do
	28/4/19	25/	do	do
	29/4/19	25/	Sunday no work	do
	30/4/19	25/	Units in Camp	do

A 5834 Wt. W4973/M687 750,000 8/16 D. D. & L. Ltd. Forms/C.2118/13

WAR DIARY.

H.Q. R.E. 16th DIVISION

MAY 1919.

WAR DIARY or INTELLIGENCE SUMMARY

Army Form C. 2118.

H.Q. R.E. 16th Division
May 1919
Page 1

(Erase heading not required.)

Instructions regarding War Diaries and Intelligence Summaries are contained in F. S. Regs., Part II and the Staff Manual respectively. Title pages will be prepared in manuscript.

Place	Date	Hour	Summary of Events and Information	Remarks and references to Appendices
AVELIN	1/5/19	15.55	7th Coy R.E. Work in Camp	
	2/5/19	15.25	do.	
	3/5/19	15.55	do.	
	4/5/19	15.25	do.	
	5/5/19	15.55	do. Cable Sec reduced to 2 Offrs. + 40 O.R. Authority 16th Div.	
	6/5/19	15.26	do. Sig. No. A 1029/32 of 5.5.19	
	7/5/19	15.52	do.	
	8/5/19	15.53	do.	
	9/5/19	15.56	do.	
	10/5/19	15.27	do.	
	11/5/19	15.57	do.	
	12/5/19	15.28	do.	
	13/5/19	15.57	do.	
	14/5/19	15.27	do.	
	15/5/19	15.57	do.	
	16/5/19	15.27	do.	
	17/5/19	15.58	do.	
	18/5/19	15.27	do.	

Army Form C. 2118.

WAR DIARY
or
INTELLIGENCE SUMMARY.

(Erase heading not required.)

H.Q. O.O.
187th DIVISION MAY 1919
Page 2

Place	Date	Hour	Summary of Events and Information	Remarks and references to Appendices
ANGLIN	19/5/19	1st Hd. Qr. O.O.	Units in Camp.	
	20/5/19	2nd " " "	do.	
	21/5/19	2nd " " "	do.	
	22/5/19	2nd	do.	
	23/5/19	2nd	do.	
	24/5/19	2nd	do.	O.C. 1st & later over 1st, 2nd, & 1st 7th Bn letters per chap	
	25/5/19	2nd	do.	Officers to replace O.O. 1st who left per chap	
	26/5/19	2nd	do.	on 5th inst.	
	27/5/19	2nd	do.		
	28/5/19	2nd	do.		
	29/5/19	2nd	do.	Order regarding the Code to be reduced	
	30/5/19	2nd	do.	& 7/5 to strength	
	31/5/19	2nd	do.	J.H. Hudson Capt/Lt.Col.	
				A/C.R.E. 187 Div.	

War Diary.
H.Q. R.E.
16th Division.

June 1919.

Final Sheets.

WAR DIARY
or
INTELLIGENCE SUMMARY.

(Erase heading not required.)

Army Form C. 2118.

H.Q. R.E.
JUNE 1919. 65th DIVISION.

Instructions regarding War Diaries and Intelligence Summaries are contained in F. S. Regs., Part II. and the Staff Manual respectively. Title pages will be prepared in manuscript.

Place	Date	Hour	Summary of Events and Information	Remarks and references to Appendices
ANZIN	1/7/19			
	5.			
	6/7/19			
	14/7/19		Conference as above.	
	18/7/19		Conference —	
	19/7/19			
	6.			
	21/7/19		All hands to	
	22/7/19			
	24/7/19			
	25/7/19			

www.ingramcontent.com/pod-product-compliance
Lightning Source LLC
Chambersburg PA
CBHW080819010526
44111CB00015B/2580